Implementing Cybersecurity

Internal Audit and IT Audit
Series Editor: Dan Swanson

A Guide to the National Initiative for Cybersecurity Education (NICE) Cybersecurity Workforce Framework (2.0)
Dan Shoemaker, Anne Kohnke, and Ken Sigler
ISBN 978-1-4987-3996-2

A Practical Guide to Performing Fraud Risk Assessments
Mary Breslin
ISBN 978-1-4987-4251-1

Corporate Defense and the Value Preservation Imperative: Bulletproof Your Corporate Defense Program
Sean Lyons
ISBN 978-1-4987-4228-3

Data Analytics for Internal Auditors
Richard E. Cascarino
ISBN 978-1-4987-3714-2

Fighting Corruption in a Global Marketplace: How Culture, Geography, Language and Economics Impact Audit and Fraud Investigations around the World
Mary Breslin
ISBN 978-1-4987-3733-3

Investigations and the CAE: The Design and Maintenance of an Investigative Function within Internal Audit
Kevin L. Sisemore
ISBN 978-1-4987-4411-9

Internal Audit Practice from A to Z
Patrick Onwura Nzechukwu
ISBN 978-1-4987-4205-4

Leading the Internal Audit Function
Lynn Fountain
ISBN 978-1-4987-3042-6

Mastering the Five Tiers of Audit Competency: The Essence of Effective Auditing
Ann Butera
ISBN 978-1-4987-3849-1

Operational Assessment of IT
Steve Katzman
ISBN 978-1-4987-3768-5

Operational Auditing: Principles and Techniques for a Changing World
Hernan Murdock
ISBN 978-1-4987-4639-7

Securing an IT Organization through Governance,
Risk Management, and Audit
Ken E. Sigler and James L. Rainey, III
ISBN 978-1-4987-3731-9

Security and Auditing of Smart Devices: Managing Proliferation of
Confidential Data on Corporate and BYOD Devices
Sajay Rai and Philip Chuckwuma
ISBN 978-1-4987-3883-5

Software Quality Assurance: Integrating Testing, Security, and Audit
Abu Sayed Mahfuz
ISBN 978-1-4987-3553-7

The Complete Guide to Cybersecurity Risks and Controls
Anne Kohnke, Dan Shoemaker, and Ken E. Sigler
ISBN 978-1-4987-4054-8

Tracking the Digital Footprint of Breaches
James Bone
ISBN 978-1-4987-4981-7

Implementing Cybersecurity
A Guide to the National Institute
of Standards and Technology Risk
Management Framework

By
Anne Kohnke, Ken Sigler, and Dan Shoemaker

CRC Press
Taylor & Francis Group
Boca Raton London New York

CRC Press is an imprint of the
Taylor & Francis Group, an **informa** business

AN AUERBACH BOOK

CRC Press
Taylor & Francis Group
6000 Broken Sound Parkway NW, Suite 300
Boca Raton, FL 33487-2742

© 2017 by Taylor & Francis Group, LLC
CRC Press is an imprint of Taylor & Francis Group, an Informa business

No claim to original U.S. Government works

Printed on acid-free paper
Version Date: 20170131

International Standard Book Number-13: 978-1-4987-8514-3 (Hardback)

Visit the Taylor & Francis Web site at
http://www.taylorandfrancis.com

and the CRC Press Web site at
http://www.crcpress.com

Contents

Foreword

Effective risk management is at the heart of good cybersecurity practice. Adopting a risk-based approach allows managers to assess the relative strengths and weaknesses of different security decisions within the context of a complex operational environment where a maze of laws, policies, and directives, along with an evolving threat landscape, can stymie even the most experienced professionals.

In an emerging area like cybersecurity, where various governments and professional entities are racing to establish protocols of professional practice, standards—such as the National Institute of Standards and Technology (NIST) Risk Management Framework detailed in this book—can assist security professionals in navigating through the challenging environment. As I have observed through my years of identifying, developing, and implementing cybersecurity best practices, when done right, standards provide a common foundation upon which practitioners can build holistic security operations. Standard frameworks offer a structure to support the full range of activities needed to secure enterprise operations. Standards also define common terminology used to support communication within single organizations and collaboration across multiple entities. Through these frameworks, practitioners can improve the efficiency of critical processes and system integration activities. By identifying a clear set of desired outcomes for security operations and the methods needed to measure progress toward meeting those goals, standards can support the assessment of security tools, services, and practices.

While consistency is a desirable state, the role of standards is not to establish uniformity. On the contrary, properly articulated standards should not lead to monolithic structures. Rather, proper standards support the application of coordinated strategies by providing a roadmap to guide organizations toward areas of alignment and by allowing for enough flexibility that individual entities can adapt internal practices to meet specific environmental constraints. The importance of having both alignment and flexibility cannot be overstated, which is critical to establishing the resilience needed as organizations face a dynamic threat environment. To ensure that standard frameworks meet both of these objectives, the development process must be conducted at a time when the core knowledge of the field has developed sufficiently to serve as a stable foundation. In addition, the data gathering process should be broadly inclusive of stakeholders across the spectrum.

Public agencies and private business of all sizes and across sectors, ranging from critical infrastructure to entertainment, should be included in the requirements gathering phase. The synthesis of these disparate inputs should be no less comprehensive and must be performed with rigorous analysis and objective processes. This is setting a high bar—one that the NIST Risk Management Framework has met. The framework was developed through 4 years of intensive and coordinated efforts to gather and synthesize expert advice. The resulting framework provides a practical, easily applicable, and understandable approach to the management of risk in any organization. As such, it serves as a valuable resource for those charged with securing the enterprise.

This book provides general guidance on applying the NIST Risk Management Framework. The text walks the readers through the central concepts, relationships between steps, and general recommendations for application across a variety of organizational types. The authors have vast experience in translating federal cybersecurity standards for both the lay reader and the seasoned professional. As with their prior efforts, see *A Guide to the National Initiative for Cybersecurity Education (NICE) Cybersecurity Workforce Framework (2.0)*, the authors construct a detailed picture that will bolster the reader's ability to use the standards. Structured as a common sense guide that addresses each component of the Risk Management Framework, managers ranging from strategic to operational levels will gain practical insights from this book.

Diana L. Burley, PhD
Professor, Human and Organizational Learning
Executive Director, Institute for Information Infrastructure Protection
The George Washington University

Preface

This book will help the reader to understand and apply the federal risk management framework (RMF). The RMF was developed and promulgated by the National Institute of Standards and Technology (NIST) in 2014. Its aim is to define a detailed and practical end-to-end process and provide an explicit methodology to manage the risk to information and communication technology (ICT) systems. The RMF is specifically oriented toward the compliance requirements of the 2002 Federal Information Security Management Act (FISMA). Thus, it provides a strategy and operational steps for installing the controls called out by Federal Information Processing Standards (FIPS) 199 and 200. The controls themselves are specified in NIST SP 800-53, Revision 4. Given the comprehensive risk management focus of the NIST RMF, the recommendations that are contained in this book will support any form of organizational risk management process.

Using the NIST RMF, it is possible for an entity to define and implement persistent day-to-day organization-wide policy–based strategic risk management control over its operations. So, the attendant stages and associated specifications of the model comprise a collection of commonly accepted, practical, and easy to implement steps to ensure systematic risk management. Thus, the NIST RMF can be seen as the detailed roadmap for implementing practical risk management in any setting. More importantly, the real-world realization of the NIST RMF's recommendations can also establish coordinated risk management across a range of organizations, which will help to ensure a robust and properly coordinated approach to the overall problem of risk management nationally.

In addition to the overall architecture of the substantive risk management process, this model also specifies an approach for creating the control set. These controls are necessary to ensure best-practice risk mitigation. The contextual control framework generated by the standard underwrites the comprehensive risk management program and it will mitigate and manage organizational risk specifically as it applies to information.

The NIST RMF framework is generally considered to be authoritative because it was prepared through a broadly inclusive, 7-year, highly rigorous process spearheaded by the federal government through NIST. However, it involved a number of other constituencies including industry and academia. The ability to put the general shape of the risk management process into an explicit and commonly accepted frame of reference underwrites the practical management of across-the-board risk. Additionally, it underwrites the standardization of the risk management process throughout all sectors of the economy.

Why the NIST RMF Is Important

The NIST RMF is a key component of the general compliance requirements of the Federal Information Management Act (2002). The aim of the NIST RMF project was to develop a strategic, risk-based approach to the deployment of real-world cybersecurity controls, which are appropriate to address latent and active risks within a given ICT situation. As a result, the NIST RMF comprises a major national influence on the overall state of cybersecurity practice. In addition to the effectiveness of its general application, the NIST RMF is the first fully sanctioned specification of a complete cybersecurity risk management process.

Comprehensive risk management is a key element in the planning, design, and implementation of any organization's operational cybersecurity program—not just that of the federal government's. This is because the unequivocal understanding of the risk environment serves as the starting point for the selection of an appropriate set of corporate security behaviors. These behaviors are always needed to protect the users and the information assets of any ICT system.

Given its intended national role, the NIST RMF initiative is understandably very ambitious in scope. To provide a comprehensive demonstration of the recommendations of the framework, we have adopted a presentation model that is based around discussions of how to embed each of the standard elements of the NIST RMF process in a tailored cybersecurity risk management process for any organization. Accordingly, this text will focus on *how* the relevant aspects of risk management will interact together to ensure suitable control selection in a practical setting.

Practical Benefits of Implementing the Risk Management Model

The NIST RMF provides a carefully researched specification of each element of the risk management process. It embodies the steps required to identify and evaluate cybersecurity risk. Thus, the time and effort that NIST expended in developing the framework comprises an all-source picture of the accepted principles of the practice of risk management. And as such cybersecurity risk management practice can be improved by building a detailed picture of the NIST RMF process and tailoring it to a specific setting. The level of detail that NIST provided for each of the steps in the RMF implementation process makes it possible to structure either a single tailored application for a given setting or an entire organization-wide strategic framework. Thus using the NIST RMF, managers and even academics can be brought to a common understanding of risk management.

The government-wide scope of the NIST RMF is necessary because compliance with information assurance best practice is mandated for all governmental entities by law. So in essence, this is a survey book. It will provide the complete strategic understanding requisite to allow a person to create and use the NIST RMF process along with recommendations for risk management. This will be the case both for applications of the NIST RMF in practical corporate situations, as well as for any individual who wants to obtain specialized knowledge in organizational risk management.

The NIST RMF is by necessity generally applicable, and therefore an initial all-in-one book seems like the most practical way to introduce the concepts of the model. In effect, what we are providing is an end-to-end explication of the six primary stages of the process. In each stage, we will introduce the central concepts and the underlying relationships with each of the steps in the prior stages, and itemize the standard process performance and task recommendations for each step. The focus of this book is to explain how to use the framework in a general organizational application rather than illustrate how it applies in an explicit sector.

Who Should Read This Book

The knowledge that is contained in this book would support managers at both the strategic as well as the project management level. It would also help to ensure specific control compliance in support of the FISMA requirements. FISMA, along with the Paperwork Reduction Act of 1995 and the Information Technology Management Reform Act of 1996 (Clinger–Cohen Act), explicitly emphasizes a risk-based policy for cost-effective security.

The management responsibilities presume that responsible executives understand the risks and other factors that could adversely affect their organization's mission. Moreover, these managers must understand the current status of their security programs and the security controls planned or in place to protect their information and information systems and must be guided by informed judgments that appropriately mitigate risk to an acceptable level.

This book is designed to give the reader a comprehensive understanding of the risk management process for all organizations. Its recommendations are relevant to every type of organization and the recommended approach must be tailored to the application. Nevertheless, it is recommended that tailoring should take place within a common framework. Therefore, the NIST RMF is also potentially applicable to risk management in all corporate settings. Thus, this book can serve as a roadmap of sorts, aimed at the practical understanding and implementation of the risk management process as an ordinary entity in the business process.

NIST is authoritative, both in the standard knowledge requirements that it specifies, as well as in terms of the definition of the specific elements of the organizational risk management process for a particular organizational application. This book is a comprehensive explication of the topic of risk management and it will allow a person to understand the application and uses of the RMF content. This also holds true for application of this book in education and training situations. The people who would benefit from this knowledge range from managers to all types of technical workers and specialists.

Organization of This Text

The chapters follow the model in a logical fashion. Some of the content of these chapters touch on concepts that are brand new; however, the general structure and approach of this model have been well established over time. And because of the extensive vetting process that was conducted by NIST in its preparation, the correctness of the approach is difficult to question. Accordingly, this book is based on nine chapters and an appendix.

Chapter 1: Introduction to Organizational Security Risk Management

This chapter presents an overview of organizational risk management through an exploration of the types of organizational risks that senior leaders must identify, the necessity and benefits of managing those risks, and the information security regulation that senior leaders must consider as they manage risk. The discussion continues with an overview of security risk management. Finally, the chapter provides an introduction to the NIST RMF.

Chapter 2: Survey of Existing Risk Management Models

This chapter briefly breaks away from the main objective of the book in order to discuss various models that can be used to implement the NIST RMF. The goal is to provide a comparative assessment of existing models and demonstrate how the NIST framework sets itself apart from other models. The models discussed include: ISO 13335, *Information Technology—Security; Techniques—Management of Information and Communications Technology Security*; HITRUST, AS/NZS, ISO 31000:2009, *Standard: Risk Management—Principles and Guidelines*; and NIST SP 800-30, *Guide for Conducting Risk Assessments*, and NIST SP 800-37, Revision 1, *Guide for Applying the Risk Management Framework to Federal Information Systems: A Security Life Cycle Approach*. This discussion will serve as the basis for the ideas that will be presented in the next seven chapters.

Chapter 3: Step 1—Categorize Information and Information Systems

This chapter begins with a definition of security impact analysis. CNSSI 1253 *Security Categorization and Control Selection for National Security Systems* and FIPS 199 *Standards for Security Categorization of Federal Information and Information Systems* are explored, compared, and contrasted as a source of guidelines for organizations to perform the information system categorization process. The major focus of this chapter centers around understanding the tables available in NIST SP 800-60, *Guide for Mapping Types of Information and Information Systems*; the security categories; and utilizing FIPS 199 as a means of implementing the security categorization; and the information classification process of the NIST RMF.

Chapter 4: Step 2—Select Security Controls

This chapter begins with an introduction of FIPS 200, *Minimum Security Requirements for Federal Information and Information Systems*. Further, this guideline is used to provide a basis for discussion of establishing security boundaries and the identification of minimum security requirements. This chapter also provides a discussion related to the contents of the security plan, and continuous monitoring strategy (which are two of the underlying outputs of the control selection process).

Chapter 5: Step 3—Implement Security Controls

This chapter starts with a review of the system development life cycle (SDLC) using ISO 12207:2008 as a basis for discussion of when activities and tasks associated with security control implementation get performed. Emphasis is placed on the standards development and acquisition processes as a means for providing details related to the development of an organizational information security architecture while at the same time integrating it into the organization's enterprise architecture.

Detailed discussion is also provided about the types of security controls (i.e., common, hybrid) together with the proper approaches to allocation of each type. This chapter concludes with a discussion of the proper procedures for documenting control implementation at the functional level and within the existing security plan.

Chapter 6: Step 4—Assess Security Controls

This chapter begins by using NIST 800-30, *Guide for Conducting Risk Assessments*, as a directive for a discussion of the process of security risk assessment. Through this discussion, the reader will understand that security risk assessment and security control assessment are not only different processes but also complimentary in nature. The major focus of this chapter is on how to use NIST SP 800-53A, *Assessing Security and Privacy Controls in Federal Information Systems and*

Organizations—Building Effective Assessment Plans. This serves as a basis for discussing the approach toward development of a security control assessment plan. An underlying objective of this chapter is to demonstrate that through security control assessment based on an established plan, the reader will be able to identify and further disclose security risks that may exist within the organization.

Chapter 7: Step 5—Authorize Information Systems

The first major component of this chapter provides a detailed discussion of the creation and dissemination of the security authorization package (security plan, security assessment report, and plan of action and milestones). This chapter begins with a discussion of the criteria included and creation of a plan of action and milestones. The reader will appreciate that the plan provides the strategies for how the organization will correct security weaknesses or deficiencies identified through security control assessment. The second major component that is discussed is the use of NIST SP 800-39 *Managing Information Security Risk: Organization, Mission, and Information System View*, as a basis for risk determination and risk acceptance.

Chapter 8: Step 6—Monitor Security State

This chapter starts by using ISO 12207:2008 as a basis for discussion of the operations and maintenance phases of the SDLC. The thrust of this discussion is on the activities associated with monitoring the security state during these two life cycle phases.

This chapter emphasizes the strategies associated with the ongoing security control assessments, remediation action strategies, procedures for implementing documentation and plan updates, implementing security status reporting procedures, strategies associated with ongoing risk determination and acceptance, and secure procedures for information system removal and decommission.

Chapter 9: Practical Application of the NIST RMF

This chapter provides specific examples of the implementation process for small-, medium-, and large-scale organizational applications. This is in the form of case studies that will be presented as model representations of the practical advantages and pitfalls of implementing the RMF as an end-to-end process. The aim of this final chapter is to give readers a concrete understanding of the real-world issues associated with enterprise risk management, as well as to suggest pragmatic strategies for implementation of the RMF within a range of settings.

Appendix: (ISC)² Certified Authorization Professional (CAP) Certification

The discussions that take place within this book have a direct relationship to the five domains of the (ISC)² CAP certification. The appendix will provide a brief introduction to (ISC)² followed by a discussion of the CAP domains, the value of this certification, its relationship to DoD 8570 standard, and the requirements to obtain certification for Information Assurance Manager Levels I and II.

Authors

Anne Kohnke, PhD, is an assistant professor of IT at Lawrence Technological University, Southfield, Michigan, and teaches courses in both the information technology and organization development/change management disciplines at the bachelor through doctorate levels. Anne started as an adjunct professor in 2002 and joined the faculty full time in 2011. Her research focus is in the areas of cybersecurity, risk management, and IT governance. Anne started her IT career in the mid-1980s on a help desk, and over the years developed technical proficiency as a database administrator, network administrator, systems analyst, and technical project manager. After a decade, Anne was promoted to management and worked as an IT Director, Vice President of IT, and Chief Information Security Officer (CISO). Anne earned her PhD from Benedictine University, Lisle, Illinois.

Ken Sigler is a faculty member of the Computer Information Systems (CIS) program at the Auburn Hills campus of Oakland Community College in Michigan. His primary research is in the areas of software management, software assurance, and cloud computing. He developed the college's CIS program option entitled "Information Technologies for Homeland Security." Until 2007, Ken served as the liaison between the college and the International Cybersecurity Education Coalition (ICSEC), of which he is one of three founding members. Ken is a member of IEEE, the Distributed Management Task Force (DMTF), and the Association for Information Systems (AIS).

Dan Shoemaker, PhD, is the principal investigator and a senior research scientist at the University of Detroit Mercy's (UDM) Center for Cyber Security and Intelligence Studies in Detroit, Michigan. Dan has served for 30 years as a professor at UDM with 25 of those years as department chair. He served as a cochair for both the Workforce Training and Education and the Software and Supply Chain Assurance Initiatives for the Department of Homeland Security, and was a subject matter expert for NICE Workforce Framework 2.0. Dan has coauthored six books in the field of cybersecurity and has authored over one hundred journal publications. Dan earned his PhD from the University of Michigan, Ann Arbor, Michigan.

Chapter 1

Introduction to Organizational Security Risk Management

At the conclusion of this chapter, the reader will understand:

- The role and importance of risk management in the cybersecurity process
- The issues associated with risk and generic risk management
- The form and content of the risk management process
- The general structure and intent of risk-oriented frameworks
- The general application and development of a risk-based strategy
- The generic elements of the risk management process

1.1 Introduction to the Book

The goal of this book is to provide a comprehensive understanding of the strategic risk management process as well as the underlying principles and a standard risk management framework. Risk management entails a formal set of steps that are carried out to protect an organization's assets from harm that may be caused by inadvertent or deliberate acts of destruction. Risk management involves a systematic architecture comprising all the necessary controls to prevent unauthorized use, loss, damage, disclosure, or modification of organizational information. Specifically, this chapter discusses the formal processes for identifying, managing, and mitigating risk as prescribed by the National Institute of Standards and Technology's (NIST) risk management framework (RMF). In this chapter, we also discuss the general uses for the framework and the contexts in which it applies.

In some respects, this book is as much about standardization as it is about risk management. Hence, Chapters 2 and 3 present an overview of the role of the standardization process in ensuring a consistent response to a given issue of importance. This includes a discussion of why information assets are difficult to protect as well as the part in which commonly acknowledged best practices apply in ensuring an informed response. The discussion will also center on how to use the NIST's RMF as a standard means of deploying an appropriate set of information technology security controls. We lay out the issues involved in implementing a standard process, including the benefits that derive from it, as well as potential pitfalls. We also try to give you an understanding of the implementation process, which is best demonstrated by applying the RMF to a specific context.

1.2 Risk Is Inevitable

Risk is a fundamental element of human life in the sense that risk is always a factor in any situation where the outcome is not precisely known (Figure 1.1). In addition, the necessary calculations that we make about the probability of some form of harm resulting from an action that we take are generally a given in our decision processes. Whether the risk assessment involves decisions about a major corporate

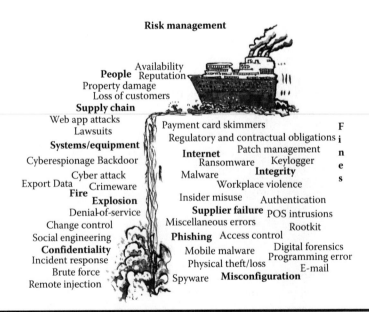

Figure 1.1 Security risk management.

initiative or just making the decision to walk down the street, we are always antici-pating, identifying, and evaluating the potential risks involved. In that respect, we can be said to be constantly managing risk in everything we do.

The reason why risk management is a particularly important aspect of the cyber-security body of knowledge (BOK) is that information and communication tech-nology (ICT) and information assets are more difficult to account for and control than most conventional physical assets, because ICT involves the production and management of virtual, highly dynamic products, which makes it difficult to iden-tify what to secure, let alone how to do it. That puts risk management center stage in the consideration of how to establish and maintain a secure ICT environment.

By definition, ICT assets are something of value to the business. The risk man-agement process specifically ensures the assurance of three generic protection cri-teria, as shown in Figure 1.2. These three criteria assure against meaningful loss of *confidentiality*, loss of *integrity*, and loss of *availability* (CIA).

From a security standpoint, the most logical generic criterion might be assur-ance against a loss of confidentiality. *Confidentiality* is a security principle that encompasses an organization's requirement to restrict access to any sensitive infor-mation or data that it keeps. Obviously, if the organization's data and information could be made public without risk, there would not be a need for this attribute; however, this is rarely the case.

From an operational point of view, confidentiality is founded on establishing and adequately enforcing access control. Data and information are essential to the business operation. And in many information-intensive organizations, it might be the only real asset that is kept. For instance, most financial data within a company is sensitive and

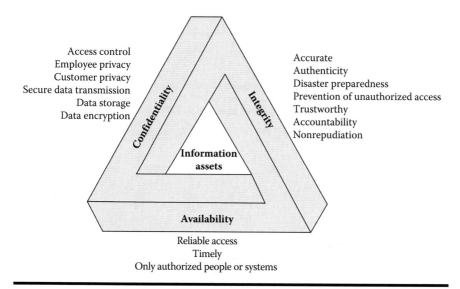

Figure 1.2 The confidentiality, integrity, and availability (CIA) triad.

access is almost always rigorously safeguarded. So, one way to view the monetary value of confidentiality is to imagine how much competitors might pay to have access to the data and information of a company or the cost of litigation if a legal requirement was violated. Thus, in that respect, the organization has a legal and ethical requirement to protect its sensitive business information as well as employee and customer privacy.

The second characteristic is *integrity*. The integrity of data or its attended processes is determined based on how authentic, accurate, and complete the data is. It is easy to appreciate the value of integrity in the context of financial business transactions. For example, if a bank could not depend on its account balances, it could potentially sustain a large loss by disbursing checks not covered by actual funds. In an inventory system, there is the potential to lose expensive materials if the counts were inaccurate due to faulty data. Or publically, the release of unreliable data that is used as background for a damaging story might expose a newspaper to legal action.

The third characteristic, *availability*, ensures that information is provided to an authorized user when it is required. The best way to understand the value of availability is to ask, "What would happen if the information was not available to support a given action or decision?" For example, what would happen if the business' payroll data were erased on payday? If the payroll program were suddenly inoperative, no one in the organization would be paid as expected. Imagine the chaos in a company the size of General Motors or IBM if they were unable to pay their employees or suppliers when they needed to. Given the potential harm that each of these principles might represent, all of the meaningful risks in each of these areas must be rationally managed.

Because every organization is unique and implements security differently, the actual process to identify, evaluate, and ensure that the meaningful risks in each of the CIA areas are properly managed generally involves the same eight requirements, which are as follows (Figure 1.3):

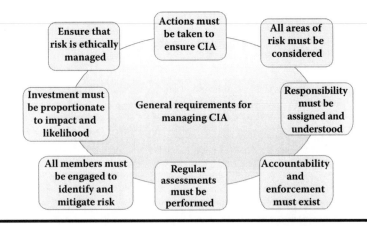

Figure 1.3   General requirements for meaningfully managing CIA.

1. Identifiable actions must be taken to ensure correct, confidential, and available information.
2. All relevant areas of risk must be considered in any given solution.
3. The responsibility for risk management must be explicitly assigned to individuals and understood.
4. A system of accountability and enforcement for risk control must exist and be documented.
5. Regular and systematic assessments of risk status must be performed.
6. All members of the organization must understand the importance of and work to identify and mitigate risk.
7. Investment in risk management must be kept proportionate to the impact and likelihood of the risk occurrence.
8. The organization must ensure that risk is ethically managed.

In practice, organizations should design, implement, and follow a systematic process to establish a persistent operational risk management process. This design and management process is a strategic activity in that it involves short- and long-range considerations. Thus, planning for strategic risk management is necessary in order to ensure continuous risk assurance. And a formal strategic planning process is necessary to implement an organization-wide risk management process. Risk management itself must incorporate all of the elements of the business within its scope and the process should reach to the boundaries of the organization.

The outcome of the implementation of a risk management process is a concrete organization-wide risk management scheme that is documented. The risk management scheme will balance the aims of a long-term risk control policy with real-world conditions and constraints. The atomic-level components of the risk management process are a set of substantive security controls that ensure the requisite level of assurance against loss. These security controls should be traceable directly to the individual policies that defined their need. This is a closed-loop process in that the ongoing alignment of risk security controls to individual policies fine-tunes the evolution of the substantive risk management process and ensures its effectiveness in the operational setting.

One problem is that the term "risk management" is rather nebulous. So, the overall process itself requires a definition of what risk management means. A concise statement and commitment to the work is needed in order to make the practice standard. Standardization is important because a lack of effective, coordinated implementation and execution of the process has made overall risk management efforts ineffective. Worse yet, employees might feel the effort is the "flavor of the day" and not take it seriously. One does not need to look any further than the increasing number of incidents in cyberspace to confirm that.

The lack of coordinated action has been so pervasive that a logical response is the formulation of a comprehensive and coherent specification of the commonly accepted best practices for risk management. The specification could then be used to guide the creation of an effective risk management scheme for all organizations. In that respect, steps were taken by the federal government to formally research and develop a standard and comprehensive risk management process.

The specification of commonly accepted standard processes is the role of the NIST, the U.S. government's standards making body. Of specific interest here, the NIST has developed and published a formal reference model for the management of risk simply called the RMF, as shown in Figure 1.4.

This large-scale standard model serves as both the specification of a fundamental process for understanding the risks involved in assuring information and ICT organizations and the foundation for deploying the common control mechanisms required to manage the risks that exist within them. It has the additional advantage of providing the umbrella definition of the processes for achieving Federal Information Security Management Act (FISMA) and NIST certifications.

An important justification for this standard is that the RMF also defines the basis for a comprehensive strategic governance approach to risk. A governance rather than a technical approach is a highly advantageous strategy because, notwithstanding the issue of whether the cybersecurity function itself can ever fully embrace all of the issues associated with assurance, a governance-based solution is more easily understood and acceptable to the managers and nontechnical people who comprise the majority of the organization.

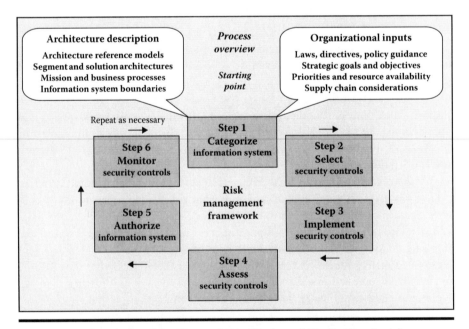

Figure 1.4 The National Institute of Standards and Technology's risk management process overview.

A governance approach is appropriate for any organizational setting. In essence, a generic governance model constitutes a flexible top-down organizational process for establishing persistent risk management actions and the formal selection and maintenance of appropriate security controls. Moreover, since the RMF is founded on an established policy and procedure approach, it is able to capture and communicate the nature of the specific risks that an organization may encounter. And finally, since the framework itself is built and maintained through a comprehensive identification and assessment process, it can assist in rationally and systematically identifying changes in the threat environment as they occur.

1.3 Strategic Governance and Risk Management

Starting from the assumption that a standardized risk management process should be applied organization-wide (which is what we believe), risk management is a strategic issue, rather than a narrow technical concern. The reason to adopt an organization-wide risk management approach is to avoid the dysfunctional effects of a typical piecemeal solution where every department is managed by its own commonly accepted business practices. These are often based on an individual unit or manager's ideas about the proper way to accomplish a particular organizational goal. And regardless of whether they are universally standard or documented, these become the corporate way of doing business. One problem is that those approaches are often not coordinated effectively in the operational environment. In some cases, they can actually cause dysfunctional conflicts. And corporate risk management has often evolved this way. Organizations develop specific one-at-a-time responses as risks present themselves, rather than addressing them by employing a single, coordinated management strategy. Moreover, as new risks appear in the corporate threatscape that have not been seen before, they are not incorporated into any specific management techniques that the organization employs to mitigate and contain them.

The alternative approach to piecemeal risk management is a formally defined and instantiated architecture of comprehensive risk management best practices, which are specifically aimed at optimizing risk controls within the company. As with any complex system, formal risk management practice can only be implemented through a rational and explicit planning process. The planning activity fits the strategic purposes and responsibilities of standards-based risk management to the security needs of the organization. From the standpoint of the rest of this text, it is the creation of that strategic risk management capability, which the RMF leverages, that will drive the presentation and discussion of the framework.

Risk management is basically built around information. In effect, risk management gathers and utilizes information from all sources, in order to decrease the possibility of future risks. The information-gathering activity is aided by a set of formal processes and technologies. And, at its core a successful risk management function relies on the ability to assure that the processes, practices, knowledge, and skills of risk management are incorporated as quickly and efficiently as possible into the organization's substantive decision-making processes.

In addition to providing the information that helps guide strategic decision-making about risks, the risk management process also makes certain that a commonly accepted and systematic set of policies and procedures are in place to handle known risks. That responsibility is operationalized through a standard set of operating procedures. Those procedures ensure that the risk planning, analysis, response, and process management function are always directly aligned to the goals of the business operation. Nevertheless, the primary purpose of risk management is to ensure a disciplined and systematic response to the risks that the organization considers a priority.

1.4 Elements of Risk Management

In simple terms, the risk management process assesses the likelihood that any given action will adversely impact something of value to any given entity. That includes things of personal value such as money, health, or even life. Once those risks are known, the risk management process deploys all of the measures that are necessary to ensure that consequent harm does not occur.

Some organizations manage risk in a highly quantified and data-driven way, for example, corporations that require high levels of integrity in their products as well as the segments of the critical infrastructure where the potential failure of a crucial system could result in a set of highly unwelcome consequences. Others tend to spend less on risk management and spending levels are influenced by the nature of the threat environment and the value and sensitivity of the assets that are being protected.

Because identification and understanding are such important aspects of risk management, assessment provides the fundamental focus of the process. Risk management is operationalized by a continuous process of assessing the organizational environment aimed at identifying and understanding all of the potential threats and the negative impacts that might affect the business. Once these have been identified and characterized, specific steps are then devised and implemented to mitigate any adverse outcomes.

Given its focus on the support of substantive decision-making, an important underlying factor in risk evaluation is the uncertainty principle. Uncertainty is a key element in assessing threats because risk entails future consequences. In essence, the outcomes of any given threat have to be fully understood in order for an intelligent decision to be made about the way forward in addressing it. However, there are usually a number of unknown, and therefore unevaluated, factors that might be associated with a given threat. Thus, the institution of standard and persistent identification, understanding, and response practices becomes an important element in the risk management process.

It goes without saying that it is easier to identify and evaluate risk in less complex environments. Yet, every aspect of cyberspace is abstract and complex. Therefore, risk management for cybersecurity requires a much different approach to the understanding and evaluation of risk. The process in the virtual world has to touch on factors than would normally not be part of the decision-making processes in the conventional physical world—such as how to authorize the acceptance of an invisible product. Accordingly, the sheer virtuality of ICT environments alone poses a threat.

The issue of threat management is important to our existence as a nation because ICT is the platform on which our modern society rests. Consequently, the huge increase in the number of strategic threats to computers and networks is a compelling danger to our modern way of life. The generic areas of threat have been variously categorized into terms such as "cyber-crime," cyber-terrorism, and "cyber-war." And in response to all of this turmoil, the past 15 years have witnessed the creation and evolution of a specialized new profession that is dedicated to addressing the many novel risks of the virtual world. The aim of that profession is to assure that ICT systems and the information that they contain, process, and communicate are protected against all logical forms of unauthorized access, use, disclosure, disruption, modification, perusal, inspection, recording, or destruction. That profession is presently termed "cybersecurity."

Cybersecurity evolved out of the practices and procedures of the older discipline of information assurance. One aspect of the original discipline was the responsibility to manage all risks related to the use, processing, storage, and transmission of information or data and the systems and processes used for those purposes. Cybersecurity incorporates a holistic approach to protection in that all aspects of risk mitigation in virtual and physical space have to be included in the protection scheme. This includes the creation and deployment of a complete and appropriate set of electronic and behavioral countermeasures.

This requirement is not simply a computer science challenge. It requires knowledge and practices from a wide range of traditional security fields, such as continuity management, forensics, audit, management science, software, and systems engineering, and even fields such as law and criminology. Consequently, what is required to manage cybersecurity risks is a complete and provably effective framework that ensures the proper coordination and use of all appropriate methods in the execution of the process. The framework should be expected to consolidate provably correct approaches into a single logical and coherent model of operation. The model contains all of the commonly accepted security best practices necessary to provide effective mitigation and management of all known risks to individuals, operations, and assets of the organization.

The key concept is "commonly accepted." A commonly accepted model of best practice establishes a standard point of reference. A unified vision is necessary to establish coordinated actions in the management of risk. Comprehensive coordination is a necessity because *all* potential risks must be identified, assessed, and responded to at all levels of the organization. The necessity for a complete, unassailable solution is a problem for the average manager. That is because conventional managers simply do not have the background or training to identify every potential risk, let alone devise foolproof methods to mitigate them. Nevertheless, particularly given the level of skill and sophistication of the large collection of malicious agents out there, it is critically important to implement comprehensive organization-wide protection since any system with an exploitable hole is a potential hazard.

As a result, there has always been an implicit requirement for the profession to establish and maintain a standard and comprehensive point of reference that practitioners can utilize to structure a practical risk management solution for their specific situation. Consequently, it is an attractive idea to consider employing a single commonly recognized standard, which specifies a single effective method for risk management.

Nonetheless, another underlying issue is how to get the most effective assurance out of the organization's limited resources. Any risk can be managed if enough money is thrown at it. However, no organization has the wherewithal to effectively put a cop on every street corner, so to speak. So, managers must weigh and balance the deployment of their risk response against the potential likelihood and material consequences of the threat. In day-to-day commercial operations, this means that it must be possible to make an informed decision about the level of risk that can be acceptable for every given situation. And given its layers of complexity, this is a particularly difficult task with cybersecurity risk, especially when the decision is weighted against the possible cost of failure.

Consequently, a coherent set of best practice methods, which let decision-makers benchmark existing and planned risk management resource usage, using the most expert advice available, is an important strategic management tool. This is because the drive for competitive advantage and the need for cost efficiency have driven corporations toward a growing dependence on technology. And thus the impacts of ICT risks have become an increasingly critical factor. Moreover, given that technology experiences rapid and dynamic change, the BOK regarding risk management must be deliberately researched, publicized, updated, and maintained. That condition justifies the role of the NIST in the development and promulgation of guidance about risk management.

The NIST's RMF was designed to offer a structured, yet flexible, means for analyzing and deciding how to alleviate the risks that arise from the information systems within an organization. The idea of adopting a coordinated set of formal risk management practices is a relatively new concept. Cybersecurity risk encompasses all of the risks that relate to the use of ICT. Thus, the risk management approaches that are specified in the RMF are intentionally broad-based. This is because those recommendations are meant to dictate how to assess risk and employ the appropriate risk mitigation strategies for all conventional ICT organizations.

This requirement implies the need for a single umbrella model that defines the elements and relationships of the risk management process. The specific steps for risk management take place within the structure created by this overarching model. And these are captured in the appropriate supporting NIST and security standards and guidelines that apply to that particular problem. The framework was derived from and builds on the collection of the International Organization for Standardization and the International Electrotechnical Commission (ISO/IEC), the Institute of Electrical and Electronics Engineers (IEEE), and NIST standards. It also consolidates information from various standard body publications, such as the Committee on National Security Systems Instruction (CNSSI) and the Department of Homeland Security Federal Continuity Directive 2 (FCD 2), and provides examples of ways to implement those standards and guidelines.

1.5 Risk Types and Risk Handling Strategies

There are four strategies that are generally employed in dealing with risk. The first strategy is to *accept* the risk and consequent losses. The second strategy is to *avoid* the loss by performing the necessary actions to eliminate the risk. A third strategy is to *mitigate* or *reduce the effect* of the risk. The last strategy involves *transferring* the risk to another party. That transfer can be achieved through contracts, insurance, or a variety of similar mechanisms. Nevertheless, no matter what approach is used, the organization has to adopt a formal strategy to decide how to address each of its risk categories. Likewise, regardless of the circumstances, the decision about what to do about the risk is purely in the domain of the designated decision-maker(s).

Accepting risk and the consequent losses is the most common approach for risks that rarely occur or where there is limited harm. Many risks pass unidentified or unacknowledged through the corporate risk management function because the cost of addressing the risk would not justify the potential cost of the harm. The decision to accept a risk can also change as the risk situation changes. After all inherent risks have been addressed by controls, there is still risk left over and an organization may decide to accept those risks. Even though the potential for harm exists, the present harm from the risk has been judged to be acceptable. Therefore, residual risks are still identified and tracked through the risk analysis process.

Risk avoidance is aimed at preventing the risk from actually occurring. Information security has three standard components: *prevention, detection,* and *response.* The prevention element and all it involves are examples of risk avoidance. Training programs, which are designed to increase the ability of employees to recognize and respond to incidents, are good examples of this type of risk handling approach. The information security process is heavily geared toward avoidance in order to reduce, as much as possible, the amount of harm by addressing the risk directly.

The last two components of the information security process, detection and response, are embodied in the risk mitigation and risk transference approaches. In the case of risk transference, the response requires an outside party to assume the impact of the risk. Insurance is a prime example of this type of assumption.

Obtaining insurance against specific risks does not prevent the risk from occurring, but it provides financial reimbursement to make up for a loss that will occur. Risk transfers work well when the risk is associated with a financial loss. Risk transfers are less effective when the loss is associated with less tangible things, such as customer service/retention, organization reputation, or in some cases regulatory requirements.

Risk mitigation approaches are the steps that an organization takes to minimize the potential loss in the event of the occurrence of a risk. For instance, an intrusion detection system will not prevent someone from actually intruding on the network. Instead, intrusion detection systems function as "burglar alarms" to limit the time that an intruder is allowed to roam undetected through a network. The limitation of time will not prevent damage. Instead, the limitation of time is meant to restrict the damage that might occur.

An important feature of the RMF is that it provides a practical basis for developing and maintaining comprehensive risk management controls for all aspects of a business's information assets. The objective of the RMF is to provide a common sense basis to develop, implement, and measure effective risk management practices. It is implemented through an organization-wide participative process and any business that has faced compliance issues with FISMA or NIST should be able to easily follow the RMF process.

The goal of the RMF initiative is to define and communicate a commonly accepted and standard basis for building risk management best practice. The RMF scheme compares the risk management practices of an organization against the threats and vulnerabilities it faces and prescribes a systematic mitigation approach for those threats (Figure 1.5).

It is designed to enable ICT managers to leverage their levels of risk awareness to a higher status. It allows companies to identify gaps in their risk management processes. It also allows companies of all sizes to demonstrate the effectiveness of their risk management program to prospective trading and investment partners. The RMF model underwrites assurance of risk management capability to any outside entity because it provides auditable and certifiable evidence that a scheme is in place to mitigate them.

Organizations have to document that they have considered the risk to their assets and have control measures in place to protect themselves against it. Those measures themselves are commonly understood as correct and specified in the NIST Special Publication (SP) 800-53 Revision 4 Standard, *Security and Privacy Controls for Federal Information Systems and Organizations,* which is the basis for verification of compliance to the FISMA. And in that respect, the RMF provides the risk-based assessment model for deploying the controls necessary to obtain formal certification of compliance with both FISMA and NIST. From a marketing perspective, certification to the RMF can also provide a basis for brand differentiation for ICT products. In that respect, the presence of an audited and certified security system becomes a true means of demonstrating the commitment of an organization to proper cybersecurity protection.

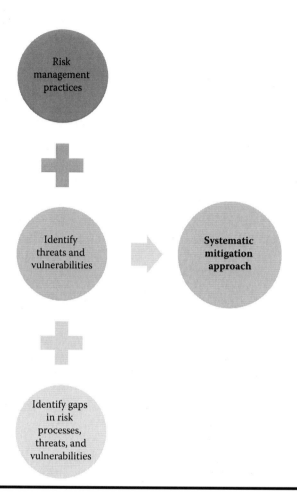

Figure 1.5   Risk management initiative goal.

Finally, in the cases where FISMA or other forms of audited proof of compliance are required, the external auditors will be able to determine that the organization has adopted a commonly accepted means to deploy a standard cybersecurity system within their organization. That is likely to make the certification and accreditation process a whole lot more efficient, as well as support the company's stance on any outcomes that could be called into question during the audit.

Besides these advantages, the RMF approach also offers some operational benefits. Cybersecurity tends to be tactical and reactive by nature, waiting for the bad guys to show up. On the other hand, if the defense-in-depth scheme is based on deterrent principles that are complete and comprehensive, the array of countermeasures can be protective rather than reactive. Organizations can initiate a full-scale set of procedures designed to prevent rather than remediate threats and work more proactively.

The RMF process supplies the management basis for identifying and organizing the comprehensive set of common best practices that the organization needs to establish and maintain control over its ICT risks. Since the RMF was designed to meet the needs of a range of target constituencies, and it is applicable to a range of ICT environments, it has the potential to deploy all of the necessary cybersecurity assurance elements to ensure an organization's systems are protected throughout their life cycle.

The RMF applies equally to building assurance as well as the long-term maintenance of assurance for information assets, embodied in organizational ICT systems. The activities in the RMF apply independently whether the actual system development and maintenance work is performed internally or externally to the organization—for example, outsourced. The risk evaluation approach applicable to the definition of a cybersecurity solution for a single system or multiple sites may even be applied on a shared basis between multiple parties. It delineates all of the elements of risk assessment that are necessary to structure a complete security response for any organization. This can be captured and expressed in everything from informal agreements up to a legally binding contract.

Since the RMF touches on every aspect of how to assess and manage risk, it forces companies through a step-by-step evaluation of their needs and responsibilities with respect to their ICT function. Nevertheless, the process itself is generic. That is, it provides the direction at the control level and not the step-by-step procedures necessary to manage risk. Thus, the generic assessment and implementation approach must be adapted to fit each given situation.

In essence, an optimum approach is engineered out of the RMF model for each individual organization. The understanding of risk that the RMF provides and the appropriate set of control objectives selected from NIST SP 800-53 Revision 4 comprise the actual form of the eventual response. Accordingly, the approach to implementing the RMF is hierarchical. Or in essence, an explicit cybersecurity solution that includes step-by-step policies and procedures is developed for each control area, at any level of definition top-down within the reference model provided by the RMF. And in that respect, the RMF assumes that specific cybersecurity approaches will be tailored to the outcomes of the common assessment process that is specified within the framework. This is accomplished in three steps. Once the threats, vulnerabilities, and weaknesses that the organization faces are assessed and their likelihood and impact are determined, policies are defined for each applicable control area. This serves as a foundation for tailoring.

Then, explicit control specifications are defined for each of the applicable areas of security risk management using the control recommendations of NIST SP 800-53 Revision 4. Finally, the real-world, day-to-day procedures/individual tasks are tailored and detailed for each individual role within the risk management process. These work instructions substantiate the standard behavioral specifications for a particular area of identified risk. The end result is an explicit set of risk management actions, which are based on the standard but accommodate all known threats.

Substantively, the actual operational response requires precise identification of the organizational context and requirements associated with each risk. Then a control is tailored that addresses those contextual requirements in the most effective way possible. Because risk contexts normally impose singular behaviors, the control procedures are usually tailored and implemented at the project level in various, project-specific ways. However, the definition and overall control selection process is executed globally for the entire business. The idea in all of these cases is to build a practical solution that will address the known threat environment, while continuing to incorporate the best practice recommendations of the framework.

This hierarchical approach creates a tangible, complete, and rational architecture of cybersecurity controls. It is imposed top-down directly out of the threat space into a precise set of security policies that define the organization's overall risk response. That definition process then continues through the practical management activities that implement these policies, right down to the level of utilitarian tasks. Tailoring can then be finalized by identifying the unique risk management issues, problems, and criteria for each instance and then making the necessary execution adjustments to fit the overall risk strategy.

The outcome of this tailoring process is a set of explicit behaviors, which become the tangible instantiation of the cybersecurity risk management scheme within any given organization. In general, the tailored set of procedures is the most visible and useful to the line manager, because it makes the recommended standard operating procedure (SOP) concrete in day-to-day practice. Moreover, the tailored set of best practices embodies and conveys the exact substance of the assigned activities and tasks for personal risk management behavior to every one of the employees working within the organization as a whole.

In concept, the controls itemized in NIST SP 800-53 Revision 4 are the general basis for tailoring out explicit control behaviors. But these control recommendations are not stand-alone elements. They are actually one facet of the aggregate set of best practices, which when properly arrayed as a set of standard activities, produces a rationally managed risk function within any organization. The controls form a complete and tightly integrated system as a set; however, in order to fulfill any aim or purpose that it might have, organizations can choose an appropriate subset from the complete set of NIST SP 800-53 Revision 4 controls.

1.6 Overview of the Risk Management Process

The steps to establish a standard risk management process involve five generic organizational functions: identification, assessment, control selection and implementation, test and measure, and continuous monitoring, as shown in Figure 1.6.

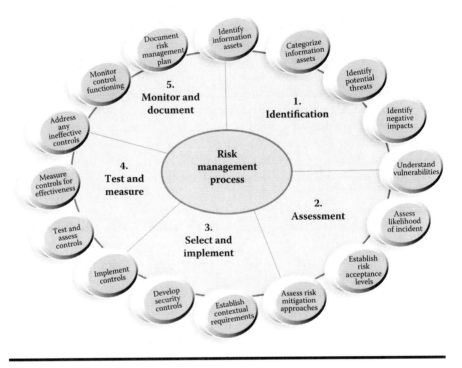

Figure 1.6   Risk management process.

1.6.1 Establishing the Risk Management Planning Process

The risk management plan shapes the risk management process. The primary role of the risk management plan is to create the framework for the detailed policies and procedures that will comprise the risk management process for the particular organization. The top-level risk management plan provides the strategic context that is needed to ensure that the organization's overall business objectives and goals are understood and then factored correctly into the decisions that are made about risk.

In that respect then, the overall plan for risk management needs to be crafted in broad, organizational terms, with the specific details of the approaches to be adopted left to lower-level operational plans. It is important that this high-level document defines the comprehensive processes and interrelationships needed to build a complete picture of the organizational risk situation. The ideal would be to create a roadmap that will let executive managers develop the strategies they will need to address existing risks.

First, the risk management plan should document the roles and responsibilities of the risk management team. The assignment of responsibility should be stated at a high enough level to allow the people on the risk management team to respond flexibly to situations covered in the plan. Nonetheless, the risk management plan has to assign specific authority to the team to act on those situations that are the responsibility of the risk management process. The assignment of high-level roles and responsibilities also ensures that the routine supervisory and budgetary authority, which is needed to conduct the process as a normal part of doing business, is expressly assigned to the individual members of the team.

Finally, the concepts associated with risk management have to be defined in clear organizational-specific terms. That definition is necessary in order to align the organization's overall security objectives with its business objectives. In that respect, a comprehensive and detailed definition of key terms has to be provided as part of the planning setup process. The purpose of those definitions is to ensure a common vocabulary throughout the organization.

Definitions are important because most people's understanding of what constitutes risk is subjective. Consequently, it is recommended that the organization provides a precise specification of what constitutes a risk, the levels of acceptable risk, and the attendant approaches that will be used to address each risk. Specific directives for how to report risks and the thresholds for acting on risk reports also have to be preestablished for the various risk elements. The reporting requirements will also apply to active, residual, and accepted risks.

1.6.2 Identifying and Categorizing the Risk Environment

The next step in establishing effective risk management is to acquire comprehensive knowledge of the threat environment. That knowledge requires an all-inclusive record of the organization's assets, a statement of the acceptable levels of risk for each asset, and the constraints that will be placed on the protection of the asset by the available resources, technology, or existing policies. The outcome of the threat cataloging process is an alignment of the policies that will be used for risk management with the business goals of the organization.

That alignment is needed to conduct the trade-off process. Trade-offs will be used to decide the risk acceptance, risk avoidance, risk transference, or risk mitigation strategy that will be used to ensure each asset is addressed. When those trade-offs are planned, they should accurately reflect the organization's business objectives. An analysis of the priority of the information that enables the business objectives versus the threats to the information is necessary in order to decide where to invest the organization's security resources. Defining risk levels needs to be done with respect to their impact on the CIA of the data in the organization's operational systems.

Risk management coordinates three highly related factors within the operation, which are as follows: (1) the risks that can be associated with the organization's systems, (2) the business functions that are associated with the information in those systems, and (3) the extent of control necessary to manage each of those risks. The key to success lies in deploying the minimum number of controls to achieve a desired level of assurance, given the intended purposes of each affected business function.

The risk control deployment process can be carried out in two different ways. The most common way to conduct the deployment is *ad hoc*. In the case of ad hoc risk control deployment, the controls are created to fulfill specific security needs. Those needs generally arise as a threat is identified. Many organizations use an ad hoc approach to risk management simply because the deployment of a coordinated set of controls is a difficult process to manage on a day-to-day basis. The ad hoc approach is cost-efficient because it only creates controls that are needed at the time. Nonetheless, it is almost certain to result in flawed protection because the organization is reacting to events that are occurring rather than deploying coordinated protection to prevent them from happening in the first place.

Another approach to risk management is the *coordinated approach*. Because it is meant to provide comprehensive protection, the coordinated approach offers more effective risk management. It deploys a series of risk mitigation baselines in a defense-in-depth scheme and is composed of a rational set of increasingly rigorous technical and behavioral controls. In most baselines, the electronic controls are automated while the behavioral controls entail a series of well-defined human-centered actions intended to produce a desired outcome. Each baseline is deployed to achieve specific risk management objectives and is prioritized in terms of the criticality of the data. Nevertheless, the creation, deployment, and ongoing monitoring of the baselines is both time-consuming and costly. Therefore, the degree of assurance justified under this scheme always has to be balanced against the level of effort and cost that is required to implement and maintain it. The aim of the coordinated approach is to deal only with the priority risks to the organization. In that respect, it takes active coordination to create and maintain an effective array of behaviors to manage the risks deemed most critical.

Because cost is a factor, a precise specification of the maximum degree of acceptable risk is a prerequisite to making a realistic plan. The specification of the maximum level of risk is necessary because much of real-world planning typically involves deciding what level of risk the organization is willing to accept. A decision about the degree of risk that the organization is willing to accept will lead to an assignment of priorities. Understanding the value of an item enables an explicit decision about its priority. The priorities then drive decisions about the practical form of the response. The value assigned is typically expressed as the level of acceptability of the risk. Consequently, acceptability is typically expressed in operational terms like, "Spend whatever it takes to ensure that this risk does not occur," all the way down to "The harm the risk would cause does not justify the cost of addressing it." Nonetheless, in order to decide about the level of risk, the decision-maker has to first know the value of the information the organization possesses.

Decisions about the acceptability of risk lead directly to a coordinated security response. Thus, the risk management process involves a technique that establishes a substantive, usually resource-based, link between every identified threat and the benefits of managing it. Operational factors that enter into that analysis include issues such as "What is the level of criticality of each particular information asset and what is the specific degree of resource involvement?" Therefore, threat/risk evaluations have to answer one key question at a minimum: "What is the trade-off between accepting the risk and the harm it can cause?"

1.6.3 Risk Assessment

The overall purpose of the risk management function is to maintain an appropriate set of risk controls. Therefore, ongoing assessments are a particularly critical part of that overall purpose. They are required because all control sets have to be periodically assessed in order to ensure that their protection is relevant and maintain their effectiveness. Risk assessments are important because they identify the specific threats to the organization, how likely those threats are to occur, and the consequences of each threat should it happen. Because knowing where risks lie is a fundamental precondition for managing them, the term "risk assessment" is sometimes used interchangeably with "risk management."

Moreover, risk assessment is not the same as risk management. Obviously, knowing the likelihood and impact of each potential threat is an essential precondition to managing it. Risk assessment is a tool that supports the larger risk management function, rather than an end in itself. Risk assessments underwrite the overall strategy that is used to deploy the risk management process. Risk assessments inform managers as to where to deploy the necessary reactive controls to respond to a risk. Risk assessments also monitor the effectiveness of those controls once they have been put in place. Thus, risk assessment maintains effective and up-to-date knowledge about the threat situation. And in many respects, risk assessment is an underlying prerequisite to the conduct of the risk management function. They are needed because a systematic risk assessment can specifically direct the maintenance of the controls that the organization has deployed to do substantive risk management. The targeted information ensures the most efficient use of security resources. Risk assessment is an information-gathering function that focuses on understanding the nature of all feasible threats. Risk assessment identifies and evaluates each relevant threat, determines the threat's potential impact, and itemizes the controls that will be needed to respond properly.

In that respect, risk assessments should always answer two distinct but highly related questions. The first is "What is the certainty of the risk?" The answer to that question is typically expressed as likelihood of occurrence. The second is "What is the anticipated impact?" The answer to that question is normally expressed as an estimate of the loss, harm, failure, or danger. Ideally, both of these questions can be answered in easily understood terms. Understandability and credibility are key factors, because the results of the risk assessment will guide the deployment and subsequent conduct of the risk management process.

All risk assessments provide two specific pieces of knowledge: (1) the probability of occurrence and (2) the estimate of the consequences. There is a logical sequence to how these two questions should be approached. Practically speaking, the first consideration has to be likelihood, since a highly unlikely event might not be worth the cost of further consideration. However, it is the estimate of the consequences that truly shapes the form of the response. That is because there is never enough money to secure against every conceivable risk and so the potential harm that each risk represents always has to be balanced against the likelihood of its occurrence.

Therefore, the fundamental goal of the risk assessment process is to maximize the operational deployment of the organization's risk controls. Risk assessment accomplishes that purpose by identifying existing and potential threats with the greatest probability of occurrence and those which will cause the greatest degree of harm. The options these created are then arrayed in descending order of priority and addressed based on the resources that are available. Since all of the decisions about the tangible form of the risk management process will depend on getting the order of those priorities correct, it should be easy to see why a rigorous and accurate risk assessment process is so critical to the overall success of any risk management program.

Risk assessments are built around tangible evidence. The evidence is usually obtained by conducting interviews and documenting observations of both organizational and human behavior as well as auditing system logs and examining any other form of relevant technical or managerial records. Because the sources of data about risk are diverse, the collection process has to be systematic and coordinated. As a consequence, every risk assessment should embody a commonly accepted and repeatable methodology, which will produce concrete evidence that can be independently verified. The gathering, compilation, analysis, and verification of data about risk can be time-consuming and resource-intensive. So, in order to ensure the effectiveness and accuracy of any particular risk assessment, the practical scope of the inquiry has to be precisely defined and should be limited to a particular question, or problem.

Risk assessments typically target the various standard areas of threat—electronic, human, and physical. The insight gained from each assessment is then aggregated into a single comprehensive understanding of the total threat picture, which serves as the basis for deciding how each threat will be addressed. Operationally, it is perfectly acceptable to approach the understanding of risk in a highly focused and compartmentalized manner, as long as the organization understands that the results of any specific risk assessment characterize only a part of the problem. In fact, the need to paint a detailed and accurate picture of all conceivable threats almost always implies a series of specifically targeted, highly integrated risk assessments that take place over a defined period.

1.6.4 Designing for Effective Risk Management

1.6.4.1 Context

Every risk management process has to be designed to fit its particular environment. Environmental considerations are the factors that have to be understood in order to fit the risk management process into the overall operating circumstances of the organization. Accordingly, the design should describe all technical and environmental factors that might impact the risk management process.

In that respect, the design has to ensure that the process is correctly aligned with the environmental, sensitivity, and security requirements within the operational context of the organization. That is because the organizational context always dictates the risk management approach. For instance, there will be a different set of risk management procedures where the operational context is top secret or highly secure and requires very rigorous approaches, versus one where the context is more relaxed. As a result, the operational context in which the process functions has to be clearly understood in order to design a proper risk management approach.

1.6.4.2 Scope and Boundaries

Once the context about the scope or area of coverage is understood, the actual assurance has to be explicitly defined. The definition should be the result of a formal planning exercise. Formal planning is required because tangible organizational resources are involved. And failure to define an accurate and realistic scope for the risk management process could result in deficient protection and wasted resources. Therefore, distinctive and meaningful boundaries have to be established for the conduct of the risk management process. In particular, the logical interrelationships have to be understood between components, since the dependencies between the various elements that fall under the risk management process have to be factored into the assurance process. Or in practical terms, an activity that is linked to one outside of the scope of protection would represent a vulnerability. Since scope is always tied to the actual resources available, understanding which components will be a part of the risk management process and their actual interdependencies will allow the organization to be more realistic about what it will be able to protect.

1.6.4.3 Roles and Responsibilities

The definition of roles and responsibilities is a critical step in designing the risk management function since they tie both personnel and financial resources to the activities that will be performed. It is also important to explicitly clarify the duties that are associated with each of those roles. Otherwise, participants are likely to bring to the party their own assumptions about what they are supposed to do, which could result in important activities falling through the cracks.

Roles and responsibilities are created by designating accountability for performance of each security activity as well as all of the organizational reporting lines that are associated with each role. In that respect, if third parties or contractors are responsible for any aspect of risk management, the responsibilities and reporting lines of both the contractor and the organizational unit must be clearly defined.

1.6.4.4 Definition of Priorities

In addition to identifying and relating the various resource elements, each of these elements has to be categorized in terms of their general priority. Priority is directly related to the criticality of the resource. It is essential to be able to know the priority of each component in order to decide how many resources to commit to its protection.

The determination of priority is based on a simple understanding of the purpose of each element. The description of purpose should convey the general importance of the element in the overall operating environment. The description of purpose satisfies two operational goals. First, it allows managers to make informed assignments of priorities for the protected components. Second, it allows managers to coordinate the implementation and subsequent execution of the information assurance functions that are assigned to each component.

1.6.4.5 Sensitivity of the Information

It is essential to specify the sensitivity of each item of information within the system. That is because the sensitivity of the information determines the levels of CIA required. Thus, this specification provides the necessary basis for determining the extent and rigor of the controls. The specification also provides the basis for deploying the selected risk controls that will be used to secure each component. The specification should not just be guided by a consideration of technical standards and protocols. Minimally, the specification of the sensitivity should also consider the policies, laws, and any relevant constraints that might affect the CIA of information within the system.

The outcome of that specification should be a detailed recommendation of how the particular requirement will be addressed by a specific control. In addition, the recommendation for each control should provide a justification for why that particular approach was taken. The aim of that justification is to explain the type and relative importance of the protection needed. Each type of data and information processed by the system should be classified based on the severity of potential negative impacts on the organization and the degree to which the ability of the organization to perform its mission would be affected, should the information be compromised.

The sensitivity of information should be characterized based on the risks a compromise would represent. The highest risk would be associated with compromises that would adversely impact critical information, or which might result in loss of life, significant financial loss, threats to national security, or the inability of the organization to perform its primary mission.

Moderate risks would be those risks that might not compromise critical information but where the losses would still have business impacts. Low-risk items would be those risks where information might be lost but it would not be vital to organizational functioning.

1.6.5 Evaluating Candidates for Control

The threats that comprise the risk environment of an organization need to be understood before precise steps can be taken to manage them. Therefore, all known threats have to be identified, their relationships to each other understood, and the potential actions that they could take to cause harm have to be characterized. This can be evaluated and understood using the RMF stages. That understanding will let the organization describe in accurate terms the factors that threaten it and what those threats are likely to cause in terms of harm and their likelihood of occurrence. This understanding can then facilitate the development of precisely targeted controls for each threat.

Threat modeling is a structured method that is used to analyze risk-related data. A successful threat modeling process requires a lot of "creative" thinking, in that every conceivable threat should be put on the table and assessed. Threat modeling allows risk data to be modeled and subsequently communicated among team members. The major steps of threat modeling begin with a determination of the scope of protected space that the model corresponds to. Then threats that might impact the components of that space are enumerated and specific details as to the potential likelihood and impact of the threat are collected.

In order to ensure that the analysis is comprehensive, data flow diagrams or similar information flow diagrams such as unified modeling language (UML)-based use-case diagrams are employed to help visualize and describe the target space. These diagrams can be very helpful to ensure inclusive coverage. Descriptions of potential attack vectors and the impacts of each of the vectors on the protected space are used to think through and then describe the actual attack behavior. In that respect then, all potential attack vectors should be able to be described and examined from an adversary's point of view.

Subsequently, the implications of each threat must be analyzed. This analysis is typically based on assigning a criticality score. A standardized criticality score is an important part of the threat modeling process because it allows analysts to classify each identified threat in terms of its likelihood and potential harm. That classification can then lead to a priority ordering of known threats from most dangerous to least dangerous. The ordering will allow management to concentrate resources on the threats that have the greatest potential for harm. It will also let managers assign fewer resources to lower priority threats. It is this classification process that allows managers to build logical and substantive defense-in-depth schemes.

A focus on priority differs from the typical low-hanging fruit approach. Nevertheless, the implementation process has to be based on some kind of quantitative or rational method for assigning priorities. Without priorities to guide the implementation, it is likely that the easiest to understand or most obvious threats will be addressed first. That approach would, in essence, disregard the business value of what was being protected. Given the requirement for thorough understanding in order to assign practical priorities, it is important to have a commonly agreed upon starting point to base the comparisons; this is the role of threat modeling. Threat modeling goes a long way toward putting quantitative and systematic implementation of the measures to control risk on a systematic and logical footing.

1.6.6 Implementing Risk Management Controls

The controls for risk management differ in their purpose and specificity. It is important to keep this difference in mind when designing and then assigning control activities because the people who will actually be executing each control need to know exactly how to perform all of the tasks that are necessary to make the control effective.

As a consequence, it is important to ensure that management types are not asked to perform highly technical tasks, just as it is equally critical that technical people are not asked to perform managerial activities. In both cases, there is the potential that the activities that underlie the control will be either misunderstood or misapplied. It is also important to understand the operational status of the control.

Knowing the existing operational status of the control, or even whether the control actually exists, is important in the design process. This is because some controls will already be present in the legacy scheme, while others will not have been created yet. Therefore, it is essential to have a complete understanding of where a procedure has already been implemented and where it has to be developed. This understanding is based on whether each necessary control item is operational and effective or not actually operational as originally planned.

It is common to have part of the control in place while other parts are still missing. If some parts of the control are implemented and others have only been planned, there should be an explicit specification of the parts of the control that are in place and the parts that are not. Where there are planned measures, this description should also include a list of resources required to make them operational and the expected timeline.

Finally, situations will exist where controls would be desirable, but it would be neither cost-effective nor feasible to implement them. If this is the case, then those controls should be noted for future planning as well as potential long-term monitoring of the risk that the measure was meant to manage.

1.6.6.1 Management Controls

Management controls are behavioral and based on policies designed to employ the organization's risk management procedures. Examples of management controls are incident response, security assessment, and planning controls. The nature of management controls is to manage risks through human-based actions rather than technology. These controls are typically designed based on a risk analysis, which should support a comparison between the costs of the applicable controls and the value of the information resource they are designed to protect.

Management controls are deployed based on the impact of the threats that they have been designed to address. It is important to design the appropriate administrative, physical, and personnel security controls into the risk management process from its inception. Because risks come in a number of forms, there can be an extensive range and variety of risk management controls.

Management controls are primarily enforced by the testing and review process. Therefore, the design must ensure that tests are performed during the development of the risk management process. The aim of those evaluations is to confirm that all of the necessary controls are an established part of the risk management process.

1.6.6.2 Technical Controls

Just as with the management process, the technical controls should also be well defined, understood, and followed. From a risk management standpoint, the most obvious technical controls are those that underlie the access control system. Technical controls are important and should be monitored closely. The monitoring of technical controls is an essential aspect of management accountability as well as a technical issue. As a consequence, the monitoring of technical controls from a managerial standpoint is often associated with audit procedures. A complete audit trail and a chronological record are evidence of adequate monitoring. The use of system log files to monitor system behavior is an example of this type of control.

1.6.6.3 Risk Type

Risks represent a threat to some aspect of organizational functioning. Moreover, the management of risk is a complex process with lots of inherent detail. As mentioned previously, in order to implement the risk management process, it is necessary to classify and understand the nature of the threats that are present in the organization's current operating environment. In general, threats can be classified into two categories, *known* and *unknown*.

Unknown threats, also known as *asymmetric* threats, are not predictable and not subject to management by standard risk management methods. Because of their unpredictability, they do not lend themselves to specific techniques for analysis. *Known* threats are those that should be logically expected to occur. Thus, another name for known threat is *intrinsic risk*. In many cases, the probability of occurrence and subsequent impact of an intrinsic risk can be estimated. Intrinsic risks can be managed and minimized by an effective risk management program.

Accordingly, the organization has to adopt and follow some kind of structured process to identify, classify, and provide a meaningful response to the intrinsic risks that fall within the scope of the risk management process. This is the general aim of the RMF process. The RMF process can be employed to organize and coordinate the risk identification, analysis, and planning activities of a comprehensive risk management program.

Areas of intrinsic risk can be classified into three generic categories: management, operational, and technical. Using these categories in some form of checklist, managers can systematically work their way through a practical risk management situation and evaluate the status of each of the standard risk items on the list.

The management risk category encompasses the potential risks to the organization's information assets or documentation, as well as any of the risks that are associated with the assignment of roles and responsibilities and the risks represented by a failure to do proper contingency or configuration management planning. These are very large areas of organizational functioning and so their analysis requires extensive coordination. And because of the sheer scope of each of these areas, the analysis process itself usually requires a large number of participants. Managers can use the identification, assessment, and the select and implement stages of the RMF process as a roadmap to guide the deployment of the necessary controls to ensure a persistent risk response.

The second category includes the operational risks. These types of risk are much more focused and detailed. Operational risks involve threats to the operational environment that the organization has to manage, such as ensuring the identify management function and making certain that the identification and authentication processes, auditing, malicious code protection, long-term system maintenance, and communications security functions are properly ensured. These areas require the coordination of complex managerial and technical activities. Because of the complexity, the assurance of these areas has to be detailed and closely controlled. The RMF stages allow managers to both coordinate the threat identification effort and aggregate the huge amount of data that is normally collected in order to ensure that risk controls are effective and persistent.

Finally, there are the risks that are associated with the technical controls. Those include the predictable threats to electronic systems; however, they also include any electronic controls over media and the physical and personnel security environment. The technical risk category even includes risks that reside in the cybersecurity education, training, and awareness function. Because of their diversity and inherent complexity, every technical risk area has to be very well defined in order to be properly analyzed. A checklist of items for analysis is useful in facilitating this process and provides the necessary structure for the analysis. A checklist will also ensure that the right data is captured for each category and that the eventual analysis is appropriate.

1.6.7 Assessing the Effectiveness of Risk Controls

Forms of process assessment and measurement are important elements of good management practice. Assessment tells decision-makers whether or not their operational objectives are being met, that the results they are getting are in line with expectations, or even whether a process is under control. Risk management is no different than any other management activity in that regard. Good risk management requires appropriate measurement that accurately reflects the present threat picture of the organization. Nevertheless, proper assessment relies on the availability of meaningful standard measures.

Qualitative and quantitative measures can both be used for risk analysis. Both qualitative and quantitative measurements allow the organization to prioritize its risks and responses. The qualitative and quantitative measurement processes both assume that risks can be analyzed and that that analysis can be used to deploy the controls necessary to manage risk.

1.6.7.1 Qualitative Measurement

Qualitative measurement does not utilize actual metrics, but rather focuses on relative differences. Graphic scales are commonly used in qualitative analysis. Numbers may also be used, but they are merely markers for comparison value, not actual representative quantities. The end result of a qualitative risk assessment is a matrix of threats that differentiates between different relative levels of likelihood and impact.

In qualitative risk analysis, the measures that are used are descriptive, typically a set of nominal values such as high, medium, and low. These categories are then assigned numbers so that the weights of relationships can be characterized. Using those nominal values, it is possible to distinguish between items receiving a score of high versus those receiving a score of medium, for instance. However, it is not possible to truly rank different elements of the same class. So, the actual measurement itself is not precise. Nevertheless, since one of the main purposes of the risk analysis function is to determine priorities, qualitative analysis can be useful.

1.6.7.2 Quantitative Measurement

If there is a need for a more granular understanding of the risk situation, then quantitative analysis methods can be used. The value of quantitative methods depends upon the quality of the data being used. For instance, in the case of something like an actuarial estimate, hard evidence like the accuracy of records of birth and death and the causes of injury and loss, coupled with other factors, can be used to build predictive mathematical models. These models can be created and studied by analysts and the results from previous time periods can be compared with current results. In the case of risk management, accurate and reliable measures are difficult if not impossible to obtain while the changing nature of the technology will restrict the application of time series studies. Therefore, in practice, a blend of both quantitative and qualitative measures is often used to arrive at the desired understanding.

1.6.8 Sustainment: Risk Assessment and Operational Evaluation of Change

Because the business environment is constantly changing, it is necessary to do continuous operational assessments of the risk environment in order to assure the validity of the risk management controls for the organization. Operational planning should be aligned with business goals and their accompanying strategies. The outcome of the assessment planning process must be a relevant monitoring of the current risk picture within business constraints.

All plans for any form of risk management process should be based on consistent standard assessment. Consistent assessment processes are important because management will use assessment data to make decisions about the degree of risk exposure as well as the types of controls that will have to be deployed. Accordingly, all of the metrics included in the risk evaluation process must be unambiguously defined in the plan. Those definitions can then be used to ensure that the data from the assessment process is consistent.

Consistency of measurement is a critical factor because stakeholders have to share a common understanding of the precise nature of the threats that the organization faces in order to trust the management response. As a result, it is important to make certain that there is reliable understanding of what a given assessment result means. If the various individuals who are involved in the risk management process interpret the information differently, there is a potential for uncoordinated and ineffective operational response. Additionally, there is the issue of credibility when it comes to the data itself. If there is no clear definition provided to function as the basis for measurement, then it is hard for decision-makers to rely on the data.

The activities that are involved in operational assessment are planned and implemented in the same way as other types of organizational assessment activities. That is, the operational risk assessment process employs risk evaluations to decide about the nature of emerging threats. Even so, rather than producing an overall risk management strategy, the goal of the operational risk assessment is to say with certainty that the currently deployed set of controls properly address the right threats. The assessment also seeks to prove that the controls continue to be effective given the overall aims of the business.

If the controls that are currently deployed do not address the aims of the business, then the operational risk assessment should provide all of the information necessary to allow decision-makers to make any changes that may be needed to achieve the desired state. Thus, any review report that contains recommendations for change is typically passed along to the people who are responsible for maintaining the operational risk management process instead of the top-level planners who initially formulated the response. The aim of that report is to provide explicit advice about changes that must be made to the current risk management controls.

Planning for operational risk assessments involves the establishment of a standard schedule for each assessment as well as a defined process for problem reporting and corrective action. The routine nature of these reviews means that the organization should treat operational risk assessment exactly as it would any other continuous organizational process. That is, the process should be resourced and staffed to ensure that it functions as a part of the everyday business operation.

Operational risk assessment does not typically entail the sort of strategic planning focus that was involved in the formulation of the security strategy. Instead, it makes use of a defined set of performance criteria to evaluate the performance of the routine operation of the risk management function. Those criteria are typically laid down during the formulation of the initial risk management strategy. Consequently, every risk control that is deployed should have a clear set of standard criteria built into its specification.

These criteria should be both quantifiable and capable of being recorded and kept in a meaningful manner. Additionally, the assumptions about cost and occurrence that were part of the original decision to deploy each control should also be stated as a means of maintaining perspective on the operational intent of that control. The purpose of standard performance criteria is to allow decision-makers to judge whether a control is performing as desired and continues to achieve its intended purpose. The organization will use the data produced by the operational assessment process to ensure the effectiveness of its risk management scheme.

1.6.9 Evaluating the Overall Risk Management Function

The real proof of a risk management program's success lies in the operational outcomes of the controls that have been deployed for risk management. The test is whether the controls have achieved the desired business outcomes when it comes to risk mitigation. Control performance audits and assessments can be used to verify that the operational controls are functioning as designed and intended. Moreover, assessments can produce quantitative evidence that the control set is effectively controlling risk.

The assessment process itself is mainly a retrospective analysis of outcomes that is designed to verify through logs, record checks, and visual confirmation that the currently deployed control set has successfully covered the priority risks. The assessment examines the operation of those controls over some defined period in order to evaluate whether the organization is actually operating as planned. The assessment also attempts to characterize the effectiveness of each control based on the historical data that is recorded about its operation.

An audit adds a series of planned tests of the actual functioning of the process in order to confirm that its control features are functioning as they were designed to do. Both assessments and evaluations are designed to cover the entire breadth of the control set. Periodic audits are necessary for any organizational function. They are needed to ensure that the program is still meeting the objectives of the organization.

Risk management programs are no different in that respect. So, one of the important elements of the risk management process is the periodic execution of an audit that is designed to assess the overall effectiveness of the risk management program. Two types of audits are commonly used, a *time-based* audit and an *event-based* audit. It is generally a good idea to utilize both types of audits in practice, in order to ensure complete assurance.

A *time-based* audit is one that occurs at regular intervals, ranging typically from 1 to 3 years. These are top-down, comprehensive audits that are designed to examine all aspects of the risk management program against the business objectives that are currently in place. The purpose of time-based audits is to ensure that the risk management operation stays current with the business strategies and the ever-changing threat environment of the enterprise.

An *event-based* audit is much less comprehensive, but much more focused on a particular aspect of the risk management process. Like lessons-learned and after-action reviews, event-based audits are meant to capture and record information about a particular aspect of the risk management operation. For instance, if a business unit is reorganized, the business objectives may change. Because that change would represent a significant modification of the operating environment, it would be a good idea to make sure that the risk management program continues to support the goals of that unit. For the same reason, it is also important to audit the risk management situation after an actual incident has occurred in order to ensure that the outcomes of the incident reflect the desired results.

The objective of both of these kinds of audits is to ensure that the risk management program stays in step with changes in the business environment. Regardless of the type of audit that is conducted, there are some common elements that should be looked at as a part of each audit. The first of these elements are the controls themselves. In essence, the audit should determine how effective these controls were in detecting and responding to the threat that they were deployed to prevent. Additionally, the audit should confirm that there was not a need for additional controls for that particular incident.

In conjunction with the assessment of the actual control set, the audits should also examine the effectiveness of the policies and procedures that guide the implementation and routine operation of those controls. Those policies and procedures should be proven to align with the criteria for accepting the residual risk levels within the environment, as well as address the threat at the level of protection that is required. If the need to add additional controls, policies, and procedures, or modify existing ones, is identified, then the audit report should itemize what those changes should be.

In addition to operational audits, a standard policy should be defined for conducting audits. As most organizations have an internal audit function, the audit of risk management processes and procedures should be built into their regular internal audit function. Conducting an audit of the risk management process as part of regular internal audit activity is an appropriate way to address the need for periodic audits of the risk management process. Rolling the assessment of the risk management function into regular internal audit activities is yet another way to institutionalize the risk management process.

1.7 Chapter Summary

In some respects, this book is as much about standardization as it is about risk management. Hence, this chapter presented an overview of the role of the standardization process in ensuring a consistent response to a given issue of importance. This includes a discussion of why information assets are difficult to protect as well as applying commonly acknowledged best practices to ensure an informed response. Specifically, we presented the issues involved in implementing a standard process including the benefits that derive from it as well as the potential pitfalls.

In practice, organizations design, implement, and follow some form of systematic process to establish a persistent operational risk management process. The design and management process is a strategic activity, in that it involves long-range considerations. Thus, planning for strategic risk management is necessary in order to ensure continuous risk assurance. And a formal strategic planning process is necessary to implement an organization-wide risk management process. Risk management itself must incorporate all of the elements of the business within its scope and the process should reach to the boundaries of the organization.

The outcome of the implementation of a risk management process is a concrete, organization-wide risk management scheme. The scheme will balance the aims of long-term risk control policy with real-world conditions and constraints. The atomic-level components of the risk management process are a set of substantive controls that ensure the requisite level of assurance against loss. These controls should be traceable directly to the policies that defined their need. This is a closed-loop process in that the ongoing alignment of risk controls to policies fine-tunes the evolution of the substantive risk management process and ensures its effectiveness in all operational settings.

One problem is that the term "risk management" is rather amorphous. So, the overall process itself requires a concrete statement of what risk management comprises. That statement is needed in order to make the practice standard. Standardization is important because a lack of effective, coordinated implementation and execution of the elements of the process has made overall risk management efforts ineffective. One does not need to look any further than the increasing number of incidents in cyberspace to confirm that.

The other important justification for this standard is that the RMF also defines the basis for a comprehensive strategic governance approach to risk. A governance rather than technical approach is a highly advantageous strategy because, notwithstanding the issue of whether the cybersecurity function itself can ever fully embrace all of the issues associated with assurance, a governance-based solution is more easily understood and acceptable to the managers and nontechnical people who comprise the bulk of the organization.

This book starts from the assumption that a standardized risk management process should be applied corporation-wide. In that respect, risk management becomes a strategic issue rather than a narrow technical concern. The reason to adopt an organization-wide risk management approach is to avoid the dysfunctional effects of a typical piecemeal solution. The alternative approach to piecemeal is a formally defined and instantiated architecture of comprehensive risk management best practices, which are specifically aimed at optimizing risk controls across the company. As with any complex system, formal risk management practice can only be implemented through a rational and explicit planning process. The planning activity fits the strategic purposes and responsibilities of standards-based risk management to the security needs of the organization. From this standpoint, and throughout the rest of the book, it is the creation of that strategic risk management capability, which the RMF leverages, that will drive the presentation and discussion of the framework.

In simple terms, the risk management process assesses the likelihood that any given action will adversely impact something of value to any given entity. This includes such things of personal value as money, health, or even life. Once those risks are known, the risk management process deploys all of the measures that are necessary to ensure that consequent harm does not occur.

Because identification and understanding are important aspects of risk management, assessment provides the fundamental focus of the process. In essence, risk management is operationalized by a continuous process of assessing the organizational environment aimed at identifying and understanding all of the potential threats and the negative impacts that might affect the business. Once these have all been identified and characterized, then specific steps are devised and implemented to mitigate any adverse outcomes.

What is required to manage cybersecurity risks is a complete and provably effective framework that ensures the proper coordination and use of all appropriate methods in the execution of the process. The framework should be expected to consolidate provably correct approaches into a single logical and coherent model of operation. That model will contain all of the commonly accepted security best practices necessary to provide effective mitigation and management of all known risks to individuals, operations, and assets of the organization.

The NIST's RMF was designed to offer a structured yet flexible means for analyzing and deciding how to alleviate the risks that arise from the information systems within an organization. The idea of adopting a coordinated set of formal risk management practices is a relatively new concept. Cybersecurity risk encompasses all of the risks that are related to the use of ICT. Thus, the risk management approaches that are specified in the RMF are intentionally broad-based. That is because those recommendations are meant to dictate how to assess risk and employ the appropriate risk mitigation strategies for all conventional ICT organizations.

The requirement implies the need for a single umbrella model that defines the elements and relationships of the risk management process. The specific steps for risk management take place within the structure created by this overarching model. And these are captured in the appropriate supporting NIST and ISO security standards and guidelines that apply to that particular problem. The framework was derived from and builds on the collection of ISO, IEEE, and NIST standards. It also consolidates information from various standard body publications and provides examples of ways to implement those standards and guidelines.

An important feature of the RMF is the fact that it provides a practical basis for developing and maintaining comprehensive risk management controls for all aspects of a business's information assets. The objective of the RMF is to provide a common sense basis to develop, implement, and measure effective risk management practice. It is implemented through an organization-wide participative process and any business that has faced compliance issues with FISMA and NIST should be able to easily follow the RMF process.

Since the RMF touches on every aspect of how to assess and manage risk, it guides organizations through a step-by-step evaluation of their needs and responsibilities with respect to their ICT function. The process itself is generic and provides only the direction; it does not dictate the specific controls necessary to manage risk. Thus, the generic assessment and implementation approach must be adapted to fit every given situation.

In essence, an optimum approach is engineered out of the RMF model for each individual organization. The understanding of risk that the RMF provides and the appropriate set of control objectives selected from NIST SP 800-53 Revision 4 comprise the actual form of the eventual response. Accordingly, the approach to implementing the RMF is hierarchical. Or in essence, an explicit cybersecurity solution is evolved for any given unit, at any level of definition top-down within the reference model provided by the RMF.

And in that respect, the RMF assumes that specific cybersecurity approaches will be tailored to the outcomes of the common assessment process that is specified within the general framework of the RMF. This is accomplished in three steps. Once the threats, vulnerabilities, and weaknesses that the organization faces are assessed and their likelihood and impact are determined, policies are defined for each applicable control area. This serves as a foundation for tailoring.

The real proof of a risk management program's success lies in the operational outcomes of the controls that have been deployed for risk management. The test is whether the controls have achieved the desired business outcomes when it comes to risk mitigation. Control performance audits and assessments can be used to verify that the operational controls are functioning as designed and intended. Moreover, assessments can produce quantitative evidence that the control set is effectively controlling risk.

Glossary

best practice: a set of lessons learned, validated for successful execution of a given task

controls: a discrete set of human, or electronic behaviors, set to produce a given outcome

control performance: the operational results of control operation within a given environment

FISMA: the Federal Information Security Management Act of 2002

impact: a specific outcome or harm that might result as a consequence of a given threat

likelihood: the probability that a given event will occur, usually expressed as percent

NIST SP 800-53 Revision 4: the National Institute of Standards and Technology Security and Privacy Controls for Federal Information Systems

risk management: formal oversight and control of the threat mitigation actions of an organization

risk management scheme: specific architecture that embodies the overall strategy for risk mitigation

standard framework: a commonly accepted formal statement of best practice for a given topic

standardization: process of ensuring systematic common execution of a responsibility, or task

strategic governance: the overall long-term management control process of an organization, always administered from the top

strategic planning: the process of developing long-term plans of action aimed at furthering and enhancing organizational goals

systematic process: a process that has been standardized and embedded in the routine operation of the organization

Chapter 2

Survey of Existing Risk Management Frameworks

At the conclusion of this chapter, the reader will understand:

- The concept and usefulness of standard best practice
- The business need for practical well-defined processes
- The function of standard organizational architectures
- The definition and function of organizational controls
- The risk management framework (RMF) implementation process
- Three alternative models for risk management: International Organization for Standardization (ISO) 31000, Committee of Sponsoring Organizations of the Treadway Commission (COSO), and Health Information Trust Alliance Common Security Framework (HITRUST CSF)
- The role and application of the National Institute of Standards and Technology (NIST)—NIST Special Publication (SP) 800-30 and NIST SP 800-39

2.1 Survey of Existing Risk Management Models and Frameworks

This chapter provides a comparative assessment of existing models and frameworks for cybersecurity. The aim is to relate the practice of risk management within the larger collection of standard processes that have been developed to implement organizational cybersecurity. Risk control is an important aspect of ensuring organization-wide security. However, the risk management process is only one element of the potential set of standardized processes that might be utilized in a secure organization, as shown in Figure 2.1. Other generic areas include secure access control models, such as the Bell–LaPadula Model and the Biba Integrity Model, or the strategic policy and procedure infrastructure frameworks, such as the International Organization for Standardization/International Electrotechnical Commission (ISO/IEC) 27000 family of Information Security Management Systems standards. Additionally, there are focused area-specific models such as the National Initiative for Cybersecurity Education (NICE) Cybersecurity Workforce Framework 2.0, and the NIST Framework for Improving Critical Infrastructure Cybersecurity (NIST CSF).

Many of these models are meant to be interoperable. So, it is possible to integrate the best practice recommendations of more than one standard into a unified specification of best practices for the profession—such as the ability to combine the NIST RMF (NIST, 2014) and NIST SP 800-53 Revision 4, *Security and Privacy Controls* (NIST, 2013). The NIST RMF specifies a standard and comprehensive architecture of processes to manage risk, which can be tailored to any organizational application using the control requirements of NIST SP 800-53 Revision 4.

The most important point to remember is that the RMF is a model for a process rather than an explicit specification of concrete steps. The process itself is strategic in its orientation and it is based on an organization-wide assessment of threats. In general, most generic standards for best practice in cybersecurity approach the problem in this manner and utilize a process rather than a checklist to manage risk.

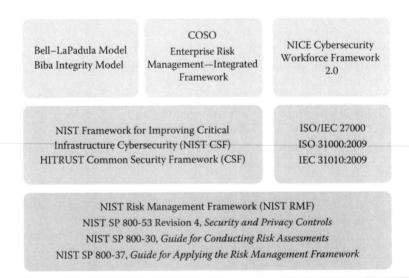

Figure 2.1 Various types of risk management models and frameworks. COSO, Committee of Sponsoring Organizations of the Treadway Commission; NICE, National Initiative for Cybersecurity Education; HITRUST, Health Information Trust Alliance; ISO/IEC, International Organization for Standardization and the International Electrotechnical Commission; RMF, risk management framework.

However, the general aims and objectives of the models and frameworks can be quite different. Consequently, our goal in this chapter is to help you understand how the NIST RMF might work with other strategic standards in the same genre. Specifically, we present a range of common, widely known, and generally accepted models for cybersecurity, which we discuss in terms of the goal of organizational risk management: ISO 31000:2009, *Risk management—Principles and guidelines*; IEC 31010:2009, *Risk management—Risk assessment techniques*; the COSO *Enterprise Risk Management Framework*; and the HITRUST CSF.

This chapter concludes with an introduction to NIST SP 800-30, *Guide for Conducting Risk Assessments*, and NIST SP 800-39, *Managing Information Security Risk: Organization, Mission, and Information System View*. These two standards provide the operational basis for the implementation of the RMF in practical settings. Accordingly, this part of the discussion serves as the basis for the conversation about the various building blocks of the RMF, which will take place in Chapters 3 through 9.

2.2 Standard Best Practice

The aim of standard best practice is to provide expert advice and a consensus in a professional area such as cybersecurity protection. As such, the RMF serves to establish the single point of reference, which can be used to evaluate whether an organization's information protection is both adequate and capable. However, the RMF standard itself essentially integrates a collection of best practice recommendations for how to conduct the process, rather than a handbook for the establishment of risk management controls. That is the role of NIST SP 800-53 Revision 4, which serves as a companion piece to the RMF.

The controls in NIST SP 800-53 Revision 4 further enhance the management of risk by instantiating the intents of the RMF risk assessment process and are meant to provide a concrete basis for the instantiation of the operational behaviors that have to be present in order for the organization to deal with the many demands and requirements imposed in its threat environment. As an added bonus, the implementation of NIST SP 800-53 Revision 4 controls within the existing organizational information and communication technology (ICT) practice will allow managers to comprehensively monitor and control the risks that are present within their own specific day-to-day operation.

2.3 Making Risk Management Tangible

As we said in Chapter 1, the goal of risk management is to add value to the business by protecting its critical assets. Capable risk management links technology processes, resources, and information to the overall purposes of the enterprise. Its specific mission is to ensure that the enterprise's information and related technology supports its purposes. Accordingly, managers have to establish a tangible internal control architecture to address identified risks. This system of controls ought to ensure the ICT function against all credible internal and external threats. There are seven universally desirable characteristics that an ICT risk management infrastructure should embody and promote, which are as follows (Figure 2.2):

1. *Effectiveness:* the operation of the risk management process should be effectively integrated with and relevant to the business process that it supports.
2. *Efficiency:* the risk management process should underwrite the mitigation of known threats in the most optimal (productive and economical) way possible.
3. *Confidentiality:* risks to sensitive information must be identified and mitigated in a manner that will ensure effective protection from unauthorized disclosure.

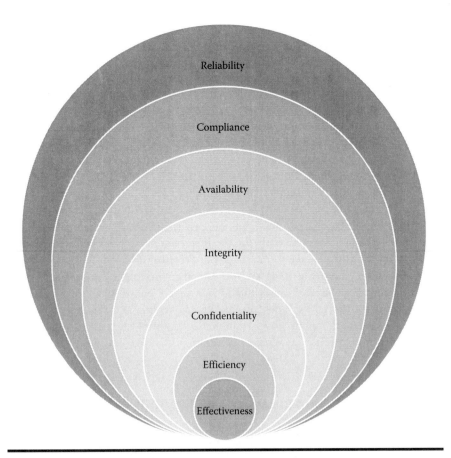

Figure 2.2   Seven desirable characteristics of effective risk management.

4. *Integrity:* the risks that may impact the accuracy and completeness of information must be mitigated in accordance with the values and expectations of the business purpose.
5. *Availability:* risks that would make information required by the business unavailable must be identified and addressed. This requirement applies to all present and future situations. It also applies to the safeguarding of the necessary resources and associated capabilities to carry this out.
6. *Compliance:* all risk management controls must comply with the laws, regulations, and contractual arrangements to which the business process is subject, that is, externally imposed business criteria.
7. *Reliability:* the risk management process must be provably robust and persistent and the continuity of the threat assessment and analysis function must be assured.

2.4 Formal Architectures

The seven characteristics are leveraged by the design, development, maintenance, and operation of a formal, organization-wide risk management capability. The purpose of this capability is to ensure that managers know the exact status of all of the identified risks to the organization's critical data, applications, technology, IT facilities, and human resource assets. And due to the many nuances and issues involved in countering threats to an intangible and widely dispersed resource, a level of detailed knowledge of contextual risk is necessary. Getting and maintaining a degree of understanding requires a much greater competency than most individuals and organizations are capable of. Consequently, some sort of formal, best practice specification of the steps to construct an ideal architecture is implicitly required in order to guide the organization in structuring the approach.

The RMF is specifically designed to meet the requirement for an ideal conceptual model. It dictates a staged organizational process that can be followed to install a complete risk management architecture. This process is assessment based and designed to guide the business in the identification and evaluation of threats and the deployment of the necessary controls to address the attendant risk.

Since they are central to the concepts in this text, we need to stop here to define security controls. By definition, a control is a precise statement of the desired outcome or purpose that a given set of defined actions are meant to achieve. As a consequence, each control objective must unambiguously specify how it will help to achieve the general requirements for mitigating the associated risk. Thus, well-defined control objectives build a clear and distinct link between the threat and the business purpose. Control objectives are defined in action-oriented terms and they must align directly with a given principle of best practice that the control is designed to address. In that respect, control objectives represent the visible aspects of the risk management system. They are concise and detailed procedures of what the organization must do to further its business goals. And they provide a concrete description of the outcome of that specific action.

Additionally, each control must generate sufficient evidence of its performance to be able to confirm its current operation. In other words, they should be measureable. Therefore, all control statements must be expressed in precise terms that provide the basis for third party audited proof of performance. For that reason, the outcomes and data that are the end product of the operation of the control must be sufficiently explicit to allow for independent confirmation of correctness and adequacy of performance.

The RMF specifies a standard umbrella process to be followed in order to develop and document a security control system. A security control system may contain controls from another standard, such as NIST SP 800-53 Revision 4, ISO 27000, or the Control Objectives for Information and Related Technologies (COBIT) Framework. The RMF was created to provide a standard comprehensive process for categorizing, selecting, implementing, assessing, authorizing, and monitoring such a control set. In essence, the RMF provides a comprehensive process for the specification of the risk controls that an organization needs to address its specific threat situations or in order to obtain a formal certification to the Federal Information Security Management Act (FISMA).

2.5 General Shape of the RMF Process

The RMF guideline is structured on one simple and pragmatic assumption: information assets should be secured and managed using a well-defined process to guide the classification, deployment, testing, and sustainment of the risk management program. Accordingly, the generic RMF process requires the organization to characterize the threat environment.

It must then formalize a control set from a standard model, implement each control, and document their effectiveness, and monitor the controls moving forward. Finally, it must sustain the control baseline as a conventional organizational function. A security control baseline is based on three levels (low, moderate, or high) of potential impact to an organization or individual in the event of a breach of security. As shown in Figure 2.3, a low-impact breach has limited adverse effects regarding the loss of confidentiality, integrity, or availability on operations, assets, or individuals. A moderate-impact breach has a serious adverse effect and a high-impact event has a severe or catastrophic adverse effect on the operations, assets, or individuals of an organization.

On the basis of the potential impact of the loss of confidentiality, integrity, or availability, a low, medium, or high potential impact baseline is designated. The baseline designation will influence the scope of security controls that are developed and implemented. The complete set of security controls that are derived from this process are expected to describe and embody all aspects of managing risk to

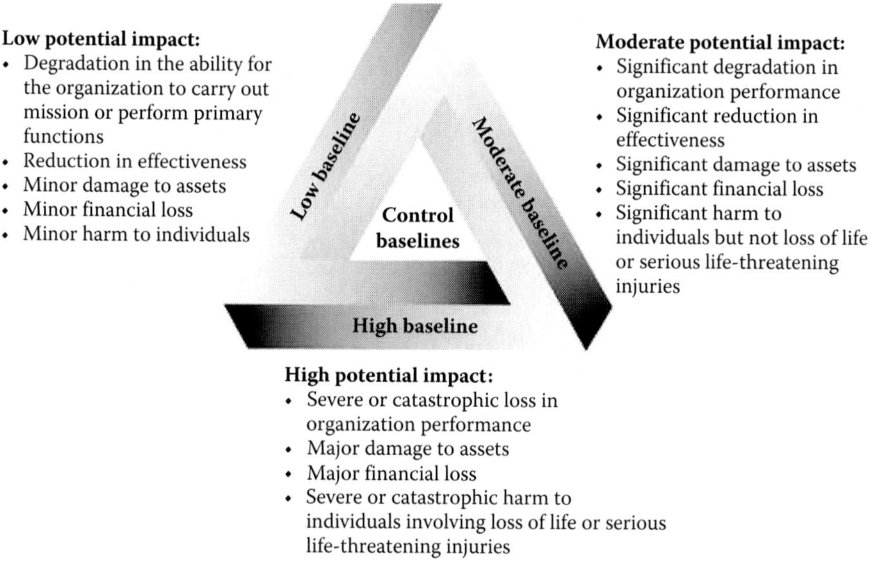

Low potential impact:
- Degradation in the ability for the organization to carry out mission or perform primary functions
- Reduction in effectiveness
- Minor damage to assets
- Minor financial loss
- Minor harm to individuals

Moderate potential impact:
- Significant degradation in organization performance
- Significant reduction in effectiveness
- Significant damage to assets
- Significant financial loss
- Significant harm to individuals but not loss of life or serious life-threatening injuries

Low baseline

Moderate baseline

Control baselines

High baseline

High potential impact:
- Severe or catastrophic loss in organization performance
- Major damage to assets
- Major financial loss
- Severe or catastrophic harm to individuals involving loss of life or serious life-threatening injuries

Figure 2.3   Low-, moderate-, and high-impact baselines.

information and ICT assets. In essence, the evaluation of security controls should be a function of the regular assessment of the threat environment.

Management can use this evaluation or audit assessment to map where the organization is in relation to the best practice ideal established by the framework. By satisfying the requirements of the process, a manager can ensure that a capable ICT control system is in place for any type of organization and at any level of security desired.

This first step of the process forces the organization to outline and examine all of the risks and organizational requirements associated with protecting its ICT operation from meaningful threats. This initial step in the RMF process forces companies to think through a step-by-step assessment of their risk posture and the specific form of their control response. The process itself is based on a set of actions meant to ensure that all of the company's risks are rationally considered and addressed. The process starts with an architectural description and threat assessment combined with an analysis of the impacts to all meaningful areas of concern. Relevant inputs to this activity might entail everything from laws, regulations, policies, and business goals to resource availabilities and supply chain issues. These concerns are categorized into a single common understanding of the threat environment and the concomitant risks. This categorization does not confine the organization to a narrowly defined or rigid mold. Instead, the determination of rigor regarding the initial security control baseline is driven by managerial decisions about the degree of security required to protect a given organizational information asset. Moreover, this evaluation phase of the RMF will likely require the organization to develop lead indicators that will allow senior management to determine whether the ICT process is meeting its overall assurance goals. This amounts to the definition of a set of critical success factors, which can be used to evaluate the performance of the most important management aspects of the overall security function.

Measures that can be defined from these factors will tell management whether the risk management process has achieved its performance goals. These critical success factors also force the organization to think through vital strategic issues such as the following: How far should we go to secure something and is the cost justifiable? What are the indicators of good security performance? What are the risks of not achieving our objectives? What do others do? And how do we compare against best practice?

2.6 RMF Implementation

The RMF process is meant to be generic or in simple terms; it is applicable to almost any conceivable threat situation worldwide. It is also proactive, in the sense that it prescribes a well-defined process that should be followed to ensure active working protection of the ICT function and its information. For the purposes of implementation, the RMF process demands that the organization should develop and document a clear policy statement of the architectural reference models that will guide the actual implementation process, the solution architectures that will result and the mission, and the business processes that will be affected. Consequent to that definition is the requirement that well-defined boundaries are drawn and related for each system. This includes executing and documenting a number of identification activities such as "information asset profiling and prioritization," which simply means that planners have to decide the practical order in which the organization's information assets will be protected and what risk mitigation factors will indicate that this has been successfully accomplished. In addition, the RMF requires that there be a precise itemization of the threats, vulnerabilities, and weaknesses associated with each of those assets ranked by their relative priority.

Three different types of documentation elements are inputs to the classification process. The first of these describe the strategic environmental factors that underlie the implementation process itself. The second set of inputs represent management issues about which a decision must be made, such as laws, regulations, policies, strategic goals, resource availabilities, and other strategic considerations such as supply chain security. These all have to be factored into the prioritization process. And the third documentation type involves performance assessment. If there are best practice benchmarks that are a part of the actual determination of this, these have to be specified and their use has to be clarified—for example, how they will be derived and used.

The organization then identifies and prioritizes the threats that it faces and the vulnerabilities that those represent, using a comprehensive assessment of the organization's threat environment as the point of reference. Decisions about priorities should be based on an understanding of the impact of all known threats on its information assets. Then a standard set of controls is selected and deployed. Because the RMF is specifically intended to address FISMA compliance, the controls in NIST SP 800-53 Revision 4 tend to be the favored set. However, other control models can be selected and utilized as part of the tailoring and implementation of the operational solution. Finally, the assessment and documentation of control performance drives the strategic development of the control set. And where specific certification is required, ongoing control assessment serves as a basis for the authorization and accreditation of the subsequent formal security control system for the purposes of management oversight and audit.

The practical RMF process is executed in six phases, the first two of which involve the establishment of a formal security architecture that is based on the setting of the boundaries of control and the definition of a security control set using a standard specification. Factors that might enter into this activity include issues such as the level of risk and criticality for each of the information assets within the scope of the system and the degree of assurance required to ensure sufficient assurance. Other architectural considerations might entail any foreseen strategic initiatives as well as any external market or regulatory trends.

The boundary setting element is particularly important since there is an obvious direct relationship between the resources required to establish the security level specified and the extent of the territory that must be secured. A concomitant set of risk management procedures are formulated and implemented once this is fully understood. These procedures must unambiguously address the findings from the risk assessment. And this must take place in the order that has been established by the priorities formulated in the prior step. Finally, these procedures must be defined in such a way that each of the basic activities encompassed by the procedure can be monitored and evaluated.

Following the actual implementation of the selected controls, the organization performs a detailed assessment of their performance. This is probably the most important element in the process because it assures the relationship between the architectural solution and the specific known threats to the business's information assets. Once the threats and their controls are satisfactorily identified and related, they are evaluated to distinguish only those issues that might create specific and undesirable outcomes. Then the outcomes are carefully analyzed with respect to the particular operational context in order to identify the presently existing day-to-day activities that the security system needs to target. The activities are prioritized so that the ones with the most critical impacts are dealt with first. Finally, a statement of applicability is prepared and documented for each control. This statement itemizes the target asset that it is meant to secure along with the reasons for its selection. Then it details the measures that will be used to determine whether that objective has been met and the resources necessary to achieve that desired result. Since the RMF is specifically intended to guide the FISMA compliance process, it is likely that there will be audited compliance certification involved. If that is the case, then this particular process will likely be followed.

A legitimate third-party auditor is typically contacted to perform the actual assessment once the organization is confident that the mandated set of security controls are in place. This is normally conducted in the same manner as any other compliance audit and it involves the presentation and evaluation of all forms of documentation relevant to and supporting the claim of compliance.

As we have seen, the RMF model is intended to guide the execution and sustainment of standard risk management practice. Given the number and complexity of the security controls that could be implemented to ensure proper manage risk, the organization still requires a means to determine whether the implemented controls are effective. Or, in simple terms, the fact that a process has been defined and controls documented does not de facto mean that its success can be assumed. So given the importance of ensuring effective risk management, it would be helpful to rate the overall capability of the actual process as well as ensure the continuous improvement of the risk management function. That is what we will be discussing in this short section.

In conventional practice, the effectiveness of a formal control process has traditionally been expressed in terms of a maturity rating scale. Logically, this scale is based on evidence of the presence—or absence—of a commonly agreed on best practice. The assumption is that capability is directly tied to the level of definition and support for the process. Every one of the currently existing capability maturity frameworks assumes that a capable process is one that embodies the following five common elements: (1) defined and documented standard processes, (2) clear lines of accountability, (3) strong support and commitment from management, (4) complete and appropriate communication mechanisms, and (5) consistent measurement practices.

So at a minimum, our maturity scale might be describable in terms of the following stages (Figure 2.4):

1. Absent: risk management controls are not identifiable in operational practice
2. Low: risk management controls are implemented ad hoc and disorganized
3. Moderate: risk management controls follow regular pattern but are not documented
4. Contained: risk management practices are documented and understood by workers
5. Managed: risk management process is continuously monitored and measured
6. Optimized: organizational change is systematically factored into risk control

These levels build on each other. For instance, the activities installed at Stage 4, the *Contained* level, are carried out in addition to the performance of the already existing practices from the prior levels. The business can benchmark itself

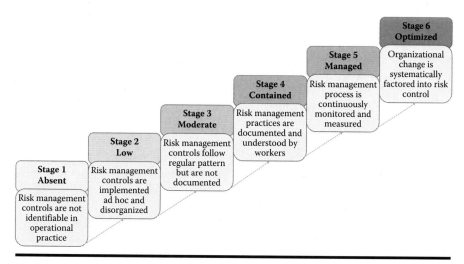

Figure 2.4 Stages of maturity scale.

along this maturity rating scale as a total entity. And the organization can shoot to achieve higher levels of maturity by increasing the level at which it deploys, documents, and commits to systematic execution of the common features. This can be supported by any explicit technique and automation that might be chosen.

The advantage of utilizing a maturity framework in the monitoring process is that it enhances psychological acceptability of the risk management control practices. Most ICT organizations do not build anything complex in a single pass. Instead, they approach implementation in an iterative manner, continually refining their understanding and the relative quality of what it is they are creating. Implementing risk management control by following a commonly accepted maturity path provides the motivation for an organization to both initiate the process and continuously enhance it. In that practical respect, a maturity framework could be as important to successful risk management as the controls themselves.

2.7 Other Frameworks and Models for Risk Management

The NIST RMF represents a measured response to the well-understood desire to organize and systematize risk management practice into a single coherent reference model that embraces all aspects of ensuring assets against known threats. The process steps that are specified in the RMF architecture span the gamut of standard threat identification and mitigation activities. These range from the requirement to create a risk management control infrastructure all the way to operational concerns such as how to ensure the continuous relevance of the practical controls that have been chosen and implemented in the solution. There are other standard models of best practice that have the same general intent as the NIST RMF. And for the sake of full contextual understanding, those standard models also need to be generally explained and discussed.

As we said in the early part of this chapter, there are the following three potential legitimate models for standardized risk management that have been developed by other organizations in approximate order of popularity:

- ISO 31000:2009, *Risk management—Principles and guidelines*, and IEC 31010:2009, *Risk management—Risk assessment techniques*
- *COSO* Enterprise Risk Integrated Framework
- *HITRUST* CSF

The rest of this chapter is devoted to outlining and explaining each of these models.

2.8 International Organization for Standardization 31000:2009

ISO 31000:2009 *Risk management—Principles and guidelines* is a membership supported standard and provides a working set of principles, an architecture, and an implementation process for managing risk. It can be used by any member organization regardless of its size, activity, or industry sector and it applies to any type of risk. Like a number of the other products from the International Organization for Standardization, ISO 31000 is a family of standards. The current family includes the following:

- ISO 31000:2009, *Risk management—Principles and guidelines*
- ISO/TR 31004:2013, *Risk management—Guidance for the implementation of ISO 31000*
- IEC 31010:2009, *Risk management—Risk assessment techniques*
- ISO Guide 73:2009, *Risk management—Vocabulary*

This family of standards is intended to define risk management practice for the global ICT community. The specific aim of ISO 31000:2009 is to promulgate a generic set of principles and guidelines for risk management. In that respect, ISO 31000 provides a commonly accepted description of the proper practice for managing risk. Its specific aim is to unify the widely dispersed common body of knowledge into a standard description of the steps and methods necessary to ensure proper practice in ICT risk management. Thus, ISO 31000:2009 is intended for a broad stakeholder group including:

- Executive level stakeholders
- Enterprise risk management groups
- Risk analysts and management officers

- Line managers and project managers
- Compliance and internal auditors
- Independent practitioners

In terms of both financial performance and reputation, ICT risks impose specific penalties on an organization. Consequently, a formally instituted process to manage risks has the potential to navigate an organization through uncertainty in a certain and secure manner. Because it was defined and sponsored by the International Organization for Standardization, ISO 31000 is in effect the global generic risk management standard. ISO 31000 is also relevant at any level and area within an organization. And it can support decisions about risk at both the strategic and operational levels of the organization. It can be used to help categorize and manage risk to processes, operations, projects, programs, products, services, and assets. Plus, it can improve the effectiveness of processes meant to identify and mitigate threats. The processes in ISO 31000 will also help an organization to more effectively allocate and use the resources that are devoted to risk response. Finally, ISO 31000 can offer explicit guidance for the internal or external auditing functions of the organization. In essence, organizations that adopt ISO 31000 are able to benchmark their risk management practices against an internationally recognized set of sound principles for effective execution of the process.

Accordingly, the overall focus of ISO 31000 is not targeted on a particular industry group, management system, or subject matter field. Rather, it is intended to provide best practice specifications and implementation guidance for any operation seeking effective risk management advice. This approach to risk management encompasses all strategic forms of risk management. Finally, it enables alignment between a common set of risk management controls and the operational tasks of an organization as they extend across its various day-to-day projects, functions, and processes. Thus, ISO 31000:2009 especially facilitates broader adoption by companies that want enterprise-level risk management but need to accommodate a number of different types of management systems (Figure 2.5).

The primary distinction between ISO 31000 and conventional frameworks lies in how risk is conceptualized. In ISO 31000, "risk" is defined as "the effect of uncertainty on objectives." In essence, it is not simply the "chance or probability of loss." In that respect, ISO 31000 considers a much broader set of potential outcomes, which enables a much broader examination and more comprehensive analysis of impacts. The aim of ISO 31000 is to leverage and improve the overall management of the organization with respect to threat, not simply to drop a stand-alone risk management system into the business process. Thus, ISO 31000:2009 involves the entire life cycle of threat and risk within a given organization and it ensures that every aspect of the design, implementation, maintenance, and improvement of risk management processes is considered within the existing governance system.

The implementation strategy for the standard reflects that intention. In ISO 31000, attention is paid to the integration of existing risk management processes

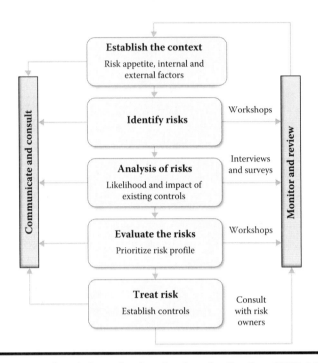

Figure 2.5   International Organization for Standardization (ISO) 31000 principles and guidelines.

into the existing management of the organization as a whole. In that respect, the ISO 31000 implementation process centers on assigning accountability and closing any accountability gaps for risk management, explicitly aligning the existing governance process with the recommendations of ISO 31000, ensuring effective communication, defining and promulgating a standard set of risk criteria and evaluation metrics, and reporting of threat and risk information. ISO 31000 focuses on reengineering existing management practices to ensure that they conform to the strategies, methods, and intentions of its recommendations rather than the across-the-board alteration of the organization's operating paradigm. Consequently, the ISO 31000 approach tends to be strategic rather than prescriptive. In that respect, organizational leadership has to be sensitive to the need to compressively integrate and align the generic risk management strategies of the standard with the current operating model for the organization and its supply chains. ISO 31000:2009 specifies the following seven options, as shown in Figure 2.6, for managing risk (ISO, 2009):

1. Avoiding the risk by deciding not to start or continue with the activity that causes the risk
2. Accepting or increasing the risk in order to pursue an opportunity
3. Removing the risk source
4. Changing the likelihood

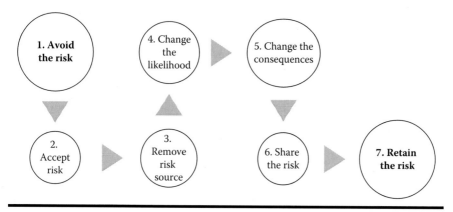

Figure 2.6   Managing the risk.

5. Changing the consequences
6. Sharing the risk with another party or parties (including contracts and risk financing)
7. Retaining the risk by informed decision

ISO 31000 embodies 11 fundamental principles, as shown in Figure 2.7, in order to accomplish its goals (ISO, 2009).

■ The *first principle* is that risk management should create and protect value. That is, risk management should be used to help achieve an organization's objectives and improve its performance.
■ The *second principle* is that risk management should be part of every process at every level. And risk management should be a responsibility of every manager.
■ The *third principle* is that risk management ought to be factored into decision-making at all levels in order to ensure informed choices and prioritize actions.
■ The *fourth principle* is that risk management methods should be the designated approach to uncertainty. That is, risk management methods should be utilized to identify and define the nature and type of uncertainties that the organization faces. Those methods should be utilized to figure out what can be done to address the uncertainties an organization always faces.
■ The *fifth principle* is that the application of the risk management process should be systematic and timely. That is, the organization's approach to risk management should be structured in a way that contributes to efficient operation and always generates reliable results.
■ The *sixth principle* is that risk management should be based on the best data. In that respect, the actual data that the organization uses to manage risk should come from the best available and most valid information sources. At the same time, decision-makers should be made to understand the limitations and shortcomings of the data that they use to manage risk.

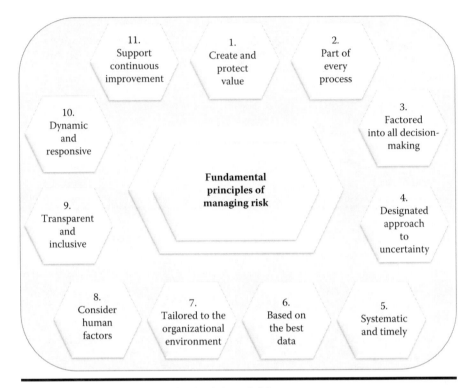

Figure 2.7   ISO fundamental principles of risk.

- The *seventh principle* states that risk management should be tailored to the organizational environment. In that respect, the organization's approach to risk management should be properly aligned with its unique internal and external contextual requirements. This is typically ensured by making certain that the organization's approach to risk management is properly aligned with its risk profile.
- The *eight principle* states that risk management should consider human factors. In essence, what this means is that the risk management approach needs to recognize and be tailored to the human and cultural factors that can influence achievement of your organization's objectives. That includes considering how human capabilities, perceptions, and intentions can facilitate or hinder the achievement of an organization's objectives.
- The *ninth principle* holds that risk management should be transparent and inclusive. In essence, the organization's approach to risk management should be open, visible, and accessible, and involve all stakeholders and also all decision-makers from all parts of the organization.
- The *tenth principle* requires the organization to make its approach to risk management dynamic and responsive. In essence, the approach to risk management should be sensing changes in the organizational environment and context

and responding to them as they occur. This approach should also be ongoing and applied whenever and wherever objectives need to be achieved.

■ Finally, the *eleventh principle* requires risk management to support continuous improvement. In essence, what this means is that the risk management process should be used to improve all aspects of the organization. In addition, there should also be a means of improving the risk management process itself.

2.9 ISO 31000 Implementation Process: Establishment

ISO 31000 style risk management is implemented in two stages. In the first stage, *Establishment*, the organization embeds formal risk management into its operational management system. This involves establishing an effective RMF and then using that framework to support the operation of the risk management process. The framework itself encompasses a set of organizational risk management policies and the risk management objectives to underwrite them. These formal policies and objectives establish the necessary risk management requirements as well as the performance indicators to evaluate whether policy goals have been achieved. This also involves assigning risk management responsibilities and allocating the necessary risk management resources. Finally, the organization has to pay close attention to its human factor issues, in that risk management benefits have to be communicated to the members of the organization in such a way that support for the operational RMF is ensured.

In the second stage, the operational elements of the RMF have to be established. This is accomplished by making effective risk management a formal part of the organization's management system. The organization should evaluate and understand its external context and the threat environment to do this. And then it should use that knowledge to design the elements of an operational risk management process. The evaluation that underwrites this includes understanding the external stakeholders and all external influences. It also involves evaluating and understanding the organization's internal environment and stakeholders in order to design the most effective set of risk management operational procedures, as well as the governance practices, capabilities, culture, and standard requirements of the overall business environment.

A set of general risk management policies and practices can then be defined for every phase of the risk management process organization wide. These policies are expanded by a clear set of well-defined management objectives. The aim is to clearly define how each policy will be implemented. Then, in order to ensure acceptance, the risk management policy and procedure set needs to be clearly communicated to the organization as a whole. An organization-wide risk management plan can be developed once the groundwork is laid and this plan should be driven by the assignment of explicit accountability. Consequently, the organization's risk owners need to be identified and given the authority and accountability to manage risk in their particular space. Finally, the formal internal and external communication mechanisms need to be defined to ensure a proper interchange of information. Performance evaluation criteria need to be developed along with formally defining the reporting and escalation procedures.

The actual implementation planning process will define how suitable human and other resources will be allocated to support the organization's risk management activities as well as support for the information and knowledge management systems. Finally, a strategy has to be developed and formally promulgated that will facilitate the implementation of the plan. This includes the steps that will be taken to put the strategy as well as the actions required to ensure continuous monitoring and improvement of the process.

Typically, the first step in the execution of the plan is to identify priority risks. This first involves defining the organization's risk criteria. This is an iterative process because the threat environment is constantly changing. Therefore, the views of the organization's stakeholders have to be factored into the definition of the risk criteria. The normal considerations of types of causes, impacts, likelihood, and level of risk and risk prioritization have to be considered here. Also, any unique combinations of multiple risks should be taken into account. Next, the operational risks can be identified, and analyzed. It is important that the level of confidence in the analysis is included with the results since credibility is an important part of risk reporting. Then, the risk analysis results can be used to assess the organization's risk picture. This will essentially state the organization's level of risk. The risk levels are then used to devise appropriate risk treatment options. The most effective risk treatment option is then used to devise the most appropriate risk treatment option. The operational application of that risk treatment option has to then be planned and executed. The risk treatment approach should be viewed as cyclical, in that risk management monitoring and review processes must accompany the plan. It is essential that arrangements to monitor and review all aspects of the risk management process, as well as to record the results of that monitoring and review activity, be in place and performed on a routine basis.

2.10 COSO Enterprise Risk Management Framework

The COSO *Enterprise Risk Management Framework* describes a continuous process that an entity undertakes as a normal part of doing business. Risk management is applied through strategy and goal setting, but it is not simply a strategic process that is developed at the C-suite level. It involves people across the enterprise and at every level of an organization. In this framework, risk management is best understood and applied by means of a portfolio approach to characterizing the organizational threat environment. It is meant to identify all of the likely events which, if they occur, will impact the organization, and then devise and implement a strategic approach to decision-making based on that particular organization's level of risk acceptance. This is geared toward the fulfillment of the organizational mission across the board.

The definition of the risk management process provided in the COSO model is purposefully broad. It captures key concepts fundamental to how companies and other organizations manage risk, providing a basis for application across organizations, industries, and sectors. It focuses directly on the achievement of objectives established by a particular entity and provides a basis for defining enterprise risk management effectiveness. Any action that an organization takes has a range of potential consequences, all of which represent both risk and opportunity. Consequences can be negative, positive, or both. Events with a negative impact represent risks, which are the potential range of outcomes of a threat to the organization. Therefore, risks have to be dealt with as part of value creation. The value that results from a given act might sufficiently offset negative impacts to be acceptable in the long term. This is because there is always the possibility that an event will positively affect the achievement of the organization's strategic goals to preserve and create value.

As shown in Figure 2.8, the COSO *Enterprise Risk Management Framework* consists of eight interrelated activities. These fundamental building blocks are derived from the general practice of business management and are integrated with each other within the management process. These components are (COSO, 2004) as follows:

1. *Internal environment:* the internal environment defines the management processes of an organization and serves as the basis for how risk is understood and responded to by the organization as a whole. The internal environment for risk management includes the risk philosophy and risk appetite, the basic level of integrity and ethical values, and the organizational context within which each of these values operate.

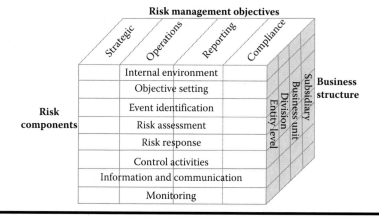

Figure 2.8 The Committee of Sponsoring Organizations of the Treadway Commission (COSO) framework. (From Committee of Sponsoring Organizations of the Treadway Commission (COSO), *Enterprise Risk Management—Integrated Framework,* **COSO, New York, NY, September 2004. With permission.)**

2. *Objective setting:* a well-defined and commonly understood set of objectives has to exist before management can begin to take the steps to achieve them. Enterprise risk management ensures that a formal process exists in which objectives are set and assurance is obtained for the selected objectives that support and align with the entity's mission and are consistent with its risk appetite.

3. *Event identification:* logically, the internal and external events that affect the achievement of organizational goals and must be identified and distinguished before decisions can be made about what risks and opportunities they represent.

4. *Risk assessment:* the risks identified in the previous step need to be analyzed. In essence, their likelihood and impact must be evaluated prior to determining how they should be managed. Risks must be assessed on both their inherent and their residual impact.

5. *Risk response:* management needs to identify and select the appropriate risk response. Responses can include avoiding, accepting, reducing, or sharing the risk. Then an explicit set of actions must be defined that will align risks with the entity's risk tolerances and risk appetite.

6. *Control activities:* policies and procedures can then be subsequently established and implemented from the decision-making process in the previous step. The aim is to help ensure the risk responses are executed effectively.

7. *Information and communication:* the relevant management information needs to be identified, captured, and communicated to the appropriate decision-maker. This has to be in a format and time frame that enables the decision-maker to carry out their responsibilities

8. *Monitoring:* the complete enterprise risk management process requires continuous monitoring in order to be effective due to the threat environment constantly changing. Therefore, it is necessary to have the appropriate responses in place as required. Monitoring is accomplished through a persistent and ongoing management process involving tests, reviews, and audits.

Finally, none of these factors are strictly stand-alone. They are essentially an interdependent and interacting set of factors where one component affects all of the others. Thus, the basic determination of effectiveness is dictated by whether these eight components are present and functioning effectively within the day-to-day operation. In that respect, these factors in-and-of themselves are also the criteria for judging whether the enterprise risk management process is functioning effectively.

The role of management is to establish strategic goals, align appropriate strategies, and implement an associated set of actions. These goals and their consequent actions apply across the enterprise and hold true for a significant portion of time. In respect to that mission, the COSO *Enterprise Risk Management Framework* helps an organization to achieve its business objectives in four fundamental categories of practice (COSO, 2004):

1. *Strategic planning and management:* the framework supports the achievement of the organization's strategies and decision-making purposes in support of its goals.
2. *Operations:* decisions made within the framework help to ensure the effective and efficient use of organizational resources.
3. *Reporting:* the framework creates the formal channels for reliable assessment and reporting.
4. *Compliance:* the framework ensures compliance with all applicable laws and regulations.

The management of risk in the four functional categories requires high-level coordination and planning because although these categories are distinct, they are overlapping. Specifically, a particular organizational goal can fall into more than one category; it might address different organizational needs and may be the direct responsibility of different executives. Much of the success of the framework relies on the establishment of reliable reporting lines and assured compliance with the dictates of the overall plan for risk management. It is assumed that if this is done properly, then enterprise risk management can be expected to provide reasonable assurance of achieving an organization's business purposes.

The achievement of any set of strategic and operational assurance objectives will always be subject to external events. Since those events are not always within the entity's control, the COSO *Enterprise Risk Management Framework* can also provide executive managers reasonable assurance of awareness and the ability to undertake a timely response to threats that might be unanticipated, but which can be managed once discovered. The strategic purpose of the COSO RMF is to always follow a course of action that will minimize risk while creating the maximum value. The enterprise orientation of the COSO model helps corporate managers deal more effectively with the uncertainty and associated risk and opportunity equation. In order to increase value, all corporations have to take risks. So, the pertinent question for all corporate managers is, "How much risk is acceptable in the context of any given decision?"

The intention of this model is to help an organization navigate uncertainty in a rational way. The value orientation is the main difference between the COSO *Enterprise Risk Management Framework* and ISO 31000. In that respect, the COSO RMF is primarily aimed at evaluating the steps that an organization plans to take in order to increase its corporate value. The COSO framework balances the need to take a given step to leverage corporate effectiveness against the potential risk of an adverse result. The organization will typically characterize effectiveness by employing a well-defined set of long-term goals and objectives. The aim is to strike an optimum balance between those corporate development strategies and any associated risks. The logical outcome of such a process would be for the organization to decide on the most efficient and effective collection of resources to ensure the fulfillment of that particular corporation's strategic objectives. In order to accomplish that goal, the COSO enterprise risk management process requires six functional elements as shown in Figure 2.9 (COSO, 2004):

1. *Definition of the precise level of risk tolerance*: this might be the most important factor of all. Risk management has to be able to incorporate the corporate willingness to accept risk into all decisions. Characterization of the level of risk tolerance has to be factored into the decisions that are made about the various strategic alternatives that will help the organization achieve its long-term goals and objectives, as well as the mechanisms it will adopt to manage attendant risks.
2. *Enhancement of the effectiveness of risk response decisions*: enterprise risk management should practice and embody all of the rigors necessary to identify the appropriate risk avoidance, reduction, sharing, or acceptance approach to a given situation.
3. *Reduction of operational surprises and losses*: this is the Saltzer and Schroeder "least astonishment" principle. The aim is to develop sufficient ability to be able to anticipate potential adverse events and then be able to establish a response that is sufficient to ensure that there are no costly surprises.
4. *Identification and management of multiple risks that are potentially cross-enterprise*: in essence, what this means is that all enterprises face risks that are likely to affect several different parts of the organization. And these appear in countless different ways. Therefore, the enterprise risk management process should be able to ensure that a coordinated and systematic response is

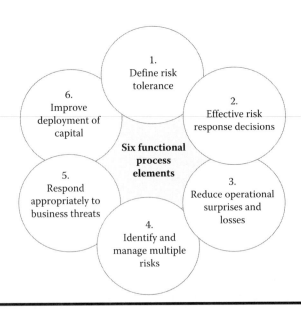

Figure 2.9   Six functional elements of the COSO process.

deployed to deal with what is likely to be a number of interrelated events embodying multiple risks organization wide.

5. *Assurance of an appropriate response to opportunities as they present themselves*: by focusing the process at the enterprise level, the risk management approach should be able to react to a full range of potential business threats, thus allowing the organization to more easily identify and respond to opportunities for advancement as they are presented.

6. *Improvement in deployment of capital*: obtaining robust risk information allows management to effectively assess the overall capital needs of any proposed or existing action as well as to enhance the capital allocated to that action.

These capabilities, which are in essence the inherent elements of the enterprise risk management process itself, are intended to ensure that management will achieve the company's strategic performance and profitability goals as well as ensure against harm that might originate from the threat environment. Enterprise-level risk management also helps ensure that all of the requisite reporting and compliance requirements are met with respect to applicable laws and regulations, and thus helps avoid damage to the entity's reputation and any associated consequences. In sum, enterprise risk management helps an entity get to where it wants to go and avoid pitfalls and surprises along the way (COSO, 2004).

One of the most valuable aspects of the COSO framework is the attention that it pays to defined roles and responsibilities. In essence, it requires everyone in an organization to share some responsibility for risk management within the enterprise. More importantly, it assigns the overall responsibility for risk ownership to the chief executive officer. The model also requires line managers to understand and properly execute the entity's risk management within their spheres of responsibility. It also makes provisions for direct supporting staff such as the assignment of a risk manager and an auditing staff to pay specific attention to the development and maintenance of a proper risk management posture. Finally, it defines the role of the board of directors in managing risk. Far too few of the top-level people understand their responsibilities with respect to risk and threat, whereas the COSO model assigns that responsibility from top to bottom in the organization and extends the process out to the customer and to the vendor community at-large.

2.11 Health Information Trust Alliance Common Security Framework

The HITRUST CSF is the product of a for-profit U.S.-based corporation called the Health Information Trust Alliance. The HITRUST CSF was developed by a consortium of leaders and experts in health care, information technology, and information security to specifically address ICT risk issues in the health-care industry.

It represents a standard process architecture that can be utilized by any organization that creates, accesses, stores, or exchanges sensitive and/or governmental regulated data. The HITRUST CSF provides a specification of the controls necessary to ensure that the risks represented by multiple regulatory environments and standards are understood and appropriately mitigated (Figure 2.10).

This model is meant to be an audit-based certification standard that will dictate ways in which organizations with regulatory compliance and risk management issues can respond in a comprehensive, flexible, and efficient manner to their individual threat environments.

The main purpose of the HITRUST CSF is to array the controls associated with health-care regulation and any associated standards into a single overarching security framework. It should be noted that based on this purpose the HITRUST CSF has both a compliance and a risk-based orientation. It allows primarily health-care organizations to tailor a set of security control baselines to a wide range of factors associated with that industry, including organization type, size, systems, and regulatory requirements. The management capabilities and monitoring potentials built into the HITRUST CSF process are a way to ensure that the health-care organizations who adopt the framework are prepared when new regulations and security risks are introduced. The HISTRUST corporation claims that their CSF is one of the most widely adopted security frameworks in the U.S. health-care industry. This has not been specifically documented; however, given its utilitarian focus on health care, the HITRUST CSF has come to represent an ideal example of a sector-specific risk model.

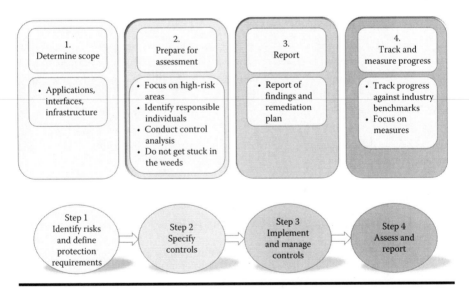

Figure 2.10   The Health Information Trust Alliance (HITRUST) assessment process and common security framework.

The auditing process that both enables and underwrites the HITRUST CSF is specifically designed to ensure effective and simplified compliance with the assessment and the related documentation and reporting requirements of the Health Insurance Portability and Accountability Act (HIPAA), and the Affordable Care Act (ACA). Any health-care or associated business organization that implements and utilizes the HITRUST CSF assures itself of commonality with respect to effectively and efficiently managing the performance of required security and compliance assessments for multiple and varied assurance requirements.

The audit and assurance methodology that is defined for the HITRUST CSF comprises all the requisite risk management oversight and assessment activities necessary to ensure the unique regulatory and business specifications of the health-care industry. Nevertheless, the HITRUST CSF is not just useful for regulatory compliance. The CSF is also very useful for organizations that simply want to quickly and efficiently assess their existing security controls in order to understand their risk exposure.

The assurance is provided by the self-assessment option that is available through HITRUST. Organizations can perform a baseline, comprehensive, or detailed control self-assessment and receive a report from HITRUST using a tool called *MyCSF*. *MyCSF* offers organizations the opportunity to compare how their *MyCSF assessment* scores fit into the general set of scores obtained by similar organizations, or even with respect to the industry as a whole.

The HITRUST CSF is a standard architectural model that seeks to normalize security control implementations in health-care organizations. The compliance target for the CSF is generally meant to be HIPAA. However, there are commercial control sets that can fit into the CSF process including payment card industry (PCI) and COBIT-based compliance efforts as well as products of the federal government such as the NIST *Framework for Improving Critical Infrastructure Cybersecurity*. The HITRUST CSF is not an attempt to create one more standard. Rather, it is an umbrella effort aimed at unifying the control requirements of many disparate standards such as the ones mentioned previously. The HITRUST CSF supplements the controls in those existing control sets with the specialized policies, practices, and procedures of the organizations in HITRUST's community. The aim is to underwrite greater clarity and consistency in the overall standard and regulatory space.

The development and maintenance of the CSF architecture is overseen by the HITRUST executive council. This executive council comprises representatives from a number of industry sectors. All of these have some form of involvement in health-care ICT risk issues. The initial development of the CSF occurred throughout 2008, prior to the release of the first version in March 2009. The development process included experts from the following (HITRUST, 2015):

- The ICT product and service vendor community
- Technology and IT infrastructure organizations
- Professional ICT service firms

- Health-care providers
- Health plans
- Pharmacies and pharmacy benefit managers
- Medical device manufacturers
- Health information networks and clearinghouses

2.12 Implementing the HITRUST CSF Control Structure

The control specifications of the CSF are similar to those of the three-level baseline concept adopted by NIST's computer security division for its SP 800 series security standards. The HITRUST CSF contains 13 security control categories composed of 42 control objectives and 135 control specifications. Each control specification can be related within the context of three levels of sensitivity. The levels of sensitivity for each of the implementation levels dictate the degree of restrictiveness for a particular control. HITRUST applies a minimum set of security requirements to all systems and organizations regardless of size, sophistication, or complexity. Two other levels of increasing rigor might be required for an organization, or system, that embodies increased risk and complexity and that judgment is made based on a set of associated organizational and system factors. For instance, the type and rigor of the controls in the authentication and authorization process would be dictated based on the protection requirements that are associated with the data in the organization. The HITRUST sensitivity levels are also meant to address the greater levels of assurance requirements that are dictated in the various standards and regulations that comprise the CSF. For example, where HIPAA requirements are satisfied at level 1 in almost every instance, the protection requirements dictated by FISMA are both more comprehensive and more detailed and thus would be captured by the more rigorous requirements defined in Federal Information Processing Standard (FIPS) 199, intermediate and high levels of control.

HITRUST has also defined a process to implement alternate control processes. These controls allow a specialized organization to adopt standardized alternate controls for their systems such as medical devices and applications. These controls are likely to fall outside of the typical CSF requirements. If a needed alternate control is not specified in the CSF, the organization itself can propose an approach that will appropriately mitigate any risk of a control failure. The alternate control process is closely integrated into the ongoing operation of the CSF and any approved alternate controls are made available to the entire industry as they are defined. The aim is to underwrite standard adoption of acceptable risk control strategies.

The HITRUST CSF also offers an alternative service that provides compliance assessment and reporting for HIPAA. The program encompasses risk management oversight and assessment methodologies that are a product of HITRUST and designed for the unique regulatory and business needs of the health-care industry. Implementation and assessment activities for the HITRUST CSF are shown in

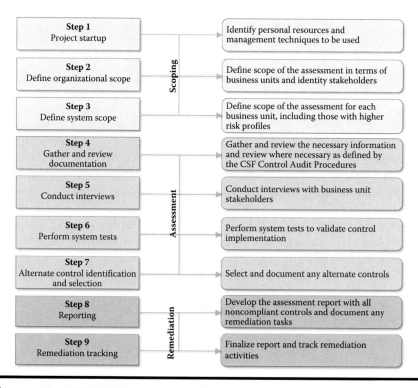

Figure 2.11 HITRUST Common Security Framework (CSF) implementation and assessment activities.

Figure 2.11. Under the CSF Assurance Program, organizations can proactively or reactively undertake an assessment that is performed against the requirements of the CSF. This assessment can be either self-initiated or undertaken due to a request from an organization that requires proof of compliance. If the assessment is self-initiated, it will give an organization insight into its state of compliance with the various standard requirements incorporated into the CSF. If the assessment is for external purposes, then the results can be used to validate third-party compliance with mandated regulatory requirements. In both cases, certified HITRUST CSF Assessors are recommended for the documentation of findings and preparation of reports.

2.13 NIST SP 800-30 and NIST SP 800-39 Standards

The NIST RMF provides a framework for the process of risk management; however, there is still the question of application. In that respect, NIST has updated SP 800-30 Revision 1, *Guide for Conducting Risk Assessments*, in order to provide guidance about the way to conduct standard risk assessments. Given its authority, NIST can only make those recommendations for federal information systems and organizations; however, it introduces a hierarchical, tier concept that is a very important concept for risk assessment and management. In essence, risk is defined in three different categories, or tiers, as shown in Figure 2.12.

In the NIST SP 800-30 model, risk assessments are carried out at all three tiers in the hierarchy of risk management. This formalizes the concept of different risk considerations for different types of decision-makers and range from the strategic to tactical. NIST SP 800-30 provides a foundation for the development of an effective risk management program. In service of that end, NIST SP 800-30 offers both the definitions and the practical guidance necessary for assessing and mitigating the risks associated with ICT systems. It also provides recommendations about how to select cost-effective security controls that can be used to mitigate risk for the better protection of sensitive information and the ICT systems that process, store, and retrieve that information. The ultimate goal of NIST SP 800-30 is to help organizations better manage IT-related mission risks. Additionally, NIST SP 800-30 provides recommendations about the best way to carry out each of the standard steps in the risk assessment process. It also provides guidance on the various ways to identify specific risk factors and then continuously monitor them as a way of tracking threat exposures that exceed organizational risk tolerances. It also suggests different courses of action that might be taken should that occur.

According to NIST, risk assessment is a key component of a holistic, organization-wide risk management process (NIST, 2006). That process is defined in NIST SP 800-39, *Managing Information Security Risk: Organization, Mission, and*

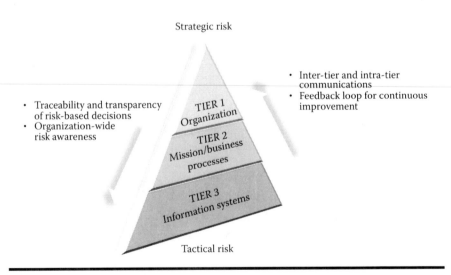

Figure 2.12   The National Institute of Standards and Technology (NIST) tiered risk management approach.

Information System View. Risk management processes cited in that publication include methods to:

- Frame risk: identify and explicitly characterize the risk event
- Assess risk: determine the likelihood and impact of occurrence
- Respond to risk: develop effective risk mitigation approaches
- Monitor risk: ensure the ongoing effectiveness of a given solution

NIST SP 800-39 specifically focuses on the risk assessment element of risk management. It provides a step-by-step set of recommendations for organizations on ways to prepare for, conduct, communicate the results to decision-makers, and maintain the risk assessment process over time. The key point that is stressed over and over in the SP 800-39 standard is that risk assessments are not just onetime activities because relevant and definitive information is needed in order to aid decision-makers in their responses to information security risks. Consequently, organizations need to know how to deploy and manage a persistent and ongoing risk assessment process in the day-to-day conduct of business and across all of pertinent levels in the risk management hierarchy. And in that respect, the frequency of risk assessments and the resources that are deployed to carry them out are always commensurate with the specific level of risk associated with the assets of the organization. The reason for the interest in SP 800-39 is that the activities that underwrite risk assessments can be naturally integrated into the six phases of in the RMF. The integration process is explicitly defined in NIST SP 800-37 Revision 1, *Guide for Applying the Risk Management Framework to Federal Information Systems* (NIST, 2010).

Assessment drives the decision-making in each of the phases of the RMF. And so each evaluation of risk has to be tailored to that particular step in the RMF based on the purpose and scope of the general decision-making. More importantly, risk assessments can also shape the type of focused security actions that have to be taken once the RMF process is embedded into the operational life cycle of the business. That in turn dictates the form and application of the general assessment program, and the level of rigor that has to be assumed during the individual assessments. This includes the methods, procedures, and tools that will be used and the types of organizational objects that the assessment will focus on. The benefit of the information that is derived from the risk assessments conducted as a routine part of the RMF process can be derived both from the results of the initial assessments and also from the updated findings that appear as the process iterates. Initially, organizations utilize the risk assessment process that is part of the *Categorization phase* of the RMF (phase one) to make decisions about the types and levels of risk that the organization is willing to tolerate. Obviously, those decisions have to be consistent with the risk management strategy that is developed by the organization's top-level policy makers.

The risk assessments in the *Categorization phase* integrate and evaluate all of the existing information about threat sources, threat events, vulnerabilities, and predisposing conditions. That understanding then lets the organization make informed decisions about how its information and the information systems have to be protected. Those decisions are based on actionable knowledge that has been gathered about the potential threats to and vulnerabilities in the organizational environment. Once risks and levels are categorized, the appropriate security controls are selected (phase two). Security categorization decisions inform the selection of initial baseline security controls. Those baseline security controls provide the starting point for the organization's tailoring and control implementation activities. Organizations use risk assessments in this second phase to direct the selection of specific security behaviors and controls for each of the organization's information systems within their specific environment. After the initial security control baseline is first put in place, risk assessment results are utilized to help the organization most effectively (NIST, 2006):

- *Apply appropriate tailoring guidance* to adjust the controls based on specific mission/business requirements, assumptions, constraints, priorities, trade-offs, or other organization-defined conditions.
- *Adjust the control baseline* based on specific and credible threat information. Threat data from risk assessments provides critical information on adversary capabilities, intent, and targeting that may affect the decisions by organizations regarding the selection of additional security controls including the associated costs and benefits.

Businesses can also utilize the results of risk assessment when common controls are selected for universal management and operational application. The definition of risk in this case is based on whether the implementation of a common control will result in a single point of failure and is a necessary consideration because common, or universal, controls affect security across a wide range of systems and organizational applications. Therefore, as risk assessments are updated and refined, the organization has to make absolutely certain that it has a complete and accurate understanding of the most up-to-date threat and vulnerability information within its operating environment. Once the initial control baseline is determined (in RMF phase two), there is still the necessity to deploy and evaluate the functional effectiveness of the control within the company's actual operating environment (RMF phase three). Risk assessment results at this phase are aimed at identifying the best practical application of a required security control. This is essentially a product evaluation and since there are always multiple ways to design an effective security control selection, it is necessary to find out for sure which products, system components, or architectural configurations should be deployed during the actual security control development and implementation phase.

In addition to the risks associated with implementation, the ongoing strength of each of the selected security controls has to be evaluated. Security control evaluations are done in light of the changing threat environment and they are not the same as a risk assessment. This is an important distinction that should not be overlooked. Control assessments can be nothing more than evaluations of individual configuration settings for an existing technology product or system component. These evaluations are done in order to determine whether the vulnerabilities identified during the initial threat assessment have been successfully mitigated. Additionally, the control evaluations can also support decisions about the cost, benefit, and risk trade-offs in using one type of technology versus another. Security control evaluations also consider the implementation of a given security control in a particular operating environment. As control assessments are updated and refined on a routine basis, the organization can use the results to help determine if the current security control set continues to remain effective given changes to the threat space.

Organizations can use the results from security control assessments to inform the risk assessments that are conducted in RMF phase four. Security control assessments identify existing vulnerabilities in the organizational information systems, especially the potential vulnerability of the partial or complete failure of a deployed security control or the absence of a planned control. Thus, organizations use the results from the risk assessments that they conduct at this stage to help determine the level of their threat exposure. That can guide and inform organizational risk responses such as the prioritization of risk response activities and the establishment of milestones for corrective action.

The organization then uses the risk assessment results to underwrite the authorization of the specific control system. This is done by providing the necessary results to the appropriate authorization decision-maker. Those decision-makers are essentially authorizing the specific security posture of the organization's operational information systems. Thus, the risk assessment results are essential to making the decision to provide that authorization. Essentially, what is being decided is that the system is safe to operate in its current environment. Otherwise, decision-makers need to define specific actions to deploy additional security controls.

Once the control system is authorized, its ongoing performance has to be monitored. Thus, the business has to perform targeted risk assessments on an ongoing basis. These are aimed at both updating the status of the current baseline set of operational and identifying any latent or new deficiencies in control system performance. These monitoring processes evaluate the continuance of the following (NIST, 2006):

- Effectiveness of security controls
- Changes to systems and operational environments that might impact security
- Compliance with laws, regulations, directives, policies, standards, and guidance

As risk assessments are updated and refined, organizations use the results to update the risk management strategy. The purpose of this is to integrate real-time operating information into the company's formal risk management process.

The purpose of NIST 8000-37 is to provide guidelines for applying the RMF. This includes the conduct of the security categorization, security control selection and implementation, security control assessment, information system authorization, and security control monitoring process. The purpose is to ensure that the management of information system–related security risks is consistent within the policies and strategic plans of the organization. This ensures that information security requirements, including necessary security controls, are integrated into the organization's enterprise architecture and system development life cycle processes.

2.14 Chapter Summary

The aim of standard best practice is to provide expert advice and a consensus in some professional area, for instance, cybersecurity protection. In this respect, the RMF serves to establish the single point of reference, which can be used to evaluate whether an organization's information protection is both adequate and capable. The goal of risk management is to add value to the business by protecting its critical assets. Capable risk management links technology processes, resources, and information to the overall purposes of the enterprise. Its specific mission is to ensure that the enterprise's information and related technology supports its purposes. Accordingly, the managers have to establish a tangible internal control architecture to address identified risks. The purpose of this system of controls is to explicitly ensure the ICT function against all credible internal and external threats. By definition, a control is a precise statement of the desired outcome or purpose that a given set of defined actions is meant to achieve. As a consequence, each control objective must unambiguously specify how it will help to achieve the general requirements for mitigating the associated risk. The RMF guideline is structured on one simple and pragmatic assumption. That is, information assets should be secured and managed using a well-defined process to guide the classification, deployment, testing, and sustainment of the risk management program. Accordingly, the generic RMF process requires the organization to characterize the threat environment.

The RMF guideline is meant to be generic. Or in simple terms, it is applicable to almost any conceivable threat situation worldwide. It is also proactive, in the sense that it prescribes a well-defined process that should be followed to ensure active working protection of the ICT function and its information. For the purposes of implementation, the RMF guideline demands that the organization develop and document an explicit statement of the architectural reference models that will guide the actual implementation process, the specific solution architectures that will result, and the mission and business processes that will be affected.

The NIST RMF model represents a measured response to the well-understood desire to organize and systematize risk management practice into a single coherent reference model that embraces all aspects of ensuring assets against known threats. The process steps that are specified in the RMF architecture span the gamut of standard threat identification and mitigation activities. Nonetheless, there are other standard models of best practice that have the same general intent as the RMF. And for the sake of full contextual understanding those standard models also need to be generally explained and discussed.

The following three potential legitimate models for standardized risk management have been developed by other organizations in approximate order of popularity:

- ISO 31000:2009, *Risk management—Principles and guidelines,* and IEC 31010:2009, *Risk management—Risk assessment techniques*
- *COSO* Enterprise Risk Integrated Framework
- *HITRUST* CSF

ISO 31000:2009, *Risk management—Principles and guidelines,* provides a working set of principles, an architecture, and an implementation process for managing risk. It can be used by any organization regardless of its size, activity, or sector. It applies to any organization no matter what size it is or what it does. It can be used by both public and private organizations and by groups, associations, and enterprises of all kinds. ISO 31000:2009 is not specific to any sector or industry. And it applies to any type of risk.

The definition of the risk management process provided in the COSO model is purposefully broad. It captures key concepts fundamental to how companies and other organizations manage risk, providing a basis for application across organizations, industries, and sectors. It focuses directly on achievement of objectives established by a particular entity and provides a basis for defining enterprise risk management effectiveness. The strategic purpose of the COSO *Enterprise Risk Management Framework* is to follow a course of action that will minimize risk while creating the maximum value. The enterprise orientation of the COSO model helps corporate managers to deal more effectively deal with the uncertainty and associated risk and opportunity equation. In order to increase value, all corporations have to take risks. So the pertinent question for all corporate managers is, "How much risk is acceptable in the context of any given decision?"

The HITRUST CSF is a product of a U.S.-based corporation. It was developed to specifically address ICT risk issues in the health-care industry. The HITRUST CSF was developed by a consortium of leaders and experts in health care, information technology, and information security. Nonetheless, it represents a standard process architecture that can be utilized by any organization that creates, accesses, stores, or exchanges sensitive and/or regulated data. The CSF provides a specification of the controls necessary to ensure that the risks represented by multiple regulatory environments and standards are understood and appropriately mitigated. The main purpose of the HITRUST CSF is to array the controls associated with health-care regulation and any associated standards into a single overarching security framework. It should be noted that based on this purpose the HITRUST CSF has both a compliance and a risk-based orientation. It allows primarily health-care organizations to tailor a set of security control baselines to a wide range of factors associated with that industry, including organization type, size, systems, and regulatory requirements.

NIST 800-30 Revision 1, *Guide for Conducting Risk Assessments*, provides explicit guidance about the way to conduct standard risk assessments. NIST SP 800-30 provides a foundation for the development of an effective risk management program. It offers both the definitions and the practical guidance necessary for assessing and mitigating the risks associated with ICT systems. It also provides recommendations about how to select cost-effective security controls that can be used to mitigate risk for the better protection of sensitive information and the ICT systems that process, store, and retrieve that information. The ultimate goal of NIST SP 800-30 is to help organizations better manage IT-related mission risks.

The purpose of NIST SP 800-37, *Guide for Applying the Risk Management Framework to Federal Information Systems*, is to provide guidelines for applying the RMF. This guideline includes the conduct of the security categorization, security control selection and implementation, security control assessment, information system authorization, and security control monitoring process. The purpose is to ensure that the management of information system–related security risks is consistent within the policies and strategic plans of the organization. This also ensures that information security requirements, including necessary security controls, are integrated into the organization's enterprise architecture and system development life cycle processes.

Glossary

application: the specific use or execution of a given system, process, procedure, or task

architecture: the formal logical structure of a given entity, as applied this refers to process

COSO Enterprise Risk Integrated Framework: Committee of Sponsoring Organizations Risk Management Model

enterprise risk management: Formal process for coordinated management of every aspect of an organization's operation

generic guideline: a standard or recommendation that is applicable in all instances

HITRUST Common Security Framework (CSF): a model for assuring healthcare organizations against risk

implementation process: a set of proscribed steps for embedding an object into a given organizational operation

internal control architecture: the set of behaviors specified to ensure the security of operation of a given organizational entity

ISO 31000:2009 Risk Management: a standard promulgated by the International Standards Organization to manage enterprise risk.

reference model: a commonly accepted standard of practice defined to structure a given concrete application of a standard process

risk management program: a formally organized and coordinated management function within an organization that is dedicated to risk mitigation

risk mitigation: the act of reducing the harm originating from a threat to acceptable levels

standard risk assessment: a best practice dictated performance evaluation process as applied to a given target for measurement

tailoring: the process of adapting the recommendations of a given standard to a specific organizational application

threat: an adversarial action that can exploit a known weakness

References

Committee of the Sponsoring Organizations of the Treadway Commission (COSO). (September 2004). *Enterprise Risk Management—Integrated Framework.* New York, NY: COSO.

Health Information Trust Alliance. (2015). *HITRUST CSF v7.* Frisco, TX: Author.

International Standards Organization (ISO). (2009). *ISO 31000: 2009 Risk management—Principles and Guidelines.* Geneva: International Standards Organization.

NIST. (2014). *Risk Management Framework (RMF).* Gaithersburg, MD: National Institute of Standards and Technology.

NIST. (January 2006). Special Publication 800-30, *Risk Management Guide for Information Technology Systems.* Gaithersburg, MD: National Institute of Standards and Technology.

NIST. (February 2010). Special Publication 800-37, *Guide for Applying the Risk Management Framework to Federal Information Systems.* Gaithersburg, MD: National Institute of Standards and Technology.

NIST. (April 2013). Special Publication 800-53 Revision 4, *Security and Privacy Controls for Federal Information Systems and Organizations.* Gaithersburg, MD: National Institute of Standards and Technology.

Chapter 3

Step 1—Categorize Information and Information Systems

At the conclusion of this chapter, the reader will understand the following:

- The role that Security Impact Analysis (SIA) plays in the overall scope of the National Institute for Standards and Technology (NIST) Risk Management Framework (RMF)
- The NIST guidelines and standards that support the activities of security categorization
- The NIST System Security Categorization process from the organization, management, and system perspective

3.1 Introduction

Recall from the discussion in Chapter 1 that the three key security requirements required by most information systems are availability, integrity, and confidentiality. These are the objectives of an information system security program and properties that must be included and deployed to most, if not all, information systems. There would be no cost-based rationalization for organizations to provide all systems with a maximum level of protection. Moreover, each system has unique requirements for different levels of these properties depending on the determined legal and regulatory requirements and, more importantly, on the impact that could result if one of these capabilities was lacking.

All information and communication technology (ICT) projects typically (or certainly should) begin with the definition of business requirements. Senior management responsible for defining these requirements, however, are not always familiar with cybersecurity and typically overlook necessary security requirements. As a consequence, those same missing requirements are often lacking in subsequent projects, thereby leaving the organization vulnerable to numerous forms of security exploitation.

Identifying security requirements is not simple and must not be dealt with haphazardly. The most experienced cybersecurity professional could, and likely does, overlook some risks. Therefore, it is imperative that the organization have a risk identification and security requirement analysis process in place. It is noteworthy to mention also that many ICT projects utilize the services of third-party vendors; sometimes those third parties are used locally, while others must be accessed across the Internet through cloud-based infrastructures. Assessing security requirements, therefore, must also address supply-chain scenarios and the associated risks that they create.

The process of understanding the business requirements and matching them to the properties of confidentiality, integrity, and availability, while also measuring each requirement for the degree of security risk it imposes, is often referred to as SIA. In an attempt to provide a process to help organizations identify the level of protection that a system requires, the first step of the NIST RMF includes the security categorization process that addresses the need of organizations to do an initial assessment on the basis of system information types and the organizational objectives that each support.

The security categorization is the most important step in the RMF; it affects information security decisions for both the organization and individual information systems and influences all remaining steps in the RMF—from the selection of security controls to the level of effort needed to assess and maintain the controls. The step of the RMF process we will discuss in this chapter uses a combination of the resources available in Federal Information Processing Standards (FIPS) Publication 199, *Standards for Security Categorization of Federal Information and Information Systems* (NIST, 2004) and NIST SP 800-60, *Guide for Mapping Types of Information and Information Systems to Security Categories* (Stine et al., 2008) in order for the organization to adequately understand the extent to which criticality and sensitivity of the information and information system can be assessed as a way of determining the underlying security impact level of the ICT system. It should be noted that the organization should have in place the appropriate processes for ongoing review of the security categorization as a means of ensuring that the resulting impact assessments clearly reflect the organization's established priorities and operational environments.

In this chapter, we will begin with a conceptualization of SIA. Next, FIPS PUB 199, *Standards for Security Categorization of Federal Information and Information Systems* and the Committee on National Security Systems' (CNSS) CNSSI No. 1253, *Security Categorization and Control Selection for National Security* Systems (CNSS, 2014) will be explored, compared, and contrasted as a source of guidelines for organizations to perform the categorization of information systems

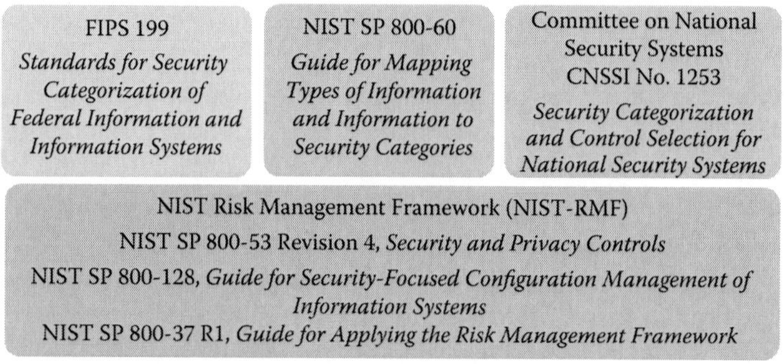

FIPS 199	NIST SP 800-60	Committee on National Security Systems CNSSI No. 1253
Standards for Security Categorization of Federal Information and Information Systems	*Guide for Mapping Types of Information and Information to Security Categories*	*Security Categorization and Control Selection for National Security Systems*

NIST Risk Management Framework (NIST-RMF)
NIST SP 800-53 Revision 4, *Security and Privacy Controls*
NIST SP 800-128, *Guide for Security-Focused Configuration Management of Information Systems*
NIST SP 800-37 R1, *Guide for Applying the Risk Management Framework*

Figure 3.1   Resources for understanding security categorization.

process. The major focus of this chapter centers on the tables available in NIST SP 800-60, *Guide for Mapping Types of Information and Information Systems to Security Categories* and FIPS PUB 199 as a means of implementing the security categorization and information classification process of the NIST RMF (Figure 3.1).

3.2 Security Impact Analysis

Before gaining an understanding of SIA, it is necessary to make two important points. The first deals with the cyclical nature of risk management. As you learn about how to implement each of the steps of the NIST RMF, it is easy to view the process from the perspective that no process for risk management currently exists within the organization. You may get the impression that there is no risk management plan, no security plan, no continuous monitoring plan, no incident response plan, and no disaster recovery plan in place. To the contrary, the opposite is often the case. Each of the pieces that make up a formal risk management process evolve over time though changes that take place within the organization and its ICT system that directly affect how security is planned, implemented, maintained, and monitored. For example, in this chapter we discuss SIA as one of the initial steps in the RMF process. Hence, you would expect that the results of this analysis would lead to the selection of a complete set of security controls that must be implemented. It is interesting to note that NIST SP 800-53 Revision 4 *Security Controls and Assessment Procedures for Federal Information Systems and Organizations* includes this process as the security control *CM-4 Security Impact Analysis*, within the configuration management (CM) category of the guideline. Therein lays the cyclic representation that we spoke to at the outset of this section.

Second, an ICT system is always in a state of change as a means for establishing new, enhanced, corrected, or updated hardware and software capabilities. Such capabilities may include software patches, mechanisms implemented to protect against new security threats, or changes that take place within the organizational environment that affect its business functions and the ICT that support them. To ensure that the required modifications to the ICT system do not adversely affect the security of the ICT system or the organization from an operational standpoint, a well-defined CM process and the establishment of a Configuration Control Board (CCB), which integrates information security into the ICT system changes, is necessary.

The purpose of establishing a CM program stems from the need for organizations to establish a baseline for the ICT changes and to track, control, and manage business development and operations from both organizational operations and the ICT support perspective. Organizations that have established a CM process must carefully consider the effect that information security has on the development and operation of ICT systems. In understanding the security impact, documentation, existing hardware, and all software applications in use or under development must be evaluated. To have an effective CM program providing adequate support of an ICT system requires the inclusion of appropriate management practices supporting secure configurations into the organization's CM processes.

As a general definition, we can say that an SIA is the analysis normally conducted by an individual who is specialized in cybersecurity risk management, to determine the extent to which the changes in the information system will affect the security state of an organization's ICT system. The analysis of the security impact of a change occurs during the analysis phase of the system or software development process, and preferably before that change is approved and implemented. Later, when the changes have been implemented and tested, an SIA should be repeated to verify that the changes have been implemented according to specification and as approved. Further, repeating the impact analysis helps to determine whether there are any unanticipated effects of the change on existing security controls.

This type of analysis, which is outlined in NIST SP 800-128. *Guide for Security-Focused Configuration Management of Information Systems* (Johnson et al., 2011), is conducted as a part of the System Development Life Cycle (SDLC) and as the first step of the risk management process to ensure that security and privacy functional (and nonfunctional) requirements are identified and addressed during the development and testing of the ICT system. Likewise, the purpose of an SIA is to identify the impacts of proposed system changes in order to develop additional security design requirements necessary to minimize the impacts of proposed system changes. Moreover, an SIA serves a benefit in assisting ICT planners, designers, and developer to:

- Identify potential risk areas (real and possible) of a proposed change
- Develop effective safeguards (design requirements) to address identified potential risks
- Develop effective security and privacy testing to integrate into overall testing, prior to promotion of changes into a production environment

Worthy of mention, the SIA process must not:

- Waive or bypass minimum regulatory or industry standard security or privacy control requirements, or other organizational policies or procedures
- Negate the direction of the CCB minimum requirements or policies, or bypass required CM phases or steps.
- Excuse systems of identified (or unidentified) security or privacy deficiencies.
- Act as a means for risk acceptance for identified (or unidentified) security or privacy deficiencies

Significant changes to an ICT system require a formal reauthorization of the system and thus trigger the need for the SIA Security Categorization. If a formal reauthorization action is required, the organization must target only the specific security controls affected by the changes and reuse previous assessment results wherever possible. Most routine changes to an information system or its environment of operation can be handled by the organization's continuous monitoring program. An effective monitoring program can significantly reduce the overall cost and level of effort of reauthorization actions. We will discuss continuous monitoring in Chapter 8. Nevertheless, NIST SP 800-37 Revision 1, *Guide for Applying the Risk Management Framework to Federal Information Systems: A Security Life Cycle Approach* (NIST, 2010) suggests that significant change to an ICT system may result from the installation or modification of:

- An operating system or middleware component that results in application modifications to system ports, protocols, or services
- New or existing hardware platforms
- Cryptographic modules or services
- New or existing security controls

From an operational perspective, significant changes to the environment may include the following:

- Moving all of part of the system to a new facility
- The addition of new organizational missions or business functions
- An awareness, through credible threat information, that the organization is being targeted
- Conformance to new or modified laws, directives, policies, or regulations

Regardless of the circumstances, changes that affect the approved security posture must be tracked through the applicable system CM and CCB processes. Several different methodologies exist by which organizations develop and implement an SIA (security categorization) process. In Sections 3.3 and 3.4, we will explore two prominent standards, FIPS 199 and CNSSI No. 1253, which serve as bases from which the security categorization is performed.

3.3 FIPS 199, Standards for Security Categorization of Federal Information and Information Systems

FIPS 199 originated in 2004 as a result of the Federal Information Security Management Act (FISMA) of 2002 that tasked NIST to develop standards and guidelines which promote the importance of information security within the United States. One of the charges that NIST took on was the development of standards that federal agencies could use to categorize information and information systems within each agency. Such standards effectively define appropriate levels of information security according to a range of risk levels.

While FIPS 199 was specifically written for implementation by the federal government, the general scope of the security categorization standards for ICT systems provide a common framework and understanding for expressing security. Through this expression, such a framework promotes the following:

■ An effective means for management and oversight of the programs that support information security
■ An effective and consistent reporting mechanism providing details related to adequacy and effectiveness of information security policies, procedures, and practices to upper management, or in the case of federal systems, to the Office of Management and Budget (OMB) and Congress

Although this standard was originally developed for the purpose of the security categorization within federal agencies, the popularity of this standard has increased to the extent that many organizations outside the federal government have adopted it for the purpose of identifying risk levels within their own risk management process.

To be used effectively by federal agencies and organizations, the FIPS 199 standard approach to categorizing information and information systems is based on the potential impact baselines driven by the objectives of providing appropriate levels of information security according to a range of risk levels. The standard defines three levels of potential impact (low, moderate, and high that were introduced in Chapter 2) on organizations or individuals should there be a breach of security (i.e., a loss of confidentiality, integrity, or availability). Figure 3.2 describes each potential impact level in more detail and provides an example of each. The definitions you see in the figure are applied within the context of the organization and in the case of the federal government, the overall national interest.

FIPS 199 provides criteria for the security categorization of information *types* and information *systems*. The former can be associated with both user information

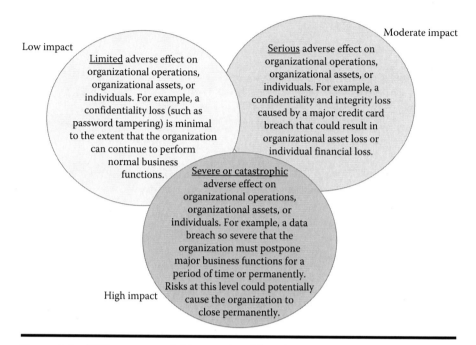

Figure 3.2   FIPS 199 potential impact level baselines.

and system information (such as password files and routing tables), which takes into consideration the information in either electronic or paper form. Likewise, the security categories assigned to information types are used, in part, when considering the appropriate security category (SC) of an information system. Both forms of categorization are interdependent and must be analyzed inclusively to identify the most appropriate risk level.

3.3.1 FIPS 199—Security Categorization of Information Types

In performing an analysis of an *information type*, the SC must take into consideration the data transit, data processing, or data storage. For each information type being analyzed, the potential impact values assigned to the three security objectives (confidentiality, integrity, and availability) are determined by using the values low, moderate, or high. The generalized format for expressing the SC of an information type, set forth in the FIPS 199 standard, is as follows:

$$SC_{\text{information type}} = \left\{ \begin{array}{l} (\text{confidentiality, impact}), \ (\text{integrity, impact}), \\ (\text{availability, impact}) \end{array} \right\}$$

where the acceptable values for potential impact are LOW, MODERATE, HIGH, or NOT APPLICABLE. (*Note that NOT APPLICABLE only applies to the security objective of confidentiality.*)

For example, an online book store managing customer information determines that the potential impact from loss of **confidentiality** is *high,* the potential impact from a loss of **integrity** is *moderate,* and the potential impact from a loss of **availability** is *moderate.* The resulting security category, SC, for this information *type* is expressed as follows:

$$SC_{\text{customer information}} = \left\{ \begin{array}{l} (\text{confidentiality, HIGH}), (\text{integrity, MODERATE}), \\ (\text{availability, MODERATE}) \end{array} \right\}$$

3.3.2 FIPS 199—Security Categorization of Information Systems

On a broader perspective, according to FIPS 199, the potential impact values assigned to the security objectives of confidentiality, integrity, and availability for a specific *information system* are categorized with the highest values assigned from among each of those security categories in consideration of each type of information transmitted, processed, or stored by an ICT system. In other words, if a mission critical system processes several types of information in which one type is considered low impact, another type is considered moderate impact, and another type is considered high impact, the resulting security category for the overall system will be the highest impact level determined. This concept is employed because of the significant dependencies among the security objectives of confidentiality, integrity, and availability. In most cases, a compromise in one security objective ultimately affects the others. To simplify the process, the worst-case potential impact for the ICT system under review is assigned to the final analysis.

The generalized format for expressing the Security Category (SC) of an information type or of an information *system,* set forth in the FIPS 199 standard, is as follows:

$$SC_{\text{information system}} = \left\{ \begin{array}{l} (\text{confidentiality, impact}), (\text{integrity, impact}), \\ (\text{availability, impact}) \end{array} \right\}$$

where the acceptable values for potential impact are LOW, MODERATE, and HIGH.

For example, an educational institution managing both sensitive student information and administrative information in a registration system determines that the potential impact (for student information) from the loss of **confidentiality** is *high* based on the criteria it must follow, which has been established by the Family Educational Rights and Privacy Act (FERPA); the potential impact from the loss of **integrity** is *high*; and the potential impact from the loss of **availability** is *moderate*. For administration information, the loss of **confidentiality** is *moderate*, the loss of **integrity** is *moderate*, and the loss of **availability** is *low*. The resulting SCs for these information *types* are expressed as follows:

$$SC_{\text{student information}} = \left\{ \begin{array}{l} (\text{confidentiality, HIGH}), (\text{integrity, HIGH}), \\ (\text{availability, MODERATE}) \end{array} \right\},$$

$$SC_{\text{administrative information}} = \left\{ \begin{array}{l} (\text{confidentiality, MODERATE}), \\ (\text{integrity, MODERATE}), \\ (\text{availability, LOW}) \end{array} \right\},$$

$$SC_{\text{registration system}} = \left\{ \begin{array}{l} (\text{confidentiality, HIGH}), (\text{integrity, HIGH}), \\ (\text{availability, MODERATE}) \end{array} \right\}$$

For its importance and relevance within the security categorization step of the RMF, we recommend examining FIPS 199. A thorough review prior to performing any of the categorization process tasks might be time well spent as it is straightforward and only a few pages in length.

3.4 CNSSI No. 1253, Security Categorization and Control Selection for National Security Systems

CNSS, a member of the Joint Task Force (JTF), sets cybersecurity policies, directives, instructions, operational procedures, guidance, and advisories for U.S. Government National Security Systems (NSS). The CNSS developed CNSS Instruction No. 1253 (CNSSI 1253) as a means of providing guidance for all NSS on the tasks associated with security categorization and security control selection (discussed in Chapter 4) of the RMF, relative to the NIST publications on these steps.

With that said, it is important to note that CNSSI 1253 is not intended to be an alternative for what was just discussed of FIPS 199 in Section 3.3.2. Rather, it is intended to be a standard by which NSS are categorized using FIPS 199 and NIST SP 800-60, *Guide for Mapping Types of Information and Information to Security Categories* as guidelines for performing the tasks of the security categorization step of the RMF. We introduce the standard here, as an example of how federal departments such as the Department of Defense (DoD) are required to implement the framework. To that extent, the major differences between this instruction and the NIST publications as they relate to categorization are as follows:

- The CNSSI 1253 standard does not adopt the high water mark concept (highest category of low, moderate, and high impact if multiple types are categorized) from FIPS 199; rather, a table in Appendix D lists each security control identified by NIST that has been mapped to each category (confidentiality, integrity, and availability) and further to the potential impact level for the purpose of determining which controls are selected for implementation.
- The definitions for moderate and high impacts in this standard are refined from those provided in FIPS 199. From a federal perspective, this was necessary because when considering national security, there is an understanding that certain losses are inevitable when particular missions are performed.
- The associations of confidentiality, integrity, and/or availability to security controls are explicitly defined in the standard.

For the purpose of NSS and as defined by CNSSI 1253, the RMF step of Security Classification is made up of two major tasks. First, the determination must be made in identifying the impact values for the information types that are processed, stored, transmitted, or protected by the information system, and for each information system within a given department. The criteria used to complete this task are similar to what was described in Section 3.3 and Figure 3.2 (with the exception of the differences between FIPS 199 and CNSSI 1253, listed earlier in this section). Second, the department must identify the overlays that apply to the information system and its environment as a means of considering additional factors (beyond impact levels identified in the first task) that could have an influence on the eventual selection of security controls, or diverge from the assumptions used to create the security control baselines. CNSSI 1253 also provides the NSS-specific information on developing and applying overlays for the national security community and the parameter values for NIST SP 800-53 security controls that are applicable to all NSS.

The remainder of this chapter will provide a detailed discussion of NIST SP 800-60, *Guide for Mapping Types of Information and Information Systems to Security*

Categories and the steps it prescribes for performing step 1, *Security Categorization*, of the NIST RMF. We will weave the discussion of CNSSI 1253 and use FIPS 199 as a basis for supporting the tasks performed throughout the process.

3.4.1 Implementation of Step 1—Security Categorization

The security categorization step of the RMF process is considered to be the most important because it draws upon the organization's mission and goals as a means of defining information system security activities. Throughout this step, FIPS 199 is used to define the requirements for categorizing information and information systems. Additionally, NIST SP 800-60 provides the guidance organizations need to assess the importance and sensitivity of each type of information and the information system from which it is inputted, processed, transmitted, and stored.

Resulting from this step, each system's impact level is further used to select a set of baseline security controls for the information system from NIST SP 800-53, *Recommended Security Controls for Federal Information Systems*, which is then customized to better meet the security needs identified of each information system. Moreover, the system's impact level also determines how aggressively the organization must apply the remaining steps in the RMF, including the assessment of security controls.

Regardless of which guideline or standard is used to identify impact levels, organizational management has the responsibility of ensuring that security categorizations are reviewed on an ongoing basis to help ensure that they continue to reflect the mission and objectives or the organization and the environment from which they exist. To that extent, NIST PS 800-60 suggests that security categorization routinely be revisited as an organization's mission and business functions change, since it is very likely the potential impact level or even information types may change as well.

On the basis of the premise that organizations enforce repetition, NIST SP 800-60 defines a four-step process for categorizing information and information systems. Those steps include:

1. *Identify information types*: develop policies regarding information system identification for security categorization purposes. The system is generally bounded by a security boundary. The deliverable for this step is a document that clearly states the organization's business and mission areas and the identification of the information types that are inputted, stored, processed, and/ or outputted from each system. Additionally, this document should include the basis for the information type selection.
2. *Select the security impact levels* for the identified information types: the security impact levels can be selected either from the recommended provisional impact levels for each identified information type using the guide, NIST SP 800-60, Volume 2 Appendix C and D or from the FIPS 199 criteria for specifying the

potential impact level based on security objective. The deliverable for this step is a document that states the provisional impact level of confidentiality, integrity, and availability associated with each of the system's information types.

3. *Review provisional impact levels* of the information impact levels for the information types: this step also include the *adjustment of the impact levels* as necessary based on the following considerations:
   a. Confidentiality, integrity, and availability factors
   b. Situational and operational drivers (timing, life cycle, etc.)
   c. Legal or statutory reasons

   The deliverable for this step includes a document of all adjustments as well as the final impact level assigned to each information type and the rationale or justification for the adjustments.

4. *Assign a system security category and overall impact level*: review the identified security categorizations for the aggregate of information types and determine the system security categorization by identifying the highest security impact level for each of the security objectives (confidentiality, integrity, and availability). The deliverable for this step is a document of final decisions made of the assignment of the overall information system impact level based on the highest impact level for the system security objectives (confidentiality, integrity, and availability).

The output of the last step can be used as input to the selection of the set of security controls necessary for each system and the system risk assessment. The minimum security controls recommended for each system security category can be found in several helpful resources such as NIST SP 800-53 Revision 4, *Security and Privacy Controls*; the Council on CyberSecurity, *Critical Security Controls for Effective Cyber Defense, Version 5.0*; SANS Institute, Top 20 Critical Security Controls; and the Payment Card Industry Security Standards Council, *Data Security Standard*.

Figure 3.3 shows each step with the job roles that are involved for each step.

Many organizations make the mistake of considering security categorization only from the perspective of the system itself. NIST recommends that as this step of the RMF is performed, considerations be made from the organizational, management, *and* system perspective.

3.5 Security Categorization from the Organizational Perspective

As a means to adequately address its security needs, an organization must have a comprehensive approach for addressing risk throughout each of its business functions. Such an approach provides the benefit of greater visibility into the integrated network of operations that exist internally and externally through the organization

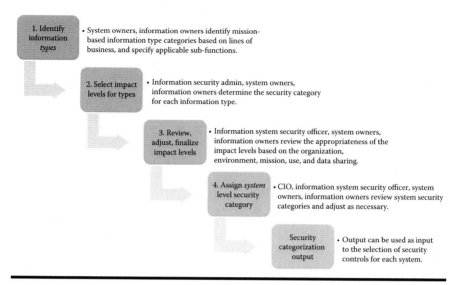

Figure 3.3   Security categorization steps.

supply chain, in addition to an understanding of all of the information flows through each of those operations.

Considering the necessity for addressing the risk of business functions beyond the scope of organizational control, it is important to note that the growing relationships among an organization's associated supply chains introduce new and difficult challenges as follows in the area of ICT security:

- Providing clear definition of the types of external services provided
- Obtaining detailed descriptions of how the external services are protected and conform to the security requirements of the organization
- Achieving adequate assurances that the risk to the organization's operations, assets, and individuals resulting from the use of the external services is at an acceptable level

In order to effectively satisfy security needs for each information system that supports business functions across the entire organization, those charged with the responsibility of implementing risk management and the underlying security program need to establish relationships with organizational entities (external and internal) that will be affected by changes that take place as a result of security initiatives. The security team is also responsible for the development of an organization-wide categorization guidance program, preparation of a catalog that identifies organization-specific information types, and the facilitation of organization-wide categorization sessions, and it serves as the organizational point of contact for those affected by the categorization process.

3.5.1 Establish Relationships with Organizational Entities

The underlying success in implementing the NIST RMF is largely dependent on a collaborative effort among all internal and external organizational entities that are directly impacted by the way in which information security practices are performed. Through a collaborative effort, senior management are able to be proactive in making security risk decisions that have an impact on the organization's ability to achieve its mission and that vital business operations remain functional while also maintaining an adequate level of security within each of those operations. The security team must continue to communicate with each business entity depending on information and the systems that provide the capacity for its processing, storage, and transmission in an effort to provide the amount of guidance and direction necessary to achieve success within the categorization process. Such outreach activities include coordinating the definition and distribution of organization-level information types, leading organization-wide categorization sessions, providing training to ensure that the categorization process is completed according to organizational directive, and developing templates or obtaining tools to provide assistance in the completion of the categorization tasks. In addition, the information security team must continue its effort in developing and maintaining relationships with the enterprise architecture team and the system operations personnel to ensure that organizational security policies based on the system's impact level are implemented properly, common security controls are implemented, and that CM includes security in the operational decision-making process.

It should be noted that the categorization process can only be successful if the appropriate level of collaboration exists between all affected individuals within the organization and its external service providers. It is vital that senior management establish a balance between the benefits gained from using the ICT system with the accompanying risk that those same systems will be the mechanism in which threats and vulnerabilities can (and often do) cause mission or business failure. By establishing a collaborative effort, senior management is in a better position to make informed decisions, while maintaining the appropriate level of security, mitigating risk, and providing assurance that the organization's missions and business operations remain functional.

3.5.2 Develop an Organization-Wide Categorization Program

The next major categorization activity performed at the organization level is for the security team to develop categorization guidance for the process in addition to formulating organization-level procedures, documentation, approval, and reporting mechanisms for completion of the process. The organization-level guidance must provide the detail of how each information or information system owner must:

■ Integrate the categorization process into the processes already established defining the system development life cycle
■ Handle the emergence of new information types
■ Conduct the categorization process for their individual information systems in accordance with organizational policies and procedures
■ Document the decisions made during the categorization process into the organizations master system security plan
■ Gain approval for decisions made during the categorization process
■ Follow appropriate reporting procedures regarding categorization decisions
■ Maintain the decisions made during the categorization process by implementing a review task for the purpose of continuously validating that the decisions made during categorization have not changed

As changes are made to the information systems, considerations related to security categorization generally take place during the project initiation. During this project phase, decisions are made based on the mission and objectives of the organization. To that extent, as systems continue to evolve, the categorization decision needs to be revisited based on proposed changes to the information system or its environment. During the maintenance phase of the SDLC, the categorization decisions must be reevaluated intermittently to confirm that the criteria from which the categorization decisions were made have not changed. The organization's System Maintenance Plan must stipulate that if any information system (including hardware, software, or networking components) is scheduled for update, the categorization process must be repeated.

As is the case with many international and domestic ICT standards and guidelines, every organization implements the NIST SP 800-60 categorization process based on the culture within their organization. Such an organization-specific process must define any required documentation, approval, and reporting requirements. Many organizations also use tools and templates to promote consistency of the categorization decisions made throughout the organization. Those same tools and templates can be used across an entire supply chain in order to increase collaboration and understanding among organizations that need to share the information. Regardless of whether these decisions are made internally or externally, they must be maintained and updated as needed throughout the life cycle of the information system. To ensure that guidelines, templates, and tools are appropriately utilized within the categorization process, the security team must ensure that the individuals using them are properly trained. Training ensures consistency throughout the organization, and provides the management the assurance that the individuals involved in the categorization process understand how the categorization process has been implemented.

You will learn in Chapter 8 of this book that one of the tasks of the continuous monitoring process requires the information and information system be monitored for changes that may occur, related to security status. Such changes that could affect the overall security of an information system include: changes in the operating environment, new threats to the system, changes to the system functions, new interconnections, or added or removed information or information technology component. When changes to the information system have been identified, measures must be taken to determine the extent to which those changes affect the systems impact level by conducting SIA on those changes.

3.5.3 Prepare an Organization-Wide Guidance Program

As we discussed at the outset of this chapter, the categorization process begins with a thorough analysis of the organization's mission and business processes integrated with the organization's enterprise architecture to identify the types of information processed, stored, and transmitted by the information systems supporting those processes. The enterprise architecture is vital to the tasks performed during this process because it draws upon the organization's enterprise architecture to provide traceability from the enterprise models through each segment of the organization: to the individual information systems and the information flows that exist within each system. The security team must determine whether there are any organization-level information types unique to their organization. In doing so, the organization's missions and lines of business are reviewed to identify information types that may not be included in NIST SP 800-60, Volume 2: *Appendices to Guide for Mapping Types of Information and Information Systems to Security Categories*. For each organization-specific information type, the security team must determine the initial security impact baseline value (low, moderate, or high) for each of the security objectives (confidentiality, integrity, and availability) and any special factors regarding the impact determination.

After an organization-specific information type has been identified and approved, the information type is documented and shared with other individuals involved in the categorization process. Each organization will have its own approach for documentation on the basis of the standards and guidelines that have been adopted; however, NIST stipulates specific descriptive criteria for each information type that must be consistent with the descriptive information provided in NIST SP 800-60, Volume 2: *Appendices*. The descriptive criteria are as follows:

- Information type title and brief description of the new organization-specific information type
- Recommended security category
- For each security objective (confidentiality, integrity, and availability):
  - Discussion of the recommended security impact value assigned
  - Special factors affecting the impact value determination (NIST, 2009b)

As each information type is documented, care must be taken to ensure that the impact values selected for the information type's security category are consistent with the impact value descriptions from FIPS 199 and NIST SP 800-60, Volume 1.

3.5.4 Lead Organization-Wide Categorization Sessions

It is vital that organizations take on the security categorization as an organization-wide effort. Likewise, without the buy-in and support of senior management and other key leaders within the organization, the work performed within the categorization process and in turn other steps within the RMF are destined for failure. By performing the tasks of the security categorization process as an organization-wide initiative, it is assured that the decisions made are indicative of the security needs and priorities of the information and information systems that provide the underlying support of the organizational mission and objectives. Moreover, the decisions made provide a high level of consistency between the security program and the organization's enterprise architecture.

In the less desirable circumstance that an organization chooses to implement the categorization process without conducting organization-wide categorization sessions, it still necessary for the identified impact levels for information systems to be consistent throughout the organization. As we mentioned in Section 3.5.2, categorization consistency is achieved by providing training sessions to individuals who perform the process tasks. Additionally, management must lead the process to completion and must accept the responsibility of reviewing and approving the categorization decisions for individual information systems.

3.5.5 Security Categorization from the Management Perspective

Recall our statement from the discussion in Chapter 1: organizations need a comprehensive approach in managing risk. Such an approach provides the capability for management to recognize the balance between the organization's defined mission and objectives in correlation with day-to-day operations (specifically those that use information systems to achieve their defined mission and accomplish business objectives). To manage organizational risk, the most effective approach is to implement a risk executive function. The underlying scope of the risk executive function is to provide appropriate senior management input and oversight for all risk management and information security processes within the organization (including but not limited to each of the steps of the RMF). The value of management input and oversight provides assurance within the organization that risk acceptance decisions are consistent across all lines of business, continue to support the defined mission and objectives, and contribute to improving the organization's overall security posture.

That said, it is important that senior management's oversight be in place within the security categorization process. We have already discussed the dependent nature of the subsequent steps of the RMF to the success of the categorization process. In the absence of management oversight, the individuals making the categorization decisions have less confidence that those decisions will be supported and approved by senior management and in turn less confidence that those decisions will directly impact the organization's ability to achieve its mission and objectives, not to mention the organizations ability to protect valuable assets. Likewise, management should be aware of errors that occur in the initial categorization process through an overspecification or underspecification of the security controls for the information systems. When overspecification occurs the organization is generally spending more on information security than necessary, thus taking resources away from other mission or business that have established a greater protection need. Conversely, underspecification of security controls results in individual mission or business processes being exposed to a greater risk due to the inadequate protection measures allocated to the ICT systems that support those processes.

In determining the extent to which the organization is able to implement security measures, the senior management must ask the question, "What security controls are needed to adequately protect the information systems that support the operations and assets of the organization in order to accomplish its assigned mission, protect its assets, fulfill its legal responsibilities, maintain its day-to-day functions, and protect individuals?" (NIST, 2009a). The security categorization provides some vital insight that will likely lead to answers to this question. It does so by considering the minimum security controls and minimum assurance requirements in relation to each identified security impact level. The net result in doing so is that the organization is demonstrating a commitment to security and ensures that the proper protocol is followed in protecting their information and information systems.

3.5.6 Security Categorization from the System Perspective

From a system prospective, the organization may consider deconstructing the information system into multiple subsystems to more effectively allocate security controls to the system in Step 2 of the RMF. One approach is to categorize each subsystem individually. Many organizations attempt to steer away from this approach claiming that separately categorizing each subsystem changes the overall categorization of the entire information system; however, the opposite is true. Evaluating each subsystem allows it to receive a separate allocation of security controls instead of deploying the higher-impact controls across every subsystem. Alternatively, the organization may choose to bundle smaller subsystems into larger subsystems within the information system, categorize each of the aggregated subsystems, and allocate security controls to them as appropriate.

Upon completion of the security categorization process, relevant information is documented in the system identification section of the security plan or included as an attachment to the plan.

In order to understand the security categorization process from the system perspective, we return to the discussion of the four steps of the process stipulated by NIST SP 800-60, Volume 1 (identify information types, select provisional impact levels, review provisional impact levels and adjust/finalize information impact levels, and select system security category). In addition to the four steps, NIST recommends organizations appropriately address proper preparation for system security categorization, tasks related to gaining approval for the system security category and impact level, and maintaining the system security category and impact level.

3.5.7 Preparing for System Security Categorization

In order to facilitate a seamless security categorization process, the individual(s) performing the tasks of the process must be adequately prepared. To begin, there must be a common understanding about which subsystem is being categorized. Recall from Section 3.5.6 that each organization will have varied approaches for how subsystems are grouped for the purpose of this process. There is a significant relationship between the system changes that take place through the organization's CM process and those subsystems requiring security categorization. It follows, then, that the subsystems chosen for inclusion in the process are those systems from which changes occurred. The objective of this process is to identify potential information types and system security impact level; therefore, it is necessary for all of the documentation related to the system components that make up the subsystem and documentation related to all information processed, stored, or transmitted by the subsystem to be available. At a minimum, the required system-specific documentation includes:

- System requirements specifications
- System design specifications
- Database design documents such as the data dictionary, database schemas, and data requirements documents
- Samples of system reports and input forms, or software code if accessible
- Maintenance plans

Additionally, it is necessary to obtain organization-specific guidance documentation that includes any additional organization-specific information types, organization categorization policies and procedures, categorization tools and templates, and preliminary risk assessment results. Other organization-specific documentation that may be valuable include: enterprise architecture documentation, the security plan, the risk management plan, and the organizational strategic plan.

Success in *any* project or organizational process is more likely achieved if strong relationships exist between pivotal individuals that have a role in that project or process. With regard to successful completion of the security categorization process, NIST recommends that organizational relationships be developed among the security team, enterprise architects, individuals involved in the capital planning and investment control process, supply-chain stakeholders, and technical operations personnel. Working collaboratively, each of these groups will provide significant contributions to the security categorization decisions and impact the organization's ability to achieve its information security strategies.

3.5.8 Step 1: Identify System Information Types

Once the appropriate documentation has been collected, the process moves on to the identification of system information types associated with the subsystem being categorized and documenting them in the system security plan. The first task of this part of the categorization process centers on the verification of the characteristics of the system, including the system boundary, and the information that it processes, stores, or transmits. Details related to this information can typically be found in the description of the information system boundary.

The system boundary separates the internal components of the information system with external entities in terms of management control. Such determinations must have been made during the initiation phase of the SDLC and before the initial risk assessment is conducted, the system is categorized, and development has begun. By establishing boundaries, the organization is effectively taking into account its underlying mission and business requirements, technical requirements required for appropriate implementation of security controls, the overall implicit and explicit cost to the organization, and the understanding of the effects that the boundaries have on authorizing the ICT system.

If the information system boundary has not yet been defined, the documentation collected at the outset of the categorization process must be reviewed. In some cases, the boundary can be identified through interviews with people knowledgeable about the system and its characteristics. Once the system boundary has been identified, the goal is to obtain as much information as possible on the following:

- Overall scope of the system
- Portions of the organization's mission, or business functions that the system supports
- Transmission of data across the system boundary
- Functions and processes performed by the system
- Types of users and their usage characteristics
- Individuals, external organizations, or other subsystems that share information with the subsystem being categorized

- Characteristics of the operational environment
- Applications supported by the subsystem and the information that they process, store, create, transmit, or delete

Once the information subsystem that is being categorized and information associated with it is understood, the security categorization process progresses to the second or lower level of abstraction in which individual data elements are identified and an understanding of how those data elements are used in the information system and grouped is achieved. Data elements are the smallest unit of information that can be understood (which is why we referred to this part of the process as "a lower level of abstraction"). For example, an inventory item usually has the following data elements: item id, description, and price. Generally, individuals that work with an information system on a daily basis are more familiar with its data elements than the information types defined within the tables in NIST SP 800-60, Volume 1. It is sometimes more beneficial to work backwards from the data element level, potentially leading to a clearer understanding of their associated information types. With each data element, a list of resultant information types can be identified.

As each data element is identified, the database documentation assembled at the outset of the process is used to gain insight into how that data element is used. For example, the data elements for an inventory item can be used by a sales application to process orders. The same data elements may be used in an accounts receivable application to calculate the total amount billed to a customer. Thus, the context in which the data elements are used is what drives the determination of each information type. Once all of the relevant data elements have been identified and logically grouped, a description of each data element is created. This description is then used to match the data elements with the information types defined in NIST SP 800-60, Volume 2, *Appendices* and the organization's supplemental guidelines.

Once data elements have been identified and documented, the next task in identifying information types is to match the data elements in the system to the available information types identified in the organization's supplement to NIST SP 800-60, Volume 1 of additional, organization-specific information types and NIST SP 800-60, Volume 2. It is important to emphasize that the NIST SP 800-60 guidelines were written for the purpose of performing security categorization on federal information systems. To that extent, the tables provided in Section 4.1 of Volume I are focused on information geared toward missions, service delivery mechanisms, service delivery support, and resource management functions of the federal government. Likewise, the appendices of Volume 2 also have a strong government theme. This is not to suggest that NIST SP 800-60 is not useful to organizations in the private sector. Rather, you will notice that there are many categories and individual information types within each of the tables in Volume

I and Appendices of Volume 2 (for the purpose of identifying provisional impact levels) that do relate to the data elements and associated information types in private sector organizations. We suggest that, in creating supplements for the guidelines, organizations begin building their own tables of categories and information types, each based on one key organizational objective that is supported for the organization's information system. Next, identify the categories and information types already provided by the guidelines that are related to the organization's objectives, then add them to the appropriate table in the supplement. In some cases, a certain data element or group of data elements may not be able to be matched to an information type in the organization's supplement to NIST SP 800-60, Volume 1 or Volume 2. This unique kind of information must be described and an initial security category determined based on the FIPS 199 categorization criteria. After identifying the new information type, a description must be written including the similar information found in NIST SP 800-60, Volume 2. At a minimum, the description must contain the following:

- A brief title and description of the information type
- A recommended security category
- A recommendation for the appropriate security impact value and the special factors affecting the impact value determination, for each security objective (confidentiality, integrity, and availability)

The description of the information type must be submitted for approval and possible inclusion in the organization's supplement to NIST SP 800-60. To determine which information type is most relevant to each group of data elements, it is important to look at the context in which the information is used.

As the organization proceeds through the task of matching data elements to information types, generally the information type will be very apparent. In other cases, the information type will not be very obvious and thus trigger the need to match the kind of information to a portion of the information type description or an extension of the information type description. In other cases, there is more than one option when matching the data elements to the defined information types. To determine which information type is most relevant to the data element, consideration must be given to the context in which the information is used. For example, a person's name (with data elements last name, first name, middle initial, and suffix) could be used in a variety of information types. How the person's name is being used in the specific application determines which information type is the best match for the data elements identified in the information system.

The final task necessary in identifying information types is for each to be documented in the organization's security plan. Figure 3.4 provides a multipurpose approach to recording all the information needed to support the categorization decision.

Information type, title, reference, description	Security category							Adjustment rationale
	Provisional				Final			
	C	I	A		C	I	A	
Corrective action, C.2.1.1, POAMs include information on noncompliant information systems within the organization								
Program evaluation, C.2.1.2, Analysis information on the status of the organization's information systems (internal or external)								
Program monitoring, C.2.1.3, Collection of data gathered to evaluate the effectiveness of the organization's information system (internal or external)								
Inventory control, C.3.4.2, List of the organization's information systems including contact information of the system owner, individual responsible for security, system components, interconnections								
Provisional system security category								
Adjusted system security category								
Information system security impact level								

Figure 3.4 Security categorization compliance tracking summary.

During this part of the categorization process, the information types are identified and added to the table. As the categorization process continues through selection of provisional impact levels and making adjustments to information types and impact levels, additional information is added to the table. The information on the information types must include the information type title and reference number (from NIST SP 800-60 or the organization's supplement to NIST SP 800-60) and a description of the information type. The example provided by Figure 3.4 is taken from draft NIST documentation related to the categorization process. It describes a compliance tracking information system used by the organization to monitor the organization's low- and moderate-impact information systems.

3.5.9 Step 2: Select Provisional Impact Values for Each Information Type

Once each information type has been identified and documented in the organization's system security plan, the categorization process includes tasks related to selecting and documenting provisional impact values for each information type. If the categorization process has been performed correctly up to this point, each information type is located in either the organization's supplement to NIST SP 800-60, Volume 1 or

NIST SP 800-60, Volume 2, *Appendices C or D*. The provisional impact values are low, moderate, or high. Confidentiality can also have an impact value of "not applicable" when the information type contains public information. If the information type is provided in NIST SP 800-60, Volume 2, the provisional impact recommendation is provided using the FIPS 199 general syntax for security categorization of information type:

$$SC_{\text{information type}} = \left\{ \begin{array}{l} (\text{confidentiality, impact}), \ (\text{integrity, impact}), \\ (\text{availability, impact}) \end{array} \right\}$$

The recommendation is then followed by a justification for how the impact type is determined for each of the three security objectives (confidentiality, integrity, and availability). Finally, *special factors* guidance is provided for each information type. The special factors guidance is applied to each information type based on how the information type is used, the organization's mission, interconnections with other systems, preliminary assessment of risk, or the system's operating environment. Documented correctly, the organizations supplement for NIST SP 800-60 must provide the same criteria for each information type not found in Volume 2. When new information types and/or categories are identified through the security categorization process, the NIST SP 800-60 supplement must be updated to include the new potential impact criteria.

Once each of the provisional impact types have been selected, the security category section of the system security plan table(s) created during the information type identification step of the categorization process must be updated to include the selected provisional impact levels for each information type. Many organizations question the need for recording potential impact types in multiple documents and too often management claims that it is a waste of time. However, it is important to remember that each created document that reflects any aspect of organizational ICT is read and interpreted by different groups of people for a variety of purposes. It is necessary to continuously provide documentation to the extent that the information is available for the right people, in the right place, and at the right time.

3.5.10 Step 3: Adjust the Provisional Impact Levels of Information Types

As the security team continues to identify net threats and vulnerabilities to the organization's ICT system, new system components continue to be added, and the organization's missions and objectives change, the established provisional impact level for many existing information types changes as well. The security categorization process of the NIST RMF builds in the ability to make adjustments to provisional impact levels when changes are a necessity.

In this step of the categorization process, the organization must perform a review and adjustment on the provisional security impact levels for the security objectives of each information type, resulting in a finalized state. Specifically, the organization must:

1. Perform a review of the provisional impact levels based on the organization, environment, mission, use, and data sharing in order to justify their appropriateness
2. Make an adjustment, based on the review, to the security objective impact levels as necessary using the special factors guidance found in NIST SP 800-60, Volume 2, *Appendices C and D*
3. Prepare and document all adjustments that were made to the impact levels, providing an appropriate rationale or justification for each adjustment

NIST recommends that when security categorization impact levels are selected as provisional security impact levels, the organization must review the appropriateness of the provisional impact levels in the context of the organization, environment, mission, use, and data sharing associated with the information system from which the categorization process is taking place. Such a review must consider organizational aspects such as defined objectives and their importance to adopted strategies and mission statement, system life cycle implications, and configuration and security policy. The potential impact factors provided in Figure 3.1, as well as in Table 1 of FIPS 199, and Section 4.2.2 of NIST SP 800-60, Volume 1, should be used as the basis for decisions regarding adjustment or finalization of the provisional impact levels. It is often the case that the security objective (confidentiality, integrity, and availability) impact levels may be adjusted one or more times in the course of the review. Moreover, the special factors guidance in NIST SP 800-60, Volume 2 provides specific guidance on how to adjust each security objective. Determination must be made as to whether or not a change to a security impact value is warranted. In many cases, no change to the security category is necessary.

If adjustments are made, the associated impact values for each security objective are added to the information type table(s) of the security plan, along with the supporting rationale to increase or decrease the values. If, for any security objective, the impact values did not change, the table must be updated to state no adjustment was needed.

3.5.11 Step 4: Determine the Information System Security Impact Level

Once each information type has been identified, assigned appropriate impact levels, and documented, the security categorization process proceeds to the task of assigning the system's provisional security category. Upon completion, the existing system impact values for each security objective (confidentiality, integrity, and availability) will have been reviewed to determine whether they are applicable to the information system or whether a more realistic view of the potential impact on the system requires increasing one or more security objectives of the security category. If the impact value of a security objective is changed, the final adjusted *system* security category will have been documented in the system security plan along with a rationale for the change, in much the same way as information type impact level adjustments were documented. The underlying objective is for the final system security category to effectively determine how an information system's security controls can be adjusted and reflect the expectations for each security objective so that an appropriate decision can be made in Step 2 *Select Security Controls,* of the NIST RMF process.

In reviewing the existing impact levels, the provisional system security category is chosen by considering the *highest value assigned* to each security objective among the system's information types. Using the high water mark (highest value) for each security objective, the value of low, moderate, or high is assigned expressed syntactically as

$$SC_{\text{information system}} = \left\{ \begin{array}{l} (\text{confidentiality, impact}), (\text{integrity, impact}), \\ (\text{availability, impact}) \end{array} \right\}$$

Having completed the provisional system security category determination, the decision needs to be made if there is a need to increase the impact provisional system security category value of one or more of the security objectives considering the potential impact a security breach could have on the information system. Consideration must be given to factors such as aggregation of information, interconnections with other systems, protection of public information, loss of system availability, use of information within critical infrastructure or key national assets, preliminary assessment of risk, and other probable circumstances. Each security objective must be reviewed from the whole system and organizational perspective rather than just considering the perspective of each individual information type. For example, a given system's confidentiality impact value in the provisional system security category may have been determined to be moderate, while other systems that are reliant on that system for information provide critical functionality to the extent that it is justified to increase the confidentiality impact value to high. From the management perspective, some decisions must be made beyond the scope of an individual system to the impact on the organization and its ability to fulfill its mission and business goals.

The *Compliance Tracking Summary* table within the organization's system security plan must provide the capability of recording the assigned impact levels for each security objective. If an adjustment must be made to a provisional security category, the final assigned values must be included within the appropriate table, along with rationale for having made the adjustment. If no adjustment is necessary after analysis of the existing provisional categories, a notation of "no adjustment needed" must be provided within the table.

It is important to remember that in determining the adjusted security category, each information type is considered as a means for identifying the high water mark for a given system. Often, the following task within the system categorization process gets confused with work that had been completed in the previous task.

Upon completing the determination of the system security category based on the high water mark of the adjusted information types, the next task is to determine the system's impact level. The impact level is easily obtained by identifying the highest value assigned to a security objective in the system security category. In the example we provided earlier in this section, the highest impact value is moderate. It follows then, that the system's impact level is moderate. Consider another example where the system security category is

$$SC_{\text{information system}} = \left\{ \begin{array}{l} (\text{confidentiality, HIGH}), (\text{integrity, HIGH}), \\ (\text{availability, LOW}) \end{array} \right\}$$

In this case, the system security impact level is high since high is the highest impact value of two of the security objectives. Remember that while this system impact level indicates that the system starts with the high baseline of security controls, based on specific circumstances the security controls can be adjusted based on the three impact values of the security category during the Select Step of the RMF.

After the determination has been made of the final system security impact level, the information is documented in the appropriate system security plan tables. In this example, the system's impact level is high.

3.5.12 Obtain Approval for the System Security Category and Impact Level

Consistent with each of the other steps of the NIST RMF, the information system's security impact level and security category must be approved based on the specific directives in the organization's categorization guidance documentation, before continuing to *Select Security Controls*, Step 2 in the RMF. The purpose of approval at this stage of the process is to validate the categorization decision, since this decision will determine the selection of the security controls that will be implemented in the information system.

The approval procedure will vary from organization to organization based on the defined governance structure. However, it is customary for the lead member of the group that has carried out the tasks of the security categorization process to submit the system security impact level, security category, and supporting rationale (e.g., the completed tables within the system security plan) to the appropriate organizational official who approves it and ensures its consistency with other organizational systems. Generally, the system's impact level is approved by the chief information security officer (CISO) or the individual charged with the responsibility of authorization or another senior information security officer. Upon submitting the request for approval, it is vital to be prepared to justify any determination of the kinds of information within the system, the selected information types, the adjusted security impact values for each information type, and the final security impact level.

During the approval decision, either the entire categorization package will be given support by the organization or the individual responsible for the approval will assist in making appropriate modifications to the final decision to make it more accurate and consistent with other systems within the organization. The system's impact level must be approved before the security controls are selected for the information system.

3.5.13 Maintain the System Security Category and Impact Levels

We said at the outset of this chapter that it is often the case that the process of security categorization is triggered through CM and requests for changes to existing information systems. It is often the case that changes to the information system or its operating environment provide new insights as to the overall importance of the system in allowing the organization to fulfill its responsibilities. It is also important for information systems that may not have frequent changes applied to them to be periodically evaluated in order to confirm the security of the system and its information to ensure that the system continues to support the organization's mission and objectives.

What is being discussed here is the application of a continuous monitoring process (which will be explored in greater detail in Chapter 8). In this case, the part of the continuous monitoring process being employed recognizes the need for the implemented security controls to be monitored on a frequent and scheduled basis. Changes or other activities performed on the information system that could affect implemented security controls include but are not limited to: changes in the operating environment, new threats to the system, changes to the system functions, new interconnections, or added or removed information or information technology components. It is vital that when changes to the information system have been identified, a determination is made as to the extent in which those changes and ongoing activities affect the system's security impact level. This is achieved by performing SIA as a means of maintaining the desired level of organizational information security.

In the event modifications to the information system do affect the system's impact level, the system categorization decisions previously made must be reviewed and any necessary changes as a result of the system modifications incorporated into the categorization documentation in the system security plan. If the review results in an increase of the system impact level, implementation of any new security controls must be implemented expeditiously.

It is important to remember that if the review does result in a change to the system security impact level, the changes must be updated in the system review documentation and security plan. Finally, the revised system review documentation and system security plan must be resubmitted for approval, following the organization's defined approval process.

3.6 Chapter Summary

This chapter used as a basis the three key security requirements required by most information systems: availability, integrity, and confidentiality. Referring to them as "objectives," they are the pivotal aspects of an information system security program and the necessary properties that must be evident within an information system. However, providing the maximum level of protection of these three objectives would not be realistic or cost-effective from an organizational standpoint. Additionally, each system is unique in terms of the security protection required. One system may require a higher level of confidentiality and lower levels of integrity and availability, while other systems within the same organization may have much different requirements. Moreover, deployed information systems are bound by legal and regulatory requirements that dictate the degree by which each objective is protected within the system. Organizations must also consider the impact that could result if one of the objectives is lacking.

All ICT projects typically begin with the definition of business requirements. Senior management responsible for defining these requirements, however, are not always familiar with cybersecurity and typically overlook necessary security requirements. As a consequence, those same missing requirements are often lacking in subsequent projects, thereby leaving the organization vulnerable to numerous forms of security exploitation.

Identifying security requirements is not simple, and must not be dealt with haphazardly. The most experienced cybersecurity professional could, and likely does, overlook some risks. Therefore, it is imperative that the organization have a risk identification and security requirement analysis process in place. It is noteworthy to mention also that many ICT projects utilize the services of third-party vendors; sometimes those third parties are used locally, while others must be accessed across the Internet through cloud-based infrastructures. Assessing security requirements, therefore, must also address such supply-chain scenarios and the associated risks that they create.

The process of understanding the business requirements and matching them to the properties of confidentiality, integrity, and availability while measuring each requirement for the degree of security risk it imposes is often referred to as

"Security Impact Analysis." In an attempt to provide a checklist process to help organizations to identify the level of protection a system requires, the first step of the NIST RMF includes a security categorization process that addresses the need for organizations to do an initial assessment based on system information types and the organizational objectives that each support.

Security categorization is the most important step in the RMF; it affects information security decisions both for the organization and individual information systems and influences all remaining steps in the RMF—from the selection of security controls to the level of effort needed to assess and maintain the controls. Security categorization uses FIPS 199, *Standards for Security Categorization of Federal Information and Information Systems*, and NIST SP 800-60, *Guide for Mapping Types of Information and Information Systems to Security Categories*, to assess the criticality and sensitivity of the information and information system to determine the system's security impact level. Security categorizations must be reviewed on an ongoing basis to help ensure that mission and business impact assessments reflect the current organizational priorities and operational environments (NIST, 2009a).

References

CNSS. (2014). *Security Categorization and Control Selection for National Security Systems*. Standard, Ft Meade, MD: Committee on National Security Systems.

Johnson, A., Dempsey, K., Ross, R., Gupta, S., and Bailey, D. (2011). *NIST SP 800-128: Guide for Security-Focused Configuration Management of Information Systems*. Guide, Gaithersburg, MD: National Institute of Standards and Technology.

NIST. (2004). *FIPS 199: Federal Information Processing Standards Publication—Standards for Security Categorization of Standard*. Gaithersburg, MD: National Institute of Standards and Technology.

NIST. (2009a). Categorize step—Management perspective. *Computer Security Division—Computer Security Resource Center*. January 27. Accessed February 14, 2016. Available at: http://csrc.nist.gov/groups/SMA/fisma/Risk-Management-Framework/categorize/QSG_categorize_management-perspective.pdf.

NIST. (2009b). Categorize step—Tips and techniques for organizations. *Computer Security Division—Computer Security Resource Center*. January 27. Accessed February 13, 2016. Available at: http://csrc.nist.gov/groups/SMA/fisma/Risk-Management-Framework/categorize/QSG_categorize_tips-and-techniques-for-organizations.pdf.

NIST. (2010). NIST SP 800-37 R 1: *Guide for Applying the Risk Management Framework to Federal Information Systems—A Security Lifecycle Approach*. Guideline, Gaithersburg, MD: National Institute of Standards and Technology.

Stine, K., Kissel, R., Barker, W.C., Fahlsing, J., and Gulick, J. (2008). NIST SP 800-60, *Guide for Mapping Types of Information and Information Systems to Security Categories*, Volume 1. Gaithersburg, MD: National Institute of Standards and Technology.

Chapter 4

Step 2—Select Security Controls

At the conclusion of this chapter, the reader will understand:

- The activities and tasks that make up the security control selection step of the National Institute of Standards and Technologies (NIST) Risk Management Framework (RMF)
- Appropriate usage of FIPS 200 in establishing a set of minimum security requirements
- Appropriate usage of NIST SP 800-53 as a means of establishing an initial security control baseline, tailoring security controls, and establishing minimum assurance requirements
- The most appropriate way to document security controls in a security plan
- What other control libraries are available for organizations to use in selecting the most appropriate security controls

A security program, whether at the organization or system level, should include an appropriate mixture of security controls: management, operational, and technical. *Management* controls are techniques that are normally addressed by management in the organization's information and communication technology (ICT) security program and focus on managing the entire program and identified risks that may inhibit the organization's ability to mitigate threats and vulnerabilities. *Operational* controls are those that are operated by people, as opposed to a technology or systems. These controls often depend on the technical expertise of network and security teams in addition to other management and technical controls. *Technical* controls are those that the system executes. These controls should be consistent with the operational context of the organization and selected management controls.

Unfortunately, many organizations stop short of selecting the proper mix of management, operational, and technical controls, allocating their entire security budget on just those technical aspects of ICT security that will limit exploitation and potentially cost the most in damages. However, relying on just technical controls will be insufficient and justifiably cost the organization even more money without the complementary management and operational controls in place. For example, an organization may choose to install the most robust firewall on the market; however, if it does not have the proper access privileges in place and in turn allows unrestricted internet access to and from the network, that organization will be prone to significant vulnerabilities.

The number and type of appropriate security controls vary throughout a system's life cycle and are selected based on the organization's understanding of the results of security impact analysis that should be performed before selection of controls begins. Thus, relative maturity of an organization's enterprise architecture and security program will have a significance influence on the types of appropriate security controls. The blend of security controls is tied to the mission of the organization and the role of the system within the organization as it supports that mission. Recall from our discussion in Chapter 3 that one of the first objectives of the RMF security categorization process is to understand the mission and objectives of the organization. ICT security impacts that mission and the defined objectives.

In Chapter 1, we emphasized that risk management is the process used to identify an effective mix of management, operational and technical security controls to mitigate risk to a level acceptable to the responsible senior official. Although it may be tempting to simply pick a product off the shelf, using a risk management process to choose the most effective blend of controls enhances an organization's security posture.

Chapter 3 introduced the activities and tasks performed in the first step (Security Classification) of the NIST RMF. In this chapter, we will begin with a conceptualization of security control selection. Next, FIPS 200, *Minimum Security Requirements for Federal Information and Information Systems* will be introduced as a means for understanding the task of establishing security boundaries and identification of minimum security requirements. The major focus of this chapter centers on the tables available in NIST 800-60, *Guide for Mapping Types of Information and Information Systems to Security Categories* (Stine et al., 2008) and FIPS 199 as a means of implementing the security categorization and information classification process of the NIST RMF.

This chapter continues the explanation of the implementation of the framework by introducing Step 2—Select Security Controls. Next, that guideline will be used to provide a basis for discussion of establishing security boundaries and the identification of minimum security requirements. The major focus of this

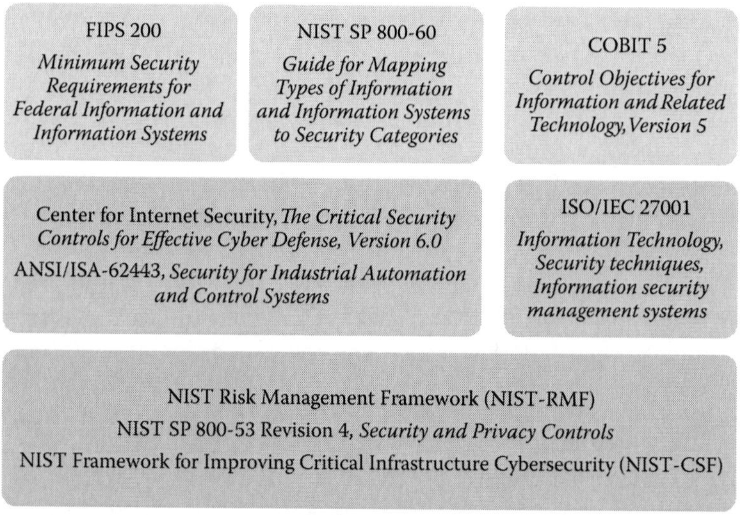

FIPS 200	NIST SP 800-60	COBIT 5
Minimum Security Requirements for Federal Information and Information Systems	*Guide for Mapping Types of Information and Information Systems to Security Categories*	*Control Objectives for Information and Related Technology, Version 5*

Center for Internet Security, *The Critical Security Controls for Effective Cyber Defense, Version 6.0* ANSI/ISA-62443, *Security for Industrial Automation and Control Systems*	ISO/IEC 27001 *Information Technology, Security techniques, Information security management systems*

NIST Risk Management Framework (NIST-RMF)
NIST SP 800-53 Revision 4, *Security and Privacy Controls*
NIST Framework for Improving Critical Infrastructure Cybersecurity (NIST-CSF)

Figure 4.1   Resources for understanding security controls.

chapter centers on understanding the guidelines for selecting security controls as defined in NIST 800-53 Revision 4, *Security and Privacy Controls for Federal Information Systems and Organizations*. Once you have gained an understanding of NIST 800-53 Revision 4, we will compare that guideline with other significant security control libraries including: COBIT5 *Control Objectives for Information and Related Technology Version 5*, CSC Council on Cyber Security (CCS) *Top 20 Critical Security Controls*; ANSI/ISA-62443-2-1 (99.02.01)-2009 *Security for Industrial Automation and Control Systems: Establishing an Industrial Automation and Control Systems Security Program*; ANSI/ISA-62443-3-3 (99.03.03)-2013 *Security for Industrial Automation and Control Systems: System Security Requirements and Security Levels*; and ISO/IEC 27001 *Information technology, Security techniques, Information security management systems*. By connecting all of these related security control standards and guidelines, you will be able to link their support and value to the NIST Framework for Improving Critical Infrastructure Cybersecurity (NSIT CSF), which we discuss later in the chapter. This chapter provides discussion on the contents of the security plan, and continuous monitoring strategy, which are two of the underlying outputs of the control selection process (Figure 4.1).

4.1 Understanding Control Selection

The second step in the security control formulation and development process, as defined by the NIST RMF, identifies the security controls necessary to satisfy an ICT system's security requirements and includes tasks associated with documenting those controls in the system security plan. From an input → processing → output perspective, the results of the system security categorization completed in Chapter 3 serve as input to the selection of security controls; the impact level assigned to the information system corresponds to a baseline set of security controls that, in combination, provide the minimum security necessary to protect systems categorized at each impact level. In this part of the process, organizations use security requirements and risk assessment documentation developed for the system in combination with the system security categorization to identify the appropriate security control baseline and modify that baseline to address the needs of the system. The outputs of the security control selection process are a tailored security control baseline, continuous monitoring strategy, and an approved initial version of the system security plan. The security control selection identifies all of the controls relevant to each ICT system regardless of which functional unit or supply chain organization is responsible for providing them. Most ICT systems include a mix of system-specific, common, and hybrid security controls. Security control baselines defined in system security plans indicate the type for each control and, in the case of common or hybrid controls, may incorporate control information in other system security plans. At the conclusion of this step, organizations have the information needed to finalize the resource allocation and timeline for the entire security control formulation and development process. The security control baseline defined during this step serves as the basis for security control implementation and assessment activities conducted in the next two subsequent steps. Therefore, the effectiveness of the remaining parts of the process depends upon the accuracy and thoroughness of the security control selection. Organizations first identify relevant controls using published standards and guidelines, as well as system-specific considerations. Based on this knowledge of relevant controls, they are able to determine how the controls will be provided and monitored once the system is operational.

The entire set of security controls selected to support an ICT system typically includes both system-specific controls provided by the system or the operational and management functions dedicated to the system and common controls provided by other systems or parts of the organization (or external organizations) that protect multiple systems. "Few ICT systems have sufficient scope or resources to provide all of the necessary security controls at a system-specific level. Instead, organizations specify common controls that their ICT systems inherit, either exactly as implemented by common control providers or with some system-specific modifications, thus creating hybrid controls" (Kohnke et al., 2016). Prior to selecting security controls, the organization needs to identify common control providers and the security controls available for their ICT systems to use, and understand common controls in sufficient detail to determine whether they meet the system's security requirements. When the available common controls do not fully satisfy ICT system security requirements, organizations must determine whether to implement a system-specific alternative or if the common control can be partially utilized as a hybrid control.

The task of identifying common controls can be performed at the organizational level, with a directory or inventory of controls made available to the management overseeing the identification process. The ability to use preidentified sources of common controls greatly simplifies the control identification for the security team members and management performing the control selection, thus eliminating the need to search for common control providers as a part of the task and allowing attention to be focused on assessing the suitability of available controls. The security team members and management performing common control identification should also be aware of the potential that more than one provider exists for one control, as is often the case when more than one operating environment is available for information system deployment, thus adding the additional activity of evaluating the provider based on characteristics such as credibility, reliability, and their own security posture.

Based on the scope and complexity of an ICT system, many security controls are generally considered to be good candidates for inheritance from common control providers. Organizations with existing ICT security programs and well-defined management structures often take advantage of common management controls such as risk management strategies, contingency plans, disaster recovery plans, and continuous monitoring strategies. The security controls, which represent security requirements that many systems share, can also be provided as common controls such as those associated with security awareness and training, personnel security, and incident response. The ICT systems housed within data centers or hosted by external organizations that could extend from the members of an organization's supply chain to systems, which take advantage of "as-a-service" technologies, typically identify the common controls that provide physical and environmental protection, maintenance, media protection, and configuration management. Note that high-impact systems or those processing other sensitive information may require system-specific controls or service-level agreements to satisfy security requirements.

We must not neglect the importance that there are also some controls for which a certain amount of system-specific implementation is expected or required, including management controls such as the system security plan, security assessments, plan of action and milestones, and privacy impact assessment. If the organization's risk management policy states that system-specific requirements are identified as part of their control implementation, then hybrid controls are likely the most appropriate.

While following the federal standards and guidelines is not a requirement within private industries, as it is in the public sector, organizations following such standards and guidelines begin security control selection by identifying the baseline security controls corresponding to the impact level assigned to the information system during security categorization. One such guideline is NIST SP 800-53, *Security and Privacy Controls*. Excerpts provided of that guide in this chapter present the controls based on three criteria, one each for (1) low-impact (2) moderate-impact, and (3) high-impact systems, that identify the subset of controls and control enhancements applicable to systems in each security category. The established baselines represent a starting point for the selection of security controls, serving as the basis for the reduction or supplementation of security controls in the ICT systems.

In some instances, organizations may find that a baseline security control applies for a system, but implementing the control specified in the baseline is beyond the organization's resource capacity from a triple constraint (scope, time, and cost) perspective. Prior to deciding to accept, avoid, or otherwise respond to the threats and vulnerabilities affecting the organization by failing to implement a required control, the management should consider the selection of compensating controls as an alternative that satisfies the same security objectives. These controls are designed to satisfy the requirement of a security measure that is determined to be too difficult or impractical to implement. For example, *segregation of duties* (SoD) is an internal control designed to prevent error and fraud by ensuring that at least two individuals are responsible for the separate parts of any task. However, SoD can be difficult for businesses with small staffs. Other types of compensating controls may include maintaining and reviewing logs and audit trails. Nevertheless, compensating controls should only be used when they can be picked from a guideline such as NIST SP 800-53 or some other appropriate resource AND the organization accepts the repercussions associated with substituting the compensating controls for those specified in the security control baseline. As with the selection of common or hybrid controls, organizations must document the selection of compensating controls and explain the rationale for choosing alternative controls instead of the ones in the baseline.

In still other cases, considering system-specific controls may also lead organizations to select supplemental security controls beyond the minimum requirements specified in the appropriate baseline for the system. Again, guidelines such as NIST SP 800-53 provide vital information for implementation of the supplemental controls and control enhancements that the organizations may choose from the requirements in a higher level baseline or from among several optional controls and enhancements in the security control catalogs, which are not assigned a baseline. Each individual organization must determine the necessity for supplemental controls by comparing the security requirements defined for each ICT system with current capabilities and the expected effect of implementing baseline controls. Moreover, any requirements that have not been satisfied by baseline controls may indicate a need for supplemental control considerations. All decisions regarding the addition of supplemental controls or enhancements should be documented to the extent that it provides supporting feasibility analysis in order for management, and other organizations within the supply chain, to understand the basis for the control implementation.

The documentation related to security controls must also include criteria related to the reductions or additions made to the security control baselines. This information not only satisfies standardized definitions of the contents of security control documentation in the system security plan, but also provides guidance to the management oversight and a security team responsible for implementing and configuring the security controls to satisfy the system's defined security requirements. In most instances, the management, operational, and technical controls include parameters associated with policy, acceptable use, time periods, frequency of execution, or other attributes that vary among the ICT systems. Selection of controls is not complete until values for these parameters have been determined and documented at the level of abstraction necessary to support effective and efficient implementation and configuration of each control.

The completion of security control selection signifies a pivotal point within the organization's security/risk management process. While performing the tasks of control categorization and selection, organizational management along with security teams document the results of all the key activities that were expected to be performed in the system security plan and submit the plan to senior executives review and approval. This interim approval evaluates the system security plan for completeness, in addition to verifying compliance with industry and regulatory requirements in terms of content, structure, and level of detail. The approval process also aims to assess the extent to which the set of security controls selected for implementation are consistent with the impact level assigned to the system and confirm that they will satisfy the system's security requirements. At a minimum, the version of the plan submitted for approval at this stage should include a statement of the system security categorization, the system description, and also a listing of security controls selected for the system including common, hybrid, and system-specific designations. The acceptance of the system security plan by senior executives is also an important milestone in the system development life cycle (SDLC) process, as the agreed-upon set of selected security controls is a key input to system development or acquisition. It also serves as a means for verified buy-in by the top-level management in terms of the significance of security requirements to the underlying efforts toward achieving the organization's strategic mission, vision, and objectives.

4.2 Federal Information Processing Standard Publication 200

FIPS 200 originated in 2006 and is the second of the two mandatory security standards that resulted from the Federal Information Security Management Act (FISMA) of 2002. Recall from the discussion in Chapter 3 that, through the enactment of this act, NIST was tasked with the development of standards and guidelines which promote the importance of information security within the United States. FIPS 200 picks up where FIPS 199 leaves off in that it was written for federal systems but can be equally utilized by private industry. Its intent is to provide a specification for minimum security requirements for information and ICT systems as well as the necessary risk-based process for selecting the security controls that satisfy those minimum security requirements. Moreover, it provides a basis for productive development, implementation, and operation of the secure ICT systems of the federal government and private industry by interjecting minimum requirements for ICT security, and in turn provides a process for selecting and specifying ICT security controls that is repeatable.

The minimum security requirements, defined by FIPS 200, cover 17 security-related areas with regard to protecting the confidentiality, integrity, and availability of systems and the information processed, stored, and transmitted by those systems. Figures 4.2 provides each of the security-related areas and a description of each.

A new 18th security-related area was added in NIST SP 800-53 (Revision 3), called *Program Management*. This new addition requires the development of an organization-wide information security program plan. We will discuss NIST SP 800-53 in Section 4.5. Specifically, FIPS 200 provides the minimum requirements that the federal agencies and private organizations must meet. In turn, NIST SP 800-53 is used to appropriately select the security controls and assurance measures that satisfy the minimum security requirements. Using the two standards interchangeably in selecting the appropriate security controls and assurance measures, organizations can be confident that their ICT systems are capable of achieving adequate security resulting from a complex and risk-based process involving the efforts of management and operational personnel within the organization.

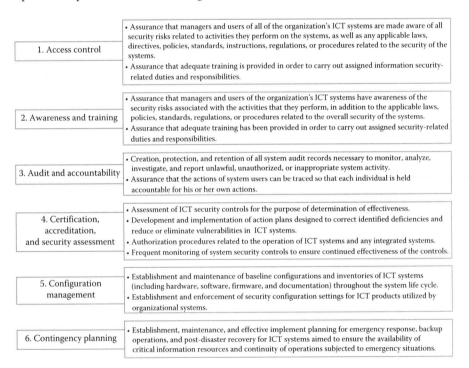

Figure 4.2   FIPS 200 minimum security requirement specifications. (Continued)

7. Identification and authentication	• Identification of system users, processes initiated by a user, or devices and verification that those users, processes, or devices are allowed access to the organization's ICT systems.
8. Incident response	• Establishment of operational incident handling capabilities for the organization's ICT systems that provide proper preparation, detection, analysis, containment, recovery, and user response activities. • Implementation of processes that track, document, and report incidents to appropriate senior officials.
9. Maintenance	• Implementation of processes that provide timely maintenance on the organization's ICT systems. • Availability of effective controls on the tools, techniques, mechanisms, and staff used to conduct ICT system maintenance.
10. Media protection	• Protection of system media provided. • Limitation of access to information on system media, making it only available to authorized users. • Sanitization or destruction of system media before disposal or release for reuse.
11. Physical and environmental protection	• Limitation of physical access to ICT systems, equipment, and the respective operating environments to authorized individuals. • Protection of the physical facilities and support infrastructure for ICT systems. • Availability of supporting utilites for ICT systems. • Protection of systems from environmental hazards. • Availability of appropiate environmental controls within facilities housing ICT systems.
12. Planning	• Development, documentation, scheduled update of security plans for an organization's ICT systems, containing the details of the security controls in place or planned for implementation into the ICT system in addition to applicable rules of behavior for individuals accessing the systems.
13. Personnel security	• Assurance of the trustworthiness of individuals holding positions of authority within organization's interface with the ICT system. • Assurance that an organization's information ICT systems are adequately protected during and after personnel terminations and transfers. • Policies that enforce formal sanctions on personnel that fail to comply with organizational security policies and procedures.
14. Risk assessment	• Scheduled assessments to the risk on the organization's operations (including mission, functions, image, or reputation), organizational assets, and individuals, as a result of operation of the ICT systems.
15. Systems and services acquisition	• Resources provided that are necessary to adequately protect the organizations ICT systems. • Implementation of system development life cycle processes that incorporate information security. • Appropriate restrictions to software usage and installation. • Assurance of adequate security measures employed by third party providers.
16. System and communications protection	• Ability to monitor, control, and protect organizational communications at the external boundaries and significant internal boundaries of the organizations ICT systems. • Implement architectural design processes, software development techniques, and systems engineering principles that promote effective information security.
17. System and information integrity	• Ability to identify, report, and correct information and information system flaws in a timely manner. • Implementation procedures that provide adequate protection from malicious code within the organization's ICT systems. • Ability to monitor information system security alerts and take appropriate actions as necessary.

Figure 4.2 (Continued)   FIPS 200 minimum security requirement specifications.

4.3 Implementation of Step 2—Select Security Controls

In order to assist organizations in the selection of appropriate security controls, an updated revision (Revision 4) to NIST SP 800-53, *Security and Privacy Controls for Federal Information Systems* was published in April 2013. This publication provides a complete set of security controls, three security control baselines (low, moderate, and high impact), and guidelines that organizations can use to tailor the standard baselines to their own specific needs according to the organization's mission and environment in which the operations or ICT systems are performed.

Prior to performing the steps of Step 2 of the RMF, we encourage you to become familiar with the detailed catalog of controls provided in *Appendix F* of NIST SP 800-53 Revision 4. To provide clarification to the assortment of controls provided, NIST has organized them into 18 families, each containing security controls related to the general security topic of the family. The security controls provided in SP 800-53 directly relate to the security of each facet of ICT with consideration made to policy, oversight, supervision, manual processes, individual actions, and automated processes performed by the ICT systems of the organization and the devices connected to the system that support its functionality. Each control listed in *Appendix F* of NIST SP 800-53 is identified using the same structure:

■ A control identification section
■ A supplemental guidance section providing a detailed description of the control
■ A control enhancements section providing the optional criteria that organizations can consider, for the control, in order to meet their individual needs
■ A references section
■ A priority and baseline allocation section matching each control to the established priorities and baselines

NIST has defined an eight-step process for selection of security controls. Each of those steps are summarized in Figure 4.3 and explained in detail throughout the rest of this section.

4.4 Document Collection and Relationship Building

To achieve success in selecting security controls for ICT systems, the organization must go through a preliminary activity involving the collection of relevant documentation specific to the ICT system. Among other valuable resources, important documents that must be readily available are the initial system security plan, risk assessment results, and any available procedural documentation issued or adopted by the organization. Moreover, this preliminary activity also utilizes a proactive

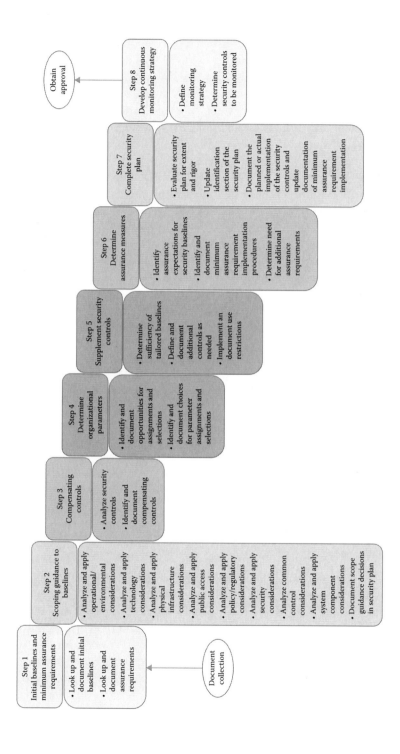

Figure 4.3   Security control selection steps.

approach to continuing relationships between individuals within and outside the organization who are impacted by the security control selection process.

Before the actual selection of security controls for an ICT system can begin, the organizations must have at their disposal the initial system security plan, risk assessment results, and any other available documentation about the ICT system. The initial security plan provides valuable information about the results of the system categorization, a description of the systems and their architecture, and the integration that exists between systems inside the organization and systems that interconnect to the organization's systems through the existence of a supply chain. The risk assessment results provide details related to the potential ICT system threats and vulnerabilities and the mitigation (planned or already in place) against those threats and vulnerabilities. Assuming consistency with the NIST 800-series, the organization will have conducted the risk assessment based on SP 800-30 Revision 1, *Guide for Conducting Risk Assessments*, which stipulates that the assessment results be documented in the system security plan or a subsequent risk assessment report.

Also valuable to the success of the security control selection process is documentation pertaining to organization-specific procedures, approved by management, that define how to select, customize, supplement, and document security controls. In most organizations, those procedures elaborate on the NIST standards and guidelines and provide implementation details, including tools, templates, or checklists to support the selection process as it is defined by that organization. The procedures also include internal requirements for reporting and approving the selected security controls for the ICT system(s) of the organization. Likewise, it is equally important that the organization's common controls and the common portion of hybrid controls have been identified. Common security controls can apply to:

- All organizational ICT systems
- A group of information systems at a specific site
- Common information systems, subsystems, or applications (i.e., common hardware, software, and/or firmware embedded within ICT components) installed at multiple operational sites

A control is considered a hybrid when one part of the control is common to multiple systems, while another part of the control is considered to be system-specific. For example, an organization may view a security control related to incident response policy and procedures as a hybrid control with the policy portion of the control considered to be common and the procedures portion of the control system-specific. It is the responsibility of the senior management to ensure that the common controls are put into place, measured for effectiveness, modified if necessary, and reassessed with the assessment results shared with pertinent individuals throughout the organization.

While gathering documentation is an important precursor to security control selection, equally important is the maintenance of relationships with others within their organization that have an impact on the success of this step of the RMF. It is the responsibility of the senior management in combination with the security officials to establish the organization-specific policies and procedures for conducting a risk assessment, selecting security controls, and documenting the selection process in the security plan. Tools, templates, or checklists to assist with the selection and documentation processes may also be provided. The organization should have information security program support services that serve as a primary contact for advice and support while individuals throughout the organization proceed through the selection of security controls for their individual ICT systems or system functions. Support can also be provided by others within the organization including the enterprise architecture group, others from within the organization from which information is shared, and the technical operations support staff. Each of these groups provides valuable information needed to ensure accurate selection of the ICT system's security controls.

4.5 Select Initial Security Control Baselines and Minimum Assurance Requirements

One of the most difficult realities of the security control selection process is that organizations must find the most cost-effective and appropriate set of security controls to adequately mitigate risk but at the same time comply with security requirements. Unfortunately, there is not a "one size fits all" set of security controls that organizations can select to adequately satisfy all security requirements. Organizations must select the most appropriate set of security controls for each situation that may arise and each ICT system to mitigate risk. To do so, the individuals responsible for selecting the controls must have an understanding of the organization's mission and business objectives, the business functions that the ICT systems support, and familiarity of the environments where the systems operate. Without question, the process of selecting, implementing, and maintaining the most effective set of security controls for an organization requires strong working relationships among management, the system users, and individuals participating in the security control formulation process to understand the changes that take place within the organization to the mission, strategic objectives, business functions that achieve those objectives, the ICT environment, and the underlying usage of the systems that support those functions.

Upon completion of the *security categorization* step of the RMF, the system's impact level has been determined and documented in the security plan. The organization can begin identifying the initial set of security controls and minimum assurance requirements. The means by which the initial set of security controls is selected is facilitated through the identification of the baselines *low, moderate, and high* listed in NIST SP 800-53, *Appendix D*. The baseline controls are chosen based on the security category and impact levels (based on FIPS 199) determined during security categorization.

The minimum assurance requirements are defined in NIST SP 800-53, *Appendix E.* Each minimum assurance requirement is grouped based on the system impact level and applies to each control within the final, selected set of security controls.

The system's security impact level is what determines the initial security baseline. Table D-2 in NIST SP 800-53 *Appendix D* lists the identified controls from each control family. For each control, the table provides a priority code of P0, P1, P2, or P3, where P0 is assigned to controls that are not selected for a baseline, P1 is the highest priority, P2 is the second highest priority, and P3 is the lowest priority. Further, each control is assigned to appropriate initial control baselines of low, mod, and high. Security control enhancements, when applicable, are indicated by the number of that enhancement under the baseline. For example, the AC-2 (1)–(5) and (11)–(13) entry in the high baseline for AC-2 indicates that the second control from the Access Control family of security controls has been selected along with control enhancements (1)–(5) and (11)–(13). Note that if a security control is not used in a particular baseline, the entry is marked as not selected. The mapping of system impact to initial baseline is such that, a system with a low-impact level would include all the security controls in the LOW column, a system with a moderate impact level would include all the security controls in the MOD column, and a system with a high-impact level would include all the security controls in the HIGH column of Table D-2 in *Appendix D* of NIST SP 800-53.

Some security controls do not make supplemental guidance or control enhancements indicative in any of the baselines. However, they are available for use by organizations, if necessary. A complete description of each security control, supplemental guidance for the control, and control enhancements is provided in NIST SP 800-53, *Appendix F.*

Once the initial baseline is identified, the security controls should be documented. One simple approach is to create a table similar to Figure 4.4. The underlying objective is to provide a summarization of decisions made during the tailoring and supplementation activities that result in the selected set of security controls for the ICT system. The table is normally included in an appendix to the system security plan, and supplements detailed information on how each of the security controls is implemented within the body of the security plan.

As mentioned earlier, NIST defines the minimum assurance requirements for an ICT system in *Appendix E* of NIST SP 800-53. In general, security assurance is the means by which trust is established within the ICT system. NIST SP 800-53 formally defines assurance as "…the measure of confidence that the security functions, features, practices, policies, procedures, mechanisms, and architecture of organizational information systems accurately mediate and enforce established security policies" (NIST, 2013). The appendix addresses five key aspects of security assurance that organizations must consider:

1. The inclusion of assurance requirements in procurements of ICT systems, or components and services that they contain

Control number	Control name	Tailoring	Rationale
AC-1	Access control policy and procedure		
AC-2	Account management		
AC-3	Access enforcement		
AT-1	Security awareness and training		
AT-4	Security training records		
AU-1	Audit and accountability		
CM-1	Configuration management		
CP-1	Contingency planning		
IA-1	Identification and authentication		
IR-1	Incident response		
MA-1	System maintenance		
MP-1	Media protection		
PE-1	Physical and environmental protection		
SC-1	System and communications protection		
SI-1	System and information integrity		

Figure 4.4 Sample baseline controls for XYZ company.

2. Establish and maintain system development processes that result in trustworthy ICT
3. Use information technology products within the SDLC processes that demonstrate appropriate security engineering techniques and provide an adequate level of assurance within the processes
4. Be conscious of security risks by deploying trustworthy ICT products within critical systems
5. Collect assurance evidence that justifies trustworthiness is maintained within the organization's ICT system

Appendix E of NIST SP 800-53 provides a description of the assurance-related controls that are included in each of the security control baselines that are listed in table D-2 in *Appendix D*. It is important that organizations take care in considering the overall characteristics of each control as the determination is made whether it is assurance related or functionality related. Assurance-related controls can be easily identified because they generally possess the following characteristics:

■ They define the processes, activities, and tasks for developing and implementing ICT systems.
■ They provide supporting processes including but not limited to the means by which quality systems are built and maintained.

- They are the mechanism by which evidence is produced justifying security within developmental or operational activities.
- They provide the means by which determination can be made relative to the effectiveness or risk of implemented security controls.
- They provide the mechanism for improved personnel skills, security expertise, and understanding.

Appendix E is broken down into four sections: (1) Minimum Assurance Requirements—*Low*-Impact Systems; (2) Minimum Assurance Requirements—*Moderate*-Impact Systems; (3) Minimum Assurance Requirements—*High*-Impact Systems; and (4) Security Controls to Achieve Enhanced Assurance. Each section describes assurance implications for each impact level by providing a description of assurance requirements, supplemental guidance, and a table of applicable assurance-related controls that should be implemented.

Once identified, the minimum assurance requirements are documented in the security plan. For example, a high-impact ICT system is expected to implement the high-impact minimum assurance requirements, recording the assurance requirements of the security plan in the general description section.

4.6 Apply Scoping Guidance to Initial Baselines

Once an initial set of baseline controls has been selected and documented in the security plan, the organization begins the process of fine-tuning or "tailoring" the baselines based on the guidelines provided in NIST SP 800-53. Throughout this activity, organizations can address specific business processes and organizational requirements, constantly evolving operational environments by adjusting the initial security control baselines. Tailoring activities include applying scope guidance to the initial baseline. Scope guidance involves the following:

- Determining the extent that a given security control applicable to a specific information technology is necessary for a specific ICT system
- Development of the specification of compensating security controls, if it becomes necessary to replace recommended security controls.
- Development of the specification of organization-defined parameter values, when required to implement specific security controls.

The activity of applying scoping guidance entails the review of the ICT system to determine whether the use of common controls, physical infrastructure-related considerations, or technology-related considerations is needed. This assessment is made for each baseline security control in the ICT system. If the scoping guidance is deemed necessary, the appropriate notation (e.g., does not apply, downgraded) is made in the table created during the selection of the initial "baseline controls step" of the security control selection process. NIST recommends that organizations take into consideration the operating environments, technology, physical infrastructure, public access, policies and regulations, security objectives, common controls, system component allocations, and scalability when making scoping guidance decisions.

It stands to reason that the controls dependent upon the type of operating environment from which they are considered are only necessary if the ICT system is contained within the environment from which the controls are necessitated. For example, alternate work-site controls may not be applicable if the organization has established policies that prohibit remote access to the ICT system.

To adequately take into consideration the degree to which the operating environment affects the selection of controls, the organization must review each baseline security control and make a decision whether the control applies to the ICT system, or to any individual components within the system's operating environment. In the case that the control does not apply, a notation of "does not apply," and an appropriate rationale (e.g., policy: off-site access is prohibited) justifying why the control does not apply, should be included in the baseline control table located in the security plan.

Many of the NIST SP 800-53 families have technology-specific controls (e.g., wireless, cryptography, public key infrastructure) that may or may not have been included within the initial baseline for the ICT system under consideration (SuC). Security controls, from within those families, that refer to specific technologies are only applicable if that technology is currently implemented or otherwise required within the ICT system. Moreover, the organization must also consider that security controls need only be applied to the ICT components that provide or support the security capability addressed by the control and components serving as sources of potential risk being mitigated by the control.

In considering technology-specific controls, it is important to note that one control will not necessarily meet all of the security needs related to one type of technology. Therefore, the organization is wise to determine whether there is a cost-effective and technically feasible automated commercial off-the-shelf (COTS) product that could provide the necessary support for a baselined control. If an automated product is not available, cost-effective, or technically feasible, compensating security controls are implemented through nonautomated techniques or procedures.

After a thorough review of each technology-specific security control identified in the initial baseline, a decision must be made about whether or not the control applies to the ICT system or a specific component within the ICT system on the basis of the awareness of the implemented technologies and available automated products. If it is found that the security control does not apply to the ICT system, a notation of "does not apply" and an appropriate rationale justifying why the control does not apply should be included in the baseline control table located in the security plan. If it is determined that the security control applies, but only to specific components within the ICT system, those components must be identified and a notation provided in the security plan.

Earlier in this section, we mentioned that organizations must evaluate the environment from which the system operates in determining the scope from which security controls are selected. In addition to considering the operating environment, organizations must also evaluate security implications to the location in which the system components are housed. In making such determinations, it is important that the organization take into account that the security controls related to organizational facilities (normally physical controls) are applicable only to the sections of the facility(s) that provide protection and support for the ICT system. Failure to stay within this scope will cause organizational expenditures in excess of what was truly necessary to physically secure the system.

An important decision to make is that a single organizational facility may not house just one ICT component or even one entire ICT system. As is often the case, particularly in large-scale organizations, several ICT resources are located within the same facility. Therefore, the physical infrastructure security controls related to organizational facilities are often implemented as common controls that apply to multiple ICT systems. If the physical infrastructure-related security controls are implemented as a common control, a notation of "common control" and identification of applicable components should be provided for the control in the baseline control table of the security plan.

Often, the common control selected to support a particular facet of an organization's physical infrastructure may not provide adequate security protection to the ICT system. Through evaluation of the facility and analysis of the system components to be housed in that facility, it may be determined that some or all of those components need system-specific infrastructure protection. In such cases, in addition to common controls that apply to the ICT system, the control is implemented as a hybrid control. For example, many organizations implement emergency power as a common control as a mechanism to keep the systems functioning within a facility in the event of a power failure. However, some of the systems housed in that facility may be so critical that a decision is made to implement a separate uninterrupted power supply (UPS) for those systems. When the selection of hybrid controls becomes necessary, a notation of "hybrid control" should be made, together with the identity of the components from which the control is applied in the baseline control table of the security plan.

Many ICT systems provide some form of public access. That access is generally made available through connection to the Internet. Any time Internet connectivity is made available, that system instantly becomes more vulnerable to security exploitation. However, organizations must carefully consider security controls associated with public access ICT systems and use discretion when considering controls from specified baselines since some of those controls may not be applicable to systems that provide public information. For example, many cities, towns, and local municipalities provide property tax information. Such a lookup capability would not necessitate identification and authentication beyond simply entering the address or parcel code that is being searched. To the contrary, access controls would be required for users accessing their personal information (such as banking, retirement, tax ID, or employee data) through a public interface or by individuals or third-party organizations that maintain and support the ICT system.

As the organization makes its selection of security controls, consideration must be made for the public access necessary of the ICT system and whether or not each baseline control meets the appropriate security needs. If the control is deemed not applicable, a notation of "does not apply" and an appropriate rationale justifying why the control does not apply should be included in the baseline control table located in security plan. If the control applies only to specific system components or a subset of system users, the specific components or user groups should be noted in the table for that control.

Security controls directly affected by laws, policies, standards, or regulations (e.g., HIPAA [Health Insurance Portability and Accountability Act], Sarbanes Oxley, FERPA [family educational rights and privacy act]) are only required if the implementation of those controls directly affects the enforcement of those laws, policies, standards, and regulations within the ICT system. For example, the federal government's "Meaningful Use" regulation for Medicare and the Medicaid electronic health record (EHR) Incentive Program requires public and private health practitioners to have specific security controls implemented within their systems in order to take complete advantage of Medicare and Medicaid benefits. If the information in the system does not contain the types of information specified by the Meaningful Use regulation, the security control does not apply.

Assuming adequate familiarity with all laws, policies, standards, and regulations, the organization must review each baselined control and determine whether the control does or does not apply to the ICT system. If it is found that the control does not apply, a notation of "does not apply" and an appropriate rationale justifying why the control does not apply should be included in the baseline control table located in security plan.

NIST SP 800-53 stipulates that security controls that are determined to have an initial baseline that is too high can be downgraded. The evaluation that prompts the downgrade of a security control takes into consideration the unique support that it provides for each of the security objectives: confidentiality, integrity, and availability. According to NIST SP 800-53, the support for a specific security objective may be downgraded to the corresponding control in a lower baseline if one or more of the following conditions apply:

▪ The downgrade provides consistency with the security category for the supported security objectives before moving to system's impact level.
▪ The downgrade is supported by an organizational assessment of risk.
▪ The downgrade does not negatively affect the level of protection for the information within the ICT system.

Organizations must consider each security control within their initial baseline and determine whether it directly supports the confidentiality, integrity, or availability of the system or it can be downgraded. For example, suppose that the analysis done during system security categorization determines that a system's impact level is *high* based on the security category for confidentiality and integrity, while the security category for availability is *moderate*. *Controls* that are uniquely related to availability may be downgraded to the moderate-impact baseline. Per NIST, Figure 4.5 shows the security controls and control enhancements that are potential candidates for downgrading.

If the decision is made to downgrade a control to one in a lower baseline, a notation of "downgraded" should be provided in the baseline controls table of the security plan.

In those instances where the impact value for a security objective in the security category is lower than the system's impact level, the organization should carefully evaluate the controls in the lower baseline in order to determine whether risk is increased if the security control of the lower baseline is used. Likewise, an assessment should be done to determine the effect the downgrading will have on the information within the system that requires security measures. To the contrary, if a security control in the lower baseline is not selected for use, an assessment should be done to determine whether risk to the system is increased if the control corresponding to the identified system impact level is not used. Moreover, an assessment should be done to gain understanding about how the absence of the control affects the security-relevant information within the system. Based on the results of the analysis, the control can either be eliminated or modified to accommodate the assessed risks.

If the control is downgraded to a lower baseline or control enhancement, again, a notation must be made in the baseline control table located in the security plan.

Potential candidates for downgrading security controls and control enhancements	
Confidentiality	AC-21, MA-3(3), MP-3, MP-4, MP-5, MP-5(4), MP-6(1), MP-6(2), PE-4, PE-5, SC-4, SC-8, SC-8(1)
Integrity	CM-5, CM-5(1), CM-5(3), SC-8, SC-8(1), SI-7, SI-7(1), SI-7(5), SI-10
Availability	CP-2(1), CP-2(2), CP-2(3), CP-2(4), CP-2(5), CP-2(8), CP-3(1), CP-4(1), CP-4(2), CP-6, CP-6(1), CP-6(2), CP-6(3), CP-7, CP-7(1), CP-7(2), CP-7(3), CP-7(4), CP-8, CP-8(1), CP-8(2), CP-8(3), CP-8(4), CP9(1), CP-9(2), CP-9(3), CP-9(5), CP-10(2), CP10(4), MA-6, PE-9, PE-10, PE-11, PE-11(1), PE-13(1), PE-13(2), PE-13(3), PE-15(1)

Figure 4.5 Potential candidates for downgrading (security controls and enhancements).

In this circumstance, an indication of "downgraded" should be added to the security control number/enhancement and a rationale for the downgrade provided. If the security control is modified in any way in order to circumvent identified risks to the system, those modifications must also be identified in the table. Finally, if it is determined that elimination of a control from the baseline will not pose additional security risks to the ICT system, a notation of "does not apply" should be indicated in the table together with the appropriate rationale.

Recall from earlier discussion that common or hybrid controls are those in which a control, in its entirety or in part, is implemented by the organization and applies to multiple ICT systems. NIST SP 800-53 does not stipulate that a common or hybrid control be implemented and assessed; however, the organization must identify whether common or hybrid controls are applicable to the system. Moreover, the assessment results must be included in the ICT system's security plan either directly or by reference. It is important that every control in the baseline be completely addressed. This is accomplished by the organization publishing each common and hybrid control in a format that provides contact information, applicability of the control, and guidance on how to obtain the controls assessment results.

One of the most confusing aspects of the security control selection is deciding whether to implement a security measure as a common or hybrid control. To make that decision, the organization must review each security control in the initial baseline and determine whether a common or hybrid control exists that is applicable to the ICT system. If a common or hybrid control does exist, then the determination must be made whether or not the common control or the common portion of the hybrid control is sufficient to meet the system's security requirements. If a common control is identified, a notation should be made in the baseline control table within the security plan indicating that the control is "common." A rationale justifying why a common control is being implemented should also be provided. In the case that only a portion of the control can be implemented as a common control, the notation should indicate that the control is "hybrid." A rationale for hybrid controls should include an explanation of which portion of the control is common and which portion is system-specific, along with a justification of why the control can be implemented as a hybrid.

It should be evident from our earlier discussion that there is a direct and inclusive relationship between security controls and components of an organization's ICT system that provide or support the security capability addressed by the control and are sources of potential risk being mitigated by the control. During the security control selection process, the organization must conduct a review of the ICT system components in order to proactively determine which security controls apply to each possible component(s) and make the decision about where to allocate the controls that adequately fulfill the system's security requirements. In retrospect, each system component and security control association should be provided within the system security documentation. During new system development projects, the system component and security control association may not be known during the *control selection* step of the NIST RMF. For new systems, control allocation will likely need to be reconsidered during the *implementation* step.

A common adage in the ICT discipline is that all systems should be built to be scalable. The same is true of security controls allocated to those systems. Scalability of controls is largely determined by the system's impact level identified during the security categorization step. Generally, there will be a substantial amount of detail provided for higher-impact systems as compared with those at the other end of the spectrum. To that extent, success in integrating scalability into selected controls can be achieved using discretion in applying the controls to ICT systems, with consideration given to the factors that influence scalability within a given environment. By doing so, the organization is assured an approach that provides cost-effectiveness and risk-awareness to a security control implementation that makes use of limited resources, while also satisfying system security requirements.

4.7 Determine Need for Compensating Controls

As the organization begins to conclude the tailoring process of the select step of the NIST RMF, NIST SP 800-53 recommends that they also consider the selection of compensating controls. NIST SP 800-53 defines compensating controls as "…alternative security controls employed by organizations in lieu of specific controls in the low, moderate, or high baselines described in *Appendix D*—controls that provide equivalent or comparable protection for organizational information systems and the information processed, stored, or transmitted by those systems" (NIST, 2013).

In making the decision about whether compensating controls are necessary, the organization should perform an analysis on each tailored and baselined security control to determine whether anything prevents it from being implemented (in whole or in part) due to technical or cost implications. If a control cannot be implemented, the organization should determine what (if any) effect failing to implement that control will have in its ability to satisfy security requirements. If it is determined that sacrificing a particular control will have negative implications, a compensating control can be used to fill the void within the organization's security posture. NIST recommends that when selecting an appropriate compensating control, every effort should be made to select the control from *Appendix F* of NIST SP 800-53. However, if an appropriate alternative is not listed in *Appendix F*, another control library can be used. We discuss other popular control libraries in Section 4.14.

Once the most appropriate compensating control has been selected, the baseline control table of the security plan should be updated to reflect that a compensating control was used, along with the rationale for the compensating control. Along with identifying the compensating control number and name, a rationale should be provided that details how the compensating control provides equivalent security protection as the control found inadequate, and justification as to why the original security control could not be employed.

4.8 Determine Organizational Parameters

Some of the security controls listed in *Appendix F* of NIST SP 800-53 include control enhancements that contain system-specific or organization-defined parameters that add a considerable amount of flexibility in defining selected portions of the controls to effectively meet specific organizational security requirements and objectives. Each parameter contains a predetermined set of values that can be assigned by the organization. Once the organization has completed an initial pass through of scoping considerations and made a selection of compensating controls, they must begin a review of security controls and control enhancements to identify appropriate assignment/selection statements and determine the most effective organization-defined values for the identified parameters. Often, the parameter values are preset and must be applied in accordance with Executive Orders and directives (for the federal systems) as well as laws, regulations, policies, and standards (for the federal systems and private organizational ICT systems alike). Once an organization has defined the parameter values and control enhancements, they become a part of the control and enhancement. Conversely, some organizations choose the parameter values before selecting compensating controls since this activity completes the control definitions and may adversely affect compensating the control requirements. After the system-specific and organization-defined security control parameters are defined, they must be documented in the security plan.

The organization should take the time to review each security control to determine whether there is a need to make a parameter assignment within the security control. If a control provides the capability for an assignment, a decision must be made about which parameters satisfy the organizational needs and the appropriate values to provide adequate protection for the ICT system.

Most organizations have an information security program office or organization-level security team that has likely made the assignment and selection decisions to ensure consistency across all systems. Thus, for individuals charged with the responsibility of control selection, the parameter assignments and associated values have already been decided for them. However, further analysis should still be completed to determine the appropriateness of each parameter and value pair for their particular ICT system or system components. To the contrary, if the organization has not made the necessary parameter decisions, that task becomes the responsibility of the group actively participating in security control selection.

Regardless of which area of the organization has the responsibility of selecting the security control parameters and values, the initial baseline table within the security plan must be updated to indicate that an assignment has been made and the specific details about the choice.

4.9 Supplement Security Controls

As organizations work through the steps of the security control selection process, many of the decisions made during the selection of the initial baseline and tailoring activities are based on risk assessment results that provide significant information that assists in determining whether the security controls adequately protect the organization's operations and assets, individuals, and third party (supply chain) organizations. Most organizations find the additional security controls or control enhancements are necessary to mitigate specific threats to and vulnerabilities in an ICT system or to satisfy the specific security requirements that have been prescribed by laws, organizational policies, standards, or industry regulations.

To thoroughly understand what supplemental controls are necessary, the organization must analyze the tailored security control baseline to determine whether the controls already selected meet the needs of the ICT system. On the basis of an understanding of the risk assessment results, mission/business requirements, system description, and applicable laws, policies, standards, or regulations, including organization-specific guidelines, reviews can be conducted to identify potential threats, vulnerabilities, and resulting system risks to better determine whether additional security controls or control enhancements are necessary to adequately protect the ICT system.

If it is determined that additional security controls are required, NIST recommends that they can be selected from *Appendix F* in the NIST SP 800-53 security control catalog. The organization must be cautious not to implement information technology beyond its ability to adequately provide protection, thus preventing the organization from implementing sufficient security controls within an ICT system to adequately reduce or mitigate risk. When technology beyond the organizations scope of protection is warranted, an alternative strategy is needed to provide the necessary protection. Such a strategy must consider all of the additional risks imposed by the additional use of technology. In other cases, the organization may adopt an approach in which instead of adding additional security controls, the implementation of a security control is modified. Such a modification could include increasing the frequency of security activities, increasing the level of detail provided in security documentation, increasing the scope of operating procedures, or increasing the frequency of security reporting during continuous monitoring activities.

Once the supplemental security controls are identified, a notation is made in the baseline control table of the security plan. The table now represents the final selected set of security controls. The rationale for supplementing a control should include the reasons supplementation was necessary, reference to the control catalog from which the control was chosen, and details that support the supplemental control's ability to satisfy system security requirements.

4.10 Determine Assurance Measures for Minimum Assurance Requirements

The NIST SP 800-53 guideline devotes an entire section to appropriately defining security assurance and trustworthiness from the perspective of security control specification, design, development, implementation, and maintenance. To understand the concept of security assurance, however, we must first define security functionality, which is security-related features, functions, mechanisms, services, procedures, and architectures implemented within organizational ICT systems or the environments in which those systems operate. Security assurance can easily be defined as the *measure of confidence* that security controls can be validated to ensure that they have been implemented correctly and perform the intended functionality, and can be verified that they meet the outcomes as specified in the security requirements. Likewise, trustworthiness can be defined as the *measure of confidence* present that supports the system's capability of preserving the confidentiality, integrity, and availability of the information that is being processed, stored, or transmitted by the systems that operate within an identified area of threat. To have trust in an ICT system is to suggest that there is a belief that the system is capable of operating within a defined risk and is still capable of carrying out the support required to keep business operations functional.

As we alluded to earlier in this chapter, the NIST minimum assurance recommendations are defined in SP 800-53, *Appendix E*. The guideline stipulates that, for security controls in low-impact ICT systems, organizations should focus on controls being in place such that there are no obvious errors and that, as flaws are discovered, they are addressed in a timely manner.

Likewise, the guideline recommends that for security controls in ICT systems categorized as moderate impact, the focus should be on actions that foster increased confidence in the correct implementation and operation of each control. NIST suggests that it is still likely that flaws will be uncovered; however, during implementation of specific capabilities, documentation should be integrated into the control in order to increase confidence but at the same time meet the required function or purpose. The documentation integrated into the control becomes important when assessors must analyze and test the functionality of the control as part of the overall control assessment step of the RMF.

Finally, the guideline recommends that, for security controls in ICT systems categorized as high impact, the focus should be expanded to *require* integration within the control, the capabilities that are necessary to provide consistent operation of the control, and continuous improvement in the control's effectiveness.

During each phase of the system life cycle, it is expected that the organization prioritize the requirement of associated design and implementation documentation to support these activities. The documentation integrated with the control is also valuable to the assessors who must analyze and test the internal components of the control as part of the assessment process.

It is clear that the responsibility of assurance requirements falls squarely on the shoulders of those individuals who perform the tasks and activities of design and implementation of the security controls. In their role of designing and implementing each control, they must ensure that the necessary control documentation is provided, essential analysis is conducted, and actions that are performed during control operation are properly defined. The objective of performing these activities is to provide a certain degree of confidence that the controls have been implemented correctly, are operating efficiently, and produce the desired outcomes on the basis of the specified security requirements. As you will learn in Chapter 6, the Assessor uses the information from these design and implementation activities during the *Assess* step of the RMF to measure control effectiveness within each application.

As each control is designed and implemented, it should be reviewed to determine whether any additional enhancements or documentation is needed to satisfy assessment criteria. *Appendix E* of NIST SP 800-53 provides assurance requirements for each of the system impact levels (high, moderate, and low). Those requirements define what degree of assurance an organization is expected to implement to satisfy assessment criteria. A table of assurance-related controls is provided for each level to identify those controls that must be implemented to satisfy the assessment expectations for that level. The appendix also provides additional assurance requirements available to developers/implementers of security controls that supplement the minimum assurance requirements for low-, moderate-, and high-impact ICT systems. Organizations should ensure that there is a process in place to capture lessons learned as they relate to each assurance-related control. In turn they should update the related policies and procedures to ensure a more consistent implementation, in addition to using the supplemental guidelines to protect against threats from highly skilled, highly motivated, and well-resourced threat agents.

When documenting in the security plan how the assurance requirements are implemented in the ICT system, it is characteristic that the extent of the detail is scaled based on the system's impact level since low-impact systems requires much less explanation than their high-impact counterparts. However, the plan should provide enough detail for a well-defined implementation of the minimum assurance requirements.

4.11 Complete Security Plan

The organization documents the decisions made during the initial security control selection, tailoring, and supplementation processes in the security plan. Each decision must be supported with a convincing rationale that leads to the conclusion that those decisions directly support prescribed security objectives and requirements. This documentation is essential when examining the overall security posture of the ICT systems, taking into consideration their impact on the organization's mission and business objectives. The selected set of security controls along with the supporting rationale for control selection decisions made throughout this step of the NIST RMF are documented in the plan.

Throughout this chapter, we have simplified the discussion of documenting security control selection decisions by referencing the initial baseline control table located in the security plan. While the table is an important resource within the plan, the details and definitions related to how each control is designed and implemented are much more extensive and must be present within the larger context of the plan. NIST SP 800-18, *Guide for Developing Security Plans for Federal Information Systems* (Sawnson et al., 2006), provides the necessary guidance organizations need to develop a security plan that adequately defines the underlying security strategy. While a discussion about the development of a security plan based on NIST SP 800-18 is beyond the scope of this book, the guideline makes a point that is relevant to our discussion of security control selection. The security plan is scalable with regard to the extent and rigor of the implementation. The scalability is largely dictated by the security categorization of the system. The security plan for a high-impact ICT system may be very detail oriented and contains a significant amount of implementation criteria. Likewise, the security plan for a low-impact information system may be much briefer and contain considerably less implementation detail. Regardless, there are many NIST-compliant security plan templates available that organizations can utilize as a basis for formulating their own security-planning strategies.

4.12 Develop Continuous Monitoring Strategy

In Chapter 7, we will introduce the *Authorization* step of the NIST RMF. Upon successful Authorization, the process of continuous monitoring of implemented security controls begins. However, once the security control selection has taken place, a strategy is developed with regard to how continuous monitoring will proceed. According to NIST SP 800-137, *Information Security Continuous Monitoring for Federal Information Systems and Organization*, "The goal is to provide: (i) operational visibility; (ii) managed change control; (iii) and attendance to incident response duties" (Dempsey et al., 2011).

As defined by NIST, the process for continuous monitoring includes the following initiatives:

- *Define* a continuous monitoring strategy based on risk tolerance that maintains clear visibility into assets and awareness of vulnerabilities and utilizes up-to-date threat information.

- *Establish* measures, metrics, and status monitoring and control assessments frequencies that make known organizational security status and detect changes to information system infrastructure and environments of operation, and status of security control effectiveness in a manner that supports continued operation within acceptable risk tolerances.
- *Implement* a continuous monitoring program to collect the data required for the defined measures and report on findings; automate collection, analysis, and reporting of data where possible.
- *Analyze* the data gathered and *report* findings accompanied by recommendations. It may become necessary to collect additional information to clarify or supplement existing monitoring data.
- *Respond* to assessment findings by making decisions to either mitigate technical, management, and operational vulnerabilities; or accept the risk; or transfer it to another authority.
- *Review and update* the monitoring program, revising the continuous monitoring strategy, and maturing measurement capabilities to increase visibility into assets and awareness of vulnerabilities; further enhance data-driven control of the security of an organization's information infrastructure; and increase organizational flexibility.

Once the continuous monitoring strategy is developed, approval is normally obtained in combination with the approval of the security plan. Many organizations take advantage of automated tools and supporting databases to conduct the continuous monitoring activities. Such tools facilitate near real-time risk management for the ICT system and provide a streamlined approach to the way security authorization activities are performed.

4.13 Approval of Security Plan and Continuous Monitoring Strategy

It is the responsibility of the organization's authorizing official to determine whether the security plan is complete, consistent, and satisfies the stated security requirements for the ICT system. The authorizing official is a senior official or executive with the authority to formally assume responsibility for operating an ICT system at an acceptable level of risk to organizational operations and assets, individuals, and other organizations that may exist within the supply chain. Authorizing officials typically have budgetary oversight for an ICT system or are responsible for the mission and/or business operations supported by the system. An authorizing official's main function is to assume accountability for the security risks associated with ICT system operations. Moreover, authorizing officials are in a management position within the organization, with a level of authority over understanding and accepting information system-related security risks.

Relative to the approval of the security plan, the authorizing official determines, to the best of their ability and based on the availability of supporting documentation, if the security plan correctly and effectively documents the potential risk to organizational operations and assets, individuals, and other organizations. The authorization official performs a review and analysis of the plan and may, in some instances, send the plan back with recommended changes.

If the security plan is reviewed and considered acceptable, the authorizing official acknowledges acceptance. The acceptance of the security plan is a significant milestone in the risk management process because, by accepting the plan, the authorizing official indicates agreement to the security controls that have been selected to meet the organization's security requirements. With the agreement in place, the risk management process progresses to the *Implementation* step. Additionally, the acceptance is also acknowledgement of the level of effort that will be necessary to complete the remaining steps in the NIST RMF.

As is the case in most ICT plans and specifications, the front matter of the security plan will provide a page with the names of reviewers and approvers of the document and a place for each to sign and date. Space should also be provided for any comments or conditions for the approval, so that they can be included directly within the plan. Depending upon the policies set forth by the organization, an opportunity for response to each comment or condition should be part of the approval process.

4.14 Other Control Libraries

This chapter has introduced the Select Security Controls step of the NIST RMF from the perspective of NIST SP 800-53, while using the control libraries of that guideline as a basis for our discussion. However, NIST recognizes several other security control libraries that organizations can utilize to ensure their ICT system provides adequate security protection and conforms to applicable laws, policies, standards, and industry regulations. Aside from NIST SP 800-53 (which has already been discussed) other control libraries include the following.

4.14.1 Control Objectives for Information and Related Technology (COBIT 5)

COBIT 5 is a framework for developing, implementing, monitoring, and improving IT governance and management practices.

The COBIT 5 framework is published by the IT Governance Institute and the Information Systems Audit and Control Association (ISACA). The goal of the framework is to provide a common language for business executives to communicate with each other about goals, objectives, and results.

COBIT 5 is based on five key principles for governance and management of enterprise IT (Figure 4.6):

Principle 1:	Meeting stakeholder needs
Principle 2:	Covering the enterprise end-to-end
Principle 3:	Applying a single integrated framework
Principle 4:	Enabling a holistic approach
Principle 5:	Separating governance from management

4.14.2 CIS Critical Security Controls

The Center for Internet Security (CIS) collaborated to create *The Critical Security Controls for Effective Cyber Defense, Version 6.0*. The 20 CSC are now governed by the Council on CyberSecurity, an independent, expert, not-for-profit organization with a global scope. The *Critical Security Controls*—also known as the *Consensus Audit Guidelines* (CAG) and formerly referred to as the SANS Institute *Top 20 Critical Security Controls* have emerged as a de facto yardstick from which cybersecurity programs can be measured. They are a recommended

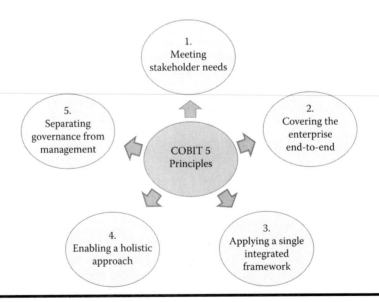

Figure 4.6   COBIT 5.

set of actions for cyber defense that provide specific ways in which organizations can stop cybersecurity attacks. They were developed and are maintained by a consortium of hundreds of security experts from across the public and private sectors (Figure 4.7).

4.14.3 Industrial Automation and Control Systems Security Life Cycle

The International Society of Automation is a nonprofit professional association that has developed a global standard called the Industrial Automation and Control Systems Security Life Cycle. The life cycle comprises three phases: Assess, Implement, and Maintain. The *Assess* phase includes both a high level and detailed cyber risk assessments, and an allocation of assets to security zones. The *Implement* phase includes cybersecurity requirements specification; design and engineering of cybersecurity countermeasures; design and development of other means of risk reduction; and installation, commissioning, and validation of the cybersecurity countermeasures. The *Maintain* phase consists of cybersecurity maintenance, monitoring, and management of change; and cyber incident response and recover. Key standard ANSI/ISA-62443-3-3-2013, *Security for Industrial Automation and Control Systems: System Security Requirements and Security Levels*, is part of a

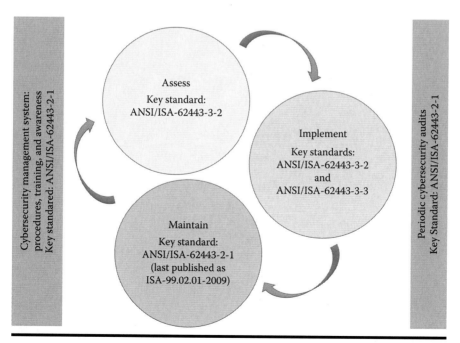

Figure 4.7   CIS critical security controls.

multipart ISA 62443 series that addresses the issue of security for industrial auto-mation and control systems (IACSs). This part, in particular, is what the standard refers to as "elements" related to cybersecurity management for use in the IACS environment and provides guidance on how to meet the requirements described for each element.

The ANSI/ISA-62443-3-3-2013 standard also provides detailed technical control system requirements (SRs) associated with seven foundational requirements (FRs) that are described in ISA-62443-1-1 (published as *ISA-99.01.01-2007*) including defining the requirements for control system capability security levels, SL-C (control system). These requirements are used by various members of the IACS community along with what the standard referred to as "the defined zones and conduits" for the SuC while developing the appropriate control system target security, SL-T (control system), for a specific asset. Figure 4.8 shows an overview of the IACS life cycle.

4.14.4 ISO/IEC 27001

The International Organization for Standardization (ISO) officially began in 1947 and is an independent, nongovernmental membership organization. ISO 27001 is the international standard that describes best practices for an information security management system (ISMS). ISO/IEC 27001, *Information technology—Security techniques—Information security management systems—Requirements* standard has become the de facto international standard for information security management. The purpose of ISO/IEC 27001 is to help organizations to establish and maintain an ISMS. An ISMS is a set of interrelated elements that organizations use to man-age and control information security risks and to protect and preserve the confiden-tiality, integrity, and availability of information. These elements include all of the policies, procedures, processes, plans, practices, roles, responsibilities, resources, and structures that are used to manage security risks and to protect information.

The comprehensive group of control objectives focus more on the organiza-tional context of information security and how an organization can respond to risks by choosing the appropriate controls. Annex A of the Requirements lists the following control groups (ISO/IEC, 2013) (Figure 4.9):

1. A.5: Information security policies (2 controls)
2. A.6: Organization of information security (7 controls)
3. A.7: Human resource security (6 controls that are applied before, during, or after employment)
4. A.8: Asset management (10 controls)
5. A.9: Access control (14 controls)
6. A.10: Cryptography (2 controls)
7. A.11: Physical and environmental security (15 controls)
8. A.12: Operations security (14 controls)

	Critical Security Control	Description
1	Inventory of Authorized and Unauthorized Devices	Actively manage all hardware, giving access to only authorized devices
2	Inventory of Authorized and Unauthorized Software	Actively manage all software so that only authorized software is installed and can execute
3	Secure Configurations for Hardware and Software	Establish, implement, and actively manage the security configuration of laptops, servers, and workstations
4	Continuous Vulnerability Assessment and Remediation	Continuously acquire, assess, and take action on new information in order to identify vulnerabilities, remediate, and minimize
5	Malware Defenses	Control the installation, spread, and execution of malicious code at multiple points in the enterprise
6	Application Software Security	Manage the security life cycle of all in-house developed and acquired software
7	Wireless Access Control	The processes and tools used to track, control, prevent, and correct the security use of wireless devices
8	Data Recovery Capability	The processes and tools used to properly back up critical information with a proven methodology for timely recovery
9	Security Skills Assessment and Appropriate Training to Fill Gaps	Identify the specific knowledge, skills, and abilities needed to support defense for all functional roles in the enterprise
10	Secure Configurations for Network Devices	Establish, implement, and actively manage the security configuration of network infrastructure devices
11	Limitation and Control of Network Ports, Protocols, and Services	Manage the ongoing operational use of ports, protocols, and services on networked devices
12	Controlled Use of Administrative Privileges	The processes and tools used to track, control, prevent, and correct the use, assignment, and configuration of administrative privileges
13	Boundary Defense	Detect, protect, and correct the flow of information transferring networks of different trust levels
14	Maintenance, Monitoring, and Analysis of Audit Logs	Collect, manage, and analyze audit logs that could help recover from an attack
15	Controlled Access Based on the Need to Know	The processes and tools used to track, control, prevent, correct secure access to critical assets
16	Account Monitoring and Control	Actively manage the life cycle of system and application accounts
17	Data Protection	The processes and tools used to prevent data exfiltration
18	Incident Response and Management	Protect the organization's information and reputation by developing and implementing an incident response infrastructure
19	Secure Network Engineering	Make security an inherent attribute of the enterprise
20	Penetration Tests and Red Team Exercises	Test the overall strength of an organization's defenses

Figure 4.8   IACS security life cycle.

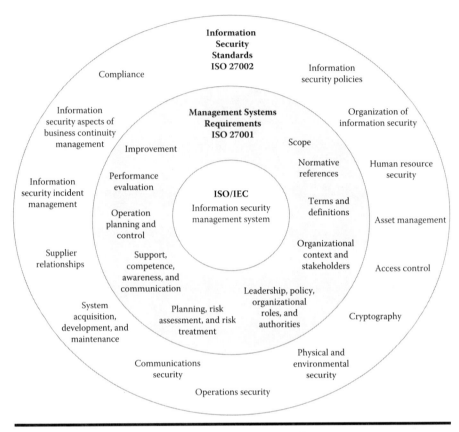

Figure 4.9   The ISO/IEC 27001 and 27002 frameworks.

9. A.13: Communications security (7 controls)
10. A.14: System acquisition, development, and maintenance (13 controls)
11. A.15: Supplier relationships (5 controls)
12. A.16: Information security incident management (7 controls)
13. A.17: Information security aspects of business continuity management (4 controls)
14. A.18: Compliance with internal requirements, such as policies, and with external requirements, such as laws (8 controls)

4.15 Chapter Summary

This chapter introduced the selection of the security controls step of the NIST RMF. The activities and tasks in this step aim to identify the security controls needed to meet the ICT system's security requirements. It also has tasks associated with documenting those controls in the system security plan and development of a continuous monitoring strategy. The results produced in system security categorization serve as input to the selection of security controls, while taking into consideration the impact level assigned to the information system. The system impact level corresponds to a baseline set of security controls that, in combination, provide the minimum security needed to protect ICT systems. During security control selection, organizations use security requirements and risk assessment documentation developed for the system in combination with the system security categorization to identify the appropriate security control baseline and tailor that baseline to address the defined requirements of the system. The outputs of the security control selection process are a tailored security control baseline, system monitoring strategy, and an approved initial version of the system security plan.

Most ICT systems include a mix of system-specific, common, and hybrid security controls. Activities within the security control selection process provide the means for each of those type of controls to be added into the initial baseline and included in the security plan. At the conclusion of this step, organizations have the information needed to finalize the resource allocation and timeline for the entire risk management process, while the security control baseline defined during this step serve as the basis for security control implementation, assessment, and authorization activities. Therefore, the effectiveness of the remaining parts of the process depends on the accuracy and thoroughness of security control selection. Organizations first identify relevant controls using published standards and guidelines, and also include system-specific considerations. Based on their knowledge of relevant controls, they are able to determine how those controls will be provided and monitored once the system is operational.

Following federal standards and guidelines is not a requirement within private industries, as is the case in the public sector. However, many organizations follow such standards and guidelines using FIPS 200 as a mean of identifying minimum security requirements corresponding to the impact level assigned to the information system during security categorization. Another such guideline is NIST SP 800-53. Excerpts of that guide present controls based on three criteria—one each for low-impact, moderate-impact, and high-impact systems—that identify the subset of controls and control enhancements applicable to systems in each security category. The established baselines represent a starting point for the selection of security controls, serving as the basis for the reduction or supplementation of security controls in ICT systems.

In some instances, an organization may find that a baseline security control applies for a system, but implementing the control specified in the baseline is beyond the organization's resource capacity from a triple constraint (scope, time, and cost) perspective. Prior to deciding to accept, avoid, or otherwise respond to the threats and vulnerabilities affecting the organization by failing to implement a required control, the management should consider the selection of compensating controls as an alternative that satisfies the same security objectives. In still other cases, considering system-specific controls may also lead organizations to select supplemental security controls beyond the minimum requirements specified in the appropriate baseline for the system. NIST SP 800-53 provides vital information for the implementation of compensating controls, supplemental controls, and control enhancements. Organizations may elect to choose from the requirement in a higher level baseline or from within a security control catalog that are not assigned a specific baseline. Each organization must determine the necessity for supplemental and compensating controls by comparing the security requirements defined for each ICT system with current capabilities and the expected effect of implementing baseline controls. All decisions regarding the addition of compensating controls, supplemental controls, or enhancements should be documented to the extent of providing supporting feasibility in order for management and other organizations within the supply chain to understand the basis for the control implementation.

The completion of security control selection signifies a pivotal point within the organization's security/risk management process. While performing the tasks of control categorization and selection, the organizational management responsible for the plan along with security teams document the results of all the key activities that were performed into the system security plan and submit the plan to an authorizing official for review and approval. The purpose of approval at this stage is to evaluate the system security plan for completeness, in addition to verifying compliance with industry and regulatory requirements in terms of content, structure, and level of detail. By having the decisions made to this point approved, the organization also affords itself the ability to assess the extent to which the set of security controls selected for implementation are consistent with the impact level assigned to the system and confirm that they will satisfy the system's security requirements. Acceptance of the system security plan by the authorizing official is also an important milestone in the SDLC process, as the agreed-upon set of selected security controls is a key input to system development or acquisition. It also serves as a means for verified buy-in by the top-level management in terms of the significance of security requirements to the underlying efforts toward achieving the organization's strategic mission, vision, and objectives.

Glossary

common controls: controls that provide a security capability for multiple information systems

compensating controls: alternate controls designed to accomplish the intent of the original controls as closely as possible, when the originally designed controls cannot be used due to limitations of the environment

continuous monitoring: a defined security process that enables information security professionals and others to see a continuous stream of near real-time snapshots of the state of risk to their security, data, the network, end points, and even cloud devices and applications.

hybrid controls: a security control that is part common control and part system-specific control. A broader definition characterizes it as a customized common control

minimum assurance requirements: a set of security-related controls, grouped based on system-impact level, which should be implemented within an ICT system

minimum security requirements: as defined by FIPS 200, "The minimum security requirements cover seventeen security-related areas with regard to protecting the confidentiality, integrity, and availability of federal information systems and the information processed, stored, and transmitted by those systems" (NIST, 2006)

scope guidance: activity in the security control selection step that allows organizations to take into consideration applicability and implementation of security controls identified in the initial security control baseline. Another term used to describe this activity is tailoring

security control baseline: the minimum set of security controls defined by an organization based on a predetermined level of impact

security plan: a formal plan that provides a systematic approach and controls necessary to protect an ICT system from security threats and other forms of exploitation

supplemental controls: controls that add a necessary additional layer of security to one or more controls provided in a systems security control baseline

system-specific controls: controls that provide a security capability for a particular information system

References

Dempsey, K., Chawla, N.S., Johnson, A., Johnston, R., Jones, A.C., Orebaugh, A. et al. (2011). NIST SP 800-137, in: *Information Security Continuous Monitoring (ISCM) for Federal Information Systems and Organizations*. Gaithersburg, MD: National Institute for Standards and Technology.

ISO/IEC. (2013). *Information Security Management Systems: Requirements*. Geneva, Switzerland: ISO/IEC. Available at: www.iso.org (accessed 28 March 2016).

Kohnke, A., Shoemaker, D., and Sigler, K. (2016). *The Complete Guide to Cybersecurity Risks and Controls*. Boca Raton, FL: Tayler & Francis.

NIST. (2006). *FIPS 200: Minimum Security Requirements for Federal Information and Information Systems*. Gaithersburg, MD: National Institute of Standards and Technologies.

NIST. (2013). NIST SP 800-53 Revision 4, in: *Security and Privacy Controls forFederal Information Systems and Organizations*. Guideline, Gaithersburg, MD: National Institute of Standards and Technologies.

Sawnson, M., Hash, J., and Bowen, P. (2006). NIST SP 800-18, in: *Guide for Developing Security Plans for Federal Information Systems*. Guideline, Gaithersburg, MD: National Institute of Standards and Technoligies.

Stine, K., Kissel, R., Barker, W.C., Fahlsing, J., and Gulick, J. (2008). NIST SP 800-60, in: *Guide for Mapping Types of Information and Information Systems to Security Categories*, Volume I. Guideline, Gaithersburg, MD: National Institute of Standards and Technology.

Chapter 5

Step 3—Implement Security Controls

At the conclusion of this chapter, the reader will understand:

- The activities defined within the two tasks of the National Institute of Standards and Technology (NIST) Risk Management Framework (RMF) implementation
- The practices associated with the implementation of management controls to support information and communication technology (ICT) security objectives
- The need for strategic management objectives, policies, and procedures at an organizational level, in support of successful control implementation processes

5.1 Introduction

Implementing security controls involves putting into action the choice that has been made for mitigating risk. There are four possible actions for mitigating risk: *accept* the risk, *transfer* the risk, *limit* the risk, or *avoid* the risk. From Steps 1 and 2, each information asset now has an assigned risk level and the controls for mitigating the risk have been chosen. Implementing the chosen controls will result in certain procedures being followed and/or new controls put in place. Limiting the risk by putting a control in place will be the most commonly chosen option to protect an organization's information assets and systems. Continual monitoring and regular updating is part of the implementation to keep the risk at an acceptable level.

Stated differently, through the tasks associated with security control implementation, the organization incorporates the controls identified and approved as part of the security plan within the functional and technical requirements identified for the system and its overall design. In considering the implementation tasks, we need to remember that there are three major categories of security controls: *managerial*, *technical*, and *operational*. The NIST RMF identifies just two tasks associated with implementation: *security control implementation* and *security control documentation*. However, on reviewing Figure 5.1, you may conclude that the focus of the implementation step of the NIST RMF puts a greater degree of weight on the implementation of technical and operational controls, without much consideration to the managerial controls, requiring implementation in order to adequately mitigate all forms of cybersecurity risk. In this chapter, we discuss the tasks that are necessary for implementing all three control categories. We do so by exploring the implementation of operational and technical controls from the system perspective. We then look at the larger scope of the implementation of controls from the management perspective.

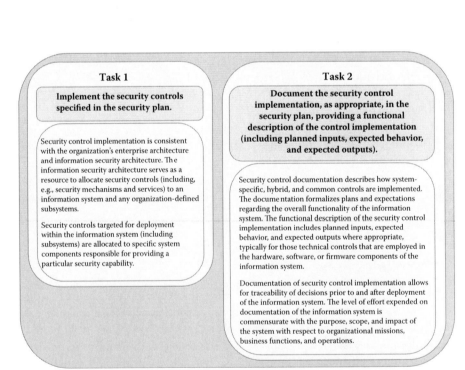

Figure 5.1 NIST Risk Management Framework control implementation tasks. (From NIST, *Guide for Applying the Risk Management Framework to Federal Information Systems—A Security Lifecycle Approach: NIST SP 800-37 Revision 1*, NIST, Gaithersburg, 2014.)

5.2 Implementation of the Security Controls Specified by the Security Plan

It is worthy of mention, up front, that this task of the implementation step of the RMF closely correlates with the supporting processes of the system development life cycle (SDLC), such as agreement, project, technical, software implementation, and software. That point, in and of itself, speaks volumes to the importance of the existence of a well-defined life cycle process that integrates with the steps of the RMF. While each organization is unique in terms of the availability of individuals or contractors to serve on implementation teams, the responsibility for completing the activities of this task generally gets assigned to all of the pertinent areas of the IT department, other affected ICT system owners (assuming supply-chain relationships), common control provider(s), the chief information security officer (CISO), and information systems security engineer. The underlying objective is to implement the system's required security controls that were selected in Step 2 of the RMF. The means by which controls are implemented is largely based on the guidance provided by NIST Special Publication (SP) 800-53A, *Guide for Assessing the Security Controls in Federal Information Systems and Organizations*. While we discuss this guideline in much greater detail in Chapter 6, it is appropriate to give it due diligence in terms of introduction in regard to the support it provides in the implementation step.

The NIST SP 800 53A guideline provides the specific requirements that are used to assess the security controls implemented in the information system. There may be confusion as to why an assessment guideline is being used in support of implementation. The clarification point is simple and rather realistic. By using the assessment guideline and taking a "back into" approach to implementation, the organization can be assured that the required security controls are implemented to the same standard required when the system is assessed. Moreover, this practice ensures that the system's security controls are developed correctly and are validated as compliant during security control assessment.

In NIST SP 800-53A, three assessment methods are defined that the organizations can use to assess the security controls implemented into an ICT system: *examine*, *interview*, and *test*. Important to note is that the requirements built into each assessment require the use of a different approach. For example, the *examination* technique encompasses the activities associated with reviewing the underlying ICT system security posture, adequate security support for each organizational business unit, security implications in terms of organizational policy, and the documentation that supports all implemented security controls. Likewise, *test* can be used to evaluate the technical aspects of individual functional units of the ICT system for security assurance. Additionally, the system outputs are tested, bearing in mind that such outputs could be user-centric or in the form of raw data. Finally, *interviews* are often conducted to evaluate that specific requirements of controls and/or control enhancements have been adequately implemented. Such interviews normally involve the assessment team and the ICT system users, managers, or individual staff members directly involved in the implementation of those controls or control enhancements.

Regardless of which technique is used to perform a given assessment, it is imperative that the organizations, the development team, and the CISO together with their security team carefully evaluate the requirements of the specific control or enhancement to ensure that the assessment technique to be used is at the same standard used to implement the system. Often, assessment techniques are performed in combination with the success of one assessment relying on the results of another. For example, an assessment performed using the examine technique could rely on system documentation as well as ICT system output, which might have been completed through a technical testing evaluation. The main point to be made is that when implementing the controls in the NIST SP 800-53 catalog, ICT system developers and security personnel should review the requirements of NIST SP 800-53A to ensure that the control or enhancement is implemented correctly based on the security requirements and assessment technique. Controls and enhancements can require compliance assessment and validation by one, two, or even all three of the assessment techniques and it is important to keep these techniques in mind while proceeding though the implementation process.

We mentioned in the introduction of this chapter that a well-defined SDLC process is vital to an organization's ability to integrate into existing processes the principles of risk management, particularly those relevant to implementation of security controls. One of the supporting SDLC processes that should already be in place encompasses the activities associated with verification and validation (V&V), which ensures that the system or component is being built correctly and according to specification. The organization can use NIST SP 800-53A to conduct self-assessments of the control in this task as a means for performing V&V in order to promote quicker corrections under circumstances that the control does not meet the documented requirements. Using control CP-9, *Information System Backup* from NIST SP 800-53A, we can easily demonstrate the key aspects that are required to implement any of the controls from the controls catalog (Figure 5.2).

In understanding the assessment objective, it is easy to match the items in section CP-9(a) with the requirements for CP-9(a) in SP 800-53. The assessment of item CP-9(b) is required to back up system-level data, CP-9(c) ensures that ICT system documentation is backed up, and CP-9(d) provides the mechanisms that support the confidentiality, availability, and integrity of the backed-up information or data. Continuing to follow the guidelines backward, NIST SP 800-53 provides a reference to NIST SP 800-34, *Contingency Planning Guide for Federal Information Systems*, where Section 3.4 provides details related to how those objectives can/should be implemented.

Each individual assessment method is a determinant on how that control will be evaluated by the security control assessment team through the activities of the next step of the RMF, based on the type of assessment, be it examination of

CP-9	INFORMATION SYSTEMS BACKUP	
	Assessment Objective: *Determine if the organization:*	
CP-9(a)	CP-9(a)[1]	Defines a frequency, consistent with recovery time objectives and recovery point objectives as specified in the information system contingency plan, to conduct backups of user-level information contained in the information system.
	CP-9(a)[2]	Conducts backups of user-level information contained in the information system with the organization-defined frequency.
CP-9(b)	CP-9(b)[1]	Defines a frequency, consistent with recovery time objectives and recovery point objectives as specified in the information system contingency plan, to conduct backups of system-level information contained in the information system.
	CP-9(b)[2]	Conducts backups of system-level information contained in the information system with the organization-defined frequency.
CP-9(c)	CP-9(c)[1]	Defines a frequency, consistent with recovery time objectives and recovery point objectives as specified in the information system contingency plan, to conduct backups of information system documentation including security-related documentation.
	CP-9(c)[2]	Conducts backups of information system documentation, including security-related documentation, with the organization-defined frequency.
CP-9(d)	Protects the confidentiality, integrity, and availability of backup information at storage locations.	
	Potential Assessment Methods and Objects: **Examine:** [*SELECT FROM:* Contingency planning policy; procedures addressing information system backup; contingency plan; backup storage location(s); information system backup logs or records; other relevant documents or records]. **Interview:** [*SELECT FROM:* Organizational personnel with information system backup responsibilities; organizational personnel with information security responsibilities]. **Test:** [*SELECT FROM:* Organizational processes for conducting information system backups; automated mechanisms supporting and/or implementing information system backups].	

Figure 5.2 Control CP-9: Information systems backup. (From NIST, *Assessing Security and Privacy Controls in Federal Information Systems and Organizations— Building Effective Assessment Plans: NIST SP 800-53A Revision 4***, NIST, Gaithersburg, 2014.)**

documentation, interviewing of staff (both users and development team), or testing of technical aspects of the security control. The cost of implementation is a clear concern of all management involved in any form of ICT implementation, whether it be a small project aimed at supporting the functionality of one business unit or a large-scale security control implementation project. To that extent, we need to consider that evaluation of the security controls during ICT development using self-assessments is substantially more cost-effective and efficient than coordinating subsequent projects in order to modify the system after the assessments are completed. Using a proactive approach during development ensures that security controls identified as not meeting the minimum requirements are corrected early in the design process. Many organizations that use in-house assessment teams assign the individuals that will be charged with the activities of assessment to a given ICT system to the development team of that system. In getting the assessment team involved early, the assessment results from the ICT system self-assessments can be, in turn, used for the system's authorization package in the security assessment report. In the case of control CP-9, system developers can use NIST SP 800-53A to determine whether or not this control is to be assessed by reviewing policy and documentation indicated by the examine assessment technique and by interviewing organizational staff with data/system backup responsibilities. The key point is that organizations must have the policies and procedures in place that ensure that the system is developed in a manner that meets the conditions for each of the controls required by the control selections made in the select step of the NIST RMF.

One viable approach to ensuring the correlation between implementation and assessment is to first consider the overall structure of the organization's ICT security posture. On the basis of the architecture that security controls are built into and the availability of organizationally approved common controls, the organization and control provider could develop methods of ensuring that the security controls within their domain of responsibility are implemented correctly, provide the required security mechanisms, and support the organization's enterprise architecture and ICT security strategies. In this case, the enterprise architecture will provide a mechanism from which specific security controls and common controls can be allocated to the ICT system, its functional units, and common control providers. The availability of a defined backup procedure, configuration management (CM), appropriate network firewall configurations, and other security mechanisms and services are just a few of several ways in which a security control may be integrated with the organization's ICT security architecture. Such services or products would then be selected, developed, and allocated, after being approved as common controls and services, to specific systems and components that require that capability.

In the case of firewall implementation, for example, many organizations require specific configuration settings to their firewall, with a defined upgrade schedule, on all network and telecommunication system components that are capable of having that form of network security applied to them. Such a standardized approach allows the ICT systems security engineer and CISO to design the system or system component such that it maintains the requirements that keep it in compliance with the organization's enterprise architecture and security strategies. Moreover, standardization assists in meeting the requirements for those controls that mandate the firewall installation be integrated to the networks and upgraded on a regular schedule. Having a clear understanding of the organization's enterprise architecture and security strategies, security control implementation can be better managed to provide leverage for system security requirements being tested and system services being developed. Likewise, as the organization continues to grow in terms of its level of security awareness, staff training in identifying and mitigating network/telecommunication threats and vulnerabilities, an overall project cost savings is likely to result.

The controls selected in Step 2 of the NIST RMF, *Select*, must now be allocated to and implemented by the specific components of the information system that will provide protection for the ICT system. Many seasoned security managers agree that control allocation is perhaps the most, if not one of the most important and sometimes time-consuming steps of the NIST RMF. Successful implementation requires the coordination of each individual organization within the system supply chain offering common controls for inheritance purposes, in addition to each affected business unit and the ICT staff facilitating and supporting the system design and development.

Too often, we speak of controls as being allocated to just one or two components of a larger ICT system. To the contrary, many controls are allocated to most if not all of the components of an organization's ICT system. Great examples of such a circumstance can come from considering the large assortment of management-related security controls identified in NIST SP 800-53. Let us use the CM controls (CM 1–11) as a basis of this discussion. CM controls must be implemented on each of the components of the ICT system as well as the systems of supply-chain organizations where CM is possible.

Aside from management controls, there are other cases where a control is only to be implemented in specific components or subsystems and is not required to be implemented across the entire system. For instance, a system may have functional units that do not require data store offsite, while a larger portion of the ICT system requires offsite storage for, among other purposes, compliance with legal and industry regulations. In these instances, the offsite data storage controls are considered separately between the larger portions of the system and would not be implemented in the part of the system where the requirement does not exist.

In general, it is the organization's underlying strategies, information processing needs, security requirements, system categorization, common control providers, and control allocation that in combination maintain a suitable balance between system- and organization-provided security control measures. A clear understanding of the organization's strategies and controls provided by common control providers helps to govern which of the required controls can be inherited, and which will be provided by the ICT system, will be a combination of the two, or will be implemented as a hybrid control.

Worthy of mention is that the development of hybrid controls results from the evaluation of common controls, and the decision made that the common control does not provide the protection necessary to meet minimum security requirements. Hybrid controls are simply the reinforcement of a control with additional protection measures to be maintained the staff responsible for maintaining the ICT system owner and supporting staff. Responsibility and maintenance of the control is then shared between the system owner and common control provider. Returning to the topic of CM control implementation, for example, the initiating organization could be responsible for development, documentation, and distribution to organizational personnel of a CM policy that addresses purpose, scope, roles, responsibilities, organization-defined values, management commitment, coordination among all organizational entities, and compliance, and procedures to facilitate the implementation of the CM policy and associated CM controls. Additionally, they would be responsible for reviews and updates of the current CM policy and procedures in accordance with legal and industry regulations, standards, guidelines, and other organizational requirements. Likewise, the common control provider(s) responsibilities include (Figure 5.3) the following:

- Develop, document, and review/update a CM control policy of greater scope to support all affiliated organizations, and define the frequency for reviews and updates.
- Provide policy and guidance for centralizing, managing, and approving IT configuration changes across all affiliated organizations.
- Ensure that system-specific CM procedures are developed, reviewed/updated, and maintained for the systems in accordance with requirements.
- Ensure that system-specific CM procedures facilitate the implementation of the CM policy.

It is important to note while understanding the general scope of this step of the NIST RMF that implementing security controls at the system level is only successful if the best practices, system and software engineering methodologies, security engineering principles, and secure coding techniques of a well-defined process are performed. By identifying and implementing security controls early in the system's life cycle development process, the organization can be confident that the system will function according to specification when all the required security controls

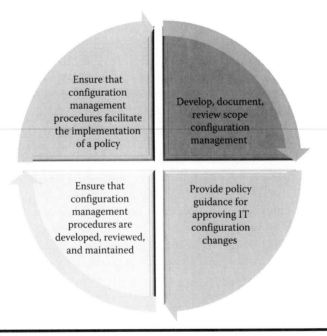

Figure 5.3   Common control provider responsibilities.

are in place. If an organization begins the security considerations as far back as the project planning process, management will have measurable data to assist in determining the cost of system development, operations, and maintenance, thus ensuring that funding is appropriately allocated for the system. Such a proactive approach does not always produce desired results.

Sometimes, the costs required to design, implement, and maintain the ICT system may be too extensive and cause the system's development to be delayed or canceled. The mistake often times made is that the development goes on, but security requirements are scaled back to accommodate the expenses. The "we will get to it later" approach is often the chosen alternative, albeit at the risk of exposure to otherwise prevented security threats and vulnerabilities.

Remember that the development of ICT systems and implementation of security controls are not a "one-size-fits-all" process. As project management begins and gives way to the other system and risk management processes, it is important to ensure that all required security controls, policies, and requirements are correctly integrated and implemented. Beyond the NIST guidelines we discuss in this book, there are a number of places to turn for assistance when implementing technical controls for an information system. It is becoming more common for each industry to have a unique set of guidelines that include specific laws, regulations, or executive orders (in the case of the federal government) that can and should be used by the organization to ensure compliance, and correct implementation of security controls.

It is not uncommon in any facet of the ICT industry for technologies and software currently existing in systems to be reused. The same holds true with regard to the implementation of security controls. In such cases, development and security teams must evaluate the existing implementation in order to determine what portions of those technologies or software can be reused. In many cases, not only can the technology be reused, but also the accompanying security policies and documentation will be applicable to the system under development as well. This process is called *reuse process management* and its purpose is to manage the life of reusable assets (technology and software) from concept to retirement.

Reuse has many advantages. It can shorten time to market, improve quality, and significantly reduce cost by utilizing existing assets while maintaining system security and compliance. However, reuse has to be managed and successful and secure reuse programs within ICT do not happen by accident. They must be based on strategic best practice. Thus, reuse is established by plan and incorporates a comprehensive strategy.

Prior to implementation, the technology components must be evaluated to ensure that what is being integrated into an ICT system is compliant with specific security standards. In some cases, that evaluation is performed by the organization that owns the system or affiliated common control providers. In other cases, the technology components are evaluated by trusted third-party organizations.

These third-party affiliates offer specific profiles for certified products, thus enabling system developers and security professionals to gain a understanding of the security status of a product before implementing or assessing the protection, detection, or monitoring services it provides. While using a third party may seem like an expense that increases the overall cost on implementation, the contrary is true. The time saved by using products evaluated by an organization other than your own will speed system development and ultimately reduce net costs.

Extra care must be taken during implementation to those systems that are critical to the organization's core business functions such as those that have the potential of causing significant setbacks within the organization if compromised, those that have been rated with high minimum assurance requirements, and those with requirements (out of the control of the organization) on how specific security controls are implemented and their operation capabilities. Such requirements of these systems may require controls that provide a higher level incidence response, backup and recovery, or access control as a means of complying with industry-based minimum security standards. Federal government systems are great examples of the type of systems that are high impact or critical to the extent that they are vulnerable to specific and credible threats or cyberattack. It is for this reason that enhanced requirements be implemented and documented thoroughly in order for the enhanced control's effectiveness to be accurately evaluated in the assessment step of the NIST RMF.

As previously stated, we mentioned that the steps of the NIST RMF (in particular, categorization and selection) should begin early in the development process. Realistically, that does not always happen. For one reason or another, the selection of controls may have been postponed until later in the development life cycle. Under those circumstances, the organization must take a reactive approach in making determinations on the selection of controls that will come from common control providers, enhanced as a hybrid control, or implemented entirely by the initiating organization. What many ICT managers fail to realize is that there is a significant amount of coordination that must be ensured in order to just correlate the inheritance of controls from a common control provider:

- The control must have been approved for inheritance by both parties.
- The control's lifetime, its approval status, and approval expiration must be determined.
- The implementing organization then must determine how the common control will be documented in the system's security plan (through reference to the provider's body of evidence or by documenting the control completely).

Perhaps the main point to be made is that the implementing organization and common control provider must collaboratively determine the most cost-effective way to implement the inherited controls into the ICT system. That can be easy or hard, depending upon the complexity of the ICT system. Given adequate time to let communications and correlations evolve between the implementing organization and common control provider will ensure that the controls meet the defined requirements.

When implementing security controls, it may be advisable to turn to vendor or industry-based security documentation. Many vendors offer security guides for the technologies they develop and support. Likewise, many industries now provide guidelines for implementation based on established standards and regulations. Because of the unique requirements of each control implementation for any given organization, there is not a single ISO, IEEE, or NIST technical standard or guideline providing a scripted approach for implementing *all* controls. Organizations must face the challenge of exploring benchmarks and other technical resources to assist in assuring security requirements are met. To the contrary, there is a guideline that was developed and released by NIST in the spring of 2016 that defines how to manage the implementation process. We discuss that guideline later in this chapter and to better understand the scope of implementation at the system and management levels, it is beneficial for us to discuss those steps from each of those perspectives.

5.3 A System Perspective to Implementation

To better understand the activities of security control implementation from a system perspective, it makes sense to review the systems implementation process given the significance of the integration of security control implementation into that process. The underlying perception of implementation is that the ICT development process is most closely associated with the discipline of software and system engineering, generally because the formal description methodologies that are used to create the end results are typically utilized by software or systems engineers. During implementation, the developer produces the technical design for each ICT component itemized in the architectural design and ensures that all requirements are directly traceable to a component that is being built. Over the past several years, many organizations have adopted the agile methodology, which makes this process iterative in terms of the flow of activities; the depiction of all system components is successively refined so they can be represented at the testing and deployment stage.

In most cases, implementation involves the requirement of constructing external and internal interfaces. The developer creates and documents an explicit design for all external and internal interfaces, including those between the components themselves. A quirk in the typical product development process should probably be explained here. In the conventional manufacturing model for ICT components, the person or team that is responsible for the technical design will separate themselves from the rest of the implementation process. Therefore, the technical design should be as self-sustaining as possible and should not require continuous "walking back and forth" between teams that could even be located on different continents.

Therefore, the design should be unambiguously understandable to all parties. This becomes especially true of implementation of common and hybrid security controls, where multiple organizations are involved.

During the development phase, the developer also produces a technical design for the database and updates the user documentation as necessary. At this point, the developer needs to define and document the testing milestones and requirements for each component in the technical design. Once these review points are known, a reasonable schedule for testing each component can be defined. Ultimately, all deliverables in this phase of the SDLC must be evaluated based on the common criteria of traceability, external and internal consistency, appropriateness of the methodology and standards employed, as well as feasibility.

Once the technical design is confirmed to be correct, it is turned over to the internal staff or outside contractors that do the actual construction. Product construction is undoubtedly the most primary activity of any ICT product development process. The developer must build the component or write the code for each required component and then create a full set of documentation for each item. Next, the test procedures that were previously defined in both the architectural and detail design phases are conducted and the data from each test are recorded. It is at this point that the evaluations, as stated earlier in this chapter, and V&V activities are performed. To support this evaluation, the developer should conduct joint reviews among stakeholders to validate the build. Next, the developer again updates the documentation, updates the test requirements if necessary, and schedules the necessary integration.

Looking at implementation from a security control standpoint, the NIST RMF stipulates that both tasks in Figure 5.1, presented at the beginning of this chapter, should be completed as part of the overall development (or acquisition) and implementation processes of the SDLC. This is achieved through a series of activities in which the members of the security team responsible for ensuring the completion of the security control implementation process collaborate with system architects and system developers working to deliver the system. The best-case scenario would include coordinated interaction between the security team and the functional and technical members of the system development team beginning early in the SDLC so that roles and expected contributions from all team members are understood by the time the system enters the development phase. Existing documentation in the form of system requirements and descriptions of system-specific and common controls developed during the system categorization and security control selection provides the mechanisms from which security control implementation activities are performed. More specifically, as we mentioned earlier, the activities performed as part of the SDLC development phase include architectural design, system engineering, testing, and preparation of supporting documentation. The details regarding the completion of these activities vary depending on the type of controls to be implemented and their source. That becomes important because different controls could have been custom developed and enabled through deployment or configuration characteristics already designed into the system. Likewise, they could have been delivered using commercially available or open-source tools, or inherited from common control providers. Upon completion of the documentation task, discussed later in this chapter, the outputs of the implementation process include a set of implemented, correctly configured controls documented at a level of detail sufficient to support security control assessment and to allow functional and technical V&V against the requirements specified for the ICT system.

Upon completion of the activities of the security control selection step, the security plan will provide criteria relative to what controls, common controls, hybrid controls, and control enhancements are required for implementation within the ICT system. Prior to engaging in control implementation, functional and technical members of the implementation project group facilitate discussions related to how each control will be implemented and assign responsibility of activities to be performed within the process to individuals with the appropriate skill level and knowledge of the system, including hardware, software, and associated configurations. Managers that assign responsibilities need to be mindful that the nature of the work required to implement a control varies considerably across operational and technical controls. The implementation team member will not have expertise in both control types inclusively. Therefore, careful planning and consideration must be made relative to the individuals performing each activity and the control type being implemented.

One of the key tasks in implementing security controls within ICT systems is the design of the security architecture. Part of that task involves distinguishing among the different types of controls and identifying the resources available within the organization to provide adequate support. The activities performed during architectural design consider the system as a whole, the functions, and services it will perform in the context of the organization's enterprise architecture. By approaching design from this perspective, it is easier to identify existing business processes, services, technologies, and capabilities the system may be able to reuse and ensure that the system does not conflict with or duplicate functions or services already deployed in the organization. The architecture design process also produces detailed diagrams, at varying levels of abstraction, showing the different components making up the system and its operating environment, points at which it connects to other systems or environments (internally and externally), and the placement or integration of security controls.

The main objective of security architecture is to specify which security controls apply to the various components of the ICT system and clearly establish the context by which common or hybrid controls are allocated. In the case of common controls, the security architecture design process must analyze the descriptions in common control documentation to understand and fulfill specified requirements for the ICT system or to determine if any of the controls are better suited for hybrid or system-specific implementation.

It is common practice for the organization to allocate security controls to an ICT system consistent with the organization's enterprise architecture relative to its security architecture. Enterprise architecture is a management practice employed by organizations to maximize the effectiveness of business processes and information resources in helping to achieve business success. The advantage of utilizing the enterprise architecture during control implementation is that it provides a clear balance between the investments in ICT and a set of defined measurable improvements, regardless if their intent is for a part of the organization or the entire business entity. Moreover, an established enterprise architecture also evaluates its ICT assets in terms of potential optimization, consolidation, and standardization. Within the scope of standardized system life cycles, both product and process standards provide a good source of generic guidance because they have to be appropriate to all situations that the standard is written to address. For that reason, the recommendations made by those standards must be customized for their guidance to apply correctly. In its applied, real-world form, this customization is typically called process engineering or enterprise architecture. Moreover, security professionals no longer view security as a product or a solution. Rather, it is commonly viewed as an in-depth system that must be incorporated throughout the business entity via computerization, managerial, or physical means. If organizations do not implement effective security controls, they place data integrity, information confidentiality, and the availability of applications critical to the capabilities and completion of core business functions at much greater risk.

With a greater insight and appreciation for enterprise architecture, we now turn our attention to security architecture. The security architecture is one of several major parts of the organization's enterprise architecture. It embodies the part of the enterprise architecture that addresses ICT system security and provides architectural information for the implementation of security controls. The value gained from using the information provided in the security architecture is that it ensures security controls that directly support individual business processes meet the requirements defined in and consistent with the organization's underlying risk management strategy.

As a security architecture evolves over time, organizations should identify and implement common security controls supporting multiple ICT systems as much as possible. Recall the discussion of reuse presented earlier in this chapter. The focus of reuse should not be isolated to individual functional components. The scope of common controls should extend to ICT systems that include existing and newly developed supply-chain management, customer relationship management, enterprise resource planning, and electronic commerce systems. When common controls are used to support a specific ICT system, they are referred to by each individual system as inherited controls. Common controls provide a cost-effective and consistent information security across the organization and can, in turn, use to simplify risk management activities. Regardless of the organization's ICT infrastructure, the main point to be made is that by applying security controls to an ICT system as system-specific, hybrid, or common, it becomes a necessity for the organization to assign responsibility and accountability to each individual organizational entity to ensure the proper development, implementation, assessment, authorization, and monitoring of each of the individual controls.

The previous point is not intended to suggest that organizations do not have a tremendous amount of flexibility in choosing the appropriate security controls intended to satisfy the functional outcomes of identify, protect, detect, respond, and recover (as specified by the NIST *Framework for Improving Critical Infrastructure Cybersecurity*—CSF) throughout the organization and its supply chain. As we discuss in Section 5.4, since the security control implementation process includes the assignment of security capabilities provided by the selected security controls, the organization must establish clear lines of communication among all affected parties that are either receiving or providing the benefits of implemented security components. To that extent, the communication must include but not be limited to making certain that common control effectiveness, continuous monitoring, and audit results are readily available to the individuals within the organization and supply chain that are directly affected by the inheriting common controls, and that any CM applied to the common controls are effectively communicated to those affected by such changes.

What has been under discussion in this section is the means by which security controls are implemented through a life cycle process called security engineering. In the same way that mechanical engineering, electrical engineering, industrial engineering, systems engineering, and software engineering serve their specific purpose to the greater scope of the engineering discipline, security engineering encompasses those processes that facilitate the execution of activities that produce security mechanisms designed to achieve those functional outcomes of the CSF that were just mentioned.

The advantage of applying security engineering principles to control implementation is that they provide a plethora of general guidance and protocols that establish a basis for security control design and development. Additionally, applying these principles leverages many security specialties and focus areas that contribute to security control implementation activities and tasks. These security specialties can include, for example: computer security; communications security; transmission security; anti-tamper protection; electronic emissions security; physical security; information; software and hardware assurance; and technology specialties such as biometrics and cryptography. Further, it provides the mechanisms for organizations to adequately define security objectives, provides specification of control design that meets minimum security requirements, integrates the viewpoints of security architecture, provides the capability for appropriate V&V, and assures the deployment of necessary controls aimed at minimizing cost and maximizing security protection and detection benefits.

5.4 A Management Perspective to Implementation

In considering the scope from which management should be understood with respect to security control implementation, the discussion can lead in two directions. First, as we have discussed the implications of security control implementation thus far, we have spent a considerable amount of time in that discussion speaking in terms of operational and technical control development and integration. However, there is another group of controls that need to be in place before implementation of technical controls and operational control implementation can even take place; that vital group of risk reducing practices is called *management controls*. Second, consider that every undertaking that enhances the capabilities of an ICT system is a project. Before security control design can even commence, project management practices at the organizational and individual project level must be engaged. In this section, we explore security control implementation from a management perspective from both of these vital angles.

Throughout this book, we have stated that a standard framework, such as NIST SP 800-37, *Guide for Applying the Risk Management Framework to Federal Information Systems* can be adapted to serve as the template for defining a practical information governance infrastructure. And we have discovered that auditable proof of conformance to the best practice recommendations of such a framework is an excellent means of demonstrating that the business is both trustworthy and secure. Similarly, in the spring of 2016, NIST published its second draft of NIST SP 800-160, *Systems Security Engineering—Considerations for a Multidisciplinary Approach in the Engineering of Trustworthy Secure Systems*. The trustworthiness of these and other frameworks can be assumed because the best practices that are embodied within such a standard model span the gamut of expert advice and consensus with respect to the correct way to ensure a given organizational application. Therefore, standard models such as SP 800-37 can be considered to be authoritative points of reference from which an organization's across-the-board cybersecurity approach can be evaluated for adequacy and capability.

However, because the NIST RMF is intended to be generic, this model essentially serves as a template rather than the actual implementation of practical controls. So in that respect, it needs to be viewed as a comprehensive specification of the functions required for instituting practical cybersecurity controls, rather than the controls themselves.

The creation of a functioning, real-world control system requires the performance of an individually planned and intentionally executed risk management process within the specific setting where the controls will be operated. That process must be able to help the business deal more effectively with the many demands and requirements of cybersecurity across the organization. Likewise, it should serve as the basis for getting that specific enterprise's information and ICT-related assets under direct security control. In addition, in compliance situations, such as those imposed by the Federal Information Security Management Act, the approach should also embody some form of explicit audit mechanism that will allow the business to demonstrate both the effectiveness and the compliance of its security controls. All of the necessities just mentioned are related to many of the management controls provided in NIST SP 800-53 and other control libraries. Such management controls should have been chosen and documented in the security plan during Step 2 of the RMF, where we categorize security controls. NIST SP 800-53 has an explicit set of security management domains associated with it and each of those domains embodies a particular collection of underlying management controls. Notice, while some domains appear more technical than others, each begins with a management control designed to enforce policy and procedures for the security measures applied within that domain. Figure 5.4 provides a summary. As can be seen by simply viewing the categories of management controls, the implementation step of the RMF could not be sufficiently accomplished in the absence of a strategic life cycle management process.

5.5 Implementation via Security Life Cycle Management

For the purposes of security assurance, security life cycle management is practiced when each of the minimally required management controls within the domains seen in Figure 5.4 is in place and capable of being improved. As in the

	Security Control Class	Security Control Family	Identifier
1	Technical	Access control	AC
2	Operational	Awareness and training	AT
3	Technical	Audit and accountability	AU
4	Management	Certification, accreditation, and security assessments	CA
5	Operational	Configuration management	CM
6	Operational	Contingency planning	CP
7	Technical	Identification and authentication	IA
8	Operational	Incident response	IR
9	Operational	Maintenance	MA
10	Operational	Media protection	MP
11	Operational	Physical and environmental protection	PE
12	Management	Planning	PL
13	Operational	Personnel security	PS
14	Management	Risk assessment	RA
15	Management	System and services acquisition	SA
16	Technical	System and communications protection	SC
17	Operational	System and information integrity	SI

Figure 5.4 NIST SP 800-53 control domain summary.

case of every other major organizational process, life cycle management becomes the practical mechanism for implementing a large-scale best practice security model in a business. The role of life cycle management is to establish and sustain the proper long-term security of any business operation. The objective is to keep proper alignment between the overall goals of the organization and the key functions created to achieve those goals. Life cycle management monitors and assures the operation of each key function in order to ensure that effective alignment is maintained.

The assumption is that each function is effective if it can be shown to contribute to the attainment of a business goal and underlying security posture. However, in order for life cycle management to accomplish that objective, the organization must create a formal process to systematically monitor the day-to-day performance of each of the many tasks that make up the overall security function. The problem with any systematic effort to ensure secure systems is that a lot of the key elements such as developers, customers, and maintainers all operate more-or-less divorced from each other. In the case of the customer, that role is always part of another unit. Often the customer is from outside the organization. The role of security life cycle management is to ensure that each of the various large processes encapsulated within the ICT system operate in the most effective manner.

In order to ensure proper integration, security life cycle management has to create and then coordinate a top-level process that combines and subsequently manages all of the underlying life cycle management functions that are required to support the security requirements of the organization. In addition to its coordination role, it also must ensure that overall security process continues to support the strategic goals of the organization. In this context, the overall security process embodies a consistent set of inherent security implementation functions, which are documented in such a way that individual managers will be able to tailor a uniform set of best practices for their units at any desired level of detail.

In much the same way that tailoring is performed, according to the RMF, to establish required security controls, life cycle management tailoring is done by identifying the unique issues, problems, and criteria associated with each required activity for which the manager is responsible. Then, the necessary adjustments are made to ensure that the resulting technologies and behaviors that are put in place in that particular instance fit within the standard requirements of the general ICT process framework. The outcome of the tailoring activity is an explicit set of practices that represent standard operating procedure for the organization.

Security life cycle management is an everyday process. Therefore, it is important to ensure the continuing day-to-day effectiveness of activities that comprise that process. Security assurance is made possible by regular assessment of the performance of each implementation activity against individual benchmarks. The comparison of performance against a stable set of benchmarks gives managers the comparative insight they need to exercise control over their operation. Particularly, benchmarks provide the consistent point of reference needed to assess the performance of technical work and allow managers to gauge its progress.

Persistent observation and quantitative assessment of performance are critical to security life cycle management. To ensure that a given process is functioning correctly, an organization must be able to independently evaluate the effectiveness of the actions that comprise the process. Such evaluations of effectiveness also lead to ongoing process improvement. Because ICT development work is complex, it is difficult for managers to know whether the return on investment in equipment, applications, information, or infrastructure is at an acceptable level unless they have objective data about performance. The existence of concrete data that characterizes actual performance against stable and reliable benchmarks can give managers the insight they need to assure that their operation is functioning properly.

There are always costs and risks associated with large security development projects. However, a well-established framework of defined processes allows the organization to better understand those risks and control the management of its resources. This is done by basing the decision-making process on quantitative factors. In return, enhanced control ensures better risk management, as well as optimum value. A defined framework of best practice also underwrites accountability. That is because responsibility and accountability can be clearly assigned as part of the management of the process.

In turn, enhanced visibility and accountability leverage return on corporate investment. That is because visibility allows the company to better manage its functions, which in turn allows managers to optimize costs and revenues. So, notwithstanding the obvious payoffs in more efficient work that the creation of a comprehensive security life cycle management control structure provides, a defined process framework also creates the potential for increased long-term profitability.

Dovetailing from the discussion of process improvement based on evaluation we just had, it is noteworthy to mention that planning is a vital component of the life cycle that aims to assure that process improvement efforts across the organization are adequately managed and implemented. Policies and procedures are documented in a process improvement plan. In addition to documenting plans for improvement, the organization's process improvement plan contains relevant details related to process action planning, pilot planning, and deployment planning. We discuss in Chapter 6 that assessment-based action plans are necessary to assure proper progress through the assessment activity. These assessment plans describe the timeline and schedule, the scope of the assessment, resources required to perform it, the reference model against which the assessment is performed, and logistics. Process action plans usually result from assessment and document how to improve weaknesses uncovered by an assessment. Improvements described in the process action plan should be tested on a small group before being deployed across the organization. In these cases, a pilot plan is generated.

5.6 Establishing Effective Security Implementation through Infrastructure Management

The purpose of any infrastructure is to serve as a foundation. So, in the simplest possible terms, infrastructure management is employed to establish another process. This process is not a management process as the name implies, in the sense that it is not ongoing. Instead, it creates a logical framework. To work properly, this structure must be explicitly stated and its elements must be explicitly related.

The infrastructure model must encompass and describe the complete structure from top to bottom of every security implementation process at every level. An organization must be able to trace and derive all of these levels and elements from each other. The most basic element of an infrastructure process model is at the task level. Each task is designed to carry out a specific functional activity within the security implementation life cycle, and is uniquely identified as such. The task has one or more defined entry conditions that are required for task initiation, including the inputs from any prior activities and from all sources. Depending upon the life cycle framework utilized (i.e., ISO 12207:2008, NIST SP 800-160), the tasks and inputs can be tailored to meet the individual requirements of that framework. Moreover, other sources can be tapped to assist in developing a detailed infrastructure specification:

- Current standard operating procedures within the organization
- Current or commonly recognized methods
- Other assigned responsibilities from the organization that might not be covered by the preceding two items
- Any contract stipulations

To be precise, the model must also specify a set of exit conditions that includes the results to be produced, the level of validation required to authenticate results, and any unusual post-task conditions that might be specific to a particular task.

Developing a defined infrastructure would be difficult if an organization could not define certain tasks as part of the basic operation of a standard security implementation process. For instance, planning and documentation tasks represent a common set of requirements across most of the life cycle processes. These tasks exhibit the same entry/task/exit (ETX) requirements for the most part. Consequently, a standard task such as planning can be defined once and then interconnected in different ways to meet the unique needs of a given process or project.

Once an organization has defined a complete set of standard security implementation process tasks, it can construct a process model by interconnecting the basic set of task in various ways. The idea is to actively construct a process that addresses expected issues and problems that may be anticipated within the process, and adequately meets the minimum security requirements identified in the select step of the NIST RMF.

An important assumption that we are making is that every organization will establish a formal infrastructure appropriately tailored to its needs. The practical mechanism for this infrastructure requires the following several steps. First, a standard process framework must be adopted for tailoring. We just mentioned ISO 12207 and SP 800-160; however, organizations have a range of widely known approaches to choose from, including the old-fashioned hierarchy. Many of these approaches are valid in their overall application, but as of this writing, only the ISO 12207 standard and NIST SP 800-160 approach the level of detail indicative of a commonly accepted framework among most of the technologically advanced nations. Politics does play a role in the widespread use of any of these standards, but because both are generally accepted, they can be considered the best legitimate source for defining a universal security implementation framework.

The next step is to formally define ETX specifications for each task to fit within the adopted framework. This set of provisions is developed directly from the ETX specifications, and it allows the organization to monitor and track the outcomes of each task as they are completed. Accordingly, the checkpoints for quality assurance must be formally designated to perform the exit assessment at relevant points in the process. An organization must define and approve measurement and reporting mechanisms for each of these planned reviews.

The overall execution of the implementation process must be uniform, yet because every component in the project is unique, it must be tailored specifically. The resulting model cannot be rigid; an organization must be able to modify it dynamically to reflect actual changes that occur as the process evolves over time. To keep track of these changes, all deviations from the process have to be documented, reviewed, and approved under CM. Because this process is not exact, the proper (highest) level of abstraction must be found, usually after experimentation.

Partly because of its monumental and somewhat indistinct scope, the infrastructure management of security implementation is one of the simplest to execute. Apart from the previously suggested approach of creating a tailored set of process activities from the standard task set and then mapping their interconnections, the key point to be made is that the organization must follow some sort of definition and documentation process (discussed later in this chapter) and then develop a plan for its implementation.

5.7 Finding the Fit: Security Implementation Projects and Organization Portfolios

In a discussion of life cycle management, it is easy to imagine such a life cycle happening in isolation. Sadly that is never the case. Small-, medium-, and large-scale organization alike must be able to manage a large portfolio of ICT projects. Adding in the priorities that exist of the urgency for implementation of security requirement, this organizational portfolio project management becomes even more complex.

Project portfolio management (PPM) is often not understood or embraced in large organizations and sometimes is managed haphazardly. Many definitions of PPM have emerged over the years. Sometimes, it is easier to describe something by explaining what it is not. PPM is neither just enterprise-wide project management (discussed in Section 5.8) nor simply the management of projects and metrics generation across various programs and projects. PPM is the construction and management of a portfolio of projects that make a maximum contribution to an organization's overall goals and objectives.

Within the context of security implementation, organizations need PPM for the following key reasons (Figure 5.5):

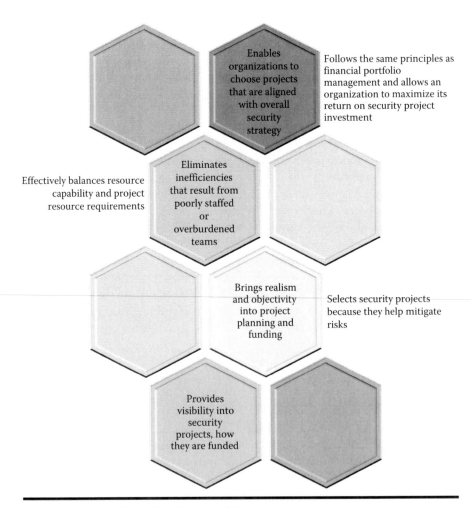

Enables organizations to choose projects that are aligned with overall security strategy

Follows the same principles as financial portfolio management and allows an organization to maximize its return on security project investment

Effectively balances resource capability and project resource requirements

Eliminates inefficiencies that result from poorly staffed or overburdened teams

Brings realism and objectivity into project planning and funding

Selects security projects because they help mitigate risks

Provides visibility into security projects, how they are funded

Figure 5.5   The value of project portfolio management.

- PPM enables organizations to choose projects that are aligned with their overall security strategy and goals.
- PPM effectively balances resource capability and project resource requirements, which eliminates inefficiencies that result from poorly staffed or overburdened teams. It also assures that resources are not being wasted while not being used on projects.
- PPM brings realism and objectivity into project planning and funding. Security projects are selected because they help mitigate that risks faced by the organization and not because of individual political agendas.
- PPM provides visibility into security projects, how they are funded, and the human and financial capabilities of the organization.
- PPM follows the same principles as financial portfolio management and allows a company to maximize its return on security project investment by selecting the right mix of projects.

In its simplest form, security PPM can be broken down into three main components. The first component deals with building the pipeline, the second assures that the right security projects are selected, and the third component deals with prioritizing the selected security projects correctly. A structured process is needed to build the project pipeline and select the right projects.

PPM focuses on decision-making about an organization's existing ICT products and services and those in development. It is a strategic function that aims to establish and maintain a balanced product portfolio that maximizes value, supports the business strategy, and makes the best use of organizational resources.

The first step of portfolio management as it would relate to security implementation is for the organization to prioritize its security strategies in combination with the other business strategies supported by an ICT system. Portfolios can then be assembled and assessed based on how they meet strategic needs. Once organizations determine the business priorities they want their projects to meet, they need to break down the portfolios. For example, New York–based Verizon Communications has a series of portfolios. ICT teams are assigned to different business functions, and each team handles a separate portfolio (both security related and nonsecurity in nature). On the basis of the established priorities, the organization can then develop metrics used to measure a portfolio's success.

Each of the projects within the portfolio must be individually evaluated. In doing so, organizations should consider the following factors: how well the project maps against the security strategies of the organization, risks in terms of technology and change management, the number of people the project will affect, and whether the project involves extensive reengineering. A good evaluation process can help organizations detect overlapping security projects up front, cut off projects with lackluster implications to the overall security posture of the organization, and strengthen alignment between ICT systems, the organization's supply chain, and senior management.

No organization consciously funds a project that it knows will fail, but changes in security requirements, business functions, economics, or market conditions can render some projects nonviable. Within the context of an investment portfolio, the decision to cancel such a project and reallocate funds to better opportunities is equivalent to selling an underperforming stock. This cancellation does not invalidate the initial decision to fund the project; at the time, the investment made sense. However, each investment must be evaluated within the context of current security conditions and whether it advances the organization's security objectives. ICT portfolio management then becomes the process of making "buy, sell, or hold" decisions, which are the same decisions made by a financial planner. Realizing that investments should be viewed as components of a unified portfolio is the first step to responsible ICT portfolio management.

5.8 Security Implementation Project Management

We stated in Section 5.7 that each security implementation initiative—whether for technical, operational, or management controls—is a project. Each individual project must, in turn, be managed. In general, project management oversees the organization's ICT acquisition, development, and sustainment processes. To that extent, it enforces the ICT policies and procedures of the organization. Project management also ensures effective coordination and control of the organization's everyday work practices. Therefore, it is a life cycle process that is always exercised across the organization. Accountability for proper project management starts at the top with strategic planning and policy making. It continues down the hierarchy or responsibilities all the way to the level of the individual ICT project manager. Because project management is hierarchical, everybody in the organization from top-level executives all the way down to the individual project managers contributes to the process in some substantive way.

Specifically, project management for security engineering projects involves defining and deployment of a fully integrated set of security implementation life cycle activities, all aimed at satisfying a given set of security requirements. In order to be effective, it must provide a considerable amount of coordination of complex combinations of everyday work practices among a diverse group of individuals. That coordination ensures that the right actions take place within a logical timeline. Coordination typically involves executing the overall security implementation life cycle process. The process itself has to be capable of ensuring a continuously appropriate alignment between the specific activities that take place within the project and the general security objectives that align with the strategies of the organization.

Project definition and subsequent coordination also ensure the efficient utilization of resources. If the activities that take place within a project are clearly understood and properly executed by the participants, then none of the resources that are allocated to carry out those activities will be wasted. For that reason alone, the ability to establish and maintain a set of well-defined project activities represents a greater degree of security assurance within the organization. Because it encompasses resource implications, the responsibility for ensuring that all project activities are properly defined and coordinated is normally vested with an immediate project manager. That project manager ensures that the ICT projects meet the requisite of the clarity and timeline criteria performance within the project plan.

The project management plan is the essential first condition for ensuring best practice at the project level. The plan defines the requisite activities and tasks for each project. In order to ensure effective communication, the plan should always be composed of concrete specifications of the work to be done. These specifications are documented using a top-down process running from general project concept down to explicit tasks (integrating the ETX specifications we spoke about earlier in this chapter) that will be performed in order to achieve the project's purposes. In essence, each general project purpose is realized through the specific procedures that are intended to accomplish that purpose. Then those procedures are provided with explicit task descriptions. The goal is to create a complete and detailed description of the work to be done as well as to communicate an understanding of how each of the various components of the project will interact with each other to achieve the project's particular purpose. Because the situation it was drawn up to address can change, that plan is typically reviewed and refined over time.

The project's manager is also responsible for actually writing the plan and then maintaining it, once it has been approved. The plan specifies the major elements for the project for the planning period as well as the resources that will be available to support each part. In effect, the project plan itemizes the execution of each of the steps within the project as well as itemizing the organizational resources that will be allocated to accomplish those goals. In addition to resources, the project plan describes that particular project's approach to management control and oversight.

Thus, the goal of the plan is to ensure that the intended business and technical work will progress down a logical timeline to a final product, which satisfies the security needs of the organization, its supply chain, and its customers. The management activities of the security implementation project should always be based on and enforce organizational and established security policies. The policies that define the general shape of the project management process of a security implementation project are developed as part of the organization's overall strategic planning process activity. Those policies dictate the organization's specific course of action as well as how it will achieve its goals and purposes. The organization's projects are one of the primary mechanisms for achieving those goals, in particular those aimed at mitigating security risk. Therefore, the planning for each security implementation project in effect implements the strategic directions of that organization.

Once the general project framework is established, each of the activities of the component processes and the tasks that populate it are planned, documented, evaluated, and adjusted as necessary. That process of documenting each task takes away from the effort that might be spent on doing specific project work. But well-defined processes lead to the repeatable outcomes, which are the hallmark of a secure ICT organization. Additionally, because the outcomes of those processes are repeatable, the organization can count on stable and predictable long-term outcomes because the planning is based on lessons learned.

Security implementation project teams actually perform most of the tasks defined within the project plan. These teams are typically composed of an integrated mix of security and ICT workers. Their primary responsibility is to execute the steps of a project under a single, unified project management process. Three big-picture questions have to be answered when forming that team:

■ What is the precise mission of the team?
■ What are the specific organizational competencies required to achieve that mission?
■ Are those competencies available for this particular project?

Defining a mission statement forces the organization to think through and fully document the application of the proposed ICT security measure. Because there can be a range of real-world variables involved, that statement might require a little soul-searching by corporate decision-makers, such as how the project will add value to the organization security posture, or the total long-term cost of operation and the trade-off of overall investment priorities. The product of that soul-searching should be a clear understanding of strategic security direction, along with how that project will meet the minimum security requirements defined in the NIST RMF select step.

The final factor, internal capability, is inward facing. An assessment of internal capability differentiates and then evaluates all of the business ability requirements to deliver a successful project. Relating the project's requisite capability requirements to the organization's ability to satisfy those requirements will provide an answer to most of the questions about whether the project is worth the investment. In doing the comparison, the business will have to identify the specific personnel and resource investment necessary that will be needed to satisfy the project's specific competency requirement. This exercise and that identification can lead to a better understanding of whether the organization is capable of delivering a successful product, and more importantly, contribute to the overall ICT security of the organization. If the company does all of the research necessary to understand how its internal capabilities align with project goals, it will be in a much better position to execute the project correctly, or conversely to decline the work if it is incapable of providing a worthwhile security product at an economical price.

5.9 Document the Security Control Implementation in the Security Plan

Throughout the discussion of implementation from a managerial perspective, we made reference to the necessity of life cycle documentation through the mention of assessment, improvement, contingency, and project plans. We purposefully kept our discussion of each of those plan's impact on individual processes of the implementation life cycle at a summary level, because the section task of the security implementation step of the NIST RMF formally prescribes the development of supporting documentation. The underlying output of this task is a set of life cycle documentation that supports the development of required controls, validation (through traceability) of documentation that supports the premise that implemented controls meet established requirements, and an updated security plan with pertinent information about each implemented security control.

The NIST RMF takes the support of documentation a step further than simply describing the activities performed to implement each security control. The documentation must also describe the categorization of each control as common, hybrid, or system-specific. Beyond the scope of life cycle project plans, this documentation serves as the formal plan and explanation resource with information about the overall function and security implementation of the system, including all required inputs and outputs. Likewise, the security control documentation defines the control's traceability to the control requirements as defined in NIST SP 800-53 and NIST SP 800-53A, and required organizational or regulatory implications affecting facilities and how a control is implemented.

Through documentation, the organization is able to effectively create a balance between the level of effort necessary for the controls to be implemented, scope, and the impact that implementing each control will have on the organization's underlying business functions, strategies, mission, or operations. At a minimum, the documentation should provide a detailed explanation about the security control implementation process, required facilities, test procedures, and appropriate references to the bodies of evidence for common and hybrid controls. Detailed control design documentation should also provide adequate descriptions of planned inputs, expected behavior, and expected output from each control implemented.

It is important to note that the documentation created during this task becomes part of the authorization package (we discuss the authorization step in Chapter 7); therefore, the security team, system engineers, and other pertinent ICT personnel must determine if each of the required security controls that are allocated as system-specific or hybrid are appropriately implemented and adequately protecting the system as designed and that the system life cycle documentation and requirements match the configuration of the system and its components. There are several ways to accomplish this. However, most organizations obtain such confirmation by executing traceability testing procedures designed to verify that the controls are documented and added to the system test processes. One common approach is for the organization to develop a traceability matrix to help document the testing results. The key point is that, much like all forms of ICT system development, through testing the end result of the implementation must be able to trace back to the requirements. In the same way, all documentation should be able to be traced backward as well. The traceability matrix simply provides the documented validation of that condition.

In addition to the authorization package requiring all of the life cycle documentation and control implementation and documentation traceability validation, it also requires an updated security plan. The documentation task of the RMF stipulates that once required security controls have been implemented, the security plan should be updated accordingly. While NIST SP 800-37 provides no formal requirements for the format of these control statements, common practice is for the organization to include a section for each of the required controls, including the required control enhancement, within the plan. The benefit of that is enhanced readability and organization to the document, especially when being evaluated by the security control assessor. Often, closely related controls in which updates occur in only one place are able to be combined into one section of the document for the purposes of clarity. This combination documentation practice promotes reduced redundancy and decreases the possibility of errors being introduced when controls or system documentation gets updated. As a consequence, if an alternate approach is chosen, it may be possible to update the required security documentation in one location while omitting needed updates in a different section. When addressing multiple controls in combination, it is advisable to include the security control's identification in the section's title: *CM (CM-1, CM-2, CM-3, CM-4, CM-5, . . . , CM-11)*. This section header is followed by specific details on how each of the controls and the required enhancements listed are implemented in the ICT system or supported in associated documentation. This is also the place to document security control inheritance or the implementation of hybrid controls.

The advantage of this method of documentation is that it ensures security control assessors are able to expeditiously identify the location of the method employed to implement a given security control. We strongly suggest that other methods of documenting security control implementation within a security plan are available and could become beneficial for the unique characteristics of a given organization. However, caution should be taken in that alternative methods may increase the time it takes the assessor to locate the security control implementation information within the security plan due to the ambiguity in some documentation styles.

5.10 Chapter Summary

This chapter presented the practice of logic that should be performed, from a system and managerial perspective, by organizations that have a vested incentive for properly implementing cybersecurity controls. Through the tasks of the NIST

RMF that are associated with security control implementation, the organization incorporates the controls identified and approved as part of the security plan within the functional and technical requirements identified for the system and its overall design. The NIST RMF prescribes two tasks in implementation: security control implementation and security control documentation. Both tasks should be completed as part of the overall development (or acquisition) and implementation processes of the SDLC. This is accomplished through a series of activities in which the members of the security team responsible for ensuring the completion of the security control formulation and development process collaborate with system architects and system developers working to deliver the system. Specifically, the security activities performed as part of the SDLC development phase include security architectural design, security system engineering, V&V, and preparation of supporting documentation. NIST defines the outputs of the implementation process, including a set of implemented, correctly configured controls documented at a level of detail sufficient to support security control assessment and to allow functional and technical V&V against the requirements specified for the ICT system.

In recognizing the need for managerial responsibility with respect to security control implementation, two vital managerial perspectives must be considered. First, it must be understood that in addition to technical and operational controls, there is a third category of controls that must be implemented, managerial controls. Given the scope in which NIST identified managerial controls within the domains of SP 800-53, it is easy to conclude that managerial controls must be in place before the life cycle implementation of technical and operational controls can commence. While senior executive and management oversight must be evident throughout the implementation of all three control categories, such management practices become even more vital during the implementation of management controls. Consideration must be given to each individual control's support of the organization's mission, strategies, and business functions. Further, consider that every undertaking that enhances the capabilities of an ICT system (whether it is enforcing management practices, implementing technical controls, or implementing operational controls) is a project. The organization must look at each project undertaking individually and measure its impact to the larger group of ICT projects. This is called PPM. Once it is deemed that one security control implementation project is a good "fit" within the project portfolio, individual project management practices must be engaged. Within the context of security control implementation, the goal of project management is to create a plan that includes but is not limited to: coordination of life cycle activities, timelines, and justifications for how scope, time, and money are going to be managed throughout the implementation process. The challenge that managers face is keeping the implementation project on track and within the originally defined scope, while providing a standard of implementation that guarantees mitigation of security risk.

In the second of two major activities of the NIST RMF security control implementation process, organizations should update the system security plan to describe the details of the implementation activities that have already taken place. The plan should be updated with details for system-specific, hybrid, and common controls (taking into consideration the details related to working with common control providers where appropriate) and provide criteria to emphasize the intention of engaging in security control assessment.

In addition to updated control descriptions provided in the system security plan, the implementation of management and operational controls also results in the development of several other documents that either directly represent required security controls or describe security controls as implemented. Documentation for technical controls includes not only technical implementation details but also functional descriptions of the expected control behavior in addition to the inputs and outputs expected for each component in the ICT system. One of the difficult tasks that managers face is determining the amount of information and level of detail to provide for each required implemented control, considering factors such as the complexity, testing, audit, and impact level of the system while also balancing the effort required to produce adequate documentation with other system development processes and security control formulation and development processes potentially competing for the same resources. Organizations should make it a priority to utilize existing sources of technical documentation whenever possible while developing security control documentation; this includes gaining access to functional and technical specifications from vendors responsible for IT products incorporated into the ICT system, policies, and procedures, in addition to plans for management and operational controls from the organization functional units that implement them. Likewise, similar documentation should also be sought from common control providers.

Glossary

assessment: the process of testing and/or evaluation of the management, operational, and technical security controls in an ICT system in order to determine the degree in which the controls are implemented correctly, operating as expected, and producing the desired outcome based on the security requirements of the system

authorization package: specific documentation collected during the *categorize, select, implement,* and *assess* steps of the RMF that is evaluated as a means for authorizing the security controls of an ICT system

compliance: a state of agreement or alignment with formally expressed criteria

configuration management: a formal process to ensure the continuing of a logically related array of ICT components; the detailed recording and updating of information that describes an organization's hardware and software

contingency plan: a plan of actions to be taken in response to a security event

customer relationship management system: an ICT system designed to coordinate all of the business functions surrounding the organization's interactions with its customers in sales, marketing, and service

enterprise architecture: a specific array of tailored practices designed to accomplish a particular task or fulfill a requirement for an entire enterprise

enterprise resource planning system: a set of integrated ICT modules that support a wide variety of business functions within an organization by allowing data to be used by each of those business functions interchangeably

infrastructure management: the role that defines, provides, and maintains the facilities, tools, communications, and ICT assets of an organization

process improvement: the improvement of an organization's ICT development

project management: a logical collection of controls instituted to ensure confidentiality, availability, and integrity of an organization's assets; the application of knowledge, tools, skills, and techniques to project activities to meet project requirements

project portfolio management: an organization's grouping and management of projects as a portfolio of investments that contribute to its objectives

security architecture: the security design that defines the requirements and potential risks involved in a specific ICT environment. It also specifies when and where to apply security controls

security assurance: a measurable degree of trust that security controls are implemented according to requirements and function appropriately

security control documentation: task within the *implementation* step of the RMF that provides specific resources pertinent to each control implemented into an ICT system

security control implementation: task within the *implementation* step of the RMF that includes all of the life cycle processes necessary to integrate security controls into an ICT system

security life cycle management: the activities performed by management to ensure that each security implementation process is completed accurately and efficiently

supply chain: a hierarchical framework of entities that work together to develop a product

system security engineering: a subset of the larger engineering discipline that engages in the life cycle processes specifically designed to implement security controls

validation: testing to ensure that the developed product provides the intended functionality

verification: the process of testing documented ICT requirements, to ensure that they have been met

References

National Institute of Standards and Technology (NIST). (2014). *Assessing Security and Privacy Controls in Federal Information Systems and Organizations—Building Effective Assessment Plans*: NIST SP 800-53A Revision 4. Standard, Gaithersburg, MD: NIST.

NIST. (2014). *Guide for Applying the Risk Management Framework to Federal Information Systems—A Security Lifecycle Approach*: NIST SP 800-37 Revision 1. Guideline, Gaithersburg, MD: NIST.

Chapter 6

Step 4—Assess Security Controls

At the conclusion of this chapter, the reader will understand:

- The underlying principles of security control assessment based on the National Institute of Standards and Technology (NIST) Special Publication (SP) 800-53A, and how it fits into the scope of the other steps of the NIST Risk Management Framework (RMF)
- The tasks associated with developing a security control assessment plan.
- How to perform a security control assessment based on the procedures of an established security control assessment plan
- The proper procedure for developing a security assessment report based on assessment findings
- The fundamental approaches of performing initial remedy actions based on the findings documented in the finalized security assessment report

Before we embark on a discussion of assessment, we should take a moment to address the cyclical nature of the NIST RMF. As information and communication technology (ICT) professionals, we think in terms of life cycles. Every project, whether the intention is to build a brand new system or add a component to an existing system, begins with a feasibility analysis and ends when the resulting system or component moves into the maintenance phase of the life cycle. It is through the activities of maintenance that subsequent projects related to the system or system component are evoked. Unlike the NIST *Framework for Improving Critical Infrastructure Cybersecurity* (CSF), in which it is clear that the intention is not to present the five functions of that framework as a life cycle, we believe NIST had different intentions for the RMF. This will become even clearer in the discussion we have in Chapter 8 of this book. Nevertheless, many make the mistake of thinking that since Step 4 of the NIST RMF refers to assessment, the framework is cycling back to the activities related to the assessment performed during Step 1 of the NIST RMF, *Categorization*. It is important to understand that the activities of Step 4, while indirectly related to those performed during the system security categorization, are intended to assess the performance of the control implementation that we discussed in Chapter 5.

Stated differently, during the system security categorization step, one of the tasks defined by the NIST RMF is to perform a risk analysis, which involves identifying the most probable threats to an organization and analyzing the related vulnerabilities of the organization to these threats. You may argue that the analysis of vulnerabilities to the organization is the equivalent of the assessment of the security controls; however, NIST more formally defined the activities of Step 4 of the NIST RMF as "The assessment methods and procedures are used to determine if the security controls are implemented correctly, operating as intended, and producing the desired outcome with respect to meeting the security requirements of the organization" (NIST, 2014).

Step 4 of the NIST RMF is *Assess Security Controls* and the intention of the activities of this step is such that once the security controls are implemented, they should be assessed to ensure that the organization is achieving the desired level of effectiveness. More specifically, security control assessment is a process put into place by the organization to review the management, technical, and operational security controls that have been implemented into the ICT system and organization's managerial structure. Such an assessment helps the organization to determine whether the controls were put into place correctly, are operating as intended, and are producing the desired outcomes as defined by the security requirements. Such an assessment goes well beyond the degree from which verification and validation activities were performed during the implementation step.

The NIST RMF identifies four tasks associated with assessment as shown in Figure 6.1.

To appropriately perform those tasks, NIST SP 800-53A Revision 4, *Assessing Security and Privacy Controls in Federal Information Systems and Organizations: Building Effective Assessment Plans* provides a set of common assessment procedures that organizations can use to evaluate the effectiveness of the security controls they have implemented. Further, the guideline provides guidance for building effective security assessment plans and managing assessment results. To support the effective assessment of technical controls, NIST has provided the guideline NIST SP 800-115, *Technical Guide to Information Security Testing and Assessment*, which presents the review, technical testing, and examination techniques which organizations can use to perform assessments.

It should be noted, up front, that there is a variation in terms of how NIST has defined the tasks in NIST SP 800-37 Revision 1, *Guide for Applying the Risk Management Framework* (NIST, 2010), and how they are subsequently defined in NIST SP 800-53A and supported by NIST SP 800-115. Nevertheless, what gets accomplished

Task	Supplemental guidance
Develop, review, and approve a plan to assess the security controls	The security assessment plan provides the objectives for the security control assessment, a detailed roadmap of how to conduct such an assessment, and assessment procedures. The assessment plan reflects the type of assessment the organization is conducting (e.g., developmental testing and evaluation, independent verification and validation, assessments supporting security authorizations or reauthorizations, audits, continuous monitoring, assessments subsequent to remediation actions). The security assessment plan is reviewed and approved by appropriate organizational officials to ensure that the plan is consistent with the security objectives of the organization, employs state-of-the practice tools, techniques, procedures, and automation to support the concept of continuous monitoring and near-real-time-risk management, and is cost-effective with regard to the resources allocated for the assessment.
Assess the security controls in accordance with the assessment procedures defined in the security assessment plan	Security control assessments determine the extent to which the controls are implemented correctly, operating as intended, and producing the desired outcome with respect to meeting the security requirements for the information system. Security control assessments occur as early as practicable in the system development life cycle, preferably during the development phase of the information system. These types of assessments are referred to as developmental testing and evaluation and are intended to validate that the required security controls are implemented correctly and consistent with the established information security architecture.
Prepare the security assessment report documenting the issues, findings, and recommendations from the security control assessment	The results of the security control assessment, including recommendations for correcting any weaknesses or deficiencies in the controls, are documented in the security assessment report. The security assessment report is one of three key documents in the security authorization package developed for authorizing officials. The assessment report includes information from the assessor necessary to determine the effectiveness of the security controls employed within or inherited by the information system based upon the assessor's findings.
Conduct initial remediation actions on security controls based on the findings and recommendations of the security assessment report and reassess remediated control(s), as appropriate	Organizations review assessor findings and determine the severity or seriousness of the findings (i.e., the potential adverse impact on organizational operations and assets, individuals, other organizations, or the Nation) and whether the findings are sufficiently significant to be worthy of further investigation or remediation. An updated assessment of risk (either formal or informal) based on the results of the findings produced during the security control assessment and any inputs from the risk executive (function) helps to determine the initial remediation actions and the prioritization of such actions.

Figure 6.1 **The National Institute of Standards and Technology (NIST) Risk Management Framework control assessment tasks. (From NIST, NIST SP 800-37, Revision 1, *Guide for Applying the Risk Management Framework to Federal Information Systems*, National Institute for Standards and Technology, Gaithersburg, 2010.)**

through the assessment process, according to all of these guidelines, does not change. NIST SP 800-37 simply defines the process in four distinct tasks, while NIST SP 800-53A uses four tasks that differ slightly from the other guideline and provide key inputs to each task, activities, and expected outcomes. In this chapter, we discuss the necessary tasks for assessing all three control categories as shown in Figure 6.2. We do so by using the 800-53A and 800-115 as a basis for our discussion.

6.1 Understanding Security Control Assessment

It may be wise to begin by defining some of the terminology we have already used in the introductory paragraphs of this chapter. On the basis of the National Institute of Standards and Technology Interagency or Internal Report (NISTIR 7298 Revision 2), *Glossary of Information Security Terms*, security control assessment is defined as "The testing and/or evaluation of the management, operational, and technical security controls in an information system to determine the extent to which the controls

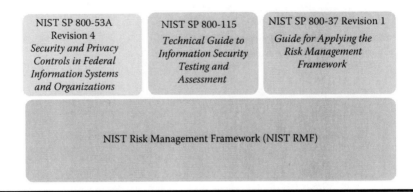

Figure 6.2 Resources for understanding security control assessment.

are implemented correctly, operating as intended, and producing the desired outcome with respect to meeting the security requirements for the system." Or, "The testing and/or evaluation of the management, operational, and technical security controls to determine the extent to which the controls are implemented correctly, operating as intended, and producing the desired outcome with respect to meeting the security requirements for the system and/or enterprise" (NISTIR, 2013).

The security control assessment process aims to gather and evaluate security control information and evidence produced by the ICT risk management program, common control providers, and individuals responsible for developing and deploying the ICT system. The security assessment process and the security control assessors/auditors who execute it typically have no prior responsibility in the development or enhancement of any of the security controls. The underlying basis on which assessment works is to consider what has already been implemented or accomplished and produce a series of conclusions as to whether the security controls implemented for the system satisfy the intended objectives. The entire process relies upon documentation and other critical artifacts developed during prior steps of the risk management process. Accordingly, it produces a separate set of documentation recording the assessment results, identifying any findings differing from expectations defined at the outset of the process, and makes recommendations for corrective actions to address any weaknesses or deficiencies found in the security posture of the ICT system.

The security control assessment, and the security assessment report that gets produced during the assessment process, provide vital information that can be used by management to make system-level decisions, but assessments support many other security, risk, and information resources management processes executed at a much higher level of abstraction than the processes associated with control formulation and development. Some of the information produced through the control assessment process can be used by an organization for the following:

■ Identify problems that may have occurred in the organization's implementation of the RMF

- Identify the security or privacy issues in the ICT system and its operating environment
- Prioritize risk mitigation decisions and activities
- Verify and validate that the identified security or privacy issues in the ICT system operating environment are adequately corrected
- Implement mechanisms for support monitoring, and information security and privacy awareness
- Make security authorization, privacy authorization, and ongoing authorization decisions
- Make data-driven budgetary decisions directly impacting the capital investment process

With regard to its role within the security control risk management process, it is important to note that the security control assessment is both the main focus under discussion in this step of the RMF and a key function in the continuous monitoring and other operational security management activities. Depending upon individual organization security objectives, security assessments can be performed at a variety of places within the system development life cycle (SDLC), where control developers and implementers can work collaboratively on specific assessment procedures to support activities in the SDLC development and implementation phases, such as design and code reviews, vulnerability scanning, functional validation, unit integration, and regression testing.

Since one of the primary objectives of the security control assessment is the identification of weaknesses or deficiencies in implementation, organizations and their common control providers also conduct security control assessments during the operations and maintenance phase of the SDLC to confirm the proper function and configuration of controls allocated to each ICT system. In the federal agencies, periodic control assessments of operational systems help satisfy requirements specified in the Federal Information Security Management Act (FISMA) and provide compliance with agency and system-specific continuous monitoring strategies developed later in the control formulation and development process. It is not uncommon for organizations to also conduct security assessments during the disposal phase of the SDLC to help ensure that sensitive information or other assets are removed from the information system and its storage media prior to disposal.

Throughout this book, we have iterated that security controls are the defense mechanisms and countermeasures specified for an ICT system and its entire supply chain that are implemented to protect the confidentiality, integrity, and availability of their information. Another appropriate interpretation is that system, security, and privacy controls are assessed to provide the information used in measuring overall effectiveness. Stated differently, it is the degree to which controls have been implemented correctly, are operating as expected, and meet the security and privacy requirements for the system and the organization.

6.2 Components of Security Control Assessment

Generally, organizations utilize security control assessment guidelines as a means for facilitating the activities of this process. For example, the federal agencies are required to use NIST SP 800-53A Revision 4, *Assessing Security and Privacy Controls in Federal Information Systems and Organizations: Building Effective Assessment Plans.* The private sector industries are also beginning to see the value of this publication and are beginning to implement regulations for its use. As you see in Section 6.6, NIST SP 800-53A provides detailed assessment procedures presented in a standard format. Each assessment procedure includes one or more assessment objectives that state specifically what the assessment team is trying to determine in order to evaluate the effectiveness of each control. Every assessment objective is further associated with the assessment methods and assessment objects that define how the assessment team should evaluate the control and what the focus of evaluations using each method should be. NIST SP 800-53A has identified the following three assessment methods that can be used individually or more commonly in combination (Figure 6.3):

■ The *examine method* uses review, inspection, observation, studying, or analyzing assessment specifications and activities.
■ The *interview method* uses discussions among individuals or groups within an organization to give the assessor greater understanding, obtain clarification

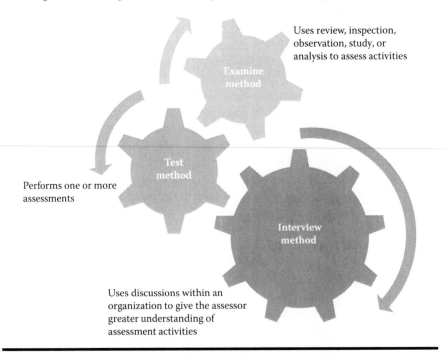

Figure 6.3   **Three assessment methods for security control evaluation.**

on observations that may have been performed, or gather evidence of implemented security controls.

- ▪ The *test method* performs one or more assessments.

The assessment team normally works closely with the organizational management, internal audit team, and other members of the security team during the security control assessment planning process to choose the appropriate methods and objects for each control and to determine the applicable scope of each assessment method. The degree to which each method is applied can vary from basic or focused, to comprehensive, resulting in a set of requirements for performing examination, interviewing, and testing with a scope and level of detail consistent with the minimum assurance requirements for the system. The guidelines that the organization uses to plan and perform the control and assessment process should describe expectations for each level defined for the examinations, interviews, and tests performed. Security control assessment teams and security teams use this guidance to plan the level of effort and amount and nature of evidence needed to perform the assessment of each control and to determine the level of detail needed for assessing the information documented during the assessment process within the security assessment reports.

While the NIST SP 800 series of guidelines is quickly becoming the de facto standard for security control formulation, in addition to all other security-related policies and procedures within the public and private sectors, organizations have considerable flexibility to adapt security control assessment procedures to suit their ICT systems and the environments in which those systems operate. Much as the security control selection process allows organizations to tailor minimum security baselines to reflect the requirements of each system, security personnel and security control assessment teams can tailor the recommended assessment procedures in SP 800-53A or use industry-specific guidelines. In either case, the degree to which assessment protocols are presented is analogous to test plans within the system or software development life cycles. The motivation for developing such a guide is to have predefined examination methods, interview topics, and test cases established in order to streamline the assessment process and to provide a presence of process repeatability.

The assessment cases defined in the NIST guidelines, or developed proprietarily, explain specific steps that the assessment team should follow to gather evidence and evaluate controls and control enhancements using each of the relevant assessment methods. Assessment cases are developed from a government or industry-wide perspective, so for organizations following procedures prescribed in industry guides, assessment cases may still need to be adjusted for organizational or system-specific requirements where available assessment cases must align well with the organization and system-level needs, so their use can reduce the time and level of effort required to develop security assessment plans.

6.3 Control Assessment and the SDLC

As we highlighted at the outset of this chapter, there is no specific point within the system or the software development life cycle (SDLC) in which security assessment activities are performed. Rather, to be proactive and assure proper security measures are in place and functional, the activities should be performed within multiple steps of the life cycle. It is important to remember that the activities and tasks of the risk management process and those of the SDLC work hand-in-hand. As such, the security control assessment tasks can and should be performed at various phases within the SDLC as a way of promoting confidence within the organization and supply chain that the system-specific or common security controls implemented within the ICT system provide the level of effectiveness necessary to defend and counter against the security attack. Some of the benefits of integrating security assessments into the SDLC include:

- Early identification and mitigation of security vulnerabilities, thus reducing the cost of implementing security controls
- Proactive action taken to reduce engineering challenges caused by mandatory security controls
- Awareness of the availability of shared security services and ability to reuse security strategies and tools, thus reducing development costs
- Capability of informed and timely decision-making through the capacities present of a risk management process
- Streamlined documentation of the security decisions that directly affect the development process and the security considerations made during those processes
- Greater flexibility in capabilities provided by systems interoperability and integration

You will find that often security control assessments are conducted by system developers during the development/acquisition and implementation phases of the life cycle. For those organizations that have implemented defined system life cycle process standards like ISO12207:2008 would have also included assessment activities within the tasks prescribed within the *technical processes* of that standard.

The major benefit of assessing controls within system development and implementation phases is that the organization can be assured that the required controls for the system are properly designed, developed, and correctly implemented while also providing evidence of consistency with the organization's ICT security architecture before the system moves into operations and maintenance phase. The main objective is to identify any security risks that may exist through nonexistent deficient controls as early as possible within the SDLC to proactively employ remediation activities in a quick and cost-effective manner.

To assure continuous security control effectiveness, security assessments are also conducted during the operations and maintenance phases of the life cycle. That gives the organization assurance that security and privacy controls continue to be effective in the operational environment and can protect against an assortment of constantly evolving threats. It is not uncommon for unplanned modifications to occur during the period in which the system is being moved into production (sometimes referred to as "going live"). In those circumstances, an assessment is typically needed in the form of a modified test of security controls, thus providing the confidence that the integrity of security controls remain intact. It is through the performance of security control assessment during operations and maintenance that this part of the risk management process becomes cyclical in nature.

The vital point to remember about this discussion is that the organization must continuously assess all implement security controls on an ongoing basis in accordance with its information security continuous monitoring plan. The frequency in which the assessments are performed is determined by the organization and supply-chain providers, and is typically documented within the organization's risk management plan.

Likewise, the disposal/retirement phase of the life cycle is the final point at which security assessment activities could and do take place. Assessments at this phase are necessary to ensure that important organizational information is deleted from the ICT system prior to disposal.

6.4 Ensuring Adequate Control Implementation

Organizations often struggle with rationalizing the expense of performing control assessment as a factor of its value to the organization's security posture. After careful consideration, it generally becomes obvious that through the assessment processes, a case is being made that the necessary security controls are implemented to the extent that priorities established in the organization's security plan are effectively achieved. To build a compelling case, the organization must do the following:

■ Compile evidence from pertinent activities within the SDLC that the controls prescribed for the ICT system are implemented correctly, operating as intended, and producing the desired outcome with respect to meeting the security and privacy requirements of the system and the organization.
■ Present the resulting evidence in a way that allows decision-makers to use it effectively in making the risk-based decisions about the operation or use of the system.

The evidence that is generated by performing assessment activities comes from the verification that the appropriate system-specific and common controls have been implemented in the appropriate ICT system components throughout the supply chain and associated management structures. As the assessment activities progress, the assessor should be building upon the existing security and SDLC specifications that have been previously established by the management and ICT requirements, designs, development criteria, and implementation details that meet the needs of the organization's security assurance plan.

Over the past decade, organizations are increasingly becoming "data-driven." In doing so, no decisions are made without the appropriate justifications provided through data collected both internally and/or externally. Considering the impact that security has on the success of an organization through the security assessment processes, assessors obtain the required evidence to allow the appropriate management staff to make objective proactive and reactive decisions about the effectiveness of the security controls and the overall security posture of the ICT system. Moreover, the collected evidence becomes an invaluable asset to the organization during the ICT security audit processes.

The assessment evidence needed to make such decisions can be obtained from a variety of sources such as the availability of the ICT component and system assessments. These ICT component assessments are often performed by third-party assessment organizations and are intended to examine the security functions of the system components in an effort to establish a set of appropriate configuration settings. Often, assessments are performed as a means of compliance to established regulations, identified security requirements, and ICT security standards and guidelines such as FISMA, the NIST 800 series, and the Payment Card Industry (PCI) certifications.

Conversely, the system assessments provide a larger scope of evidence of effectiveness. These assessments are typically performed by assigned members of the system development team and often work collaboratively with the user representatives from the functional units of that system, common control providers, assessors assigned to that system, and system auditors. When the system assessments are performed, the assessment team works together to collect as much documentation as possible about the ICT system including specifications, security plans, risk management plans, and other such information collected from organizational knowledge bases. Additionally, the results from individual component product assessments are useful in conducting system-level assessments using the predetermined assessment methods, some of which we discuss in Section 6.6. The vital goal of the system assessments is to collect and assess the evidence necessary for the management to determine the effectiveness of security controls deployed in the ICT system and throughout the organization in terms of their likelihood of mitigating risk. Important to note is that when we speak of evaluating security controls, all three implementation control types (management, technical, and operational) must be considered.

6.5 Assessment Plan Development, Review, and Approval

In many ICT management books (if not all), the statement is made that successful completion of ICT projects requires the cooperation and collaboration of all the parties having a vested interest in the scope of that project. This includes ICT professionals, system users, senior executives, business partners, and so on. Establishing an appropriate set of expectations before, during, and after the project is important to achieving an acceptable outcome. The preparation for security control assessment is no different. Organizations should develop an information security assessment policy that adequately provides the necessary direction and guidance for security assessments on their systems. Such a policy should identify the necessary security assessment requirements, and ensure that individuals responsible for ensuring that the assessments conform to defined requirements are held accountable. The policy should also include:

- Defined organizational requirements that affect the compliance of assessments
- Defined roles and responsibilities of the individuals approving and executing the assessments
- Strategies for adherence to established methodology
- Established assessment frequency requirements
- A list of documentation requirements (such as assessment plans and assessment results) and a procedure for storage and retrieval

The underlying planning process comprises activities associated with preparing for assessments and developing the security assessment plans. Security control assessors develop security assessment plans for each ICT system; however, care must be taken to complete the necessary organization-level preparation activities in addition to system-specific preparations. In combination with the criteria provided in guidelines such as NIST SP 800-53A, many organizations find it useful to develop their own assessment procedures specifically tailored to their organizational requirements, operating environments, and risk tolerance levels while making these procedures available for use in ICT systems. Moreover, organizations may choose to develop templates for recording control assessment results and producing the security assessment reports as part of their ICT security program. Still other organizations deploy automated assessment tools or other mechanisms to facilitate persistent assessment activity across the organization and throughout the supply chain.

In much the same way as other ICT projects, the security control assessment process begins with information gathering, the identification of assessors and necessary resources (external and internal), and other activities to confirm that the system, its operating environment, and its resources are ready for the assessment.

NIST identifies the following assessment preparation criteria that must be considered prior to any planning taking place:

- Appropriate policies covering security and privacy control assessments must be established and understood by organizational personnel affected by the assessment.
- The objective and scope of assessments must be created.
- Appropriate development and implementation organizational entities must have been assigned security and privacy controls that were identified as common or the common portion of hybrid controls.
- Pertinent management staff must be made aware of the assessments and appropriate resources allocated.
- Communication channels among management staff must be established.
- Project planning in the form of timeframes and key milestone decision points must be completed.
- A competent assessor/assessment team must be identified.
- Document artifacts that will be useful to the assessment team must be collected and readily available.
- A mechanism must be established between the organization and the assessment team that aims to minimize ambiguity or confusion about the implementation of security or privacy controls and assist in the security/privacy control weaknesses or deficiencies identified during the assessments.
- An understanding of the assessed ICT system's role in support of the organization's mission and business processes.
- A thorough understanding of the structure of the ICT system and the security or privacy controls being assessed.
- The organizational units responsible for the development and implementation of the common controls (or the common portion of hybrid controls) must be identified.
- Management at all levels of the organization must have a common understanding of the assessment objectives and the proposed rigor and scope of the assessment.
- Points of contact throughout the organization needed to carry out the assessment must be established.
- If an assessment has been performed on the ICT system previously, pertinent results must be obtained to assist in the productivity of the current assessment.
- A security assessment plan must be developed, disseminated, and understood.

As may be expected, the amount of effort necessary to properly prepare for a security control assessment is contingent upon the scope of the assessment. In this context, the assessment scope is measured by the number and types of security controls to be assessed, the assessment procedures to be performed, and the extent to which evidence is needed to support the objectives of the methods of those procedures. NIST recommends that the following three factors be considered in the selection of procedures:

- The system security categorization
- The set of security controls selected for the system that fall within the scope of the assessment
- The level of assurance the organization needs to satisfy to determine the effectiveness of implemented security controls

The first task in planning and preparing for assessment is to identify the controls that are to be assessed. As mentioned in Section 6.2, NIST SP 800-53A contains assessment procedures for every control and control enhancement in the security control catalog of NIST SP 800-53. While that may give some organizations an incentive to use NIST's control catalog, it is not uncommon for organizations to adapt proprietary or industry-based assessment procedures to achieve the intended assessment objectives. However, regardless of the means by which assessment methods are chosen, the selection of those procedures must take into consideration criteria such as the impact level of the system and assurance requirements that must be satisfied.

Once the organization has effectively established the scope of the assessment, other factors can be considered. At this point, a timeline for activities performed throughout the assessment can be established. Additionally, the organization can make the necessary decisions regarding the allocation of sufficient resources to the assessment, including the decision about how many assessors should be assigned to the project. When multiple assessors are assigned, it is important that each assessor have sufficient expertise to evaluate their assigned controls and that all assessors have a common understanding of what constitutes a *satisfied* finding.

The security control assessment plan is intended to provide the necessary details about the controls being assessed. The plan should define the scope of the assessment (determined in the previous task), in particular indicating if the intention is to perform a complete or partial assessment. Additionally, it should specify if it provides assessment planning criteria for a new or significantly changed system or criteria for ongoing assessments of operational systems. The plan must also describe the procedures (including the selection of assessment methods and objects and assigned depth and coverage attributes) to be used for each control, whether that be from NIST SP 800-53A or another source tailored as necessary to satisfy organizational or system-specific security requirements. Finally, the assessment plan should include sufficient detail to clearly indicate the schedule for completing the project, the individual or individuals responsible (assessor or assessment team), and the assessment procedures planned for assessing each control. It is important that the information contained within the plan be clear and concise since organizations rely on the information within the plan to allocate appropriate resources to the assessment process.

Regardless of the circumstances surrounding the need for creating the assessment plan, in order for an organization to develop a complete and comprehensive NIST compliant document, the following steps, shown in Figure 6.4, should be completed in order (NIST, 2014):

1. *Step 1*—Determine the set of security controls and control enhancements to be included in the scope of the assessment.
2. *Step 2*—Select the appropriate assessment procedures to be used based on the set of controls and control enhancements within the scope and on organizational factors such as minimum assurance levels.
3. *Step 3*—Tailor the assessment methods and objects to organization or system-specific requirements and assign depth and coverage attribute values to each selected method.
4. *Step 4*—Develop additional assessment procedures to address any security requirements or controls implemented that fall outside the scope of the security control catalog in NIST SP 800-53.
5. *Step 5*—Document the resource requirements and anticipated time to complete the assessment, considering opportunities to sequence or consolidate procedures to reduce duplication of efforts.
6. *Step 6*—Finalize the assessment plan and obtain the necessary approvals to execute the security control assessment according to the plan.

As in the case of all ICT projects, there are legal implications that must be considered before the organization begins implementing the assessment plan. In the event that an organization obtains an external assessment organization to conduct an assessment, the legal departments of each organization may be involved. Each department may play a role in reviewing the assessment plan and providing specific clauses into the contracts that dictate what can and cannot be done, as it relates

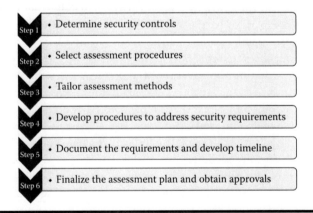

Step 1 • Determine security controls

Step 2 • Select assessment procedures

Step 3 • Tailor assessment methods

Step 4 • Develop procedures to address security requirements

Step 5 • Document the requirements and develop timeline

Step 6 • Finalize the assessment plan and obtain approvals

Figure 6.4 Steps to develop a security assessment plan.

to the security assessments being performed. Confidentiality of information is also a concern. The legal department may require external assessment organizations to sign nondisclosure agreements that prohibit assessors from disclosing any sensitive, proprietary, or restricted information to unapproved parties. Within the agreement, privacy issues should also be addressed. The legal department should be aware of any privacy concerns that the organization may have and address potential privacy violations before the assessment begins. Finally, captured data may include sensitive attributes that do not belong to the organization, or personal employee data which may create privacy concerns. The legal department has the responsibility to determine data handling requirements to ensure that data confidentiality is intact.

6.6 Security Control Assessment Procedures and Methodologies

While there are many methodologies in existence aimed at performing assessment on security controls, the recommendation set forth by the NIST RMF is that organizations utilize the most effective approach for the set of security controls they have implemented and the security priorities the organization has established. NIST defines an assessment procedure as "a set of assessment objectives, each with an associated set of potential assessment methods and assessment objects" (NIST, 2014). Many ICT professionals associate assessment procedures as being analogous to a test plan developed within the traditional SDLC. Test plans provide predefined statements and scenarios (also called test cases) that are evaluated to test the validation and verification criteria of an ICT system or software component. Each test case is further specified to the level of detail describing the approach to be taken in order to generate adequate test results and document evidence. In much the same way, NIST defines assessment objectives as a set of predefined statements related to the particular security control under assessment. When performing quality assurance (QA) activities associated with the ICT systems or software components, the individual who develops the associated test plan ensures that the statements contained within the plan can be effectively traced back to the requirements specification of the system or software. Likewise, the security control assessment objectives must be linked to the content of the security control being assessed to ensure traceability of assessment results back to the prescribed control requirements. The outputs from performing the assessment procedures become the evidence that determines the level of effectiveness provided by the control being assessed. These findings in turn should be documented in an effort to provide the management the knowledge it needs for making decisions that impact the underlying security posture of the organization.

Assessment methods define *how* the assessment objects are evaluated. Although numerous methodologies exist and organizations are encouraged to identify and employ the approach that meets their own particular needs, NIST SP 800-115 suggests that a phased information security assessment methodology is an optimal approach.

The structure is easy to follow, and provides natural breaking points for staff transition. Such a methodology should contain the following phases at a minimum:

- *Planning*—The planning phase aims to ensure that information needed for assessment execution is collected and made available. Such information includes the assets to be assessed, the threats of interest against the assets, and the security controls to be used to mitigate those threats and develop the assessment approach. A security assessment is an ICT project and should be treated as such. A project management plan that effectively identifies the criteria for managing the scope, time, and cost should be created and communicated.
- *Execution*—During the execution phase, the underlying objective is to identify vulnerabilities and validate them when appropriate. During this phase, activities are performed that are associated with the predetermined assessment method and technique. The intended outcome of this phase is for assessors to have identified system, network, and organizational process vulnerabilities.
- *Postexecution*—The postexecution phase is sometimes referred to as the "analysis phase" because the objective is to analyze identified vulnerabilities as a means for determining the causes of those vulnerabilities, establishing mitigation recommendations, and developing a final report.

Regardless of the varying degree to which the methods are employed, the end result is to achieve the objective defined by each individual control assessment procedure. Figure 6.5 summarizes each method provided by the NIST guidelines and examples of objects associated with them.

The procedures followed for interview-based assessments are fairly straightforward and the only differential from one organization to the next, or one system to the next, are the questions asked during the interviews to meet that particular assessment. Exams and tests and tests require a bit more discussion. Examinations

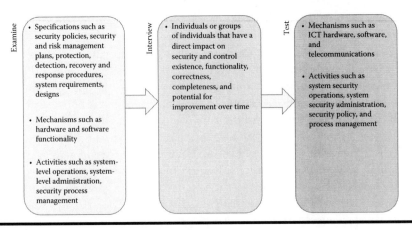

Figure 6.5   NIST security assessment phases.

generally consist of the review of documents (policies, procedures, security plans, security requirements, standard operating procedures, architecture diagrams, engineering documentation, asset inventories, system configurations, rulesets, and system logs) to determine whether there exists proper documentation to support the system or process, and to understand the components of security that are available only through such documentation (i.e., management controls). The assessor is looking for the intended design, installation, configuration, operation, and maintenance of the systems and communication system, as well as performing a review and traceability measures to ensure conformance and consistency.

Testing consists of manual and automated techniques performed directly on the systems and networks as a way of identifying security vulnerabilities. Such tests can be performed on an entire enterprise or on selected systems. An advantage of testing is that it enables organizations to measure levels of compliance to federal, state, and local regulations in addition to established industry benchmarks. Nevertheless, extreme care must be taken while forming assessment tests. While most ICT professionals will agree that they provide the best way to identify an organization's current security posture, they are also more intrusive and can negatively impact systems or networks in the target environment if the tests are not performed accurately and according to plan. The degree to which testing impacts the system or network depends upon the type of test being performed. Any time that a test or tester directly interacts with a system or network, the potential exists for unexpected system or network failures. As part of the security control assessment planning process, organizations must gauge what is acceptable in terms of intrusiveness when deciding which testing techniques to use. Excluding tests known to create denial of service conditions and other disruptions can help reduce these negative impacts. While testing in and of itself does not provide a complete picture of an organization's security posture and testing is less likely than examinations to identify weaknesses or deficiencies in management controls, organizations generally combining testing and examination techniques can provide a more accurate view of security.

We should point out here that each of the security controls defined in NIST SP 800-53 has an associated assessment procedure defined within NIST SP 800-53A, as exemplified in Figure 6.6, thereby eliminating the need for an organization to develop their own procedure for each control. This is not to suggest that an organization should feel obligated to adopt the controls specified within NIST SP 800-53. However, the guideline serves as a basis from which the organization can build its security control framework.

Each of the assessment methods provided by the NIST guidelines have a set of associated attributes that are described from the perspective of depth and coverage. These attributes assist the assessor in determining the amount of effort required in employing that method. The depth aspect of each attribute identifies the level of detail and precision that is required when applying that method. Values for the depth attribute include: *basic, focused,* and *comprehensive.* All three methods provide their own definition of what constitutes each value. The coverage attribute

SC-6	Resource Availability	
Assessment objective *Determine if:*		
SC-6[1]	*The organization defines resources to be allocated to protect the availability of resources*	
SC-6[2]	*The organization defines security safeguards to be employed to protect the availability of resources*	
SC-6[3]	*The information system protects the availability of resources by allocating organization-defined resources by one or more of the following:*	
	SC-6[3][a]	*Priority*
	SC-6[3][b]	*Quota*
	SC-6[3][c]	*Organization-defined safeguards*

Potential assessment methods and objects
Examine: [*SELECT FROM*: System and communications protection policy; procedures addressing prioritization of information system resources; information system design documentation; information system configuration settings and associated documentation; information system audit records; other relevant documents or records].

Interview: [*SELECT FROM*: System/network administrators; organizational personnel with information security responsibilities; system developer].

Test: [*SELECT FROM*: Automated mechanisms supporting and/or implementing resource allocation capability; safeguards employed to protect availability of resources].

Figure 6.6 Sample security assessment procedure definition. (From NIST, Special Publication 800-53A Revision 4, *Assessing Security and Privacy Controls for Federal Information Systems and Organizations: Building Effective Assessment Plans,* **National Institute for Standards and Technology, Gaithersburg, 2014.)**

defines the scope at which each method is employed. The guidelines accomplish this by including the number and type of specifications, mechanisms, and activities to be examined or tested, and the number and types of individuals to be interviewed. In the same way that the levels of depth were identified as basic, focused, and comprehensive, the same values are assigned to each method according to the level of coverage each method provides to the overall assessment process. The organization must make the decision as to the appropriate level of depth and coverage of each method it must employ to adequately verify and validate the security control implemented within the organization and its supply chain. Figure 6.7 provides a summary of each depth and coverage level defined by NIST.

6.7 Assess Controls in Accordance with Assessment Plan

The second task of Step 4 of the NIST RMF stipulates that once the assessment plan has progressed through the appropriate approval process, management oversight must ensure that security control assessment proceeds according to the schedule and approach specified in the plan. One way to look at the activities associated with

Level	Depth	Coverage
Basic	• High-level reviews, observations, or inspections of the assessment objects, discussions with ICT professionals, or tests on the basis of no previous knowledge of internal control implementation details. • Conducted using limited evidence, generalized questions, or functional control specifications. • Results are basic assessments providing a high level of understanding of the security control necessary for determining whether the control is implemented and error free.	Uses a sample set of assessment objects that provide just enough coverage necessary for determining whether the security control is implemented and error free.
Focused	• Greater depth of analysis is performed on each assessment object. • Conducted using a substantial amount of evidence, detailed questions, or high-level design and process descriptions for controls. • Provide a level of understanding for determining whether the control is implemented and error free, and the assurance that the control is implemented correctly and operating according to specification.	Uses a sample set of assessment objects and other pertinent assessment objects considered important to achieving the assessment objective to provide a higher level of coverage necessary for determining whether the security control is implemented and error free and there exists assurance that the control is implemented correctly and operating according to specification.
Comprehensive	• Activities that can range from basic or focused levels to a very detailed depth of analysis of the assessment object. • Conducted using an extensive amount of evidence, in-depth interview questions, or detailed technical control specifications. • Provide a level of understanding of the security control necessary for determining whether the control is implemented and error free, and the assurance that the control is implemented correctly and operating as intended on an ongoing and consistent basis. • There is evidence that supports continuous improvement in the effectiveness of the control.	Uses a large sample set of assessment objects and other pertinent assessment objects considered to be important to achieving the assessment objective to provide the greatest level possible of coverage necessary for determining whether the security control is implemented and error free, and there exists assurance that the control is implemented correctly and operating according to specification, and that there is support for continuous improvement in the effectiveness of the control.

Figure 6.7   NIST assessment depth and coverage level summary.

performing the assessment is to think of it as building an *assurance case*, which is a term built from the work of the Software Engineering Institute (SEI) of Carnegie Mellon University. NIST identifies building an assurance case for security and privacy control effectiveness as a process that involves:

■ Evidence obtained through performing activities of the SDLC justifying that the controls implemented in the ICT system have been done so correctly, are operating as intended, and are producing the desired outcome based on established security and privacy requirements

■ Presenting the evidence in a way that assists decision-makers in making risk-based decisions effectively

Stated more generically, the assessment should adequately verify the implementation of security controls documented in the system security plan by examining the evidence produced through interviewing members of the security implementation team with knowledge of specific aspects of the system, testing the controls based on the criteria specified in the assessment plan to validate that they function as expected, and verifying that evidence shows that the security controls continue to meet documented requirements.

Progression through the assessment process should follow the predetermined procedures specified for each control in the security assessment plan, examining, interviewing, or testing applicable assessment objects and reviewing available evidence in order to make a determination for each assessment objective. The goal of the assessor is to find adequate evidence within each assessment procedure in order to render a result in a finding of *satisfied* or *other than satisfied*.

Assessment objectives for each control are achieved by performing the defined assessment methods on individual assessment objects and then documenting the evidence. A finding of *satisfied* is reached if the evidence associated with each determination statement of the assessment objective is able to conclude that the control meets the assessment objective. A finding of *other than satisfied* indicates that the evidence associated with the determination statement is unable to demonstrate that the control meets the assessment objective.

In most cases, the finding of *other than satisfied* indicates weaknesses or deficiencies in a control's implementation. However, the assessor may provide the same finding in other circumstances. For example, the assessor may not be able to obtain adequate evidence to evaluate the determination statement for a control, in which case a finding of *other than satisfied* would have to be recorded. Each *other-than-satisfied* finding must be documented with details that include what aspects of the security control were considered to be unsatisfactory or were unable to be assessed, and how the control implementation is different from what was planned or expected.

Regardless of the procedure, it is important that security control assessment findings be objective, evidence-based indications of the way the organization has implemented each security control. Since documentation and observation are generally used as a source of evidence for assessed controls, such evidence must be correct, complete, and present a level of quality that provides its own evidence of accuracy. Moreover, the documentation of security control assessment results should be presented at a level of detail appropriate for the type of assessment being performed and include required criteria consistent with organizational policy. One of the benefits of following the NIST guidelines is that they provide recommendations to assessors in terms of what actions to take and what sequence of steps to follow. However, they do not define what constitutes a satisfactory assessment objective implementation.

6.8 Prepare the Security Assessment Report

The third task of the security control assessment step, as defined by the NIST RMF, stipulates that the initial result of the security control assessment process is a draft security assessment report. Included within the report are the assessment findings and indications of the effectiveness determined for each security control implemented for the ICT system. For ease in creating the report and ensuring that it contains the correct content, we recommend the general format provided by NIST in SP 800-53A. NIST suggests that the results of security and privacy control assessment directly impact the way controls are implemented (which would be expected). Moreover, the assessment has an influence on what is contained within the security plans and privacy plans, and other plans of action and milestones that directly impact the security posture of the organization.

Once prepared, the organizational management together with the ICT system users and common control providers review the security assessment reports, privacy assessment reports, and updated risk assessment to determine the next steps required in response to the identified weaknesses and deficiencies. In doing so, NIST recommends that the labels of (S) for *satisfied* and (O) for *other than satisfied* be used as a means for providing visibility into specific weaknesses and deficiencies of security or privacy controls that have been identified within the ICT system or other influential systems within the supply chain. To effectively communicate the conclusions drawn from engaging in the assessment process, the report should, at a minimum, document assessment findings and provide recommendations for correcting control weaknesses, deficiencies, or *other-than-satisfied* determinations made during the assessment. The assessor should document the findings for each implemented control similar to the example shown in Figure 6.8.

Specifically, NIST SP 800-53A stipulates the following content be included within the report:

- The information system name
- The impact level assigned to the system
- Results of previous assessments or other related documentation
- The identifier of each control or control enhancement assessed
- The assessment methods and objects used and level of depth and coverage for each control or enhancement
- A summary of assessment findings
- Assessor comments or recommendations

SC-6	Resource objective	
Assessment objective *Determine if:*		
SC-6[1]	*The organization defines resources to be allocated to protect the availability of resources* **(S)**	
SC-6[2]	*The organization defines security safeguards to be employed to protect the availability of resources* **(S)**	
SC-6[3]	*The information system protects the availability of resources by allocating organization-defined resources by one or more of the following:* **(O)**	
	SC-6[3][a]	*Priority*
	SC-6[3][b]	*Quota*
	SC-6[3][c]	*Organization-defined safeguards*
Comments and recommendations:		
SC-6[3] was marked as other than satisfied because the assessors could not find any evidence, within any ICT specifications or plans that the organization allocates resources based on one of the three defined criteria as indicated in SC-6[3][a],[b], or [c].		

Figure 6.8   Sample assessment finding summary.

We need to emphasize that organizations and associated common control providers rely heavily on the technical knowledge and judgment of the security control assessment team to accurately assess the controls implemented for the ICT systems and provide recommendations as to how corrections can be made to alleviate weaknesses or deficiencies identified during the process. The assessment team normally provides their assessment results in an initial security assessment report to communicate missing evidence or provide corrective actions for the identified control weaknesses or deficiencies before the security assessment report is finalized. Likewise, it is common for the assessment team to reevaluate any security controls added or revised during this process, and it includes the updated assessment findings in the final security assessment report.

6.9 Initial Remedy Actions of Assessment Findings

The finalized security assessment report provides awareness about specific weaknesses and deficiencies in the security controls within an organization or through their control provider that were not resolved during system development. The findings generated during the security control assessment can be thought of as a disciplined and structured approach to mitigating risks according to the priorities set forth by the organization. During this fourth and final task in Step 4 of the NIST RMF, the organization should use the security assessment report to develop a plan to resolve (or remedy) those security control weaknesses and deficiencies discovered through the assessment process. Generally, those inefficiencies are the result of the combination of the organization and common control provider's not properly configuring or inadequately or completely failing to implement a required control. During this part of the assessment process, organization officials and control providers engage in discussions about the report and work collaboratively to make decisions related to "next steps." The collaborative effort may result in a decision that certain findings are frivolous and realistically present no significant risk to the organization. Such controls should be highlighted and a rationale for "no further action required" should be documented in the security plan. On the other hand, the organizational officials and control providers may rationalize that specific findings within the report are substantial enough to require immediate remediation actions. Often, the organization will perform an updated risk assessment based on the results of the security control assessment as a way to determine the initial remedial actions and prioritize those actions. Some security controls which were identified as weak or deficient may be so significant to the vulnerability of the system that remediation is necessary prior to the system moving into production. In all cases, organizations review the security assessment report findings and determine the degree of severity or seriousness of each finding. Ultimately, a decision must be made as to whether the findings are sufficiently significant to be worthy of further investigation or remediation.

Once the findings of the security assessment report are understood, severity determined, and remedies prioritized, the information is used to update the assessment of risk for the system and organization. The traceability of such security control information assists the organization in assigning resources to those items which have the highest degree of impact to the organization, and not to just one system or control family.

For those controls that have identified weaknesses or deficiencies, once corrections are made they must be tested and reassessed, ensuring that all corrective actions are compliant with the organization's *Configuration Management* policy and have gained appropriate approval through the IT governance structure that is in place. As such, actions implemented to mitigate risk are implemented and in turn verified as a means for ensuring that the implementation process was completed accurately. *Verification* is the process in which the organization conducts an audit of the system; the system is retested against predetermined test cases and documentation prepared as a means for holding the individuals performing the verification processes, accountable.

The advantage of a system audit is that it includes details of technical verification of the changes that have been implemented on the system and can be conducted by internal security personnel or an external security test organization. The audit team should use the defined mitigation strategy as a checklist throughout the process as a means of ensuring that each action is completed. Retesting the system helps to validate that the mitigation actions were indeed completed. Nevertheless, the test team will only be able to verify mitigation implementation if a mirror copy of the original test is performed. As technology evolves, it is inevitable that additional vulnerabilities are uncovered during follow-up security tests. Organizations sometimes also elect to use documentation as a means for verifying the implementation of the mitigation strategy through a nontechnical approach.

The process of security control reassessment is intended to determine the extent to which the remediated controls have been implemented correctly, are operating as intended, and are producing the desired outcome based on the defined security requirements for the ICT system. Organizations should approach reassessment with caution since there is a reflexive desire to change the original assessment results. During the reassessment process, assessors must be conscious to update the security assessment report with only the findings from the reassessment. Moreover, the security plan must be updated based on the findings of the security control assessment and any remediation actions taken. The updated security plan should always reflect the actual state of the security controls after the initial assessment and any modifications made by the organization or common control provider in addressing recommendations for remediation resulting from deficiencies in any ICT life cycle or security process. At the completion of the assessment, the security plan contains an accurate list and description of the security controls implemented (including compensating controls) and a list of residual vulnerabilities.

In a postmortem of the remediation process, some organizations and control providers choose to prepare an addendum to the security assessment report in response to the initial findings of the assessors. The addendum normally includes details relevant to the initial remediation actions taken by the organization or common control provider in response to the assessment findings provided in the report, or provides the organization or control providers perspective on the findings. For example, the addendum may include additional explanatory material beyond what may have been made available to the assessor during the original assessment, such as rebuttal comments and justifications related to certain findings, and correcting the record.

We must emphasize that the addendum to the security assessment report does not change any of the findings documented within it, and is not intended to be influential in any manner. Once the original report is written, it is baselined and can only be amended. The details that are provided in the addendum are considered by the authorizing officials in their risk-based authorization decisions.

It is not uncommon for organizations to choose to employ an issue resolution process designed to assist in determining the appropriate actions to take with regard to the security control weaknesses and deficiencies identified during the assessment. The practice of utilizing issue resolution can help address vulnerabilities and associated risk, false positives, and other factors that may provide useful information to the organization regarding the overall state of security of the ICT system including system-specific, hybrid, and common control effectiveness. Likewise, the issue resolution process provides value in providing assistance to ensure that only substantive items are identified and transferred to the plan of actions and milestones.

6.10 Chapter Summary

This chapter introduced the selection of security controls in Step 4 of the NIST RMF. The security control assessment process aims to gather and evaluate security control information and evidence produced by the ICT risk management program, common control providers, and individuals responsible for developing and deploying the ICT system. The security assessment process and the security control assessors who execute it normally have no prior responsibility in the development or enhancement of any security controls. The underlying basis on which assessment works is to consider what has already been implemented or accomplished and produce a series of conclusions as to whether the security controls implemented for the system satisfy intended objectives. The entire process relies on documentation and other critical artifacts developed during the prior steps of the NIST RMF. Accordingly, it produces a separate set of documentation recording the assessment results and identifying any findings differing from the expectations defined at the outset of the process and makes recommendations for corrective actions to address any weaknesses or deficiencies found in the security posture of the ICT system.

The security control assessment plan and the security assessment report that are produced during the assessment process provide vital information that can be used by the management to make system-level decisions, but assessments support many other security, risk, and information resources management processes executed at a much higher level of abstraction than the processes associated with control formulation and development.

With regard to its role within the security control RMF, it's important to note that security control assessment is both the main focus under discussion in this step of the process and a key role player in the continuous monitoring and other operational security management activities in the subsequent step. Depending upon individual organization security objectives, security assessments can be performed at a variety of places within the SDLC, where control developers and implementers can work collaboratively on specific assessment procedures to support activities in the SDLC development and implementation phases, such as design and code reviews, vulnerability scanning, functional validation, and unit, integration, and regression testing.

Since one of the primary objectives of security control assessment is the identification of weaknesses or deficiencies in implementation, organizations and their common control providers also conduct security control assessments during the operations and maintenance phase of the SDLC to confirm the proper function and configuration of controls allocated to each ICT system. For federal agencies, periodic control assessments for operational systems help satisfy requirements specified in FISMA and provide compliance with agency and system-specific continuous monitoring strategies developed later in the control formulation and development process.

It is not uncommon for organizations to also conduct security assessments during the disposal phase of the SDLC to help ensure that sensitive information or other assets are removed from the information system and its storage media prior to disposal.

Generally, organizations utilize security control assessment guidelines as a means for facilitating the activities of this process. For example, federal agencies are required to use NIST SP 800-53A. Private sector industries are also beginning to see the value of the publication and are beginning to implement regulations for its use. NIST SP 800-53A provides detailed assessment procedures presented in a standard format. Each assessment procedure includes one or more assessment objectives that state specifically what the assessment team is trying to determine in order to evaluate the effectiveness of each control. Every assessment objective is further associated with assessment methods and assessment objects that define how the assessment team should evaluate the control and what the focus of evaluations using each method should be. According to the NIST SP 800-53A guideline, assessment methods include examine, interview, and test.

The assessment team normally works closely with organizational management and other members of the security team during the security control assessment planning process to choose the appropriate methods and objects for each control and to determine the applicable scope of each assessment method. The degree to which each method is applied can vary from basic or focused, to comprehensive, resulting in a set of requirements for performing examination, interviewing, and testing with a scope and level of detail consistent with the minimum assurance requirements for the system. The guidelines that the organization uses to plan and perform the control and assessment process should describe expectations for each level defined for the examinations, interviews, and tests performed. Security control assessment teams and security teams use this guidance to plan the level of effort and amount and nature of evidence needed to perform the assessment of each control and to guide the level of detail needed for assessment information documented during the assessment process, within security assessment reports.

The NIST SP 800 series of guidelines is quickly becoming the de facto standard for security control formulation, in addition to all other security-related policies and procedures within the public and private sectors. Organizations have considerable flexibility to adapt security control assessment procedures to suit their ICT systems and the environments in which those systems operate. Much as the security control selection process allows organization to tailor minimum security baselines to reflect the requirements of each system, security personnel and security control assessment teams can tailor the recommended assessment procedures in SP 800-53A or use industry-specific guidelines. In either case, the degree to which assessment protocols are presented is analogous to test plans within the system or software development life cycles. The motivation for developing such a guide is to have predefined examination methods, interview topics, and test cases established in order to streamline the assessment process and to provide a presence of process repeatability.

The assessment cases defined in the NIST guidelines or developed proprietarily explain specific steps that the assessment team should follow to gather evidence and evaluate controls and control enhancements using each of the relevant assessment methods. Assessment cases are developed from a government or industry-wide perspective, so for organizations following procedures prescribed in industry guides, assessment cases may still need to be adjusted for organizational or system-specific requirements where available the assessment cases must align well with organization and system-level needs. Thus, their use can reduce the time and level of effort required to develop security assessment plans.

Based on the criteria contained within a preapproved security control assessment plan, the process attempts to verify the implementation of security controls documented in the system security plan by examining evidence produced by control implementers, interviewing personnel with knowledge of the system, and testing relevant controls to determine whether they function as expected. The assessment follows defined procedures included for each control in the plan, examining, interviewing, or testing relevant assessment objects and reviewing available evidence to make a determination for each assessment objective. For each determination statement included in selected assessment procedures, the evaluation of evidence by the assessment team results in a conclusion of *satisfied* or *other than satisfied*. The assessment team realizes assessment objectives for each control by performing the prescribed assessment methods on appropriate assessment objects and documenting the evidence used to evaluate each determination statement. The assessment team will render a conclusion of *satisfied* if there is substantive evidence that the control meets the assessment objective. A finding of *other than satisfied* indicates that the evidence found, is insufficient to meet the assessment objective.

It is important to note that, while the discovery of weaknesses or deficiencies in a control's implementation may result in an *other-than-satisfied* conclusion, that same conclusion may be acceptable in other circumstances, such as cases where the assessment team cannot obtain enough information to evaluate the control to the level of detail necessary. Security control assessment findings should be objective, evidence-based, and indicative of the way the organization implements each security control. The assessments must be supported by documentation and observation as sources of evidence for each assessed control and must demonstrate completeness, correctness, and a high level of quality of evidence presented.

To justify each *other-than-satisfied* conclusion, the assessment team documents what aspects of the security control were deemed unsatisfactory or were unable to be assessed and describes how the control, as implemented, differs from what was planned or expected. It is important that the assessment team document the security control assessment results at a level of detail appropriate for the type of assessment being performed consistent with organizational policy and any requirements or expectations specified by the management and senior executives who will review the assessment results.

Upon finalization and review of the security assessment report, the organization begins the final task of the security control assessment step, by implementing initial remedies to the controls which the findings of the report deemed *other than satisfied*. Organizations must coordinate this effort by properly prioritizing the remedy actions. Some organizations may conclude that some of the findings of the report are not consistent with the security goals previously established. In such cases, an addendum can be included with the assessment report that identifies the questionable finding and provides justification for the current state of that control.

Glossary

assessor: in the context of security control assessment, he/she is responsible for leading the activities performed throughout the assessment process

assessment method: one of three types of actions (i.e., examine, interview, test) taken by assessors in obtaining evidence during an assessment

assurance case: a term developed out of the Software Engineering Institute; it is a structured set of details about a system and a body of evidence to support those details by showing that an information system satisfies specific claims with respect to a given quality attribute

quality assurance: the process of checking to see whether a product or service being developed is meeting specified requirements; in the context of security controls, it is the process of checking to see whether the controls are implemented to the extent that they meet predefined requirements

security control assessment: the process of testing and/or evaluation of the management, operational, and technical security controls in an ICT system in order to determine the degree in which the controls are implemented correctly, operating as expected, and producing the desired outcome based on the security requirements of the system

security control assessment plan: a set of predetermined activities and tasks that provide details of how a security control assessment will be performed. Some of the criteria of the plan include assessor identification, timelines for completing the assessment, controls to be assessed, and methods to be used in assessing each control

security control assessment report: provides the specific details of the controls assessed, methods used, and the findings and conclusions made during the assessment process

system auditor: similar to a security assessor to the extent that in the context of security audit, he/she is responsible for leading the activities performed throughout the audit process

target: the ICT system or system component being tested or examined through a security control assessment of security audit process

References

NIST. (2010). NIST SP 800-37, *Guide for Applying the Risk Management Framework to Federal Information Systems.* Gaithersburg, MD: National Institute for Standards and Technology.

NIST. (2014). Special Publication 800-53A Revision 4, *Assessing Security and Privacy Controls for Federal Information Systems and Organizations: Building Effective Assessment Plans* Gaithersburg, MD: National Institute for Standards and Technology.

NISTIR. (2013). National Institute of Standards and Technology Interagency or Internal Report 7298 Revision 2, *Glossary of Key Information Security Terms.* Kissel, R. (Ed.). Gaithersburg, MD: National Institute of Standards and Technology.

Chapter 7

Step 5—Authorize: Preparing the Information System for Use

At the conclusion of this chapter, the reader will understand:

- The concept and usefulness of formal authorizations for security accreditation
- The purpose and business advantage of authorizations to operate (ATO)
- The function of standard controls and frameworks in the authorization process
- The function of a formally organized certification and accreditation (C&A) process
- The need to maintain ongoing organizational risk assessment
- The specific role of audit findings in supporting decision-making

7.1 Authorizing the Formal Risk Response

This chapter describes the fundamental concepts associated with *Authorize Information System,* Step 5 of the National Institute of Standards and Technology (NIST) Risk Management Framework (RMF) (NIST, 2014). The *Authorization* phase includes the documentation of the acceptance of a formally sanctioned, organization-wide, and systematic approach to the risk management needs of a given situation. The aim of this chapter is to present and discuss the standard steps for authorization of well-defined risk management approaches for a modern multifaceted and highly complex organization. This chapter introduces a three-tiered approach to practical risk management. This three-tiered model will be focused at the strategic organizational policy level (Tier One); the business management/business process level (Tier Two); and the day-to-day operational risk management practice (Tier Three).

As shown in Figure 7.1, the actual management of risk is an intricate and multilayered process, which requires top-to-bottom involvement of the entire organization. In that respect, risk management is intended to leverage trust and confidence for any given system across the entire spectrum of the organizational culture. Trust is an important concept in the consideration of good risk management practice. It is the means which an organization adopts to ensure trust will influence its long-term corporate relationships as well as the internal and external aspects of doing business.

There are a variety of risk-related concepts related to trust. These concepts do not operate in a vacuum, rather, there is often a strong interplay among them. For instance, an organization's culture along with its formal governance structures and processes will often influence the level of rigor and the degree of change

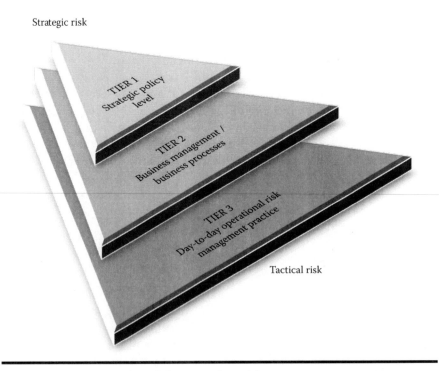

Figure 7.1 Three-tiered model approach to risk management.

possible with respect to its risk management strategy. Thus, every individual who is involved in organizational risk-based decisions needs to have an awareness and appreciation for the underlying concept of trust. For example, the governance process is built around a risk tolerance philosophy, that is, the risk management strategy is meant to underwrite an acceptable level of trust in the correctness of the organization's overall functioning. The need for tangible assurance of correctness and capability ties directly to the authorization/certification process such as a third-party certification of an accredited system demonstrating sufficient due diligence in managing risk to other entities and organizations. In business, this is an important thing to document because potential partners who are risk averse are likely to require some form of documentary evidence that a given organization is trustworthy. And in that regard, third-party certification of the system operation, which is based on a commonly accepted model of proper risk management practice such as the NIST RMF, can serve as a universal basis for establishing trusted business relationships among diverse organizations.

Therefore, for the purposes of our discussion, risk management is understood to be a thorough and systematic process conducted organization-wide. To ensure trust, the process must address all forms of risk ranging from strategic level concerns, all the way down to the day-to-day operational level. The general aim of the risk management process is to ensure that risk-based decision-making is integrated into every aspect of the organization. There are four elements in classic risk management. According to NIST SP 800-39, *Managing Information Security Risk: Organization, Mission, and Information System View*, risk management is a comprehensive process that requires organizations to systematically (NIST, 2011) (Figure 7.2):

1. Frame risk (i.e., establish the context for risk-based decisions)
2. Assess risk
3. Respond to risk once determined
4. Monitor risk on an ongoing basis for continuous organizational improvement

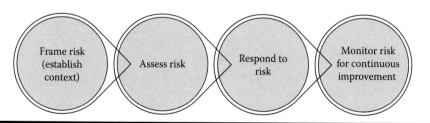

Figure 7.2 Elements of classic risk management.

7.2 Elements of Risk Management

The first component of the risk management process involves making the risk real. The manner in which the organization understands and characterizes the risk establishes the security context, which will serve as the basis for authorization. In essence, the security context comprises the specific environment in which the relevant risk-based decisions will be made. Thus, the outcome of the risk-framing stage is an explicit risk management strategy. The strategy defines how that specific organization will assess any identified risk, respond to the risk, and subsequently monitor the risk within the particular environment of that system.

The aim of this step is to make clear and transparent any and all forms of risk or threat across the organization. The specific understanding will then routinely drive both the organizational investment in mitigating a given set of risks. It will also shape the operational decisions that are made about a risk in a given situation. Consequently, the function of the risk frame is to make the specific form of the risk environment explicit and able to be commonly understood across the organization. The accurate understanding forms the basis for the delineation of the scope of any related risk-based decision making and the long-term management of the risk environment.

Establishing a realistic and credible risk frame requires the organization to lay out all of its underlying assumptions about the current threat environment. The aim is to provide an explicit motivation for addressing any particular risk. This includes all specifically identified harm resulting from threats, vulnerabilities, and their impacts as well as the likelihood of occurrence. Any of these factors will influence how the risk will be assessed, responded to, and monitored over time. To do this properly, any and all constraints on the risk management process have to be identified and factored into the solution. This includes each constraint on the risk assessment process, the risk response, and the ongoing monitoring alternatives.

More importantly, the organizational risk tolerance, or appetite, has to be made clear up front. This includes the levels of risk, types of risk that must be addressed, as well as the acceptable degree of risk uncertainty. The final understanding leads to the assignment of the relative level of importance of each of the effected risks and their related system functions. The prioritization process will normally trigger a rigorous trade-off activity where every different type of risk is examined in the light of how it will be mitigated within defined time and resource constraints. The risk-framing component and the associated risk management strategy that emerges from it also incorporates any strategic level decisions about how general risks to organizational operations and assets, individuals, and other organizations are to be specifically addressed by executive leadership.

The second component of risk management is risk assessment. This component involves the decisions about how the organization will understand the risk within the context of the formally established risk frame. The purpose of risk assessment is to identify all relevant threats to the organization's operations, assets, or even its individuals. All the meaningful vulnerabilities are characterized by the identification, including both internal and external sources of threat. And as part of the vulnerability identification activity, all of the impacts and likelihood of consequent harm have to be assessed and understood. The aim is to understand all priority threats in terms of the way that they might exploit a given vulnerability. The end result of this stage in the process is a risk classification for every threat. This includes the estimated degree of harm and likelihood of occurrence. The classification drives the authorization function in that it provides the point of reference for decision-making about the accuracy of the implementation.

To provide a tangible point of comparison to underwrite the actual proof of system correctness, it is necessary for the organization to adopt and document an unambiguous set of standard methods and tools that will be employed in the risk assessment/management process for that given situation. This transparency requirement includes making clear all of the underlying assumptions, constraints, roles and responsibilities of the risk assessment team. This includes statements regarding how the regular, organization-wide risk assessment process will be carried out, as well as the frequency that regular risk assessments will be performed. It also includes the standard sources and methods for information about risk. In addition, the means for ensuring that the relevant risk information is properly collected, processed, and communicated to the relevant decision-maker also has to be made clear.

The third component of general risk management involves the development of the organizational response to risk. In essence, this phase requires documentation of a standard approach to mitigating risk, once it has been identified. The purpose of the risk response component of the process is to provide a reliable, organization-wide, solution to risks as they appear in that particular organizational environment; the response must fit within the constraints of the previously drawn organizational risk frame. It normally involves the development of alternative scenarios for risk response. Within that process, all alternative courses of action are identified and the appropriate course of action is laid out based on organizational risk tolerance policy. Finally, alternative approaches are devised for responding to risk depending upon the alternate factors that drive a given scenario.

The actual execution of this stage of the process depends on the organization's ability to acceptably choose between the classic types of risk responses that might be implemented for a given situation. The classic options are *acceptance, avoidance, mitigation, sharing,* or *transfer*. It is, at this stage, that organizations identify the tools, techniques, and methodologies that will be used to ensure the ongoing effectiveness of the specific course of action and milestones for responding to a given risk. This includes stating any evaluation criteria for selection as well as the organization-wide communication process.

The establishment of the way in which the organization will monitor risk over time is the final component of standard classic risk management. This is appropriately called the *monitoring stage* and it leads directly to Step 6 of the NIST RMF, *Monitor Security Controls*. The purpose of the risk-monitoring stage is to verify that each of the prearranged risk response measures are in place and properly implemented. This involves a specific determination of the relative value of the risk response measures that have been put in place in the earlier stages of the process. Since change is given in all system operations, it is also necessary to ensure that all novel or previously unidentified risks to the organization are subsequently identified and placed under standard risk management.

To enforce this final aspect of the risk management process, it should be made clear how the current risk-monitoring activities will be evaluated in order to effectively ensure that any requisite compliance requirements are adequately verified and that the ongoing effectiveness of the risk response will be ensured. Moreover, if specific risk mitigation measures have been implemented, it must be possible to judge whether those measures are operating correctly and as intended.

7.3 Certification and Accreditation

Authorization typically involves the concepts and general practices of the formal C&A process. There are an impossibly wide range of approaches to C&A; however, given the fact that this entire book is focused on the NIST RMF, we will quite reasonably center the discussion on the federal government's Federal Information Security Management Act (FISMA) process certification requirements. As a consequence, this will necessitate a detailed discussion of the NIST SP 800-37 Revision 1, *Guide for Applying the Risk Management Framework to Federal Information Systems: A Security Life Cycle Approach*, recommendations for creating and disseminating a FISMA security authorization package, for example, the security plan, security assessment report, and plan of action and milestones. The discussion will also involve a more general exploration of the necessary mechanisms for establishing the exact criteria to be included in the plan as well as how an action plan and milestones can be created to ensure practical direction. The reader will understand how the accreditation plan documents the organization's specific approach and strategy for finding and remediating a particular security weakness or operating deficiency that has been identified through security control assessment.

Finally, in service to the applied development of the RMF process, the second part of this chapter discusses and makes specific recommendations for the implementation of NIST SP 800-39. This will be utilized as a basis for the discussion of risk determination and risk acceptance within the overall C&A process.

As the term is most frequently employed, *Certification and Accreditation* describes a well-defined and systematic procedure for evaluating, describing, testing, and authorizing systems and their associated activities prior to or after a system is put into operation. The C&A process is used across the world and in many settings, not just the US Federal Government. As it is normally applied, *Certification* simply entails a formal process for confirming a given set of characteristics of an object, person, or organization. This confirmation is often, but not always, provided by some form of external review, education, assessment, or audit. An audit typically includes a comprehensive evaluation of a process, system, product, event, or skill typically measured against some existing norm or standard.

Accreditation is a formal and well-defined organizational process for performing certification. Accreditation is the specifically defined approach that is taken to certify competency, authority, or credibility of a given organization, practice, or product within a defined set of criteria. Accreditation is normally provided by a third-party institution. Organizations that issue credentials or certify third parties against official standards are themselves formally accredited by accreditation bodies, which are usually national in nature, such as the German organization DAkkS, *Deutsche Akkreditierungsstelle*, or the UKAS, *United Kingdom Accreditation Service*.

These credentialing bodies are also known as "notified" or "accredited" certifiers. The accreditation process ensures that the testing and audit practices of the certifying body are sufficient to distinguish conformance with a given standard, or regulation, as well as to certify that the audited parties behave ethically and employ appropriate control assurance.

Various professions, economic sectors, and even commercial bodies rely on certification processes to test and evaluate the skills of those organizations or individuals who operate within a given area of defined interest. Nevertheless, there are also formal testing organizations that provide certification services for a fixed set of products within the security space. These laboratories certify that a particular individual product or service meets preestablished performance criteria. And in some special cases, these labs might also certify that a given product or company meets the stipulations of a requisite law or regulation.

Accreditation also provides audited third-party assurance that a specifically targeted undertaking such as a quality system or security system certification process has been executed in such a way that the relevant testing and assurance outcomes meet the relevant norms or standards of given process standard, such as ISO 17024, *Conformity assessment: General requirements for bodies operating certification of persons*. Many nations have established specific oversight bodies to provide the overall level of corroboration. For instance, most European nations maintain official, formal accreditation bodies to provide accreditation services within their borders. Unfortunately, there is no such universally recognized "official" accreditation body within the United States. Instead, over the years, multiple accreditation bodies have been established to address the accreditation needs of specific industries or market segments. Some of these accreditation services are for-profit entities; however, the majority are not-for-profit bodies that provide accreditation services as part of their mission.

The certification process itself is meant to evaluate, test, and audit security control behaviors in order to confirm that those behaviors meet predetermined criteria. Because of the influence of FISMA, this often implies that the behaviors themselves are based on the type and sensitivity of the data which are handled by the information system. The evaluation process compares the current system's security state with specific control stipulations contained in the relevant standard. In federal settings, the standard is NIST SP 800-53 Revision 4, *Security and Privacy Controls for Federal Information Systems and Organizations* (NIST, 2013). The certification process ensures that security weaknesses as defined by this standard are identified and plans for mitigation strategies are in place. In addition to control planning, the accreditation process also provides a means for justifying the acceptance of residual risks that might be associated with the continued operation of a system. In this case, the approval to operate is granted for a specified period of time, until the necessary rework can be done.

7.4 Application of the RMF

It is commonly recognized that risk management is a holistic activity that must be fully integrated into every aspect of the organization in order to be effective. Coordination of the management of risks is both complex and demanding. It is a multifaceted top-down undertaking that involves everybody in the organization from senior policy leaders, all the way through mid-level leaders to the individuals on the shop floor who actually develop, implement, and operate the systems that facilitate the essential mission and pragmatic business processes of the organization. Risks requiring management fall into many categories. The traditional security risks related to the operation and use of information systems are just one of many components of organizational risk. In order for the organization to be truly secure, the organization's decision-makers have to address a wide range of other considerations as part of their ongoing risk management responsibilities. For instance, besides general security risks, there are program management risks, investment risks, budgetary risks, legal liability risks, safety risks, inventory risks, supply chain risks, and technical infrastructure security risks (Figure 7.3).

Thus, decision-makers have to reach unequivocal, well-informed risk-based decisions that balance the benefits and utility of the systems that they oversee against the risk of those same systems causing organizational operation or routine business harm due to persistent attacks, environmental disruptions, or human error. So, to ensure both the necessary and proper risk response, the managers of information system security risk, like risk managers in general, do not practice an exact science. Rather risk management requires an artistic blend of collective decision-making among all of the individuals and groups within organizations who are responsible for strategic planning, oversight, management, and day-to-day operations.

The complex interactions between the organization's business purposes and the information systems that ensure proper fulfillment of those purposes requires an integrated, organization-wide approach to managing risk. The role of generic risk management in mitigating operational risk is also critical to the long-term

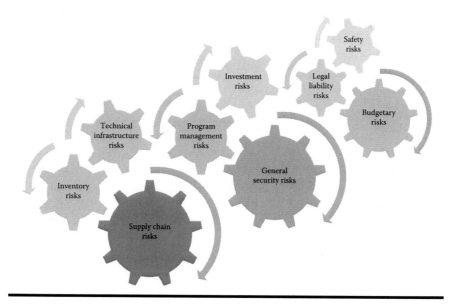

Figure 7.3   Categories of risk management.

strategic aims of the organization. That is because risk management ensures that the organization as a whole is fully protected from all reasonably anticipated threats.

The concept of organization-wide, top-down risk management is somewhat groundbreaking. That is because, in the past, traditional leadership has taken a very narrow view of information security. Senior managers have tended to view information security as being either as a technological problem or stove-piped in a separate category from the other forms of organizational risk, as well as the traditional management and life cycle processes. This extremely limited perspective often resulted in inadequate consideration of how information security risk, like other organizational risks, affects the likelihood of organizations successfully carrying out their missions and business functions (NIST, 2011).

In response to the problem of this sort of limited view of risk, NIST has promulgated a standard common information security framework and implementation model for the federal government and its contractors. This was published in February 2010 as NIST SP 800-37 Revision 1 and in March 2011 as NIST SP 800-39. It was a broadscale effort including input from various sources including the Department of Defense (DoD), the Office of the Director of National Intelligence (ODNI), and the Committee on National Security Systems (CNSS).

The objective of the NIST SP 800-37 and NIST SP 800-39 combination is to (NIST, 2010, 2011):

1. Ensure that senior leaders/executives recognize the importance of managing information security risk and establish appropriate governance structures for managing such risk
2. Ensure that the organization's risk management process is being effectively conducted across the three tiers of organization, mission/business processes, and information systems
3. Foster an organizational climate where information security risk is considered within the context of the design of mission/business processes, the definition of an overarching enterprise architecture, and system development life cycle (SDLC) processes
4. Help individuals with responsibilities for information system implementation or operation better understand how information security risk associated with their systems translates into organization-wide risk that may ultimately affect the mission/business success

The primary thrust of these two documents is to establish the fact that risk management is a basic requirement of successfully doing business. The focus on achieving a top-level, executive commitment is designed to ensure an effective, organization-wide risk management program. It makes identifying, characterizing, and mitigating risk a strategic responsibility of the organization and it leverages the success of business performance across every aspect of the organization. On the basis of these two standards, the effective organization-wide management of risk to information systems requires the following four key factors (NIST, 2011):

1. Assignment of risk management responsibilities to senior leaders/executives
2. Ongoing recognition and understanding by senior leaders/executives of the information security risks to organizational operations and assets arising from the operation and use of information systems
3. Establishing the organizational tolerance for risk and communicating the risk tolerance throughout the organization
4. Accountability by senior leaders/executives for their risk management decisions and for the implementation of effective, organization-wide risk management programs

The aim of the NIST RMF, which these two standards support, was to create an omnibus approach that would specifically incorporate the traditional federal C&A process into a six-step standard model (the NIST RMF). The ultimate outcome of that effort was intended to emphasize the critical need to integrate explicit information security capabilities and controls into federal information systems.

The broad aim of the NIST RMF project was to specify a framework of best-state-of-the-practice management, operational, and technical security controls as a single operational model that would ensure continuous awareness of the security state of information systems on an ongoing basis though enhanced monitoring processes. The monitoring processes would be designed to provide essential information to senior leaders to facilitate decisions about the acceptance of risk to organizational operations and information assets arising from the operation and use of information systems.

The NIST RMF was designed to promote the concept of the ongoing information system authorization requirements of FISMA. The effectiveness of the authorization was meant to be supported by effective continuous monitoring processes. The aim was to integrate standard and approved information security practices into both the architecture of the enterprise, as well as the overall SDLC. This was supported by formal authorization of the correctness of the implementation of a set of standard security controls. Thus, the risk management process described in NIST SP 800-37 alters the traditional static focus of C&A into to a much more dynamic approach that underwrites the capability to manage information system–related security risks in highly diverse environments involving complex and sophisticated cyber threats, ever-increasing system vulnerabilities, and rapidly changing missions (NIST, 2010).

In effect, NIST SP 800-37 was developed to ensure that the general management of information system–related security risks is properly aligned and consistent with the organization's business goals and purposes. Like the ISO 27000 Information Security Management System standards, NIST SP 800-37 is also designed to ensure that strategic policies for overall risk management are established at the top. The aim is to make certain that the necessary policies and procedures are in place to ensure that the practical controls deployed by the organization to mitigate risk are fully and correctly integrated into the operational and life cycle processes of the business.

Because well-informed and effective decision-making serves as the fundamental basis for good security management, it is necessary to maintain a capable level of day-to-day operational management of risk. Nevertheless, given the widespread implications and impact of the FISMA the primary practical purpose of the recommendations in NIST SP 800-37 is to provide a practical means of ensuring that the target organization complies with the requirements established by the Office of Management and Budget (OMB) in Circular A-130. The guidelines in this publication are applicable to all federal information systems other than those systems designated as national security systems as defined in 44 U.S.C. Section 3542 (NIST, 2010).

NIST SP 800-37 specifies a fundamental set of best practices that are designed to productively manage all forms of risk related to information systems and their security. Along with policy level considerations, the NIST SP 800-37 practice set is designed to ensure that risks in the basic SDLC process are properly managed and controlled and that practical and meaningful boundaries for organizational information systems can be drawn. This set of practices is derived from a well-defined set of lessons learned from the profession. The principles suggest the most effective way to integrating risk management principles and best practices into organization-wide strategic planning considerations.

NIST SP 800-37 approaches the management of risk at three distinctly different tiers of the organization. *Tier One* approaches the management of risk from a *strategic* perspective. It centers on the creation of a comprehensive governance structure and organization-wide risk management strategy that includes (NIST, 2010):

1. Techniques and methodologies the organization plans to employ in order to assess information system–related security risks and other types of risk of concern to the organization
2. Methods and procedures the organization plans to use to evaluate the significance of the risks identified during the risk assessment
3. Types and extent of risk mitigation measures the organization plans to employ to address identified risks
4. Level of risk the organization plans to accept (i.e., risk tolerance)
5. How the organization plans to monitor risk on an ongoing basis given the inevitable changes to organizational information systems and their environments of operation
6. The degree and type of oversight the organization plans to use to ensure that the risk management strategy is being effectively carried out

Because it is broad spectrum in focus, the organization-wide risk management strategy is circulated to a wide range of organizational officials and contractors by means of the overall governance structure established by the organization. These recipients generally all have some form of governance, planning, development, acquisition, operational, or oversight responsibilities.

Tier Two addresses risk from a mission and business *process* perspective. Actions at this level are guided by the overall strategic planning and policy-making which is developed in Tier One. Tier Two activities tend to be associated with the process of defining and maintaining the active set of policies and procedures for enterprise operation. They include such activities as the definition and refinement of the organization's core mission and business processes, as well as the ongoing prioritization of those mission and business processes in accordance with the changing goals and objectives of the organization. It is at Tier Two that various types of information are identified and prioritized. This is the information that the organization will use to carry out its stated mission and perform its necessary day-to-day business functions.

The organization-wide information protection strategy is defined at Tier Two, which involves developing and incorporating into the overall operation of the business the high-level practices for assessing, evaluating, mitigating, accepting, and monitoring risk as well as the assignment of a set of accountabilities for performing those duties on a routine basis. NIST SP 800-37 allows subsets of the organization, who might have already developed their own methods for assessing, evaluating, mitigating, accepting, and monitoring risk a greater degree of autonomy in order to minimize costs.

Tier Three addresses risk from an *operational* perspective. Decisions made at this level are always derived from and guided by the risk decisions that have been made at Tiers One and Two. The risk decisions made at Tiers One and Two influence the practical selection and deployment of the operational controls and defense-in-depth countermeasures at the day-to-day operational system level.

For the sake of satisfying NIST SP 800-37's specific purpose, the requirements for practical risk management are fulfilled through the deployment of an appropriate collection of management, operational, and technical security controls derived from NIST Special Publication 800-53 Revision 4. Those pragmatic security controls are then allocated to the various risk management requirements of the particular information system in accordance with the specific information security plan that has been developed by the organization.

7.5 Security Authorizations/Approvals to Operate

Formal authorization of federal systems is required by the E-Government Act of 2002. Specifically, these authorizations are mandated by Title III of that Act: FISMA. In essence, security authorizations represent the official sanction that must be obtained to operate a federal information system under FISMA.

Because of their importance, these authorizations are always granted by a senior organizational official. The authorization permits the organization to operate the given information system; it categorically accepts the risk of system operation to organizational functioning. This acceptance is based on audited evidence of the proper operation of an agreed-upon set of security controls (NIST, 2011). The organizational official granting the approval to operate explicitly accepts security responsibility for the operation of the system under evaluation and officially declares the ATO.

The security authorization process involves comprehensive testing and evaluation of all of the designated security controls within an information system. It attests to the correctness of specific software and hardware security controls. In addition, it also authorizes the correctness of the procedural, physical, and personnel security measures that provide the system context. It also considers the procedural, physical, and personnel security measures employed to enforce information security policy. Finally, it establishes the extent to which the implementation of a particular design, or architecture, configuration meets a specified set of life cycle security requirements.

Every system that falls under the purview of FISMA must have an *Authority to Operate* granted before it becomes operational. *Operational* is generally defined as whenever an information system begins processing real or live data (NIST, 2011). To ensure consistency, the system must be reauthorized at least every 3 years under

FISMA. In addition, if significant changes are made that might affect the potential risk level of system operation, it is necessary to reauthorize it.

The assessment results and the authorization decision are all captured in an *Accreditation Decision Letter* that is typically issued prior to system launch. An approval to operate may be granted in the form of an *Interim Authorization to Operate* (IATO). This latter decision applies to any system that is undergoing development testing or is in a prototype phase of development. IATOs are typically granted in the instance of a nonoperational development information system testing with production data; however, they are not authorized for operational systems. By law, the applicable authorizing official may grant an IATO for a maximum period of 6 months and may grant a single 6-month extension.

In general, the process for conducting a reauthorization is the same, which is used to conduct the initial security authorization. The primary difference is that an initial security authorization is typically begun early in the *System Engineering Life Cycle*, while the process of reauthorization of a system will usually start 4–6 months before the current ATO expires. The 4–6-month timeframe assumes that resources are available to begin the security authorization process. Additional lead time might be needed to obtain the resources that will be required to conduct the security authorization.

The interest from the standpoint of this book is that the security authorization process is the current end result of the implementation of the NIST RMF. The NIST RMF process satisfies all of the requirements for official certification of correctness. This process involves conducting the requisite authorization activities of security categorization, security control selection and implementation, security control assessment, information system authorization, and security control monitoring.

7.6 Certification of the Correctness of Security Controls

Within the federal government, all unclassified systems including general support systems and major governmental applications fall under FISMA. Therefore, they must be assessed and authorized in accordance with a well-defined and commonly accepted process sanctioned by the government. Accordingly, at its core the authorization process accredits the effectiveness of a categorical set of controls that have been put in place to manage risks to a given system based on a set of government criteria established in NIST SP 800-53 Revision 4.

NIST DP 800-37 defines three types of controls that might be potentially certified as effective. Those are the *system-specific controls*, which are the controls that ensure a given security capability for a single, particular information system. Then there are the *common controls*. Common controls ensure a security capability for a number of related systems. Finally, there are the *hybrid controls*. Those controls have both system-specific and common characteristics.

The security controls are typically traceable to the strategic security requirements of the organization. Their purpose is to ensure that those requirements are fully addressed during design, development, and operation of the information system. Risk management tasks begin early in the SDLC and are important in shaping the security capabilities of the information system. Moreover, by regulation each risk management requirement must be satisfied prior to placing the information system into operation or continuing its operation.

It has to be demonstrated by means of clear evidence that all identified information system security–related risks have been correctly and certifiably addressed on an ongoing basis and that the authorizing official explicitly understands and accepts the risk for a defined set of security controls and the current security state of the information system. The NIST RMF provides a disciplined and structured process that integrates information security and risk management activities into the SDLC. The NIST RMF operates primarily at Tier Three in the risk management hierarchy but can also have interactions at Tiers One and Two.

The organization designs and deploys the risk management mechanisms that are appropriate to the purposes and intents of the organization's enterprise architecture. Thus, the design and deployment of the specific control set is strategic, in that it is carried out as an organization-wide management activity. This activity involves the appropriate authorizing agents including such roles as information system owners, chief information security officer, senior information security officer, enterprise architect, information security architect, information system security officer, common control providers, and risk executives (NIST, 2010).

The enterprise can exercise substantial discretion in deciding which families of security controls or specific controls from selected families might be employed. For government authorizations, those controls are specified in NIST SP 800-53 Revision 4. The process includes a set of well-defined risk-related tasks that are to be carried out by selected individuals or groups within well-defined organizational roles. Those roles include (NIST, 2010):

- Risk executive
- Authorizing official
- Authorizing official designated representative
- Chief information officer
- Senior information security officer
- Enterprise architect
- Information security architect
- Information owner/steward
- Information system owner
- Common control provider
- Information system security officer
- Security control assessor

7.7 Risk Management and Enterprise Architecture

This chapter is focused on the formal process for certifying the correctness of a set of well-defined risk management controls for federal information systems. The actual control structure is created by means of a formal design activity. So, risk management is substantively enabled through the design and implementation of an organization-wide enterprise architectural process. This process designs and implements the tangible proof that the various strategies the organization has adopted to facilitate its day-to-day operation are in place and functioning properly. Because the architectural design process is essentially executed top-down, the initial definition of risk management requirements takes place at two conceptual level tiers (Policy Tier One and Procedure Tier Two). This strategic definition then leads to the selection of tangible risk/security controls at the Tier Three operational level.

A top-down conceptual approach to coherent design is capable of ensuring a tightly integrated operational risk management process for the organization. This ensures that all of the people accountable for the design, development, implementation, operation, maintenance, and evolution of the risk response function in a coordinated fashion. The coordination process should be driven by a documentation set comprising all of the relevant information necessary to ensure full situational awareness at all Tiers in the process. The information that is factored into the organization's risk management process can include testing and review data, any evolving documentation from system operation, and all other artifacts generated for information security–related purposes. It can comprise such data points as operational monitoring feedback about the functioning of common organizational controls, including security controls.

Under the standard, the elements of the NIST RMF are installed alongside the activities of the conventional SDLC. This helps to ensure that organizations are effectively integrating the management of information system–related security risks with SDLC activities. The concurrence between the risk management function and the traditional SDLC is of special interest when it comes to enterprise architecture, because the SDLC can be employed to characterize the various legitimate operational states that an information system might be in. The life cycle itself is typically understood in terms of the classic waterfall steps of requirements gathering/design specifications, analysis and design, development/coding/system build, testing, acceptance, implementation and training, and operations and maintenance. At various times, every aspect of information technology operation will be in one of these life cycle stages. This includes normal states like the routine functioning of an operational system. It can include new or evolving systems under development. Most often it includes all systems that might be going through modification, patching, or upgrade processes (Figure 7.4).

These SDLC stages all have a critical part to play in ensuring information system security; however, from the standpoint of the management of risk, perhaps the most important stage of all is the initial requirements gathering stage. This is

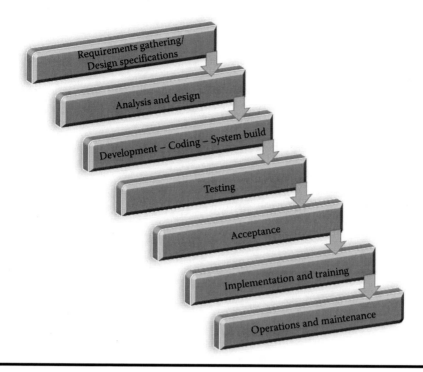

Figure 7.4   Phases of the SDLC.

because all of the strategic decision-making with respect to the security architecture takes place at this stage and if you get the requirements wrong, everything else is negatively impacted.

7.8 Particular Role of Requirements

General requirements definition is a critical part of any system development process as it defines the shape of the system and all subsequent activity devolves from that understanding. Security requirements are a critical element within that phase, since they are derived as part of the overall definition of the functional and nonfunctional requirements set for the information system. In essence, security requirements are a subset of the general functional and nonfunctional requirements. Nevertheless, without the early integration of security requirements into the overall requirements set, the security cannot be "baked in." Instead it is "bolted on" later in the SDLC.

The early integration of risk management thinking into the requirements phase of the SDLC ensures that the risk management strategy is an integral part of the overall life cycle process. It also ensures that the specific risk management processes are not isolated from the other routine management functions that are employed by the organization as it develops, implements, operates, and maintains the systems that underwrite its business purposes and the underlying functions that enable them. In addition to incorporating a comprehensive set of risk management requirements directly into the developing systems, those same strategies can also be integrated into the organization's overall policy, planning, and resourcing activities.

7.9 Drawing Hard Perimeters

With regard to risk management and enterprise architecture in general, the term system boundary, or perimeter, is synonymous with the authorization boundary, for example, the precise limits of the system that is being certified. The set of management resources devoted to the management of risk for a given system is also synonymous with the authorization boundaries for that system.

Thus, the important point to stress here is that the boundary comprises the elements that will be authorized. Therefore, authorizing officials, chief information officers, senior information security officers, information security architects, and the risk management function need to be involved in establishing or changing system boundaries. The process of establishing information system boundaries and the associated risk management implications is an organization-wide activity that includes careful negotiation among all key participants—taking into account mission and business requirements, technical considerations with respect to information security, and programmatic costs to the organization.

Because that definition is conceptual in nature, the organization has significant flexibility in determining what constitutes an information system and its associated boundary. The definition has to be tangible because the protected assets that are placed within the defined perimeter will essentially be under the same direct management control, and enforcing this control will require the allocation of personnel, equipment, funds, and system-processing power. More importantly for the purposes of this chapter, this control will involve the assignment of the authorization authority and associated responsibility and accountability.

One of the most challenging aspects in creating an effective risk management scheme, or any security scheme for that matter, is the need to draw a precise and unambiguously understood boundary around the system elements that will be assured. This perimeter does not simply encompass the system, it also circumscribes the people, processes, and related systems that will be involved in the management of the particular set of risks for that system. Well-defined perimeters are essential because they establish the precise operational space that the tangible risk management function will be accountable for. In essence, the explicit perimeter of the system comprises exactly those system elements that the organization will, and will not, agree to control.

Getting the boundaries right is an important consideration in the real-world implementation of a tangible risk management architecture, because a boundary that encompasses an inappropriate number of system components or which is need-lessly architecturally complex runs the risk of making the risk management pro-cess unwieldy and complicated. However, the boundaries that are too narrow will increase the risk that a known risk negatively impacting that system will not be included in the management scheme.

There are some simple decision rules that can be followed for practical bound-ary setting. Specifically, the organization needs to ask the question whether all of the elements within the perimeter support the same set of business goals, objec-tives, and functions, and reside within the same general operating environment, or, in the case of a distributed information system, reside in various locations with similar operating environments. Since that commonality can change over time, the boundary determination needs to be revisited periodically as part of a continuous monitoring process.

7.10 Preparing the Action Plan

The authorize phase of the NIST RMF is where the authorizing officer makes a deci-sion whether or not to authorize the system for operation. This decision is based on the documented security plan, security assessment report, and the plan of action for remediation and maintenance milestones. This documentation provides the autho-rization officer (AO) with all necessary information with respect to risk impact. The eventual risk acceptance should always be a strategic level policy decision. In essence, every Tier in the risk understanding, risk mitigation decision tree has to be involved in the final decision; however, the decision itself has to come from, and be supported by, the executive decision-makers of the organization. In essence, to ensure comprehensive accountability, the risk acceptance decisions at this stage in the process have to apply organization-wide and be accepted by all levels.

The responsibility for ensuring properly documented authorization lies with the organizationally designated authorizing official. In essence, the acceptance of risk is an accountability of the authorizing official and cannot be delegated to other officials within the organization (NIST, 2010). The authorizing official has to blend many factors into the risk acceptance decision. This includes such considerations as the impact of a given system on business goals and objectives, intangible things like effect on corporate reputation, and the obvious tangible elements of the operation such as the information assets and people that fall within the system boundary. This is never a cut and dried decision. An acceptable authorization decision requires balancing mitigation of all of the known risk factors against the efficient and effec-tive operation of the business.

The security assessment report contains the findings from the testing and iden-tifies which findings may be deemed as acceptable risk and which findings are not acceptable as it would adversely impact the system's security posture and inad-equately protect the data should the system be compromised. Unacceptable risks, also called residual risks, are findings that are detrimental for the operation of the system. These must be a plan for implementing solutions and mitigating the risks.

The information system owner or the accountable manager prepares the plan of action and milestones for remediation and mitigation. This is then submitted to the authorizing official and is one of three key documents in the security authorization package that describes the specific tasks that are planned to remediate any weaknesses or deficiencies in the security controls that were noted during the assessment. The plan also conveys the risk acceptance strategy to address any residual vulnerabilities in the information system. Specifically, the plan of action and milestones identifies (NIST, 2011):

1. The tasks to be accomplished with a recommendation for completion either before or after information system implementation
2. The resources required to accomplish the tasks
3. Any milestones in meeting the tasks
4. The scheduled completion dates for the milestones

The plan of action and milestones provides the point of reference for the authorizing official to monitor progress in remediation or rework each identified weakness/deficiency that has been noted in the security control assessment. All security weaknesses and deficiencies identified during the security control assessment are documented in the security assessment report with the purpose of this report being the maintenance of an effective audit trail.

This action plan and the associated milestones are then utilized by the authorizing entity to monitor the organization's progress in correcting weaknesses or deficiencies that were noted during the security control assessment. To maintain an effective audit trail, all security weaknesses and deficiencies identified during the prior security control assessment phase are documented in the security assessment report and passed up to the authorization phase. Organizations then develop specific plans of action and milestones on the basis of the results of the security control assessment. Where the situation is regulated, for instance in the federal space, this plan must adhere to all relevant laws, directives, policies, standards, guidance, or regulations.

Organizations define a strategy for developing plans of action and milestones. The aim is to facilitate a rational and orderly approach to risk mitigation which is consistent across the organization. The strategy must be able to ensure that organizational plans of action and milestones are directly referenced to the earlier findings of the NIST RMF process, and it must specifically align with (NIST, 2010):

1. The security categorization of the information system (NIST RMF Step 1)
2. The specific weaknesses or deficiencies in the security controls (NIST RMF Step 2)

3. The organization's proposed approach to mitigate the identified weaknesses or deficiencies in the security controls (NIST RMF Step 3)
4. The direct or indirect effect that the weakness or deficiency might have on the overall risk exposure of the organization (NIST RMF Step 4)

Like most large organizational processes, the activities that are carried out in the authorization stage are guided by a formal action plan. Thus, the development of a tailored plan of action is the first stage in the authorization phase. This plan is, in essence, a conventional project management artifact in that the activities and milestones for the anticipated authorization process are laid out in an organized and sequential fashion.

The role with the primary responsibility at this stage is the actual information system owner, or stakeholder. The stakeholders for that particular system prepare a plan of action, which includes all checkpoints and milestone. The aim is to give the independent authorizing official a working description of the specific steps that will be carried out to remediate any previously identified weakness or deficiency in the security controls. The information supporting this is passed along from the prior assessment stage (Step 4). The aim is to address any residual vulnerabilities in the system that is undergoing authorization.

This action plan is a key document in the security authorization package. It drives the authorization process in that it specifies the actions that will be taken and the milestones will be met to ensure proper certification of system capabilities. A risk assessment guides the prioritization process for items included in the plan of action and milestones. This document details the precise set of activates that will be carried out along with a set of tailored recommendations for how all necessary remediation, rework, or additional development work will be carried out prior to implementation. Obviously that also includes a precise listing of resources required to effectively accomplish those tasks as well as the scheduled completion dates for each milestone.

7.11 Preparing the Security Authorization Package

The final step before an information system is placed into day-to-day operation is the acceptance of risk by the authorizing official. This is called an *authorization*. In many aspects, the authorization phase serves the same general purpose as the "acceptance" phase of the general SDLC. It is here that the organization obtains formal proof of risk management correctness sufficient to approve the routine operation of the system.

Once a viable plan has been agreed to, the next step in the authorization phase is to assemble the security authorization package and then submit the package to the authorizing official for a decision about its acceptability. The system owner or stakeholder is the role with the primary responsibility for doing this. The security authorization package contains: (1) a detailed security plan, (2) the security assessment report, and (3) the plan of action and milestones for addressing any identified weaknesses, or deficiencies. The information in these key documents is then used by authorizing officials to make a risk-based authorization decision (Figure 7.5).

Because the security authorization package is so critical to the overall process, the best practice advice contained in NIST SP 800-37 strongly encourages the organization to use automated support tools to prepare and manage the content. The aim is to easily and effectively maintain and update the necessary control status information for authorizing officials. The security authorization package should provide an orderly, disciplined, and timely way to update the security plan, the security assessment report, or the plan of action and milestones. The aim of this support is to achieve near real-time risk management and the concomitant ongoing authorization for each system. Obviously, automation also facilitates more cost-effective and meaningful reauthorizations.

The organization ensures that the information needed for authorizing officials to make risk-based decisions about system correctness and functionality is always available. Additional information can be included in the security authorization package at the request of the authorizing entity that might be carrying out a given authorization action. Because the continuing integrity of the authorization package is critical to certification of correctness, the organization maintains strict version control over the changes or updates to the key documents in the authorization package. This change management process is often automated in the same fashion

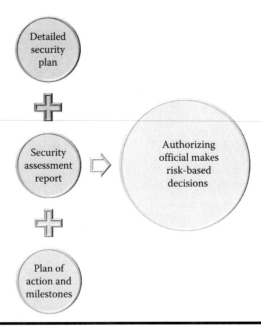

Figure 7.5   Security authorization package.

as configuration control is carried out for other important organizational artifacts. The assurance of ongoing integrity allows the organizational leadership to maintain their confidence in the ongoing effectiveness of system-specific, hybrid, and common controls.

7.12 Standard Risk Determination

In the end, every decision to authorize has to be made in light of the level of risk that is represented by a given state or condition of the system. Therefore, the next stage in the process is the determination of the degree of risk that is represented by a given assessed state of system security. The role that is primarily responsible for this is that of the authorizing agent, or their designate. This is almost always a third party to the system operation itself. To carry out this task, the authorizing official or designated representative goes over the documentation that is provided by the system owner or stakeholder with respect to the current security status of the system. This involves reviewing recommendations for addressing rework or residual tasks that might be identified in the assessment report. The stakeholder, or owner's representative, is an important player in this part of the process and is normally included in this part of the process. It is at this stage that formal or informal risk assessments might be employed. The aim is to get a complete picture of the potential impacts of any threats, vulnerabilities, or deficiencies that might still exist in the system architecture. These are all examined in light of impact and likelihood analyses that should be carried out for all risk mitigation recommendations. The risk manager role provides all of the relevant information to the authorizing official. This describes the entire set of factors that play a part in the final determination of the level of acceptable risk that can be authorized for a given system.

In most instances, the actual work of risk evaluation is done by a security assessment team. This team has the primary responsibility for conducting security authorization tasks. Those activities include collecting data, developing documents, and preparing the security authorization package for the control adequacy assessment review. The security authorization team may also conduct the actual adequacy assessment depending on the need for separation of duties in a given organization.

In general, the role of the security assessment is to test the security controls documented in the select (NIST RMF Step 2) and implement (NIST RMF Step 3) stages in order to test that they have been implemented properly and are operating as intended. The control assessment is usually conducted using the security assessment plan that has been developed by the security authorization team.

To avoid conflict of interest, the members of the security assessment team should not also be the security authorization team. However, most information processing systems members do NOT have to function in isolation from each other. In essence, if the confidentiality, integrity, and availability requirements are normal and conventional, it is acceptable to have team members interact. The only condition is that the test results themselves must be reviewed by an independent source to validate their completeness, consistency, and veracity. The members of the organization who are accountable for the authorization process can normally set the required level of independence based on the criticality and sensitivity of the system and the ultimate level of risk.

The risk acceptance decision normally hinges on *criticality*. That is, the centrality and sensitivity of a given information system that is under study for authorization will go a long way in deciding the amount and degree of risk management control that is acceptable for that system. The degree of confidence in the risk acceptance decision is typically based on the rigor of the process of risk analysis (i.e., the precise methods and analytic tools that are employed in the risk assessment process). The level of rigor is then factored into the assessed level of vulnerability or criticality of a given system and the known threats that are associated with each of these individual risks. Finally, a formal statement of risk tolerance is prepared with a statement of assessed criticality, risk tolerances, and concomitant risk controls. This is promulgated along with a plan for monitoring each mitigated risk over time.

A final review of the plan of action and milestones is then performed by the organization prior to submission of the authorization package to the approving authority. The point is to provide a final cross-check of the solution that is being proposed to any issues that might have been raised during the risk analysis. The aim is to ensure that all concerns and issues have been accurately and acceptably characterized and addressed before the final package is submitted to the authorizing official. The general purpose of this step is to (NIST, 2011):

- Review and/or update the individual plan of action and milestone elements to ensure everything has been included, analyzed, planned, and prioritized
- Perform the final review of the plan of action and milestone report itself

Plans of action and milestones are created either in response to an identified deficiency or to meet a mandated requirement. A plan is required to address each of the risk elements identified during the risk analysis for the system that is undergoing authorization. This step allows the organization to take the steps necessary to address the identified risk elements and document the schedule of actions that will be taken to remove, or mitigate, the risk to the system.

This is usually the implementation of the appropriate NIST SP 800-53 control, but it can also include such conventional actions as implementation of security patches, vulnerability mitigation work, or changes in procedure. This information can be updated throughout the entire authorization process and it is formally documented in the plan of action and milestones documentation. The plan of action and milestones specifies (NIST, 2011):

1. The weakness description and related findings
2. Remedial actions to be taken for each named weakness
3. The severity rating if the weakness is not addressed
4. The date scheduled for full implementation
5. The point of contact, or person accountable
6. The amount of resources (time and effort) required to implement the solution
7. Milestones—a list of critical objectives for the implementation of the plan
8. Items identified during security assessment, vulnerability scan, and so on
9. Any additional comments

After reviewing all of the relevant information and consulting with the executives of the target system, the authorizing official then issues a formal authorization decision. This decision is based on an evaluation of the content of the security authorization package and, where appropriate, outside consultation and advice. The authorization package should detail all of the information necessary to understand the present state of the system including the current state of the security controls, both developed and inherited, that are employed by the system. The authorization package should also explain the organization's risk posture, including the policy and procedure structure for risk mitigation. Finally, any information that is relevant to understanding the risk environment but is not part of the standard authorization package requirements should also be documented for the authorizing official. Completion of this task leads to the document review.

The goal of document review is to ensure that applicable controls have been properly documented. Where applicable, the document review team will enforce the creation of mitigation plans for control requirements that have not been met. The objective of the documentation process is to:

- Assess the completeness of the information provided by the security assessment against organizational quality standards
- Improve the informational and educational feedback process to assist units across the organization in developing a more consistent and repeatable security assessment process
- Complete a review of a security assessment package for a particular information system or major application before it has been signed by the authorizing official
- Provide feedback to help refine the general authorization process
- Identify trends across units to help determine the root causes of deficiencies

Typically, the security authorization package is conveyed under cover of a security authorization package transmittal letter. This letter is a formal artifact and it is the accepted means of officially conveying all relevant and required information to support the authorization decision. The letter identifies the location of the testing, and the personnel who conducted the testing. It is the final step in creating a security authorization package for submittal to the authorizing officer. This step is used to publish the security authorization package to the appropriate personnel for subsequent action.

To make an *ATO* decision, the authorizing official reviews the accreditation package and makes the decision to grant or deny ATO. To perform this task, the authorizing agent will (NIST, 2011):

- Use the officially sanctioned documentation to review the accreditation package
- Use the ATO letter to review the granting of the ATO
- Update the project accreditation, if this is a renewal

If an ATO is granted, the authorizing agent will sign the ATO letter thereby granting approval to operate. The ATO letter includes ATO information systems or approval to use security controls inherited by a given system. Additionally, the accreditation document is used to indicate the authorization type granted to projects based on the results of the assessment effort as well as to maintain a project's authorization history. It states:

- The authorization status of the information system
- The date the system is authorized to operate
- The date the system's ATO expires
- The date the system's authorization is reviewed
- Any comments from the authorizing agent regarding the authorization

The security authorization decision is conveyed to the interested parties within the organization. The authorization decision document expresses the ultimate security authorization decision. It is a form of contract between the authorizing official and the stakeholders of the target system. The authorization decision document contains the following information (NIST, 2010):

1. The authorization decision
2. The terms and conditions for the authorization
3. The authorization termination date
4. Whether the system is authorized to operate or not authorized to operate
5. Any specific limitations or restrictions on the operation of the information system or inherited controls

The authorization termination date indicates when the security authorization expires and a new reauthorization process must be undertaken. In the case of federal systems, authorization termination dates are often established by federal law or regulation. These laws or regulations might establish a given authorization period that is dictated by mandate rather than based on an assessment or the outcomes of a continuous monitoring process. Nevertheless, if the ongoing monitoring process is carried out with the proper degree of rigor it is possible for the monitoring outcomes to serve as a standing basis for a form of ongoing authorization.

Authorizing officials may eliminate the requirement for reauthorization if the formal continuous monitoring program (NIST RMF Step 6) is proven to be sufficiently robust to ensure continuous understanding of the risk environment and the associated risk acceptance activities. If this is the case a periodic authorization decision document can be issued and attached to the original security authorization package. This is then transmitted to system stakeholders and the organization at large. Upon receipt of the updated authorization decision document and the original authorization package, the information system stakeholder must acknowledge the terms and conditions of the reauthorization and implement any additional recommendations for changes to controls or procedures.

Finally, the authorizing official verifies on an ongoing basis that the terms and conditions established as part of the authorization process are being followed by the information system owner. In addition, the organization ensures that the authorization documents for the system are made available to the organizational decision-makers as appropriate. Information in the authorization documents, especially any information that describe system vulnerabilities, is appropriately protected and then retained in accordance with the requirements of the authorization process.

The initial system authorization is based on evidence that is gathered at one point in time, but systems and environments change. Therefore, to address the dictates of constantly changing system environments, it is necessary to implement some form of continuous process for evaluating system control effectiveness. The aim is to facilitate a continual state of awareness among system owners and decision-makers. The process itself is based around event-driven monitoring and analysis. The purpose of this approach is to collectively evaluate the status of existing controls. In essence, this is an ad hoc, incident-based evaluation and testing process encompassing the security control set for a given system. The process itself is activated where security events or "triggers" occur that may have an impact on the system's security status. Following an event, a formal review is conducted to determine the impact of the incident on the status of controls and risk to the system. An *Incident Review Board* composed of various subject matter experts evaluates all relevant aspects of the precipitating incident, and makes a set of risk-based recommendations. From this report, the relevant organizational stakeholder or manager prepares a formal proposal to the authorization officer about the ongoing status of the authorization.

7.13 Chapter Summary

This chapter describes the fundamental concepts associated with the authorization phase of the NIST RMF. The authorization documents the acceptance of a formally sanctioned, organization-wide, and systematic approach to the risk management needs of a given situation. The risk management is intended to leverage trust and confidence for any given system across the entire spectrum of the organizational culture. The risk management strategy is meant to underwrite an acceptable level of trust in the correctness of the organization's overall functioning. The need for tangible assurance of correctness and capability ties directly to the authorization/certification process. That is, third-party certification of an accredited system demonstrates sufficient due diligence in managing risk to other entities and organizations. There are four elements to classic risk management:

1. Frame risk (i.e., establish the context for risk-based decisions)
2. Assess risk
3. Respond to risk once determined
4. Monitor risk on an ongoing basis for continuous organizational improvement

Authorization typically involves the concepts and general practices of the formal C&A process. This discussion will involve a more general exploration of the necessary mechanisms for establishing the exact criteria to be included in a risk management and milestone plan, as well as how an action plan and milestones can be created to ensure practical direction. The accreditation plan documents the organization's specific approach and strategy for finding and remediating a particular security weakness or operating deficiency that has been identified through security control assessment. As the term is most frequently employed, C&A describes a well-defined and systematic procedure for evaluating, describing, testing, and authorizing systems and their associated activities prior to or after a system is put into operation. The C&A process is used across the world and in many settings, not just the US Federal Government. As it is normally applied, certification simply entails a formal process for confirming a given set of characteristics of an object, person, or organization. This confirmation is often, but not always, provided by some form of external review, education, assessment, or audit. An audit typically includes a comprehensive evaluation of a process, system, product, event, or skill typically measured against some existing norm or standard.

Accreditation is a formal and well-defined organizational process for performing certification. Accreditation is the specifically defined approach that is taken to certify competency, authority, or credibility of a given organization, practice, or product within a defined set of criteria. Accreditation is normally provided by a third-party institution. Organizations that issue credentials or certify third parties against official standards are themselves formally accredited by accreditation bodies, which are usually national in nature such as DAkkS or UKAS.

Accreditation provides audited third-party assurance that a specifically targeted undertaking such as a quality system or security system certification process has been executed in such a way that the relevant testing and assurance outcomes meet the relevant norms or standards of given process standard, such as ISO 17024. Many nations have established specific oversight bodies to provide that overall level of corroboration. For instance, most European nations maintain official, formal accreditation bodies to provide accreditation services within their borders.

The certification process itself is meant to evaluate, test, and audit security control behaviors in order to confirm that those behaviors meet predetermined criteria. Because of the influence of FISMA that often implies that the behaviors themselves are based on the type and sensitivity of the data that are handled by the information system. The evaluation process compares the current system's security state with specific control stipulations contained in the relevant standard. In federal settings, the standard is NIST SP 800-53. The certification process ensures that security weaknesses as defined by the standard are identified and plans for mitigation strategies are in place. In addition to control planning, the accreditation process also provides a means for justifying the acceptance of residual risks that might be associated with the continued operation of a system. In this case, approval to operate is granted for a specified period of time, until the necessary rework can be done.

It is commonly recognized that risk management is a holistic activity which must be fully integrated into every aspect of the organization in order to be effective. Coordination of the management of risks is both complex and demanding. It is a multifaceted top-down undertaking that involves everybody in the organization from senior policy leaders, all the way through mid-level leaders to the individuals on the shop floor who actually develop, implement, and operate the systems that facilitate the essential mission and pragmatic business processes of the organization. Thus, decision-makers have to reach explicit, well-informed risk-based decisions that balance the benefits and utility of the systems that they oversee against the risk of those same systems causing organizational operation or routine business harm due to persistent attacks, environmental disruptions, or human error.

The complex interactions between the organization's business purposes and the information systems that ensure proper fulfillment of those purposes requires an integrated, organization-wide approach to managing risk. The role of generic risk management in mitigating operational risk is also critical to the long-term strategic aims of the organization, because risk management ensures that the organization as a whole is fully protected from all reasonably anticipated threats. The aim of the NIST RMF was to create an omnibus approach that would specifically incorporate the traditional federal C&A process into a six-step standard model (the RMF). The ultimate outcome of that effort was intended to emphasize the critical need to integrate explicit information security capabilities and controls into federal information systems.

The broad aim of the NIST RMF project was to specify a framework of best-state-of-the-practice management, operational, and technical security controls as a single operational model that would ensure continuous awareness of the security state of information systems on an ongoing basis, which would be accomplished though enhanced monitoring processes. Those processes would be designed to provide essential information to senior leaders to facilitate decisions about the acceptance of risk to organizational operations and information assets arising from the operation and use of information systems. The NIST RMF was designed to promote the concept of the ongoing information system authorization requirements of FISMA. The effectiveness of the authorization was meant to be supported by effective continuous monitoring processes. The aim was to integrate standard and approved information security practices into both the architecture of the enterprise, as well as the overall SDLC. This was supported by formal authorization of the correctness of the implementation of a set of standard security controls.

Risk is managed at three distinctly different tiers of the organization. *Tier One* approaches the management of risk from a strategic perspective. It centers on the creation of a comprehensive governance structure and organization-wide risk management strategy. *Tier Two* addresses risk from a mission and business process perspective. Actions at this level are guided by the overall strategic planning and policy making that is developed in Tier One. *Tier Three* addresses risk from an operational perspective. Decisions made at this level are always derived from and guided by risk decisions that have been made at Tiers One and Two. Risk decisions made at Tiers One and Two influence the practical selection and deployment of the operational controls and defense-in-depth countermeasures at the day-to-day operational system level.

Formal authorization of federal systems is required by the E-Government Act of 2002. Specifically, these authorizations are mandated by Title III of that Act: FISMA. In essence, security authorizations represent the official sanction that must be obtained to operate a federal information system under FISMA.

The security authorization process involves comprehensive testing and evaluation of all of the designated security controls within an information system. It attests to the correctness of specific software and hardware security controls. In addition, it also authorizes the correctness of the procedural, physical, and personnel security measures that provide the system context. It also considers the procedural, physical, and personnel security measures employed to enforce information security policy. Finally, it establishes the extent to which the implementation of a particular design, or architecture, configuration meets a specified set of life cycle security requirements.

The interest from the standpoint of this book is that the security authorization process is the current end result of the implementation of the RMF. The RMF process satisfies all of the requirements for official certification of correctness. This process involves conducting the requisite authorization activities of security categorization, security control selection and implementation, security control assessment, information system authorization, and security control monitoring. The actual control structure is created by means of a formal design activity. Therefore, risk management is substantively enabled through the design and implementation of an organization-wide enterprise architectural process. The RMF process designs and implements the tangible proof that the various strategies the organization has adopted to facilitate its day-to-day operation are in place and functioning properly. Because the architectural design process is essentially executed top-down, the initial definition of risk management requirements takes place at two conceptual level tiers (Policy Tier One and Procedure Tier Two). That strategic definition then leads to the selection of tangible risk/security controls at Tier Three operational level.

The authorize phase of the NIST RMF is where the authorizing officer makes a decision whether or not to authorize the system for operation. The decision is based on the documented security plan, security assessment report, and the plan of action for remediation and maintenance milestones. This documentation provides the AO with all necessary information with respect to risk impact. The information system owner or the accountable manager prepares the plan of action and milestones for remediation and mitigation. This is then submitted to the authorizing official. This plan is one of three key documents in the security authorization package and describes the specific tasks that are planned to remediate any weaknesses or deficiencies in the security controls that were noted during the assessment. The plan also conveys the risk acceptance strategy to address any residual vulnerabilities in the information system.

Once a viable plan has been agreed to, the next step in the authorization phase is to assemble the security authorization package and then submit the package to the authorizing official for a decision about its acceptability. The system owner or stakeholder is the role with the primary responsibility for doing this. The security authorization package contains: (1) a detailed security plan, (2) the security assessment report, and (3) the plan of action and milestones for addressing any identified weaknesses, or deficiencies. The information in these key documents is then used by authorizing officials to make a risk-based authorization decision.

Because the continuing integrity of the authorization package is critical to certification of correctness, the organization maintains strict version control over the change or updating of the key documents in the authorization package.

In the end, every decision to authorize has to be made in light of the level of risk that is represented by a given state or condition of the system. It is at this stage that formal or informal risk assessments might be employed. The aim is to get a complete picture of the potential impacts of any threats, vulnerabilities, or deficiencies that might still exist in the system architecture. These are all examined in light of impact and likelihood analyses that should be carried out for all risk mitigation recommendations. The risk manager role provides all of the relevant information to the authorizing official. This describes the entire set of factors that play a part in the final determination of the level of acceptable risk that can be authorized for a given system.

Glossary

accreditation: the formal attestation that all requirements and criteria have been met

approval to operate: formal permission to operate a federal system based on satisfaction of a requisite set of performance criteria

architecture: the explicitly designed structure of a given entity, this also refers to process

certification: formal documentation that an object under evaluation has met requirements

enterprise risk management: single organization-wide process for managing risk

plan of action and milestones: organization's proposed approach to risk mitigation

reference model: a commonly accepted standard of practice defined to structure a given concrete application of a standard process

risk assessment: estimate of likelihood and impact of all known threats; drives risk tolerance decisions

risk controls: specific behaviors executed to protect against a given threat

risk frame: the precise environment that will be subject to the authorization process

risk tolerance: the degree a given system needs to be trusted, normally expressed in terms of sensitivity/criticality

security authorization package: the security plan, security assessment report, and plan of action and milestones

standard: a commonly accepted recommendation for executing a given process

implementation: the establishment of a persistent organizational process

References

NIST. (2010). Special Publication 800-37 Revision 1, *Guide for Applying the Risk Management Framework to Federal Information Systems: A Security Life Cycle Approach.* Gaithersburg, MD: National Institute of Standards and Technology.

NIST. (2011). Special Publication 800-39, *Managing Information Security Risk: Organization, Mission, and Information System View.* Gaithersburg, MD: National Institute of Standards and Technology.

NIST. (2013). Special Publication 800-53 Revision 4, *Security and Privacy Controls for Federal Information Systems and Organizations.* Gaithersburg, MD: National Institute of Standards and Technology.

NIST. (2014). *Risk Management Framework (RMF).* Gaithersburg, MD: National Institute of Standards and Technology.

Chapter 8

Step 6—Monitor Security State

At the conclusion of this chapter, the reader will understand:

- The concept and process for long-term sustainment of a secure system state
- The purpose and business advantage of security system configuration management
- The function of standard monitoring of the threat environment and control response
- The function of a formally organized control remediation process (patching)
- The need to maintain ongoing environmental threat assessment
- The specific role of security system status checks in maintaining security authorizations

8.1 Sustaining the Organization's Risk Management Response

We discussed the authorization process in Chapter 7 and it should be remembered that the end result of that process is the issuance of a formally documented approval to operate an information system that has undergone a formal controls assessment process. The approval to operate documents an independent authorization decision on the part of an approval authority and is a form of contract between the approval authority and the stakeholders of the target system. By standard, the authorization decision document contains the following information [National Institute of Standards and Technology (NIST), 2011]:

1. The authorization decision
2. The terms and conditions for the authorization
3. The authorization termination date
4. Whether the system is or is not authorized to operate
5. Any specific limitations or restrictions on the operation of the information system or inherited controls

The initial system authorization is based on evidence that is gathered at the time of the initial controls assessment; however, as was stated previously, systems and environments change over time. Thus, there is always a need to ensure that a suitable security response continues to be maintained for the specific threat environment. Therefore, a formal control-monitoring process is needed and must be capable of continuous assurance of the appropriateness and sufficiency of the control response within the known threat environment and in accordance with any documented risk acceptance decisions.

As we said in Chapter 7, the monitoring process is based on incident-driven responses. In essence, the monitoring entails the analysis of individual occurrences in the system environment that might pose a threat. The status of existing controls is evaluated in light of each new instance. The process itself is activated when an event occurs that may impact the overall system security status. From this analysis, the relevant organizational stakeholder or manager of the affected system is given a set of recommendations that might include options such as *change* or *patch*. They might also simply recommend *accept*. This all requires an ongoing, formally organized and managed sustainment process and it is the structure of that process that will be the subject of this chapter.

The risk management process embodies the organization's commitment to identify and mitigate any relevant threats and vulnerabilities. Risk management applies to all types of life cycle threats from technical work through to the execution of policy. The goal of the risk management process is to identify, analyze, treat, and monitor each of the currently active as well as latent risks that are known to exist in the organizational threat environment. Therefore, at its heart, risk management is an information gathering function. It focuses on understanding all feasible risks and then identifies and evaluates those risks in order to determine their potential impact. Risk management ensures sufficient knowledge about each relevant threat. Then, risk management takes the necessary steps to respond to all priority threats. Risk management also monitors the effectiveness of the mitigations for those threats once they have been put in place. Risk management is information based and, therefore, threat assessments are a prerequisite to the implementation of the risk management function. Threat assessments ensure that all of the relevant risks are properly identified and categorized. After the initial identification and characterization, the risk management process typically involves five generic steps: planning, oversight, risk analysis, risk response, and continuous monitoring.

Because it is a formal process, all of the operational steps of the risk management process have to be planned. Every one of the day-to-day practices that dictate the organization's specific risk management strategy have to be planned right down to the who, what, when, and where of execution. Then a formal oversight process has to be established to stay actively involved and knowledgeable of the organization's threat situation. The oversight process should be able to describe the present status of all identified threats and to distinguish and report on new threats as they appear.

In order to maintain a sufficient understanding of the risk picture, the organization has to institute a properly targeted *risk-monitoring function*. That function should be able to perform ongoing qualitative and quantitative analyses of any newly identified or emerging risk event. The risk-monitoring function should also be able to perform the analyses that are required to confirm that currently existing risks are fully characterized and contained. The ideal outcome of the execution of the risk-monitoring process should be the continuing certainty that the risks that the organization considers priorities are understood and mitigated and that any emerging risks will be identified and dealt with as they manifest themselves.

Once the analysis operation is established, the formal responses in which the organization will utilize to mitigate all priority risks have to be maintained. The response to each priority risk should always be a substantive and sufficient mitigation as well as feasible and understandable. Finally, the response should be shown to mitigate the known impacts of any identified risk. The organization also has a duty to continuously monitor the existing threat environment in order to identify and mitigate any new threats that might arise. Constant vigilance is necessary in the case of risk because dangerous threats can appear at odd times and in unanticipated places. The risk-monitoring function is typically underwritten by formal testing and reviews.

The overall purpose of the risk-monitoring function is to establish and maintain a continuously appropriate set of risk controls. Because of this purpose, risk assessments are a particularly critical part of the overall monitoring process. Risk assessments ensure effectiveness because they identify the specific threats to the organization and then determine how likely those threats are to occur, as well as the consequences of each threat should it happen. Correctly done, the existing threat environment is periodically assessed to ensure that the current risk mitigation scheme is relevant and maintains its effectiveness (Figure 8.1).

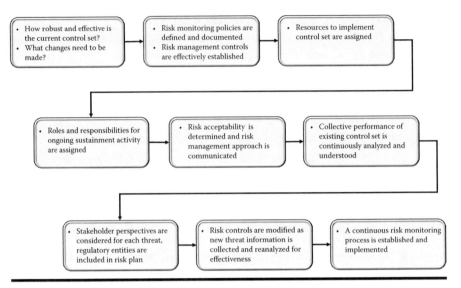

Figure 8.1 Overview of the risk monitoring process.

8.2 Overview of the Process: Sustaining Effective Risk Monitoring

Because there can be an infinite number of risks in the threat environment, the means for sustaining the risk management process over time has to be well-defined and yet flexible. Essentially, the ongoing monitoring of risk answers two highly related questions. The first issue is "How robust and effective is the current control set?" The second is "What changes need to be made in order to sustain the control set at a given status?" The answer is normally supported by ongoing evaluation of the control set performance within a given timeframe, and for a given situation.

Once optimum risk-monitoring policies are sufficiently defined and documented and the resulting risk management controls are effectively established, the collective performance of the control set has to be continuously analyzed, and the individual purpose and role of each control has to be understood on a priority basis. The latter step is necessary because the resources required to implement the control set have to be assigned and such priorities determine investment. Then, once all of the necessary risk controls have been systematically implemented, their performance has to be assessed in the operational space in order to ensure their continuing effectiveness.

The risk control set that is established through the NIST Risk Management Framework (RMF) process and authorized in the prior step is a formally executed organizational process, especially where certification is involved. Nevertheless, once instituted the risk management process must be consistently effective over time. And it is the effectiveness that must be maintained through continuous monitoring of the performance of the control set. In most cases, the outcomes of the monitoring will dictate a set of specific actions that are necessary to sustain effectiveness. Those outcomes then run through a decision process, which sustains the continuous organizational control over the risk management process. The aim of continuous assessment is to understand the present status of the control set, and, in addition, to maintain an effective practical approach to the management of risk. Nevertheless, the sustainment of the risk management function is still an operational responsibility, no different than any other organizational function like accounting, or human resources.

Consequently, the control-monitoring process also needs to be properly resourced and specific roles and responsibilities for the ongoing sustainment activity have to be assigned. Moreover, in order to maintain its ongoing relevance and effectiveness, the overall risk management process has to be evaluated and strategic decisions have to be made about the optimum set of next steps in the risk management process. Those decisions are normally based on the lessons learned from the ongoing performance evaluations.

Because resourcing is always a factor, the maximum degree of acceptable risk must be made explicit with the organization. It is this statement of risk appetite that will guide the ongoing decisions about the degree of control the organization is willing to pay for. Global decisions about risk acceptability will subsequently drive decisions about the practical form of the response. In essence, the actual response will typically be referenced to the level of practical acceptability of the risk. Consequently, the risk management planning process normally involves the establishment of a substantive, usually resource based, link between each risk and the various options for mitigating it. Thus, the global specification of the maximum level of acceptable risk will drive the trade-off process necessary to make real-world planning decisions about the shape and contents of the control set.

Risk acceptance decisions establish the link between the risk management approach of the organization and the contextual threat environment. This linkage is established by the control set and maintained by the continuous risk-monitoring process. The continuous risk-monitoring process assesses the specific threat environment at a given point in time, the probability of occurrence, and the consequences if it does. The risk-monitoring process also factors in the changing stakeholder perspectives for each category of threat, and often involves the technical and managerial objectives, assumptions, and constraints of any regulatory entity. The evolution of the risk management process is then guided by changes to the threat and stakeholder perspectives.

The continuing risk-monitoring process provides the guidance for the operational risk management function and the evolving priorities for risk mitigation serve as the basis for determining resource allocation. Since priorities are a business decision, the risk assessment results are circulated to relevant stakeholders for assignment of the necessary resources. The results then dictate the routine decision-making about the allocation of resources and these results support periodic decision-making as changes occur in the risk environment. The overall purpose of the risk-monitoring process is to mitigate evolving risk. The proviso is that all risks must be identified, characterized, and subjected to a risk acceptance decision. When viewed over the long term, continuous monitoring becomes an essential activity because the risk environment changes over time. Thus, sustainment of the relevance and effectiveness of the control set is a critical requirement. The ongoing assessment of the controls that have been put in place as a result of any risk management process ensures the most effective use of the organization's security resources, because the alignment between the control set and the risk environment is a fundamental precondition for ensuring long-term information security. However, the sustainment of the risk controls is not the same activity as the institution of the general risk management function, as outlined in the NIST RMF (NIST, 2014). Rather than being an end in itself, the activity that maintains the effectiveness of the control set is a means that supports the larger end of the general risk management process. The ongoing control set sustainment should always ensure against any loss, harm, failure, or danger that has been identified and mitigated as a result of the establishment of the risk management function. The effectiveness of the control set is evaluated and any changes, remediations, patches, or additions are instituted to maintain a given level of risk protection for the overall risk management process.

Mainly, the sustainment function ensures the long-term application of the strategy that the organization has adopted to manage risk. Risk management ensures effective and up-to-date alignment between each identified threat and a deliberately assigned set of control behaviors intended to mitigate the risk. This alignment is established by the overall risk management policy. The continuous assessment feature of the sustainment process then documents that all potential risk mitigation alternatives have been considered and that the mitigation strategy has been effectively maintained.

Risk management combines all of the relevant technical, environmental, and stakeholder controls into a single coherent and systematic process to control risk. The controls are developed, tested, validated, and approved in earlier stages of the NIST RMF (NIST, 2014). The assumption is that these series of stages will create an effective approach to addressing organization risk. Any system has to be maintained in order to stay aligned to the changing environment; this especially true with technology. Therefore, continuous monitoring of the threat environment is a necessity in order to determine the future actions that have to be taken in order to maintain proper alignment.

All of the factors that make up the organizational context have to be evaluated in order to be able to assure the continuous effectiveness of the risk management controls for a given organization. The formal definition of the required level of assurance provides the primary point of reference in ensuring alignment. A clear specification of the acceptable level of requisite performance for the control set, as a whole, and each individual control in particular, has to be documented because the long-term sustainment of any systematic solution will always be dependent on the goals that have been set for its performance.

Roles and responsibilities for execution of control operations also have to be specified and accurately maintained. The human factor is often overlooked in the risk management process due to the focus often being on the activities that will be performed rather than the human and technological resources that will actually have to do the work. Thus, it is important to have a well-defined definition of all relevant duties associated with the execution of the risk control function.

Roles and responsibilities are originally assigned by the designation of accountabilities for performance of each control task as well as all of the organizational reporting lines that are associated with that task. It is the responsibility of the continuous monitoring process to ensure that all of those accountabilities are maintained as required and to bring any deviations in the execution of those duties to the attention of management. In addition to evaluating the degree of alignment between the risk management control framework and the known threat environment, it is also essential to ensure that all of the decision-makers in the organization are able to make informed, data-driven decisions in their assigned areas of responsibility. The comprehensive flow of information throughout the organization will allow decision-makers to coordinate the execution of their own operational tasks with the overall risk control objectives of the organization.

In general, what this means is that the organization's decision-makers must be able to tell whether their risk mitigation objectives are being achieved and whether the risk control framework as a whole continues to function in line with expectations. The threat environment has to be continuously monitored throughout the life cycle to identify any new or emerging risks. This monitoring is an important element of good management practice. All of the known risks should be monitored for change and any emerging risks must be identified and characterized. This includes any existing risk that has undergone change and implies the need for an appropriate and accurate measurement process. The qualitative and quantitative measurement processes assume both that the risk picture can be accurately analyzed and that analysis can be used to manage risk. Good risk monitoring requires the development and use of meaningful quantitative measures that accurately reflect the current risk picture. Proper measurement relies on the availability of a set of relevant standard measures of risk likelihood and impact. A combination of both qualitative and quantitative measures will help the organization to prioritize its control implementation activities.

Qualitative measures do not attempt to produce actual metrics, but rather focus on relative differences in control set performance. However, since one of the main purposes of the risk-monitoring function is to determine priorities, qualitative analysis can be useful. Therefore, graphic scales, such as comparative risk levels over time, are commonly used to support the qualitative analysis reporting function. In qualitative risk analysis, the measures that are used are typically a discrete set of nominal values such as *high, medium,* and *low.* These categories are then given numbers so that the weights of relationships can be objectively characterized for decision-makers.

Quantitative analysis methods are also used in ongoing risk monitoring. The value of well-defined quantitative methods is that they generate objective data. Unfortunately, the abstract nature of risk management operations will tend to restrict the availability of quantitative measures. Therefore, in practice a blend of both quantitative and qualitative measures is often employed to arrive at the desired understanding.

8.3 Structuring the Risk-Monitoring Process

Information about control performance needs to be gathered throughout the life cycle of any risk management control set. This is done for the purpose of ensuring proper continuous alignment between the risk management function and the threat environment. However, a collection of valid performance information can also be useful for the purpose of improving the risk management process itself. Therefore, designated points are needed in the continuous monitoring process where the overall performance of the process is evaluated for effectiveness.

A standard evaluation of the overall risk-monitoring process can generate useful lessons learned for improvement purposes. Risk-monitoring data include such things as the threats identified and the specific controls that have been assigned to mitigate them. These are normally specified by individual risk. Finally, any meaningful measure of the effectiveness of the risk control set and a detailed assessment of the performance of the individual controls that make up that set can ensure sufficiently correct ongoing operation of the risk management control process.

The risk-monitoring process assessment process is normally not continuous. It involves well-defined, periodic stop-out places where the organization determines whether the control set continues to meet the risk management objectives established in the beginning of the process. Risk management is really no different than any other organizational function in that way. Its focus can wander off the initial goals of the process. Therefore, one of the important elements of the risk management process is the execution of a series of reviews that are designed to assess whether the risk-monitoring process itself continues to achieve its objectives.

Two types of reviews are commonly used to do this, a *time-based review* and an *event-based review*. A *time-based* review is one that occurs at regularly scheduled intervals. The intervals are typically established when the continuous monitoring function is set up. These are top-down, comprehensive examinations that are designed to assess all aspects of the risk management control operation against stated protection goals. The purpose of a time-based review is to ensure that the risk management control set stays current with respect to both the correctness of its actions, and the ever changing risk environment.

An *event-based* review is less comprehensive, but much more focused on a particular occurrence within the operational risk management process. Like lessons-learned and after-action reviews, event-based reviews are meant to capture and record information about breakdowns of a given aspect of the risk management program, whether it is improper control functioning, or improperly defined policies, or procedures. It is generally a good idea to utilize both types of reviews in practice, in order to ensure complete coverage (Figure 8.2).

The objective of both of these types of reviews is to ensure that the risk management control set stays aligned with its initial purposes. Regardless of the type of review conducted, there are some common elements that should be looked at as a part of each review. The first of these elements are the controls themselves. In essence, the review should determine how effective each control continues to be in its response to the risks that they were designed to mitigate. In addition, the review should confirm that there is no need for changing, patching, or a different application of a given control.

In conjunction with the assessment of the actual control set, the reviews should also examine the effectiveness of the policies and procedures that have been put in place to guide the routine operation of the risk management control set. The policies and procedures should be proven to be properly aligned with the threat environment, the organization's risk acceptance policies, as well as the presence of *all known* risks. If there is a need to add additional policies or controls, or modify existing ones then the review report should itemize what those changes should be.

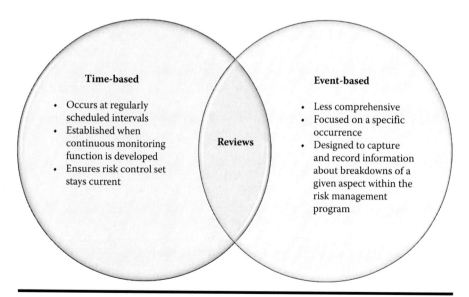

Figure 8.2   Time- and event-based reviews.

8.4 Sustaining an Ongoing Control-Monitoring Process

The ongoing control-monitoring process implies the establishment of a fully planned and integrated set of activities. These are all aimed at maintaining the alignment between the control response, which has been authorized and documented in the *approval to operate*, and the evolving threat environment. In order to be effective, the complex and diverse things that have to be kept in alignment by this process must be well-defined and closely coordinated. The coordination ensures that the right control behaviors take place as required in order to address as planned any anticipated incident or react to changes in the threat environment or detect and remediate misaligned controls. The coordination process normally includes a well-defined set of tasks. The tasks themselves have to be capable of assessing the current status of the authorized system and then continuously documenting the appropriate alignment between those controls and the general threat environment. This all takes place in light of the business goals and assurance criteria of the organization.

Control system assessments and the subsequent coordination of outcomes ensure efficient utilization of the organization's resources. If the activities that take place within the defined control perimeter are clearly understood and properly executed by the stakeholders, then ideally none of the resources that are allocated to ensure the authorized control state will be wasted. For that reason alone, the ability to establish and maintain a set of well-defined continuous monitoring activities will provide a distinct assurance advantage for any organization.

Due to compliance implications and certainly in the case of certified systems, organizations must ensure that authorized control activities are properly defined and continuously monitored. The responsibility has to be vested with the stakeholders who are accountable for the management of the system. The stakeholders ensure that the prior authorized control system meets the requisite compliance criteria as stated in the authorization.

The management stakeholders are also the people who are responsible for actually overseeing the day-to-day control-monitoring process and then making the appropriate decisions to maintain authorized compliance. The goal of decision-making is to ensure that the authorized system and the necessary technical work to maintain it progresses into a well-defined and appropriately documented set of steps. The control assessment activities themselves should always be based on and enforce the organizational policies that underwrote the authorization. The policies that define the general shape of the continuous control system assurance process need to mesh with business goals. Therefore, those policies should be developed as part of the organization's overall strategic planning process. The policies dictate the organization's overall conduct of the control-monitoring process. In addition, they dictate the criteria for how any risk acceptance or modification to the control system decisions will be made; all of this should be integrated and operationalized by a strategic plan.

The plan specifies the major assessment and response elements for the authorization period as well as itemizing the general set of resources that will be available to support the ongoing control performance assessment process. In effect, the plan itemizes the general timing and execution of each of the steps in the ongoing control performance assessment as well as stating the organizational resources that will be allocated to accomplish each of those steps. In addition to resources, the plan describes the ongoing control system monitoring approach as well as the methods that will be employed to ensure that there is adequate management of the control performance assessment process.

The ongoing control system assessment plan is the essential first condition for ensuring continued authorization of the system. The plan defines the requisite activities and tasks for each of the system controls and this is done in substantive terms. To ensure that the plan provides concrete specifications, it is normally developed using the same top-down process that is used to lay out the control system in the first place. Thus, it starts with the general control assurance policies and continues down to explicit tasks that reference those policies. In essence, each of the general control performance requirements is examined by means of a specific set of assessment procedures, which are designed to accomplish a given purpose. Then those procedures are given explicit criteria and performance expectations. The aim is to provide a complete and detailed description of the exact assessment outcomes required to maintain sufficient authorization assurance. Because the precise environmental situation that the control assessment specification is drawn up to address can change, the plan and expectations are typically reviewed and refined over time.

Once the routine continuous assessment process is established, each of the component elements of that process are evaluated for correctness and then adjusted as necessary over time. The responsibility for documenting each task might seem like busy work; however, well-defined processes, activities, and tasks lead to the repeatable outcomes that are the hallmark of an effective and capable continuous control assessment process. In addition, because the outcomes of these well-defined processes are repeatable, the organization can count on predictable long-term authorization of system operation based on lessons learned.

8.5 Establishing a Continuous Control Assessment Process

The control performance assessment process that underlies continuous monitoring is normally done by a designated assessment team. The team is typically composed of control audit and performance measurement personnel. These people typically operate as a distinct, unified assessment team under a single manager. Three big-picture questions have to be answered when forming that team. The first question is: What is the precise goal of the overall control process? For instance, is it certification, compliance, or general proof of capability? The second question is: What are the specific control understanding and assessment competencies required to carry out an effective assessment? And finally, there is the obvious question of whether the organization presently has the requisite competencies available to formulate a capable assessment team.

The first logical step in the process is to establish the scope of the general monitoring activity. Typically, this will entail explicit definition of the control system's objectives, purposes, and boundaries. The aim is to identify what the assessment will or will not cover. This is done so that the ensuing control-monitoring activities can be realistically organized. Once the assessment boundaries are established, ongoing control system monitoring will seek to establish the correctness of the system controls. This is done by assessment, which in practice involves the continuous auditing, testing, and reviewing the outcomes of the operation of the system.

A successful control assessment process usually monitors a diverse range of controls, ranging from electronic through human behavior and to physical security mechanisms. Therefore, a comprehensive set of assessment methods is required to ensure that all of the logical factors in control performance have been considered and that effective testing and review processes are in place to evaluate them. A well-defined set of routine control assessment steps are necessary because the technical elements are often a black box to managers and managerial processes are hard for technical workers to understand. Therefore, the definition both guides implementation and also serves as a mechanism for the entire organization to understand the purpose and outcomes of continuous monitoring.

The essential condition is addressed and managed by means of standard coordination and communication. Since the process participants on the business and technology level are different from each other, it might seem over-simplistic to suggest that an important aspect of ongoing control system monitoring is just getting the various key players on the same page. However, a key aspect of good ongoing control system monitoring involves nothing more than the need to ensure that the performance of all of the certified controls are properly overseen and their outcomes included in the general understanding of the continuing correctness of a given approval to operate.

A critical problem in assuring a comprehensive monitoring process is the ability to formally guarantee the active and effective cooperation of all of the target system's stakeholders. The ability to leverage the cooperation of all of the system users and beneficiaries will ensure that every aspect of the control set has been properly monitored. However, in many cases there is a necessity to bring people who are typically not involved in process considerations to the party. Specifically, that is the IT work force itself. In most organizations, information technology workers have had a long history of isolation from any aspect of the business process. It does not seem logical to exclude technical people, who are experts in the actual operation of the system, from the ongoing control system monitoring process. However, most of the authorization and monitoring decisions take place several management layers up from the actual IT workforce. The consequences of this unfortunate lack of involvement can create critical failures in the execution of an organizational process that by definition has to be executed on a coordinated and continuous basis.

Logically, this first area institutionalizes the ongoing control system monitoring process as an organizational function. The assessment and control-monitoring planning process pertains specifically to the implementation of the routine control evaluation process. The real purpose of monitoring is to obtain data that decision-makers can utilize to fine-tune the operational control system—or make changes where necessary. Therefore, part of the assessment process is the consideration of routine management decision support. Management decision support ensures effective decision-making in the ongoing monitoring of the effectiveness of the controls.

Effective risk measurement and analysis are a critical part of the process of system monitoring due to the management decisions being made about risk. The measurement of risk guides the evolution and sustainment of the general configuration of the control set. Finally, to ensure that the control configuration evolves in a rational and controlled fashion, it is necessary to factor proper configuration management practice into the overall planning for the organization's system control performance monitoring process.

8.6 Implementing a Practical Control System Monitoring Process

Just as with any other large-scale organization, the control system monitoring process is established by a strategic planning effort. The overall goal of the strategic planning is to develop an effective and realistic way forward for the overall monitoring process. Strategic planning determines the overall scope and focus of the ongoing system assessment and monitoring elements as well as the general timing and explicit assessment activities involved at each of those steps. The plan provides a detailed description of all tasks, deliverables, and outcomes of each assessment activity as well as the schedule for routine execution and the criteria that will be used to confirm the correctness of performance. Finally, it specifies the practical resource considerations of the process.

The actual planning outcomes characterize the precise scope of the work to be done. Scoping the evaluation activity is part of the perimeter setting process that was mentioned in Chapter 7. It ensures that the specified work can be carried out within the organization's available resources and known constraints. The ongoing control system monitoring process seeks to ensure proper alignment between the formal control set and the reality of the threat environment. Thus, once the organization is certain that the control set and the threat environment are aligned properly, it is possible to do accurate effort and resource estimations for the prospective work. As part of the sizing and estimation of the discrete control system monitoring activities themselves, the organization also has to identify any relevant interfaces with organizational units that are required to be involved in the actual monitoring in order to ensure effective coordination of all essential tasks.

As with any other organizational function, the process is initiated by plan. The initiation typically involves a standard planning procedure aimed at creating a living organizational process. The goal of this process is to perform all of the necessary work to sustain a continuous and correct ongoing effort. The merger of the requisite activities of the effort into an effective set of routine work practices is not a simple matter of identifying the various participants and then telling them what to do. The establishment of a persistent organizational control assurance process involves making certain that all of the required actions of all of the various stakeholders in the process are correctly and properly coordinated with each other to ensure sustainment of a proper organizational control system.

One challenge with the ongoing control performance assessment process is that it involves evaluating technology. Thus, the requisite planning for that process involves factoring the complex details of the specific technologies that sit within the evaluation perimeter into a continuously evolving assessment and assurance procedure. The ongoing control system monitoring process has to be carried out in such a way that it will assure the integrity of the technology and the associated technical work, while at the same time ensuring that the much broader set of compliance constraints and long-term strategies of the organization are effectively monitored for correctness. To ensure such a balanced understanding, the activities that establish the monitoring process have to oversee both managerial and technical activities and tasks, and therefore, the assessment activities have to be clearly specified and understood down to a level of actionable detail, which will ensure that all of the participants in the process do exactly what they have to do in order to ensure achievement of the organization's risk management goals.

At the same time the conduct of the assessment activity has to be such that adequate lines of communication are established among all participants. The aim of all of this is to guarantee effective management of the various required evaluation activities. The tangible outcome of the design and implementation of a routine monitoring and oversight process is a validated set of well-defined activities and tasks that will satisfy the general compliance goals of the certification standard. Successful documentation of those activities and tasks is normally the point where the continuous monitoring process starts.

8.7 Conducting Continuous Monitoring

Once the scope of the assessment has been defined and all of the resources that are necessary to execute it have been put in place, the actual scheduling of the requisite activities and tasks takes place. This schedule itemizes the timing and execution of all of the activities that are identified as part of the continuous monitoring process. The schedule usually states the timing, intervals and milestones, staffing and resource assignments, and the specific roles and responsibilities that are necessary to execute each task. The schedule might also include a detailed execution plan for each requisite activity as well as the organizationally approved life cycle measures that will be utilized to measure the performance of the process.

Like any other organization-wide activity, the continuous oversight process has to be formally launched; this is typically included as part of the scheduling process. The launch requires management to assign start dates as well as checkpoint activities for each activity, which will ensure that all of the continuous monitoring tasks are performed under direct control of the organization as a whole. There also has to be a formal managerial decision to assign the resources required to carry out the evaluation activities. This decision is normally attached to the official schedule of activities.

Once all of the prep work is done, the individuals who have been assigned accountability for the execution of each task can now perform the actual work. The work itself is officially defined in a set of formal work instructions with the aim to establish management control over the continuous monitoring process down to the task level of the operation. Considerable evidence over time has shown that it is particularly important to get the work instructions right and to make them clearly visible and understandable to all of the participants in the process, because management's ability to ensure successful execution of a given task depends on the individual manager's ability to oversee the work. A properly written collection of work instructions specifies the precise mechanism that each manager needs to employ in order to ensure their individual control. In addition, a well-defined set of work instructions will also ensure that the required steps are communicated, understood by the workforce, and enforceable.

The day-to-day continuous monitoring process is designed to understand and document the status of the control set that has been established by the NIST RMF process. It is based on a documented set of plans, schedules, budgets, and technical objectives that are organized in previous phases of the overall continuous monitoring process. The ability to measure and quantitatively assess the performance of the control set is an important practical consideration for managers because it helps them make informed decisions about overall risk and threat. To make those intelligent choices, managers have to be able to understand and evaluate the effectiveness of each individual control in the entire organizational array. As a result, the ability to obtain quantitative measurement data is an essential concept within the risk management process. The existence of quantitative data gives individual managers the objective basis to make informed choices about the performance of the controls in which they have been assigned and are accountable. Managers in the information technology parts of the organization need to have the capability to judge the performance of the items under their supervision; however, given the dynamic and generally complex nature of information technology work, it is almost impossible to develop practical, objective indicators of performance. This is because information technology work involves mainly abstract things and the complex activities that are associated with execution and management of that technology are hard for nontechnical people to understand, let alone successfully manage. Therefore, it is sometimes impractical to expect an informed decision by members of management who operate above the level of the actual technical work, which is the reason why quantitative ongoing monitoring information about the performance of the control system is so important for ordinary decision-makers up-and-down the organizational ladder. Data that are obtained from quantitative measurement helps corporate decision-makers make decisions about the performance of their risk controls. And if consistent data are analyzed over time, it will also ensure that the organization makes its decisions against well-established and reliable corporate benchmarks.

The ability to empirically understand how information technology risks are being managed will also ensure that corporate decision-makers are able to more responsively identify problems as they emerge. In addition, it will allow them to judge the potential risks and rewards of any contemplated response to an identified threat. Every organization has a basic need to understand how well it is performing its important tasks. And to understand that, it is necessary to have the ability to evaluate the effectiveness of its actions against a concrete set of criteria, which is what measurement provides.

Thus, quantitative measurement is an important element of the management of information technology work but it is particularly important when it comes to the management of IT risk. Proper understanding of the risk situation is a necessity for making intelligent long-term decisions. Therefore, the systematic and ongoing collection of standard control performance data is a prerequisite to making intelligent management decisions. Continuous and reliable data ensure the continuous appropriateness and cost-effectiveness of the control set. Nevertheless, control performance measures have to be formally defined, instituted, and the outcomes routinely collected in order to support that kind of quantitative decision-making.

Specifically, standard quantitative measures are required to enable benchmarking. The measures have to be standard because continuous measurement requires that the definition of the data itself remains stable over the measurement period. That stability allows for the kind of causal and comparative analyses necessary to ensure good decision-making. Also, in conjunction with their support of everyday ongoing control system monitoring, stable quantitative metrics can also be employed to improve the effectiveness of the overall quantitative measurement process as well as the efficiency of the resource utilization necessary to support it. In addition to the need for stable definitions, different decision-makers up-and-down the decision hierarchy will require a well-defined understanding of the quantitative risk data that they receive. This understanding is necessary to ensure that decision-makers at each level have an effective understanding of the status of the risk controls for the organizational elements under their supervision. Such standard metrics include considerations like the reliability, effectiveness, usability, efficiency, and maintainability of the risk controls that they oversee within a given area of responsibility.

8.8 Practical Considerations

Overall, the aim of the continuous control oversight process is to ensure that the compliance objectives necessary to maintain an approval to operate are successfully achieved and properly documented. In addition to supporting the authorization to operate, continuous ongoing assessment of risk controls also assures that appropriate actions are taken if an anomaly or deviation from requirements occurs. Since the *approval to operate* the system is dependent on consistent execution of the approved control set, any identified issue must be addressed and steps taken to prevent reoccurrences of the problem in order to maintain that certification.

Continuous control monitoring and oversight assures that the status of the risk environment is monitored and reported as necessary to ensure that the organization's overall information security process is continuously measured for effectiveness. The continuous monitoring requirement applies to all formal risk controls that have been established under the NIST RMF process. In addition, it applies to any additional controls that the organization might decide to utilize to address a threat that does not fall under classic risk management doctrine.

Naturally, the sustainment of the correctness of the organization's formally established risk controls that have been put in place to provide the basis for the granting of an authorization to operate the system is a primary goal of the continuous monitoring process. In many respects, the term *effective risk monitoring* describes the overall purpose of the entire information security management process. In effect, the tasks that underlie continuous risk monitoring also serve to ensure that the execution of the information security management process is always correct and that the outcomes of the risk control activity are suitably managed by all of the process stakeholders, both internal and external. Moreover, because there is an outside threat aspect to risk control, the monitoring process also has to know the status of the threat environment as it affects every aspect of the overall information security management approach of the organization.

The ongoing status assessment outcomes that are a routine part of the risk-monitoring activities of the organization are the other side of the coin from the monitoring that is part of sustaining the *approval to operate* certification. In order to respond effectively to the changing threat picture, it is necessary to know what the current status of that environment is; however, simply knowing the status is not sufficient to ensure the organization's ongoing security. It is also necessary to have a systematic process in place to remediate and assure the ongoing effectiveness of the actual operational risk management control array itself.

Effective management of the actual control set requires constant awareness of the risk picture and the ability to respond to any identified deviations or anomalies. The occasional deviation from the intent of a given control has to be expected. This is because the threat picture is constantly changing and the technology that is arrayed to mitigate risk is highly dynamic. Nevertheless, the impact of change and evolution over time can introduce very substantive changes in the security status of an organization. Therefore, continuous active monitoring of the alignment between the threat environment and the existing control set is an absolute necessity if the organization wishes to remain secure.

To enforce the need for accurate alignment between threat and risk management controls, it is necessary for the organization to be able to investigate, analyze, and resolve any identified deviations from the intended purpose of the control set. Thus, the general purpose of the overall control-monitoring activity is to ensure that the impact of any deviation from the intended outcome of a control is evaluated, authorized, and subsequently addressed by substantive rework.

Of course a properly executed organizational reporting process, which is fully integrated into the overall monitoring activity, will also ensure that managers who operate above the technical level are directly involved in any substantive decision about overall organizational security.

Routine reporting is also an important function if the aim is to ensure general organizational oversight over the risk management process. Consequently, it is also helpful to designate formal points in the performance of the continuous system monitoring process where overall effectiveness is reviewed and reported to stakeholders. Essentially, these reviews are the routine stop-outs where the organization as a whole can take a moment to assess its general level of security. And from that assessment it can formally plan, identify, and resolve any actual or emerging concerns that might need to be addressed. In addition, those stopping-out places can also serve as the mechanism for ensuring that any procedural or regulatory issues regarding the approval to operate have been properly addressed.

8.9 Quantitative Measurement Considerations

We referred to quantitative measurement in Section 8.8. In effect, the need to maintain a full, complete, and continuous understanding of the overall risk mitigation status of the organization's security controls is an essential part of good risk management practice. Since each control functions within a carefully designed set, it is also important to have specific data about every single control's performance. The aim of quantitative measurement is to ensure continuing knowledge of the functional status of each control, and the control set in general (Figure 8.3).

The aim is to ensure that the day-to-day risk management operation satisfies all criteria for approved operation as well as documenting the fact that the system meets regulatory requirements. Therefore, the organization utilizes systematic measures of performance in order to ensure that the specific set of controls it has

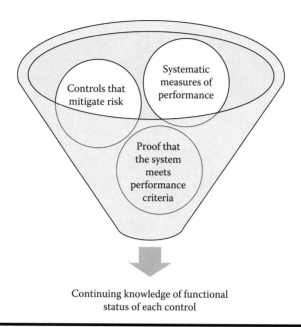

Continuing knowledge of functional
status of each control

Figure 8.3   Aim of quantitative measurement.

established mitigates known risks and to develop proof that the system meets the
stipulations of the approval to operate criteria it is intended to address. Where problems in either control performance or process execution are identified, the organization will utilize the quantitative assessment results to make decisions about the
necessary steps to achieve proper realignment and to prevent future recurrences.

The measurement process requires a well-defined and systematic standard process, which the organization needs to establish. Establishing a formal risk control
measurement capability involves the establishment of a standard, routine, sustainment schedule for performing each assessment, as well as putting in place a defined
process for collecting and reporting results. The need to collect standard, routine
risk status data implies that the organization needs to treat the risk measurement
function exactly like it would any other ongoing organizational process, that is,
the risk measurement activity has to be fully resourced and staffed to ensure that it
operates as a routine part of the everyday business operation.

Done properly, quantitative risk measurement is a routine organizational function and typically does not have a long-term focus. Instead, it makes use of the
criteria that the risk management controls have been designed to address in order
to systematically gather data about the performance of the overall process against
standard benchmarks. The criteria are typically outlined and stated in the formal
compliance document that motivates the creation of the risk management controls
in the first place, such as the *approval to operate* requirements of FISMA, or they are
specified in the overall organizational risk management strategy.

Consequently, every single metric that is utilized in the process needs to have an explicit connection to either regulatory requirements, or a documented organizational goal. The measures themselves should be both objective and capable of being recorded in some meaningful fashion. Additionally, the assumptions about what each measure represents in terms of practical operational control outcomes should also be documented and used as a means of maintaining perspective on the data that are produced. The organization can then use the data that are produced to ensure the ongoing performance of its risk management process.

The measurement process itself executes a pertinent set of operational measurement activities that can be used to judge the appropriate performance of the risk management control system. The risk control performance measurement process then provides a consistent and ongoing data stream that makes it possible for decision-makers to draw informed conclusions about the relative correctness of the control set. These data can be used to identify and prioritize the security concerns of each decision maker.

The set of measures that are used to address the concerns are carefully designed to satisfy the specific information needs of each participant in the reporting line. The aim is to define the data collection, analysis, and reporting process that allows each effected decision maker to understand the performance of both the control set that they are accountable for as well as the meaning of the data itself with respect to the overall security state of the organization. Because of the tie between quantitative data and management decision-making, the ongoing control assessment process has to collect as much objective information as possible about the performance of each control within the organization's immediate threat environment. Likewise, the measurement process also has to ensure that the threat environment at-large continues to be understood over time. This understanding is vitally important because accurate knowledge of the status of the environment is essential to maintaining the relevance of the controls for the threats that an organization faces.

Quantitative assessment is also useful to ensure ongoing improvement of the control set. The people who manage the risk control process have to have some systematic means to evaluate the ongoing effectiveness of the organization's formal set of risk mitigation measures. The challenge is that the performance of the actual risk mitigation process is hard to assess, because barring a simple count of incidents (which is not particularly useful to long-term decision-making), there are few standard measures that are geared toward evaluating the effectiveness of a risk management system. Therefore, it is essential to have a mechanism in place to provide the most accurate and in-depth information about control system performance within the context of its specific threat environment. Therefore, the first step in implementing a systematic control performance measurement process is to develop the best set of comparative measures possible. These measures have to accurately characterize the real-world interaction between the formal risk controls and the threats in the organization's immediate environment. This is the reason why often the only way to evaluate the performance of the risk mitigation process is through benchmarks. Benchmarks capture and record the outcomes of a target process over time. Because they are comparisons rather than measures, benchmarks are the best means of understanding the actual performance of something as abstract as risk management. For this reason, the first step in creating a risk management evaluation program is to confirm that all of the elements involved in the overall risk management function have been evaluated and documented accurately at a consistent point in time. At a minimum, the documentation of the accuracy should include an overall assessment of the status of each control and an accompanying set of operational testing and review results that are capable of ensuring current effectiveness.

Once the status is understood, the outcomes of the measurement process can be baselined and tracked against prior assessments across the complete set of controls. The aim of the evaluation activity is to ensure and improve the long-term effectiveness of the control set. The fact that a running assessment of the current status of the controls against their prior performance will provide a meaningful point of reference to judge the present effectiveness of the control set.

The scope of the consideration might include threats that occur in the larger organization ranging from policy breakdowns at the upper management level, right down to precise threats to the hardware, software, and network elements that appear in the operational space. The data points recorded through that information gathering process will then serve as a useful basis for analyzing ways to better improve the protection scheme. And that knowledge can then also be used to develop and fine-tune any necessary change, or response.

The measures themselves have to generate quantitative data and ideally, the data must describe the performance of each relevant control within the control set. The information that is gathered should be as quantitative as possible since measurement-based data can be statistically analyzed for such things as inferential and descriptive trends. An analysis that is based on a rich and comprehensive pool of objectively gathered, quantitative performance data will help decision-makers make more informed decisions about the immediate risk environment, as well as chart the course for the long-term response to risk.

The measurement of risk management control performance involves the collection, storage, and verification of quantitative data. Decision-makers analyze that data and develop new and more relevant responses based on the general requirement to accurately align the risk management controls to the threat environment. These types of decisions are always part of the ongoing security operation and can range from decisions about routine patching or changes all the way up to emergency action decisions aimed at responding to some unanticipated occurrence. Because of the complex nature of technology and the decision maker's likely unfamiliarity with the nuts-and-bolts of the work, there has to be a systematic process to assist them in coming to optimum decisions. The outcome of any decision ought to be the best possible response to any given concern and a formal decision process is an essential component of operational risk management. Essentially, the organization is able to design a set of standard, rational procedures that will help decision-makers utilize organizational data to arrive at the best course of action for any given situation.

A structured decision-making process within the risk management sustainment operation might not guarantee ideal decisions, but it will ensure that a quick and rational information-based decision is made. The process itself is based around the documentation, categorization, and objective analysis of threat data as it emerges from the conventional risk management operation. Because influential threats can appear quickly, a quick but rational response method is one of the best practical arguments for structuring and running a formal risk decision-making process. So along with the need to sustain a persistent framework of risk management policies, one of the other important roles of the ongoing risk-monitoring process is to provide a set of best practice steps to arrive at an optimum decision.

The overall aim of the ongoing operational risk management function is to ensure that decisions that are made in the day-to-day functioning of the risk management process underwrite the alignment between the threat picture and the risk response. Therefore, the elements of operational decision-making need to follow a well-defined and documented decision-making criteria to create a standard template or model approach to practical risk issues as they arise.

As stated previously, the identification of the issues comes from the control system monitoring process. Nevertheless, the response requires decision-making. Systematic decision-making is a fundamental management activity that seeks to ensure the optimum outcome for any given concern that might arise in the organizational threat environment. The decision-making process should also involve alternative solutions. The aim is to evaluate all of the options among an available set of alternatives and choose the one that will provide the likeliest benefit.

The overall aim of the decision-making that is performed during the routine sustainment phase is to devise a response that will underwrite the best possible outcome for a given situation. Executed properly, the ongoing risk-monitoring process is an information gathering and response oriented function, which ensures the most satisfying decision options for any given range of alternatives. In the process of reaching the optimum decision all of the outcomes, consequences and contingencies for every possible option have to be considered and the optimum alternative arrived at. In general, risk decisions are guided by two things: *policies* or *regulatory* requirements. If a policy exists, then the decision should be shaped by its recommendations. If there is no policy, which is frequently the case with risk situations, then there has to be a decision-making strategy or protocol in place to ensure that a quality decision will be made. The strategy itself should be geared toward achieving a specific set of identified outcomes and should be expressed in a way that will make them measurable, in order to judge their performance.

The decision-making strategy should also be supported by a set of formal decision-making criteria. Standard, organizationally sanctioned criteria are necessary in order to ensure a generally appropriate decision. Needless to say, those criteria have to be documented in advance. So logically the development and long-term management of an effective set of decision criteria is an integral part of the overall sustainment phase. Once a set of criteria are developed, their documentation, monitoring, and enforcement has to be organized and implemented. The implementation process involves the categorization and prioritization of all categories of likely risk events and in conjunction with categorizing risk, the authorizations and responsibilities for decision-making have to be delegated to the appropriate personnel. Effective policies are then defined to guide decisions for each of the decision-making categories. It is also important to identify and involve all of the pertinent parties in the decision-making process.

Criteria are also required to guide the selection of alternatives for any given decision. In the case of many routine decisions, the point of reference is provided by a well-defined policy or procedure. The existence of an existing policy that dictates a given response for a foreseen event will likely make the eventual outcome optimally efficient; however, there are many unique or unforeseen situations that also require decision-making. In the case of unforeseen events, it is important to follow a rationale process to arrive at the optimum course of action.

This process typically involves gathering timely information to help the decision maker understand the context and contingencies of a given event, and the analysis of that information to arrive at an optimum conclusion. The development of a standardized decision-making process as well as the formal decision-making approach to unforeseen contingencies is a critical success factor in the operation of an ongoing monitoring and sustainment process. Because the threat environment is fluid and the technology constantly changes, much of operational decision-making is often ad hoc.

If this is the case, then a standard decision-making process is required to ensure uniformity of approach. In essence, decisions have to be made within the context the new event or circumstance. Because it is novel, there is no standard solution; however, it is possible to—at least—implement a standard process for rationally considering the logical alternatives. This process does not address the problem itself; instead, it provides a structure milieu within which the problem can be evaluated and responded to. The process provides standard guidance for all decision-makers as to the best approach for responding to an unforeseen circumstance.

The only difference between foreseen and unforeseen decision-making is whether there is already a policy or direction in place to guide subsequent actions. The actual policies and procedures to guide decision-making during the operational risk management sustainment phase are planned in advance and are meant to address situations that are known to happen. However, many decisions arise where no policy or procedure exists. If the required decision is unforeseen, the aim of the standard decision-making process is to ensure that a systematic set of best practice steps are followed to think through the risk management data and reach the most rational possible decision. In order to utilize that data, there has to be a process to analyze the various contingencies.

Once a decision is reached, it has to be proven effective otherwise there is a need to reconsider the alternatives that might better achieve the organizations goals. Reconsideration requires knowledge of the current status of the situation; each decision should be recorded, and the outcomes then tracked, evaluated, and reported. The aim of this part of the process is to ensure that all identified problems have been effectively resolved, or that the desired benefit has been gained. If this is not the case, then the knowledge gained from the tracking can provide the guidance for fine tuning. In order to properly document those outcomes, the organization has to maintain an operational record of the problems and resolutions that the process has produced. The actions associated with the implementation of a given decision have to be monitored by means of organized reviews, inspections, or even audits and data captured that will both describe the complete set of results. This activity will also provide lessons-learned that might guide the development of new policies for decision-makers in similar situations.

8.10 Keeping the Control Set Correct over Time

In essence, the NIST RMF model creates and recommends the implementation of a properly validated set of correct security controls. These controls are specifically aimed at addressing risk within a given organization. In this final stage of the NIST RFM framework, the aim is to ensure the effectiveness of the control set over time. The purpose of this monitoring process is to ensure the continuous correctness and authorized integrity of the entire set of explicitly implemented human and electronic control behaviors that have been installed to ensure against risk.

It is essential to continuously monitor alignment between controls and the threat environment because threats can arise at any point and can represent a range of unanticipated impacts. So alignment with the threat picture must be ensured on a routine and disciplined basis.

There is a conventional well-defined formal process for the rational management of change to any abstract entity called *sustainment*. In concept, *sustainment* refers to any formal set of practices undertaken to organize and maintain a set of control objects. In essence, sustainment rationally manages changes to the control set and is carried out in such a way that it preserves the overall integrity of the control system. Sustainment entails all of the processes that are implemented to assure the continuing correctness and effectiveness of the organization's established set of security controls. Security controls are created and deployed in order to facilitate the organization's security goals and each goal has operational performance requirements. The control behaviors themselves are always continuously executed in the operational space, which is necessary because risks in the threat environment and the requirements for control are continuous.

Therefore, confidence in the accuracy and effectiveness of the control set must be renewed. Typically, sustainment monitors the control set's ability to ensure confidence in the continued proper functioning of the control set as well as monitors the control set's ability to accurately identify and record problems, analyze those problems, take the appropriate corrective, adaptive, perfective, or preventive action, and confirm the restored capability of the controls. The operational sustainment process encompasses four domains. These domains represent the four primary activities that taken together ensure rational alignment of any given object to changes in the environment. Those activities are: *sensing, analyzing, responding,* and *improving* (Figure 8.4).

Operational monitoring to *sense threats* is instituted by a selected set of policies, procedures, tools, and standards and are deployed to monitor, test, and review the control set or system. Operational monitoring also identifies and resolves security and control vulnerabilities within the control set, the system, the data, the policies, and the users. Because vulnerabilities can be associated with everything from applications, the operating system, network or device configurations, policies and procedures, security mechanisms, physical security, and employee usage, operational monitoring is not typically limited to the technical control set alone.

The control set must be maintained in a trustworthy state and that state must be understood and documented as performing operational monitoring to the organization's defined requirements. Therefore, a requisite of good practice is to develop and utilize a continuous operational testing process to identify security threats and vulnerabilities and control violations in control set and control set–intensive

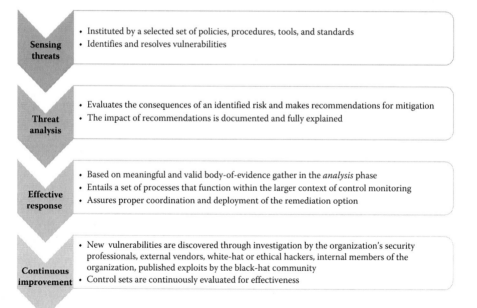

Figure 8.4 Operational sustainment process.

systems. Technical monitoring practices include intrusion detection, penetration testing, and violation analysis and processing. Reviewing is a periodic activity that evaluates the control set, the system, the policies and procedures, and the users' usage against established standards. Reviews may consist of walkthroughs, inspections, or audits and they can be both managerial and technical.

Environmental threats are always present in the real-world context. In this respect, the environment represents the place where early warning of impending hazards or attacks can be best spotted. Therefore, a requisite of good practice is to continuously monitor the operating environment that surrounds the control set to identify and respond to new threats, exposures, vulnerabilities, and violations as they arise.

Security incidents must be reported through a standard and disciplined process. The aim is to respond as quickly as possible to any trouble arising from the exploitation of vulnerabilities, malfunctions, or incidents that might exist in the control system. The process must be both standard in its procedure and fully documented and also must be well understood within the organization. Therefore, a requisite of good practice is to institute a systematic procedure to document and record threat exposures and vulnerabilities.

The *threat analysis* function then evaluates the consequences of an identified risk and makes recommendations for mitigation along with documenting the impact of the recommended change. All control sets, and control intensive systems, policies, processes, or objectives impacted by the change must be included in the evaluation. This degree of documentation is necessary to ensure a coordinated response. Analysis entails identification of the affected control set and systems including cascading or ripple effects, along with affected policies or processes. Affected control set and systems elements are examined to determine impacts of a prospective change. Impacts on existing control set and systems, as well as any interfacing systems and organizational functioning, are also characterized. Security and safety impacts of the change must be fully examined and documented and communicated to the appropriate decision-makers for authorization.

In order to implement a correct *response,* it is necessary to know what the implications of a particular response strategy or action might be. The analysis should be based on a formal methodology aimed at ensuring a comprehensive and unambiguous understanding of all operational implications for the control set, its requirements, and its associated architecture.

In order to support the requisite executive decision-making about the form of the response, a meaningful and valid body-of-evidence has to be developed in the analysis phase. This must be communicated in a clear and understandable fashion to the designated approving authorities of the organization. That authority will then provide the actual authorization of any changes necessary to ensure the continued effectiveness of the control set.

The results of the analysis are reported to the appropriate manager with a full explanation of the implementation requirements for each remediation option. This report must clearly outline the impacts of each option and it must be plainly and explicitly understandable to lay decision-makers. The feasible remediation options must be itemized. These must be expressed in a manner that is understandable to lay decision-makers and each option recommended must be fully and demonstrably traceable to the business case.

Response management entails a set of processes that function within the larger context of the generic control-monitoring activities of the organization. Response management assures proper coordination and deployment of the remediation option that is selected by the decision authorities. One major responsibility of the response management function is to maintain the security and integrity of the control set throughout its useful lifetime. The reality is that over that lifetime, a significant number of new vulnerabilities, which might threaten the control management process, will be discovered. The vulnerabilities might be discovered through investigation by the organization's security professionals, vendors who are external to the organization, white-hat hackers, internal members of the organization, or any other interested party, including published exploits by the black-hat community. Whatever the source, any vulnerability that has been discovered requires risk management decisions on patching or other risk mitigations.

The agent performing the authorized fix or change to the control set must understand all of the requirements and restrictions involved in making the change. Thus, a process must be established to unambiguously convey all of the technical and contextual specifications of the remediation option to the change agent. Although a change is implemented through other organizational functions such as maintenance or development, it is the change monitoring process that ensures that the change meets established criteria for correctness. This monitoring entails a continuous oversight process, which involves various types of management review and problem resolution activities carried out by the organization's designated decision-makers.

Documenting the outcomes of the monitoring activity requires an audit trail that provides traceability between the change authorization and the eventual change to the control set. For potential compliance reasons that audit trail must be maintained for a specified period of time into the future operation. Changes must be reintegrated into the operational environment of the organization. Thus, the decision maker who has authorized a change must provide the formal authorization to perform the reintegration. Once authorization is granted, the change is reintegrated into the operational control set. It is then necessary to conduct a technically rigorous process to assure that this reintegration has been done correctly.

In addition to certifying of the correctness of the reintegration, it is also necessary to fully document the new control set's baseline configuration and then maintain it under strict configuration control. The documentation is kept as a current baseline configuration description. That baseline is stored in an organizationally designated repository. In the case of certain regulatory requirements, it might be necessary for the control set and related systems to be assessed and authorized by an appropriate third-party evaluator and then baselined.

8.11 Chapter Summary

There is always a need to ensure that a suitable security response continues to be maintained for the specific threat environment. Therefore, a formal control-monitoring process has to be put in place to ensure continuing alignment. That process must be capable of continuous assurance of the appropriateness and sufficiency of the control response within the known threat environment and in accordance with any documented risk acceptance decisions.

In order to maintain a sufficient understanding of the risk picture, the organization has to institute a properly targeted risk-monitoring function. That function should be able to perform ongoing qualitative and quantitative analyses of any newly identified or emerging risk event. The risk-monitoring function should also be able to do the analyses that are required to confirm that currently existing risks are fully characterized and contained. The ideal outcome of the execution of the risk-monitoring process should be the continuing certainty that the risks that the organization considers priorities are understood and mitigated and that any emerging risks will be identified and dealt with as they manifest themselves.

Because there can be an infinite number of risks in the threat environment, the means for sustaining the risk management process over time have to be well-defined and yet flexible. Once optimum risk-monitoring policies are sufficiently defined and documented and the resulting risk management controls are effectively established, the collective performance of the control set has to be continuously analyzed, and the individual purpose and role of each control has to be understood on a priority basis. The latter step is necessary because the resources required to implement the control set have to be assigned and such priorities determine investment.

The aim of continuous assessment is to understand the present status of the control set, and in that respect also maintain an effective practical approach to the management of risk. Accordingly, the control-monitoring process also needs to be properly resourced and specific roles and responsibilities for the ongoing sustainment activity have to be assigned. Moreover, in order to maintain its ongoing relevance and effectiveness, the overall risk management process has to be evaluated and strategic decisions have to be made about the optimum set of next steps in the conduct of the risk management process. Those decisions are normally based on the lessons learned from ongoing performance evaluations.

Information about control performance needs to be gathered throughout the life cycle of any risk management control set. This is done for the purpose of ensuring proper continuous alignment between the risk management function and the threat environment. However, a collection of valid performance information can also be useful for the purpose of improving the risk management process itself. Therefore, there needs to be designated points in the continuous monitoring process where the overall performance of the process is evaluated for effectiveness.

The risk-monitoring process assessment process is normally not continuous. It involves well-defined, periodic stop-out places where the organization determines whether the control set continues to meet the risk management objectives established in the beginning of the process. Risk management is really no different than any other organizational function in that way. Its focus can wander off the initial goals of the process. Therefore, one of the important elements of the risk management process is the execution of a series of reviews that are designed to assess whether the risk-monitoring process itself continues to achieve its objectives.

The ongoing control-monitoring process implies the establishment of a fully planned and integrated set of activities. These are all aimed at maintaining alignment between the control response that has been authorized in the approval to operate and the evolving threat environment. In order to be effective, the complex and diverse things that have to be kept in alignment by this process must be well-defined and closely coordinated. That coordination ensures that the right control behaviors take place as required in order to address as planned any anticipated incident, react to changes in the threat environment, or detect and remediate misaligned controls.

That coordination process normally includes some sort of well-defined set of tasks. The tasks themselves have to be capable of assessing the current status of the authorized system and then continuously documenting the appropriate alignment between those controls and the general threat environment. This all takes place in light of the business goals and assurance criteria of the organization.

Just as with any other large-scale organization, the control system monitoring process is established by a strategic planning effort. The overall goal of that strategic planning is to develop an effective and realistic way forward for the overall monitoring process. Strategic planning determines the overall scope and focus of the ongoing system assessment and monitoring elements as well as the general timing and explicit assessment activities involved at each of those steps. The plan provides a detailed description of all tasks, deliverables, and outcomes of each assessment activity as well as the schedule for routine execution and the criteria that will be used to confirm the correctness of performance. Finally, it specifies the practical resource considerations of the project.

Continuous control monitoring and oversight assures that the status of the risk environment is monitored and reported as necessary to ensure that the organization's overall information security process is continuously measured for effectiveness. The continuous monitoring requirement applies to all formal risk controls that have been established under the NIST RMF process. In addition, it applies to any additional controls that the organization might decide to utilize to address a threat that does not fall under classic risk management doctrine.

Naturally, the sustainment of the correctness of the organization's formally established risk controls, which have been put in place to provide the basis for the granting of an authorization to operate the system, is a primary goal of the continuous monitoring process. Nevertheless, in many respects the term "effective risk monitoring" describes the overall purpose of the entire information security management process. In effect, the tasks that underlie continuous risk monitoring also serve to ensure that the execution of the information security management process is always correct and that the outcomes of the risk control activity are suitably managed by all of the project stakeholders, both internal and external. Moreover, because there is an outside threat aspect to risk control, the monitoring process also has to know the status of the threat environment as it affects every aspect of the overall information security management approach of the organization.

In many respects then, the ongoing status assessment outcomes that are a routine part of the risk-monitoring activities of the organization are the other side of the coin from the monitoring that is part of sustaining the approval to operate certification. Obviously, in order to respond effectively to the changing threat picture, it is necessary to know what the current status of that environment is. However, simply knowing the status is not sufficient to ensure the organization's ongoing security. It is also necessary to have a systematic process in place to remediate and assure the ongoing effectiveness of the actual operational risk management control array itself.

It is essential to continuously monitor alignment between controls and the threat environment. This is because threats can arise at any point and can represent a range of unanticipated impacts. So alignment with the threat picture must be ensured on a routine and disciplined basis. There is a conventional well-defined formal process for the rational management of change to any abstract entity. It is called sustainment. In concept, sustainment refers to any formal set of practices undertaken to organize and maintain a set of control objects. In essence, sustainment rationally manages changes to the control set. Sustainment is always carried out in such a way that it preserves the overall integrity of the control system.

Therefore, confidence in the correctness and effectiveness of the control set must be renewed. Typically, sustainment monitors the control set's ability to ensure confidence in the continued proper functioning of the control set. Sustainment monitors the control set's ability to (1) accurately identify and record problems; (2) analyze those problems; (3) take the appropriate corrective, adaptive, perfective, or preventive action; and (4) confirm the restored capability of the controls. The operational sustainment process encompasses four domains. These domains represent the four primary activities that taken together ensure rational alignment of any given object to changes in the environment. Those activities are sensing, analyzing, responding, and improving.

Security incidents must be reported through a standard and disciplined process. The aim is to respond as quickly as possible to any trouble arising from the exploitation of vulnerabilities, malfunctions, or incidents that might exist in the control system. The process must be both standard in its procedure and fully documented. The process also must be well understood within the organization. Therefore, a requisite of good practice is to institute a systematic procedure to document and record threat exposures and vulnerabilities.

In order to support the requisite executive decision-making about the form of the response, a meaningful and valid body-of-evidence has to be developed in the analysis phase. This must be communicated in a clear and understandable fashion to the designated approving authorities of the organization. That authority will then provide the actual authorization of any changes necessary to ensure the continued effectiveness of the control set.

The results of the analysis are reported to the appropriate manager with a full explanation of the implementation requirements for each remediation option. This report must clearly outline the impacts of each option and it must be plainly and explicitly understandable to lay decision-makers. The feasible remediation options must be itemized. These must be expressed in a manner that is understandable to lay decision-makers and each option recommended must be fully and demonstrably traceable to the business case.

Glossary

accountabilities: assigned management responsibility for the execution of some element of the continuous monitoring process

alignment: the state of having all known threats evaluated and addressed by appropriate controls

continuous monitoring plan: the specification of how long-term assessment of the control set alignment will be carried out

criterion: formal documentation of an organization requirement used to judge success

quantitative data: empirically derived and methodically collected information about a process

quantitative decision support: measurement-derived information to guide managerial decision-making

response management: a planned, formal process for ensuring proper execution of the risk response process

risk appetite: the degree of willingness of the organization to tolerate a given risk

risk controls: specific behaviors executed to protect against a given threat

risk mitigation: the explicitly designed control for a given organizational threat

risk monitoring: a formal process, continuously executed to ensure alignment between threats and controls

RMF life cycle: the six stages of the Risk Management Framework Process ending in a continuously maintained approval to operate the system

stakeholder: a party who owns or is affected by a given operation or system

sustainment: the formal, rational process for ensuring control set correctness over time

threat analysis: quantitative examination of the implications of a given threat with respect to the organizational risk picture

References

National Institute of Standards and Technology (NIST). (2011). NIST Special Publication 800-39, *Managing Information Security Risk Organization, Mission, and Information System View*. Gaithersburg, MD: National Institute of Standards and Technology.

National Institute of Standards and Technology (NIST). (2014). *NIST Risk Management Framework (RMF)*. Gaithersburg, MD: National Institute of Standards and Technology.

Chapter 9

Practical Applications of the National Institute of Standards and Technology Risk Management Framework

At the conclusion of this chapter, the reader will understand:

- The various certification and accreditation (C&A) options applicable to the National Institute of Standards and Technology Risk Management Framework (NIST RMF)
- Where the RMF fits into Federal Information Security Management Act (FISMA) compliance
- The U.S. government's legal basis for accrediting the security of its systems
- The potential applications of the RMF outside the government
- The standard basis for implementing risk controls using Federal Information Processing Standard (FIPS 199 and FIPS 200) and NIST SP 800-53
- The potential long-term application of a risk-based approach to control formulation

9.1 Applying the NIST RMF

The NIST RMF was developed by the NIST as a specific way to ensure standard compliance with various federal information assurance certification programs. The goal was to create a standardized basis for documenting the effectiveness of a range of assurance models such as the Department of Defense Information Assurance Certification and Accreditation Process (DIACAP), Department of Defense (DoD) Policy Series 8500, and FIPS 200. More specifically, the purpose of the NIST RMF was to provide the common life cycle basis for assessing the explicit compliance of federal government systems with the dictates of the FISMA.

FISMA is Title III of the E-Government Act of 2002 and in conjunction with FISMA compliance, the NIST RMF also supports the information resources management policies of the Office of Management and Budget (OMB) as stated in Circular A-130. It is the law of the land as far as the requirement for secure operation of federal systems goes. The specified goals of the NIST RMF (NIST RMF, 2014) are as follows (Figure 9.1):

1. To improve information security
2. To strengthen risk management processes
3. To encourage reciprocity among federal agencies
4. Through implementation of the RMF, achieve compliance with policy directives.

9.2 RMF Application

The DoD and other federal agencies require all information technology systems, including medical devices, to comply with a large number of well-defined information assurance requirements. Thus, in effect, the NIST RMF specifies a standardized

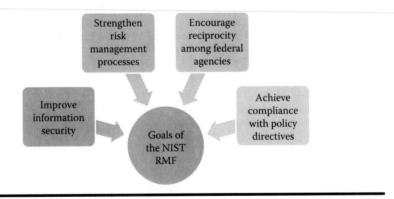

Figure 9.1 Goals of the National Institute of Standards and Technology Risk Management Framework (NIST RMF).

process for performing the traditional C&A functions. Since the discussion of the NIST RMF has occurred throughout this book, we only need to summarize this process. It involves six life cycle stages, as shown in Figure 9.2, consisting of the following:

1. Categorization of information systems (ISs)
2. Selection of security controls
3. Implementation of security controls
4. Assessment of security controls
5. Authorization of ISs
6. Monitoring of security controls

The primary use of the NIST RMF in the C&A process is to underwrite the issuance of Approvals to Operate (ATOs) for ISs operated by the federal government. C&A is essentially inaccurate as it applies to the NIST RMF, in the sense that the actual purpose of the RMF process is to assess and then support the long-term development of a comprehensive information security control set, rather than certify those controls. After completion of the initial four stages of the RMF process, the outcomes are sent to a Designated Accrediting Authority (DAA). The DAA's signature actually completes the "authorization" portion of the process and allows the system to go live or continue in operation if it is an existing system. Consequently, the DAA's role is to authorize the correctness of the RMF assessment process rather than actually accredit the system.

Figure 9.2   Six stages of the NIST RMF life cycle.

In the typical C&A process, a system is first identified and its stakeholders are registered. Then a formal risk analysis is performed in order to categorize the general sensitivity of the information in the system. The method for doing this within the present federal space is specified in FIPS 199. Once the system has been described in terms of the impact and priority using FIPS 199, a list of controls is selected and implemented. The current federal standard for control selection is FIPS 200, *Minimum Security Requirements for Federal Information and Information Systems.* This standard works in conjunction with NIST Special Publication (SP) 800-53 Revision 4, *Security and Privacy Controls for Federal Information Systems and Organizations* (NIST, 2013).

Once the requisite behavioral and electronic controls are in place, a designated third-party certifier assesses the established control set for explicit effectiveness. If the controls are documented sufficiently, then a responsible party accredits the system. The accreditation certifies a fully correct control set, which underwrites the granting of a formal ATO endorsement for that system. The actual endorsement is based on audited proof of the presence of an effective life cycle-based management function that is capable of identifying, implementing, and managing the enterprise-wide security capabilities and services of the system undergoing certification. The fact is that every federally operated system must supply documentary evidence of compliance with all of the applicable security requirements that have been mandated for its operation. This compliance is within whatever regulations that might apply and because of the compliance implications, the documentation process itself has to be designed, instituted, and then carried out on a persistent and organized basis.

The process must be able to support an in-depth policy and technical analysis of the degree of compliance with a standard set of security controls. In the federal space, those controls are specified in NIST SP 800-53 Revision 4. Compliance with the required behaviors of those controls provides an index of the level of risk that is represented by the operation of the system. And in that respect, a formal ATO accreditation simply states that the system operates within an acceptable degree of risk. The credential issued is based on whether the designated decision authority can accept the known level of risk identified in the compliance auditing process.

9.3 Certification and Accreditation in the Federal Space

Since it began in 1997, the formal C&A process for the ISs that operate within the federal government has been evolving through several incarnations. Because of the sensitivity of its systems, the overall requirement for the formal certification of system capability originated with the DoD. The Pentagon called the first of these formal certification processes the *Defense Information Technology Security Certification and Accreditation Process* (DITSCAP). DITSCAP's primary justification was that it provided a form of documented performance certification; however, it had some significant weaknesses. The primary problem was that the systems that were being overseen were treated in isolation from each other and the systems that were part of the enterprise as a whole. Even worse, there were no common, well-defined, standard control sets published to guide the compliance process and the proof of compliance itself required a lot of documentation to support the accreditation process. As a result, the DITSCAP was criticized as being nothing more than a paperchase rather than an actual enhancement of the organization's security posture.

Given the unhappiness with the DITSCAP, in 2007 the DoD defined a new certification process called the *Defense Information Assurance Certification & Accreditation Process* (DIACAP). The primary advantage of DIACAP was that it was built around well-defined implementation standards and specific goals for information assurance (DoD 8500.01, 2002). This included the specification of a standard set of auditable controls (DoD 8500.2, 2010). These two standards serve as a basis for the actual certification.

DoD 8500.01 defines a multitiered set of cybersecurity controls. All of the information technology owned by the DoD is governed by a comprehensive cybersecurity program that ensures an appropriate level of assurance for each asset based on the value of the information technology that might potentially be affected by a given threat. In order to ensure the right level of assurance, the DoD has promulgated a set of controls that ensure the security status of everything from an individual device or software object to the aggregated systems of systems.

These controls are made precisely for system stakeholders and operators throughout the DoD and are based on the specifications of DoD 8500.01. The DoD 8500.01's procedural specifications underwrite the premise that cybersecurity must be fully integrated into system life cycles and made candidly as an element of organizational function within the joint and DoD-specific information technology portfolios. The integration goal is ensured by hooking compliance to an overarching set of integrated decision structures and processes that are itemized in DoD 8500.01. The primary aim is to ensure a commonly acceptable level of resilience in the operation of all DoD systems.

Performance of the assurance mission is then assessed for overall effectiveness and managed in accordance with DoD regulations. This is a data-driven process that is meant to support explicit life cycle decision-making. In accordance with DoD 8500.01, all DoD information technology is acquired, configured, operated, maintained, and disposed of consistent with a set of 75 high-level controls that are specified in DoD 8500.2. These controls range in specificity from operational details like, "Unauthorized use of VOIP," all the way up to successful implementation of Saltzer and Schroeder's principles (1974). The actual control behaviors are specified and evaluated based on the individual system's level of classification. The paperwork requirements for DITSCAP were reduced; however, one major problem still remained. While DIACAP served as the certification basis for the DoD, the rest of the federal government and specifically the intelligence community at large still utilized a completely different set of processes and control sets to secure their information resources. The lack of coordination meant that shared trust and even practical interconnectivity between the DoD and other systems was nearly impossible to achieve without a drawn-out articulation process. Consequently, over the past 8 years NIST collaborated with the Office of the Director of National Intelligence (ODNI) and the Committee on National Security Systems (CNSS) to establish a unified framework and common foundation for information security across the federal government. The intention of this common framework model was to provide the intelligence, defense, and civilian sectors with more uniform and consistent ways to manage risk that resulted from the operation and use of ISs. A common foundation and framework is considered to be important, because it can then serve as the basis for reciprocal acceptance of security authorizations and facilitate information sharing among all types of federal agencies.

The government-wide effort to develop a new, universal, commonly understood, and accepted process for risk management produced the NIST RMF. The true advantage of the RMF is that it is designed to fully integrate all of the many C&A processes and control sets across the government into a single approach. On the surface, this integration would be capable of enhancing interagency cooperation. In effect, if all of the government's systems were categorized, analyzed, secured, assessed, and authorized using the same common process, it would be possible for diverse systems from a range of agencies to be able to be certified trustworthy without first having to undergo a time-consuming and costly articulation process.

Essentially, the NIST RMF is intended to be the fundamental methodology that will be used to establish and document the compliance of all federal systems with relevant regulatory requirements. The NIST RMF integrates directly with the Systems Development Life Cycle (SDLC), which ensures that security is included in the development process from the very beginning. Security is strongest when it is "baked" into a system. Unfortunately, many systems are still designed and implemented without security considerations resulting in inadequate levels of trust and assurance. Theoretically, when the NIST RMF is fully implemented across the federal space, reciprocal relationships can be established between all of the federal systems of equal classification. In that case, it will be possible to achieve truly automated interconnection between ranges of agencies. The interconnectivity will enhance the prospects for immediate data exchange and availability of information as needed.

Like all other broad scale initiatives, the NIST RMF has a history. It has essentially evolved from a growing awareness in the federal space in which threats to information and the systems that process it are real and have to be dealt with by systematic policy. The evolution has to be understood to fully comprehend the overall purpose and application of the NIST RMF in today's governmental risk environment. So, in order to understand where the RMF is coming from, we need to begin at the beginning.

9.4 In the Beginning: The Clinger–Cohen Act (1996)

There are a number of mandated accreditations required in the federal space. Most of these stem from the *Clinger–Cohen Act* (CCA), enacted by Congress in February 1996 to reform and improve the way federal agencies acquired and managed their information technology assets.

The law underwrites the coordinated development of overarching federal information technology management policy by mandating a comprehensive approach to the way that information technology resources are acquired and managed. It applies to all of the agencies under the executive branch. The passing of the CCA brought about a number of changes in the roles and responsibilities of federal agencies, particularly in how they operate and acquire their IT resources. One of the most significant changes to the overall method of agency operation was that the CCA highly encouraged the procurement of commercial off-the-shelf technology as opposed to specialized development of federal systems, which in effect integrated procurement into the general set of responsibilities for information technology management and operation.

Most importantly, the CCA centralized the overall mandate for federal information technology management oversight with the Director of the OMB. The CCA assigns the Director of the OMB with the direct accountability to improving the acquisition, use, and disposal of information technology by the federal government (CCA, 1996). The OMB was made officially responsible for the improvement of the productivity, efficiency, and effectiveness of all federal systems (CCA, 1996). OMB circular No. A-130 (2000) is the single most significant artifact in the entire Clinger–Cohen implementation process and provides officially sanctioned practical guidance for implementing the act itself.

The OMB requires each agency to establish clear accountability for IT management activities by appointing an agency Chief Information Officer (CIO) with the visibility and management responsibilities necessary to carry out the specific provisions of the act (CCA, 1996). While the actual law is complex, all agency stakeholders need to be aware of the CIO's leadership in implementing the requirements of the Clinger–Cohen Act. In the subsequent 20 years, the CIO's role was made much more universal and substantive by the formation of the *US Federal CIO Council*, originally established in 1996. This group was an informal interest assembly for the first 6 years; however, the E-Government Act of 2002 codified the overall role and purpose of the CIO Council into a law. Now, the Council has assumed an official role in developing policy recommendations for government information technology management policies, procedures, and standards, identifying opportunities to share information resources and assessing and addressing the needs of the federal government's information technology workforce (CCA, 1996).

Besides mandating roles and responsibilities for information technology management, the OMB also has an architectural focus. It specifically mandates the requirement for each agency to develop a formal information technology architecture (ITA) in order to rationally align and coordinate the use of ISs within the government. The OMB suggests that these architectures should fully align with existing federal and agency architectures. The outcome of the CCA's architectural guidance is the *Consolidated Reference Model of the Federal Enterprise Architecture Framework* (FEAF).

The OMB mandates an integrated system framework aimed at efficiently executing the assigned role and responsibility of a given department. Thus, all aspects of capital planning are taken into consideration in its implementation. The operational goal of the FEAF is to define a common model and nomenclature across the federal space. The FEAF actually comprises an interrelated set of subframeworks that are designed to facilitate coordination and alignment of cross-agency system acquisition and development. As a set, the reference models that make up this framework coordinate and normalize all of the fundamental aspects of federal agency operations into a single understanding. The intention is that the standard FEAF and its common vocabulary will enhance interagency collaboration and ultimately standardize the federal government information technology management process.

The OMB supplements the existing policy about how federal agencies will collect public information, stated 10 years earlier in the 1986 *Paperwork Reduction Act* (PRA, 1995). It does this by requiring an agency-wide methodology for the improvement of IS acquisition and management through specific work process redesign measures and by linking strategic information resource planning and investment directly to the budgeting process.

From the standpoint of the evolution of the NIST RMF, the most relevant outcome of the Clinger–Cohen Act is the mandate that the OMB Director develop a process for analyzing, tracking, and evaluating the risks and results of all major capital investments made by an executive agency for ISs (CCA, 1996). Specifically, the requirement is that the process be applicable to the entire life cycle of each system and should include an explicit set of benchmarks for analyzing risks associated with information technology investments.

The CCA also requires the Director of the OMB to oversee the development and implementation of standards and guidelines pertaining to federal computer systems. This requirement tied the Clinger–Cohen initiative directly to NIST and its many standards for best practice. In that respect, the OMB was tasked with the responsibilities to (CCA, 1996) do the following:

1. Evaluate the information resources management practices of the executive agencies with respect to the performance and results of the investments made by the executive agencies in information technology. This in effect established the principle of uniform assessment of system security practices, which was later turned into a law by FISMA (2002).
2. Establish effective and efficient capital planning processes for selecting, managing, and evaluating the results of all of its major investments in ISs. This in

effect serves as the basis for assessment of federal system performance, which underlies the principle of ATO.

3. Ensure that the information security policies, procedures, and practices are adequate to guide efficient and effective interagency and government-wide investments in information technology. This essentially serves as the basis for the alignment of policy to implementation, which is at the core of FISMA's continuous performance assessment requirement.

4. Perform periodic reviews of selected information resources management activities of the agencies in order to enforce accountability of the head of an agency for information resources management. This in effect establishes the principle of periodic ATO.

As can be seen, much of the purpose and intent of the formal C&A process that was formalized in the subsequent *E-Government Act* (2002) has its origins in the Clinger–Cohen Act. And in many respects, that seminal act still serves as the contextual "godfather" for the specific mechanisms that the U.S. government employs to perform the various processes supported by the NIST RMF.

9.5 The E-Government Act of 2002: FISMA

The central legislative piece in any discussion about the RMF is FISMA (2002). As we mentioned earlier, FISMA was enacted 6 years after the Clinger–Cohen Act as *Title III of the E-Government Act of 2002* and it was FISMA that formally established the importance of cybersecurity as a national security priority for the United States. It is FISMA that establishes the mandate for every agency of the federal government to document, implement, and sustain an organization-wide program to ensure the confidentiality, integrity, and availably of federal proprietary information and the systems that process it.

It is probably oversimplistic to call FISMA the *Federal Cybersecurity Act*, but in effect that is exactly what it is. FISMA explicitly establishes the need for formal risk-based responses to information security threats and it requires annual reviews of information security programs and the documenting of those outcomes. In particular, FISMA requires the accountable people in each agency to implement policies and procedures to reduce any potential unauthorized access, use, disclosure, disruption, modification, or destruction of information technology to an acceptable level (FISMA, 2002).

FISMA assigns NIST the responsibility for developing standards, guidelines, and associated methods and techniques to guide that effort. And on that basis, the RMF is one contributor in the effort to satisfy FISMA's provisions. NIST works closely with federal agencies to improve their understanding and implementation of FISMA and publishes standards and guidelines, which serve as the basis for standard implementations of the FISMA requirements. In support of its standards work, NIST also develops standards, metrics, tests, and validation programs to promote, measure, and validate the FISMA compliance work. At its heart, FISMA is an information security management framework and all systems used or operated by a U.S. federal government agency must comply with its requirements. The requirements are stated in a series of standards that have been defined by NIST over the past 8 years and will all be part of the discussion. The NIST RMF does not provide compliance criteria; however, it does provide a well-defined process for putting those stipulations in place.

FISMA applies to all of the systems within a given enterprise and the universality of its application within a given government organization is one of its chief characteristics and advantages. Essentially, FISMA requires every agency to inventory all of the systems it operates and includes characterizing both the applicable software and hardware assets as well as all of the major interfaces between each system and the networks in which they are attached. Additionally, the information within those systems needs to be identified and categorized on the basis of the level of sensitivity and risk. The identification and categorization process provides the requisite understanding of the exact protection requirements for each system as well as drawing a roadmap of potential areas of threat.

The key to this process is the ability to know and describe the overall sensitivity level of the system and its information, which dictates the level of security required. The procedure for performing this is explained in FIPS 199, *Standard for Security Categorization of Federal Information and Information Systems*, which is the first of the required security standards that underlies the FISMA legislation. FIPS 199 provides the official definition of the standard security categories.

As a consequence of the passage of FISMA, Congress tasked NIST with the job of developing standards and guidelines to be used by all federal agencies to categorize all information and ISs operated by the federal government based on levels of information security required. This categorization is based on a range of risk levels (FIPS 199). FIPS 199 offers a common framework and advice on how to define appropriate security categories for both information and their attendant ISs. Security categories are to be used in conjunction with vulnerability and threat information in assessing the risk to the organization.

FIPS 199 is built around security impact categorizations, a common sense way to approach the assignment of controls since it orders the investment to focus on the most important security issues first. As discussed in Chapter 2, the security categories are based on the potential impact should the information and ISs be threatened. Thus, the information is categorized according to its potential impact on the functioning of the organization. FIPS 199 defines three levels, *low, moderate,* and *high,* of potential impact on organizations or individuals should there be a breach of security. The application of these definitions must take place within the context of each organization and the overall national interest (FIPS 199). Besides impact, the other side of the classification process is deciding about the relative sensitivity or importance of the information. Thus, the other factor that is brought into the decision about priorities is the issue of information sensitivity. Or in simple terms, the security category of any information type is used to decide the right sensitivity category of the system.

Once the organization makes a decision about the sensitivity and impact of a given system, security controls are assigned. Federal ISs must meet minimum security requirements defined in the second mandatory security standard that is specified in FISMA FIPS 200, *Minimum Security Requirements for Federal Information and Information Systems*. Policies and procedures play an important role in the implementation of an enterprise-wide information security program. Thus, organizations require guidance in the most effective way to develop and promulgate formal security policies.

This standard specifies 17 control areas for which policies might be required. The 17 areas represent a broad-based, balanced information security program that addresses the management, operational, and technical aspects of protecting federal information and ISs. In order to satisfy the requirements of these 17 categories, the organization must select the appropriate security controls and assurance requirements as described in NIST SP 800-53 Revision 4, *Security and Privacy Controls for Federal Information Systems and Organizations*. The process of selecting the appropriate security controls and assurance requirements for organizational ISs is a multifaceted, risk-based activity involving management and operational personnel within the organization. Security categorization of federal information and ISs, as required by FIPS Publication 199, is the first step in the risk management process. Subsequent to the security categorization process, organizations must select an appropriate set of security controls for their ISs that satisfy the minimum security requirements set forth in this standard. As discussed in Chapter 2, the selected set of security controls must include one of three appropriately tailored security control baselines from NIST SP 800-53 that are associated with the designated impact levels of the organizational ISs as determined during the security categorization process.

Agencies have flexibility in applying the baseline security controls in accordance with the tailoring guidance provided in NIST SP 800-53. This allows agencies to adjust the security controls to more closely fit their mission requirements and operational environments. The controls selected or planned must be documented in the system security plan. The combination of FIPS 200 and NIST SP 800-53 describes a foundational level of security for all federal information and ISs. The agency's risk assessment validates the security control set and determines whether any additional controls are needed to protect agency operations, agency assets, or individuals.

The resulting set of security controls establishes a level of "security due diligence" for the federal agency and its contractors. The 17 areas, as shown in Figure 9.3, are (FIPS PUB 200, 2006) as follows:

Security Control Class		Security Control Family	Identifier
1	Technical	Access control	AC
2	Operational	Awareness and training	AT
3	Technical	Audit and accountability	AU
4	Management	Certification, accreditation, and security assessments	CA
5	Operational	Configuration management	CM
6	Operational	Contingency planning	CP
7	Technical	Identification and authentication	IA
8	Operational	Incident response	IR
9	Operational	Maintenance	MA
10	Operational	Media protection	MP
11	Operational	Physical and environmental protection	PE
12	Management	Planning	PL
13	Operational	Personnel security	PS
14	Management	Risk assessment	RA
15	Management	System and services acquisition	SA
16	Technical	System and communications protection	SC
17	Operational	System and information integrity	SI

Figure 9.3   NIST security control library families.

1. *Access control* (AC): organizations must limit IS access to authorized users or processes acting on behalf of authorized users.
2. *Awareness and training* (AT): organizations must ensure that personnel are made aware of the risks associated with their activities and ensure that organizational personnel are adequately trained to carry out their assigned information security-related duties and responsibilities.
3. *Audit and accountability* (AU): organizations must create, protect, and retain IS audit records to the extent needed to enable the monitoring, analysis, investigation, and reporting of unlawful, unauthorized, or inappropriate IS activity.
4. *Certification, accreditation, and security assessments* (CA): organizations must periodically assess the security controls in organizational IS to determine if the controls are effective in their application, correct deficiencies, and reduce or eliminate vulnerabilities, and authorize the operation of those systems.
5. *Configuration management* (CM): organizations must establish and maintain baseline configurations and inventories of organizational IS (including hardware, software, firmware, and documentation) throughout the respective system life cycle.
6. *Contingency planning* (CP): organizations must establish, maintain, and effectively implement plans for emergency response, backup operations, and post-disaster recovery.

7. *Identification and authentication* (IA): organizations must identify IS users, processes acting on behalf of users or devices, and authenticate their identities prerequisite to allowing access to organizational ISs.

8. *Incident response* (IR): organizations must establish an operational incident handling capability for organizational ISs that includes adequate preparation, detection, analysis, containment, recovery, and user response activities.

9. *Maintenance* (MA): organizations must perform periodic and timely maintenance on organizational ISs; and provide effective controls on the tools, techniques, mechanisms, and personnel used to conduct IS maintenance.

10. *Media protection* (MP): organizations must protect IS media, both paper and digital and limit access to information on IS media to authorized users.

11. *Physical and environmental protection* (PE): organizations must limit physical access to ISs, equipment, and the respective operating environments to authorized individuals.

12. *Planning* (PL): organizations must develop, document, periodically update, and implement security plans for organizational ISs.

13. *Personnel security* (PS): organizations must ensure that individuals occupying positions of responsibility within organization are trustworthy and meet established security criteria for those positions.

14. *Risk assessment* (RA): organizations must periodically assess the risk to organizational operations resulting from the operation of organizational ISs.

15. *System and services acquisition* (SA): organizations must employ system development life cycle processes that incorporate information security considerations and ensure that third-party providers employ adequate security measures to protect products and services outsourced from the organization.

16. *System and communications protection* (SC): organizations must monitor, control, and protect organizational communications at the external boundaries and key internal boundaries and employ principles that promote information security within organizational ISs.

17. *System and information integrity* (SI): organizations must identify, report, and correct information and IS flaws in a timely manner and provide protection from malicious code.

9.6 Implementing Information Security Controls—NIST 800-53

NIST SP 800-53 Revision 4, *Security and Privacy Controls for Federal Information Systems and Organizations*, is intended to supply the specific process and behavioral specifications for the controls that implement each of these 17 general areas. It recommends security controls for all federal ISs and documents security control requirements and comprehensively catalogs the requisite set of overall security controls for all U.S. federal ISs. NIST 800-53's primary mission is to assist federal agencies in implementing FISMA (2002) along with underwriting any other formal program meant to promote information security. NIST SP 800-53 contains an entire selection of primary baseline security controls. There are a set of standard security controls specified in the document. Additionally, there is also a process for developing a specialized set of security controls in accordance with a targeted organizational risk assessment.

NIST SP 800-53 subdivides security controls into *common, custom,* and *hybrid* categories. *Common controls* are those that are most frequently used throughout an organization, such as conventional access controls. *Custom controls* are those controls that have been specifically designed for a given, distinct application or device. *Hybrid controls* start with a standard control and are customized as per the requirements of a particular device or application. These controls are assigned as a result of a FIPS 199 worst-case impact analysis. The security controls are the embodiment of the 17 areas, ranging in focus from incident response, access control, and disaster recovery all the way down to encryption.

The specific responses in each of these global areas are implemented by means of a risk-based process, which is the current purpose of the NIST RMF. Logically such a process begins with the identification of all of the potential threats and vulnerabilities in the risk environment. This leads to the mapping and implementation of specific controls to address each of the individual vulnerabilities. The residual risk is estimated by calculating the likelihood and impact of any given vulnerability that could be exploited, taking into account existing controls. In the end, the culmination of the risk assessment process itemizes the estimated risk for each identified vulnerability and then makes a decision about whether that risk should be accepted or mitigated. If the risk is mitigated through the implementation of a specific control, then the organization needs to describe the specific actions taken and purpose of that control.

The overall risk management process is initiated and guided by means of a plan. NIST SP 800-18, *Guide for Developing Security Plans for Federal Information Systems* (NIST, 2006), introduces the concept of a *system security plan*. Under the NIST SP 800-18 process, the organization develops an appropriate set of policies during the system security planning process. Following that, the system security plan is maintained as a living document. Consequently, there has to be a clear specification of who reviews the plan and keeps it current. Moreover, there has to be an organized and well-defined specification of who follows up on the implementation of planned security controls. The plan itself undergoes scheduled assessments for the purpose of determining whether a modification is required and if that is the case, then plans of action and milestones for implementing security controls are drawn up.

The system security plan is the major input to the security C&A process for the system. During the security C&A process, the system security plan is analyzed, updated, and accepted. The certification agent confirms that the security controls described in the system security plan are consistent with the FIPS 199 security category determined for the IS and the threat and vulnerability and initial risk are identified and documented in the system security plan, risk assessment, or equivalent document.

Once the system documentation and risk assessment have been completed, the system security controls must be reviewed and certified to be functioning appropriately. Based on the results of the review, the IS is accredited. The certification and accreditation process is defined in NIST SP 800-37, *Guide for the Security Certification and Accreditation of Federal Information Systems* (2004). Security accreditation is the official management decision given by a senior agency official to authorize operation of an IS and to accept the risk to agency operations, agency assets, or individuals based on the implementation of an agreed-upon set of security controls. This is required by OMB Circular A-130, Appendix III. Security accreditation provides a form of quality control and challenges managers and technical staffs at all levels to implement the most effective security controls possible in an IS.

By accrediting an IS, an agency official accepts responsibility for the security of the system and is fully accountable for any adverse impacts to the agency if a breach of security occurs. Thus, responsibility and accountability are core principles that characterize security accreditation. It is essential that agency officials have the most complete, accurate, and trustworthy information possible on the security status of their IS in order to make timely, credible, and risk-based decisions on whether to authorize operation of those systems.

The information and supporting evidence needed for security accreditation are developed during a detailed security review of an IS, typically referred to as security certification. Security certification is a comprehensive assessment of the management, operational, and technical security controls in an IS, made in support of security accreditation, to determine the extent to which the controls are implemented correctly, operating as intended, and producing the desired outcome with respect to meeting the security requirements for the system. The results of the security certification are used to reassess the risks and update the system security plan, thus providing the factual basis for an authorizing official to render a security accreditation decision.

All accredited systems must be monitored and the aim of the monitoring is to ensure that the selected set of security controls and the system documentation are kept current in order to reflect changes and modifications to the system or the threat environment. Major changes to the security profile of the system might even trigger an updated risk assessment. In addition, any controls that are significantly modified might need to be recertified. All of this is implemented by a formal continuous monitoring process.

Continuous monitoring activities include configuration management and control of IS components, security impact analyses of changes to the system, ongoing assessment of security controls, and status reporting. The organization establishes the selection criteria and subsequently selects a subset of the security controls employed within the IS for assessment. The organization also establishes the schedule for control monitoring to ensure that adequate coverage is achieved.

9.7 Evaluating the Control Set

It is one thing to specify controls and it is another to exemplify those controls in an effective practical process. As a result, NIST produced a companion work to NIST SP 800-53, called NIST SP 800-53A, *Assessing Security and Privacy Controls in Federal Information Systems and Organizations: Building Effective Assessment Plans.* If NIST SP 800-53 was written to address the real-world need for designing and developing an appropriate control set for each IS, NIST SP 800-53A defines the necessary approach to determine how well those controls are operating. Because they are companion documents, NIST plans to keep SP 800-53 and SP 800-53A in alignment with each other as the two develop.

NIST SP 800-53A specifies a set of procedures that can be used to conduct a practical assessment of the specific security controls that have been implemented for a given IS. The assessment procedures apply at various phases in the life cycle of the system and they are focused on the security and privacy controls that have been stated in NIST SP 800-53, Revision 4. The RMF development and implementation process also provides valuable lessons learned and in that respect, the NIST RMF and NIST SP 800-53A are easily interoperable.

The assessment process itself can be easily tailored to the risk management needs of any given organization. The NIST SP 800-53A approach is not monolithic—it gives organizations the necessary flexibility to concentrate on the parts of the system that might need greater oversight and control. The organization can tailor the scope and effort requirements of the assessment to practical intervals and it can also ensure that the parts of the system that might need greater oversight are given the requisite attention.

The NIST SP 800-53A process is built around the belief that proper assessment of security controls is not established on simple pass–fail evaluations of checklists. Instead, the authors of NIST SP 800-53A operated under the assumption that suitably effective security assessments can best be used to ensure alignment between the organization and its stated business and assurance goals. Thus, NIST SP 800-53A (NIST, 2014) was written to facilitate the assessment of security and privacy controls within a well-defined RMF. The intention is to provide decision-makers with the following:

1. Evidence about the effectiveness of implemented controls
2. An indication of the quality of the risk management processes employed within the organization

3. Information about the strengths and weaknesses of the IS, which are supporting organizational missions and business functions in a global environment of sophisticated and changing threats

The outcomes of the assessment can then be used to determine the overall effectiveness of the system-specific, common, and hybrid controls that have been put in place for a given system. The aim of the assessment then is to provide credible and meaningful inputs to the organization's formal risk management decision-making process. Thus, a properly executed NIST SP 800-53A assessment process will ensure that the organization is able to determine the validity of the controls that have been implemented based on the organization's overall security strategy and subsequently utilized it as a means of securing the operation. It will also better define the means that must be employed to correct the identified weakness or deficiency in a way that best aligns with organizational goals.

From the standpoint of this book, it has to be understood that both SP 800-53A and SP 800-53 are meant to provide guidance for implementing the specific phases of the RMF. Specifically, NIST SP 800-53 applies to Step 2 in the RMF, *Select* security and privacy control selection. And NIST SP 800-53A applies to RMF Step 4, *Assess*, and RMF Step 6, *Monitor*. NIST SP 800-53A guidelines includes the mechanism for building effective assessment plans and it also recommends the best way to analyze and manage assessment results.

NIST SP 800-53A allows organizations to tailor the basic assessment procedures applicable to the standard. Tailoring involves customizing the assessment procedures to more closely match the characteristics of the IS in its operating environment. The tailoring process gives organizations the flexibility to use assessment approaches that best fit the capability and culture of the workforce while simultaneously meeting the assessment requirements that are built into the NIST RMF. Tailoring of the process can also include the addition of assessment procedures or assessment details to effectively satisfy the risk management needs of the organization.

According to NIST SP 800-53A, those tailoring decisions are left to the individual discretion of the organization. This is done in order to maximize organizational flexibility in developing assessment plans—applying the results of risk assessments to determine the extent, rigor, and level of intensity of the assessments (NIST, 2014). The overall reliability and consistency of outcomes are also important considerations in the overall assessment process. Therefore, a major design objective for NIST SP 800-53A is to provide a standard assessment framework and starting point that is geared toward achieving the necessary reliability and consistency. The actual assessment procedures that will be utilized as well as the depth and thoroughness of the examination depend on the following three common factors (NIST, 2014):

1. The security categorization of the IS based on FIPS 199
2. The assurance requirements that the organization intends to meet in determining the overall effectiveness of the security and privacy controls

3. The security and privacy controls from NIST SP 800-53 as identified in the approved security plans and privacy plans (Figure 9.4).

The assessment process itself constitutes an information-gathering activity and includes the organization gathering the necessary background on the control environment. Decision-makers will then choose a course of action that best fits the

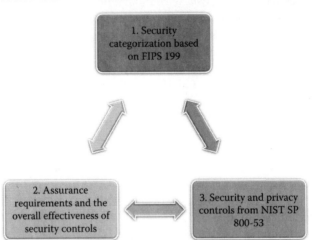

Figure 9.4 Three common factors in effective assessment and examination.

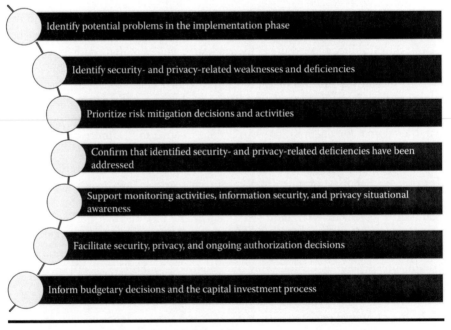

Figure 9.5 Control assessment information.

findings of the assessment. The designated decision-makers consider all relevant factors and utilize the results of the risk assessments that have been conducted to date. However, they should also consider the relative maturity and current level of capability of the organization's risk management process. Then they use NIST SP 800-53A as a starting point in planning the actual practical procedures that will be employed to assess the security and privacy controls that currently exist within the organizational environment. In general, this approach is designed to establish a consistent overall level of security and privacy in the organization as a whole. At the same time, it is also designed to ensure the flexibility that is needed to identify and mitigate any unique threats that might be present within a particular organizational environment. Based on these assessment results, the organization is able to customize its policies and resultant security procedures to address all identified threats and vulnerabilities.

The important point is that it is possible to do this within the considerations of the practical operation and in compliance with the organizational risk appetite. The information produced during control assessments, as shown in Figure 9.5, can be used by an organization to (NIST, 2014) do the following:

1. Identify potential problems or shortfalls in the organization's implementation of the RMF
2. Identify security- and privacy-related weaknesses and deficiencies in the IS and in the environment in which the system operates
3. Prioritize risk mitigation decisions and associated risk mitigation activities
4. Confirm that identified security- and privacy-related weaknesses and deficiencies in the IS and in the environment of operation have been addressed
5. Support monitoring activities and information security and privacy situational awareness
6. Facilitate security authorization decisions, privacy authorization decisions, and ongoing authorization decisions
7. Inform budgetary decisions and the capital investment process

Organizations are not expected to employ every one of the assessment methods and the assessment objects that have been specified in NIST SP 800-53A. Instead, the organization is given the inherent freedom to determine the level of effort needed and the assurance required. This determination is made on the basis of the best approach to accomplishing the goals of the assessment within that organization. The aim is to always provide trustworthy decision-making information that can assist managers in their subsequent decisions about the tactics that they need to employ to mitigate an identified set of business risks. An example of one methodology recommended by NIST SP 800-53A is the *Security Content Automation Protocol* (SCAP). This project provides an actual concrete way of actually doing assessments. SCAP is a NIST product that is designed to work with NIST SP 800-53A (NIST, 2014). Its purpose is to tailor the organization's particular assessment approach into a consistent, cost-effective security control assessment process.

The primary objective of SCAP is to standardize the format and nomenclature of the activities that are used to gather the data and then execute the necessary resource trade-offs necessary to evaluate a given set of organizational functions. SCAP is also designed to help organizations identify and reduce vulnerabilities associated with products that are not patched or insecurely configured.

The regular and consistent assessment of the system under examination is normally executed by members of the development staff. Other possible participants in the process could also include the owners themselves, integrators, the stakeholders for the common controls, third-party assessors and auditors, or the information security staffs of the target organization. The assessors or auditors are the people who are responsible for gathering the relevant data from all of the sources listed in the assessment plan. The assessments themselves include tests, reviews, and other forms of component assessments for the product. The fully integrated set of components is also subject to system-level testing using a variety of methods and techniques. The assessors or auditors compile and analyze the information that they gathered in order to develop the evidence necessary to support decision-makers in their conclusions about the correctness and effectiveness of the controls employed in that particular IS.

The recommended assessment procedure is organized and itemized in the assessment plan. The plan states that the formal assessment objectives and each objective should have a prescribed set of tasks and their associated work instructions and assessment methods specified for it. The assessment objective also includes a specific set of criteria that can be used to judge the present state of performance of that objective. Each of these criteria is linked to the control that is under evaluation and this linkage is necessary to ensure that the assessment results can be directly associated with the requisite performance requirements of the control. The actual performance of the specified assessment will produce a formal set of assessment findings. These findings will then be used by the organization's decision-makers to judge the overall effectiveness of the given control.

The assessment plan also identifies the specific items being assessed, which include things like document-based artifacts such as the specifications and design documentation, the underlying mechanisms of the system itself such as the platform, and the dedicated security activities of the system and its users. Specifications entail documentation items such as the functional and nonfunctional requirements and the final design documents for the operational version of the system. Mechanisms entail characteristic things such as the actual hardware, software, or firmware safeguards and the specific countermeasures that will be employed to assure the system itself. Activities are the specific protection-related actions that are performed by the workforce to ensure the day-to-day security of the system. This includes things such as system backup operations, network traffic monitoring, and contingency planning (NIST, 2014).

The assessment methods outlined in the plan specify the exact process that will be used by the assessors to ensure a proper and correct evaluation of system performance. Assessment methods include things such as reviews, inspections, and audits as well as static and dynamic testing procedures. The reason why assessment methods must be made explicit is that every system is different in its particulars and most of the assessment objects are abstract. Therefore, it is the common methodology and explicit examination procedures that provide the fundamental uniformity that is necessary to facilitate assessor understanding and to achieve clarification of the evidence that has been gathered. The evidence set will be both *subjective* and *objective*.

Subjective evidence is gathered from discussions with individuals or groups of individuals within an organization. These are the stakeholders and the people who are directly responsible for the actual day-to-day performance of the system. Thus, their insights are valuable in understanding the fundamental operation of the system. *Objective evidence* is gathered from testing and the testing can be both static and dynamic. Each method involves executing the functions of one or more assessment objects under a given set of testing conditions. The aim is to confirm that actual behavior conforms to expected behavior. Both forms of assessments are used in making the necessary determinations that are the actual purpose of a given set of assessment subjective and objective analyses.

Naturally, every assessment process is unique in that each has its own particular requirements, attributes, and degree of rigor associated with each. Thus, the assessment plan should specify the precise level of thoroughness required by the examination. In essence, for the degree of assurance required, there ought to be a hierarchy of reviews and tests associated with the process. This increasing level of rigor is what aligns the appropriate rigor and scope of the assessment to match the level of assurances required for each system. Thus, the rigor and level of detail that is exercised in the examination, interview, and testing processes will also dictate the degree of trust that can be placed in the system operation. Consequently, as trust requirements increase, the rigor and scope of the assessment process tends to increase as well.

After the security assessment plan is approved by the organization, the assessment team executes the plan in accordance with an agreed-upon schedule. Part of the risk management decision-making is the determination of the size and organizational makeup of the assessment team. The results of the subsequent evaluations are then recorded in the assessor's report, which is a key contributor to the authorization package that is developed in Step 5 of the NIST RMF life cycle process.

Assessment objectives are achieved by applying the designated assessment methods to the system objects under assessment and then compiling the evidence necessary to judge the performance of each assessment objective. Each determination will produce one of the following findings: *satisfied (S)* or *other than satisfied (O)*. A finding of *satisfied* indicates that the assessment objective for the control has been met based on the evidence collected. A finding of *other than satisfied* means that the assessment information for the control indicates potential anomalies in its operation or implementation. A finding of *other than satisfied* may also indicate that the assessor was unable to obtain sufficient information to make the particular assessment that is called for in the determination statement. For each finding of *other than satisfied*, assessors indicate which parts of the control are affected and describe how the control differs from the planned or expected state. For assessment findings that are *other than satisfied*, organizations may choose to specify the level of severity, or criticality of the weaknesses. Defining criticality levels can help to establish priorities for needed risk mitigation actions and the potential for compromises due to *other than satisfied* findings are also noted by the assessor.

This notation reflects the lack of a requisite safeguard and it itemizes the exploitation that could occur as a result. Risk determination and acceptance activities are conducted by the organization postassessment as part of the risk management strategy and should involve more than just technical personnel. They should also involve the senior leadership of the organization and the authorizing officials as the involvement of the senior people ensures that the necessary rework and mitigations that might result are properly overseen and closed out.

The stakeholders of the system and any common control providers rely on the expertise and technical judgment of assessors to both determine the status of the security control set, as well as provide recommendations about corrective action to mitigate weaknesses or deficiencies in the controls. The assessment results produced by the assessor are provided to IS stakeholders and common control providers in the initial security assessment reports. System owners and common control providers may choose to act on selected recommendations before the assessment reports are finalized if there are reasonable opportunities to correct weaknesses or deficiencies.

This leads directly to the issue of tailoring. The NIST SP 800-53 control set has to be tangibly adapted to the mission, business purpose, and goals of the system that is being assured. This requires the organization to tailor the NIST SP 800-53 control set to the specific characteristics of the system within its given operating environment. The tailoring requirement also applies to the control assessment procedures. The steps that will be followed to characterize and describe control performance must be clearly stated and accepted as correct by the stakeholders in the assessment process. According to NIST 800-53A, organizations should tailor their assessment processes to encompass all of the ISs at the organization level (NIST, 2014). In addition, there is a need to tailor the individual information system-level assessments to align with the overall organizational-level approach as well as the evaluation needs of the specific system.

The actual people who are performing the assessment are the ones who are accountable for determining the form of the tailoring process. In general, the tailoring process, as shown in Figure 9.6, follows these six recommended steps (NIST, 2014):

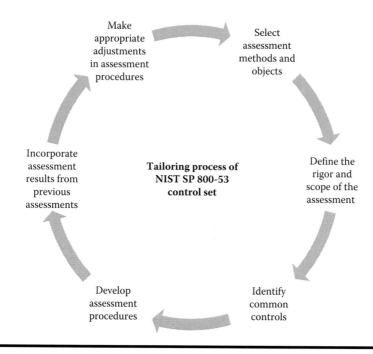

Figure 9.6   Tailoring process of the NIST SP 800-53 control set.

1. *Step 1:* select the appropriate assessment methods and objects that are needed to satisfy the stated assessment objectives.
2. *Step 2:* select the appropriate depth and coverage attribute values to define the rigor and scope of the assessment.
3. *Step 3:* identify the common controls that have been stipulated by a separately specified security assessment plan, and do not require the repeated execution of the common assessment procedures.
4. *Step 4:* develop IS/platform-specific and organization-specific assessment procedures (which may be adapted from NIST 800-53A Appendices F and J).
5. *Step 5:* incorporate assessment results from previous assessments where the results are deemed applicable.
6. *Step 6:* make appropriate adjustments in assessment procedures in order to be able to obtain the requisite assessment evidence from external providers.

Because organizations are diverse, the arrangement and day-to-day operation of the systems themselves cannot be approached in any lock-step manner. Thus, it is both understandable and acceptable that organizations will document and configure their ISs in a wide variety of ways. As a consequence, the substance and general acceptability of the resulting assessment evidence will also differ. The best mechanism for ensuring reliability of results is to employ a broad range of assessment methods in evaluating any given set of assessment objects. The aim is to look at the performance of the security of controls from a variety of different perspectives and a range of directions in order to be certain that the assessment evidence is valid.

Therefore, the approach to every assessment project is based on a set of potential assessment methods that might be applicable to a given object; however, the initial assumption is that those methods will have to be tailored to their application. The aim of the tailoring process for a specific assessment is to be able to apply precisely the right methods and their attendant objects. The assessment methods and objects chosen are those deemed the best possible means of generating the evidence that is needed to make the determinations that are described in the assessment plan. NIST 800-53A contains appendices that document a set of potential methods and objects in the assessment procedure. The references are provided as a resource to assist in the selection of appropriate methods and objects. However, the intention of NIST 800-53A is to not be prescriptive since that would limit the selection process.

Organizations are instructed to use their judgment in choosing from the list of possible assessment methods and the list of assessment objects associated with each selected method is meant to suggest rather than propose. Organizations select the methods and objects that they feel provide a reasonable contribution to making the right decisions about a given assessment objective. The accompanying justification for how the various assessment methods and procedures have been selected and applied also underwrites confidence in the general quality of the assessment results. In most cases, the aim of the assessment process is to review, audit, and test every aspect of every assessment object, because proper scope and consistency of assessment results is an important element of trust.

In addition to providing a justification for how an assessment method has been appropriately aligned to an object, each assessment method must be characterized in terms of the standard depth and coverage attributes prescribed in 800-53A. This description identifies the rigor and scope of that particular assessment activity. The depth and coverage attributes that have been selected by the organization are generally referenced to the sensitivity of the information and processing for the specific system being assessed as well as the type of certification required. More importantly, the depth and coverage attribute values essentially underwrite trust. Therefore, these values have to be traceable to the overall security requirements that have been specified by the organization. The standard suggests that SCAP checklists can be used to provide a profile-based point of reference that will assist in the tailoring of attribute values.

At the end, the foundation of organization-wide security rests on the common controls that are utilized across all systems. Since the assessment of common controls is the responsibility of the organizational entity that developed and implemented them, the part of any individual assessment that involves the evaluation of the adequacy of common controls has to include all of the results of all of the previous assessments organization-wide. This is because common controls have most likely been assessed in other places as part of the organization's overall information security program. Thus, the stakeholders for the IS under assessment have to coordinate their assessment of the common control set with the responsible parties for the common controls within the organization. Additionally, they have to obtain previously existing results of common control assessments or make arrangements to include or reference prior common control assessment results in the current assessment.

Another consideration in the use of common controls is that there are occasionally times when system-specific aspects are combined with a common control. These types of controls are referred to as *hybrid controls*. For example, legal compliance controls may be considered a hybrid control if the individual system has additional regulations that it has to comply with above and beyond the requirements specified for all organizational ISs as a whole. Therefore, the stakeholders in the IS under assessment would have to tailor the common controls in their compliance plans to meet the enhanced regulations. So, for each hybrid control, assessors have to evaluate the system-specific aspects of the control as well as the results from the common control assessment. This is necessary to ensure that all aspects of the control are assessed.

Within the 800-53A standard, assessors have a great deal of flexibility in planning for each assessment. The aim is to always obtain the best evidence available to judge the performance of a security or privacy control. Given that, an important area for consideration is the sequence in which security controls are assessed. The assessment of some controls before others may provide useful information that facilitates understanding of other controls in the control set. For example, there are a number of exploit controls within 800-53A that will ensure a better picture of the shape of the IS. Assessing these controls early in the assessment process is likely to provide a better basic understanding of the IS, which knowledge can then guide the assessors in their evaluation of other types of more specific security controls.

The results of security control assessments ultimately influence control implementations, the content of security plans and privacy plans, and the respective plans of action and milestones. Accordingly, the stakeholders of the system and the common control providers review the security assessment reports and make a final decision about the residual risk. Then with the concurrence of the designated approving authority, they make a determination about the appropriate steps that will be required to adequately mitigate any weakness or deficiency that has been identified during the assessment.

By using the labels of *satisfied* and *other than satisfied*, the reporting format for the assessment findings provides visibility for organizational officials into specific weaknesses and deficiencies in the control set for that particular IS. This facilitates the execution of a disciplined and structured approach to responding to risks in accordance with organizational priorities. For example, IS owners or common control providers may decide that certain assessment findings marked as *other than satisfied* are of an inconsequential nature. Therefore, they might make a decision to accept the implicit risk. Conversely, the same stakeholders might decide that findings that are marked as *other than satisfied* represent a clear and present danger that requires immediate remediation actions. In all cases, the organization reviews each assessor finding of *other than satisfied* after the assessment and applies its judgment with regard to the severity or seriousness of the finding and whether the finding is significant enough to be worthy of further investigation or remedial action.

Senior leadership has to be involved in this decision-making process to ensure that the post-assessment decisions are promptly and correctly implemented. This is primarily reinforced by the allocation of resources in accordance with organizational priorities. That is, the most critical and sensitive issues are corrected first since they pose the greatest degree of risk. Ultimately, the assessment findings and any subsequent mitigation actions that are initiated by the stakeholders will result in actual updates to the system as well as the need to commensurately update key documents used in the authorization to operate. The documents include security plans and privacy plans, security assessment reports and privacy assessment reports, and the respective plans of action and milestones.

9.8 Chapter Summary

The DoD and other federal agencies require all information technology systems, including medical devices, to comply with a large number of well-defined information assurance requirements. Thus, in effect, the RMF specifies a standardized process for performing the traditional C&A functions.

In the typical C&A process, a system is first identified and its stakeholders are registered. Then a formal risk analysis is performed to categorize the general sensitivity of the information in the system. The method for doing that within the present federal space is specified in FIPS 199. Once the system has been described in terms of impact and priority using FIPS 199, a list of controls is selected and implemented. The current federal standard for control selection is FIPS 200, *Minimum Security Requirements for Federal Information and Information Systems.* This standard works in conjunction with NIST 800-53 Revision 4, *Security and Privacy Controls for Federal Information Systems and Organizations.*

There are a number of mandated accreditations required in the federal space. Most of these stem from the CCA that was enacted by Congress in February 1996 to reform and improve the way federal agencies acquired and managed its information technology assets.

The law underwrites the coordinated development of overarching federal information technology management policy by mandating a comprehensive approach to the way that information technology resources are acquired and managed. It applies to all of the agencies under the executive branch.

The CCA centralized the overall mandate for federal information technology management oversight with the Director of the OMB. In this respect, the OMB is made officially responsible for the improvement of the productivity, efficiency, and effectiveness of all federal systems (CCA, 1996). OMB A-130 (2000) provides officially sanctioned practical guidance for implementing the act itself. The OMB mandates an integrated system framework aimed at efficiently executing the assigned role and responsibility of a given department. Thus, all aspects of capital planning are taken into consideration in its implementation. The operational goal of the FEAF is to define a common model and nomenclature across the federal space. The FEAF actually comprises an interrelated set of subframeworks that are designed to facilitate coordination and alignment of cross-agency system acquisition and development.

From the standpoint of the evolution of the NIST RMF, the most relevant outcome of the Clinger–Cohen Act is the mandate that the OMB Director develop a process for analyzing, tracking, and evaluating the risks and results of all major capital investments made by an executive agency for ISs (CCA, 1996). Specifically, the requirement is that the process be applicable to the entire life cycle of each system and should include an explicit set of benchmarks for analyzing risks associated with information technology investments. Much of the purpose and intent of the formal C&A process that was formalized in the subsequent E-Government Act (2002) has its origins in the Clinger–Cohen Act. And in many respects, this seminal act still serves as the contextual godfather for the specific mechanisms that the U.S. government employs to perform the various processes supported by the NIST RMF.

The central legislative piece in any discussion about the RMF is FISMA (2002). FISMA was enacted 6 years after the Clinger–Cohen as Title III of the E-Government Act of 2002. And it was FISMA that formally established the importance of cybersecurity as a national security priority for the United States.

At its heart, FISMA is an information security management framework. All systems used or operated by a U.S. federal government agency must comply with its requirements. The requirements are stated in a series of standards that have been defined by NIST over the past 8 years. The NIST RMF does not provide compliance criteria; however, it does provide a well-defined process for putting those stipulations in place.

FISMA applies to all of the systems within a given enterprise. The universality of its application within a given government organization is one of its chief characteristics and advantages. Essentially, FISMA requires every agency to inventory all of the systems it operates. That includes characterizing both the applicable software and hardware assets as well as all of the major interfaces between each system and the networks that they attach to. Also the information within those systems needs to be identified and categorized based on the level of sensitivity and risk. In essence, this identification and categorization process provides the requisite understanding of the exact protection requirements for each system, as well as drawing a roadmap of potential areas of threat.

FIPS 199 offers a common framework and advice on how to define appropriate security categories for both information and their attendant ISs. Security categories are to be used in conjunction with vulnerability and threat information in assessing the risk to the organization. The security categories are based on the potential impact should the information and ISs be threatened. Thus, the information is categorized according to its potential impact on the functioning of the organization. FIPS 199 defines three levels of potential impact on organizations or individuals should there be a breach of security. The application of these definitions must take place within the context of each organization and the overall national interest (FIPS PUB 199, 2004).

Besides impact, the other side of the classification process is deciding about the relative sensitivity, or importance, of the information. Thus, the other factor that is brought into the decision about priorities is the issue of information sensitivity. Or in simple terms, the security category of any information type is used to decide the right sensitivity category of the system. The determination of the security category has to consider the range of security levels of the information that is in each IS.

Once the organization makes a decision about the sensitivity and impact of a given system explicit security controls are assigned. Federal ISs must meet minimum security requirements defined in the second mandatory security standard that is specified in the FISMA legislation. That standard is FIPS 200, *Minimum Security Requirements for Federal Information and Information Systems*. Policies and procedures play an important role in the implementation of an enterprise-wide information security program. Thus, organizations require guidance in the most effective way to develop and promulgate formal security policies.

This standard specifies 17 control areas for which policies might be required. The 17 areas represent a broad-based, balanced information security program that addresses the management, operational, and technical aspects of protecting federal information and ISs. To satisfy the requirements of these 17 categories the organization must select the appropriate security controls and assurance requirements as described in NIST SP 800-53, *Recommended Security Controls for Federal Information Systems*.

The process of selecting the appropriate security controls and assurance requirements for organizational ISs is a multifaceted, risk-based activity involving management and operational personnel within the organization. The security categorization of federal information and ISs, as required by FIPS 199, is the first step in the risk management process. Subsequent to the security categorization process, organizations must select an appropriate set of security controls for their ISs that satisfy the minimum security requirements set forth in this standard. The selected set of security controls must include one of three appropriately tailored security control baselines from NIST SP 800-53 that are associated with the designated impact levels of the organizational ISs as determined during the security categorization process.

The combination of FIPS 200 and NIST SP 800-53 describes a foundational level of security for all federal information and ISs. The agency's risk assessment validates the security control set and determines if any additional controls are needed to protect agency operations, agency assets, or individuals. The resulting set of security controls establishes a level of "security due diligence" for the federal agency and its contractors.

NIST SP 800-53, *Security and Privacy Controls for federal Information Systems and Organizations*, is a publication of the federal government. It is intended to supply the specific process and behavioral specifications for the controls that implement each of these 17 general areas. It recommends security controls for all federal ISs and documents security control requirements. It comprehensively catalogs the requisite set of overall security controls for all U.S. federal ISs.

Nevertheless, NIST 800-53's primary mission is to assist federal agencies in implementing FISMA (2002) along with underwriting any other formal program meant to promote information security. NIST SP 800-53 contains an entire selection of primary baseline security controls. There are a set of standard security controls specified in the document. In addition, there is also a process for developing a specialized set of security controls in accordance with a targeted organizational risk assessment.

NIST 800-53 subdivides security controls into common, custom, and hybrid categories. Common controls are those that are most frequently used throughout an organization, such as conventional access controls. Custom controls are those controls that have been explicitly designed for a given, distinct application or device. Hybrid controls start with a standard control and are customized as per the requirements of a particular device or application. These controls are assigned as a result of a FIPS 199 worst-case impact analysis. The security controls are the embodiment of the 17 areas, ranging in focus from incident response, access control, and disaster recovery all the way down to encryption.

The specific responses in each of these global areas are implemented by means of a risk-based process. That is the current purpose of the NIST RMF. Logically such a process begins with the identification of all of the potential threats and vulnerabilities in the risk environment. That leads to the mapping and implementation of specific controls to address each of the individual vulnerabilities. The residual risk is estimated by calculating the likelihood and impact that any given vulnerability could be exploited, taking into account existing controls. In the end, the culmination of the risk assessment process itemizes the estimated risk for each identified vulnerability and then makes a decision about whether that risk should be accepted or mitigated. If the risk is mitigated through the implementation of a specific control, then the organization needs to describe the specific actions and purpose of that control.

The overall risk management process is initiated and guided by means of a plan. NIST SP 800-18 introduces the concept of a System Security Plan. Under the NIST 800-18, Revision 1 process, the organization develops an appropriate set of policies during the system security planning process. Following that, the system security plan is maintained as a living document. Consequently, there has to be an explicit specification of who reviews the plan and keeps it current. Moreover, there has to be an organized and well-defined specification of who follows up on the implementation of planned security controls. The plan itself undergoes scheduled assessments for the purpose of determining whether a modification is required. And if that is the case, then plans of action and milestones for implementing security controls are drawn up.

The system security plan is the major input to the security C&A process for the system. During the security C&A process, the system security plan is analyzed, updated, and accepted. The certification agent confirms that the security controls described in the system security plan are consistent with the FIPS 199 security category determined for the IS, and that the threat and vulnerability identification and initial risk determination are identified and documented in the system security plan, risk assessment, or equivalent document.

All accredited systems must be monitored. The aim of that monitoring is to ensure that the selected set of security controls and the system documentation are kept current in order to reflect changes and modifications to the system, or the threat environment. Major changes to the security profile of the system might even trigger an updated risk assessment. In addition, any controls that are significantly modified might need to be recertified. All these are implemented by a formal continuous monitoring process.

Continuous monitoring activities include configuration management and control of IS components, security impact analyses of changes to the system, ongoing assessment of security controls, and status reporting. The organization establishes the selection criteria and subsequently selects a subset of the security controls employed within the IS for assessment. The organization also establishes the schedule for control monitoring to ensure adequate coverage is achieved.

NIST produced a companion work to 800-53, that is, NIST SP 800-53A, *Assessing Security and Privacy Controls in Federal Information Systems and Organizations: Building Effective Assessment Plans.* If SP 800-53 was written to address the real-world need for designing and developing an appropriate control sets for each IS, SP 800-53A defines the necessary approach to determining how well those controls are operating. Because they are companion pieces NIST plans to keep 800-53 and 800-53A in alignment with each other as the two develop.

NIST SP 800-53A specifies a set of procedures that can be used to conduct a practical assessment of the specific security controls that have been implemented for a given federal IS. The assessment procedures apply at various phases in the life cycle of the system and they are focused on the security and privacy controls that have been promulgated in NIST SP 800-53, Revision 4. The RMF development and implementation process also provided valuable lessons learned. And in this respect, the NIST RMF and NIST SP 800-53A are easily interoperable.

The assessment process itself can be easily tailored to the risk management needs of any given organization. The NIST 800-53A approach is not monolithic.

It gives organizations the necessary flexibility to concentrate on the parts of the system that might need greater oversight and control. The organization can tailor the scope and effort requirements of the assessment to practical intervals and it can also ensure that the parts of the system that might need greater oversight are given the requisite attention.

SP 800-53A allows organizations to tailor the basic assessment procedures applicable to the standard. Tailoring involves customizing the assessment procedures to more closely match the characteristics of the IS in its operating environment. The tailoring process gives organizations the flexibility to use assessment approaches that best fit the capability and culture of the workforce while simultaneously meeting the assessment requirements that are built into the RMF. Tailoring of the process can also include the addition of assessment procedures or assessment details to effectively satisfy the risk management needs of the organization.

Therefore, a major design objective for SP 800-53A is to provide a standard assessment framework and starting point that is geared toward achieving the necessary reliability and consistency. In general, this approach is designed to establish a consistent overall level of security and privacy in the organization as a whole. At the same time, it is also designed to ensure the flexibility that is needed to identify and mitigate any unique threats that might be present within a particular organizational environment. Based on those assessment results, the organization is able to customize its policies and resultant security procedures to address all identified threats and vulnerabilities.

The assessment plan identifies the specific items being assessed. These normally include things like document-based artifacts such as the specifications and design documentation, the underlying mechanisms of the system itself such as the platform, and the dedicated security activities of the system and its users. Specifications entail documentation items such as the functional and nonfunctional requirements and the final design documents for the operational version of the system. Mechanisms entail characteristic things such as the actual hardware, software, or firmware safeguards and the specific countermeasures that will be employed to assure the system itself. Activities are the specific protection-related actions that are performed by the workforce in order to ensure the day-to-day security of the system. That includes things such as system backup operations, network traffic monitoring, and contingency planning (NIST, 2014).

The results of security control assessments ultimately influence control implementations, the content of security plans and privacy plans, and the respective plans of action and milestones. Accordingly, the stakeholders of the system and the common control providers review the security assessment reports and make a final decision about the residual risk. Then with the concurrence of the designated approving authority, they make a determination about the appropriate steps that will be required to adequately mitigate any weakness or deficiency that has been identified during the assessment.

Glossary

agency: an executive department or a wholly owned corporation subject to federal oversight

assessment: process of evaluating security controls to determine the extent to which they are implemented correctly, operating as intended, and producing the desired outcome

assessment results: produced by an assessment procedure culminating in either a "satisfied" or "other than satisfied" condition

assessment method: one of three types of actions (i.e., examine, interview, test) taken by assessors in obtaining evidence during an assessment

assessment object: the item upon which an evaluation method is applied

assessment objective: statements that expresses the desired outcome for the assessment

assessment procedure: evaluation methods and their objects

assurance: confidence that security controls are effective in their application

authorization: the official permission to operate an information system based on the evaluation of system security controls

authorizing official: executive with the authority to formally assume responsibility for operating an information system

common control: control that is inherited by one or more organizational information systems

common control provider: entity responsible for the development of common controls

coverage: attribute that describes the scope or breadth of the assessment objects

depth: attribute that describes the rigor and level of detail associated with the method

federal information system: information system operated on behalf of the government

hybrid control: security control that is part common control and part system-specific control

information owner: official with statutory or operational authority for specified information

information security program plan: formal document that describes planned program management controls and common controls

information system: discrete set of information resources organized for the collection, processing, maintenance, use, sharing, dissemination, or disposition of information

information system owner: official responsible for the overall procurement, development, integration, modification, or operation and maintenance of an information system

information type: a specific category of information referenced to sensitivity and impact

risk: a measure of the extent to which an entity is affected by a potential event

risk assessment: the process of identifying risks to organizational operations

security categorization: the determination of the relative sensitivity and impact of an information type

security control assessor: responsible for conducting a security control assessment

security controls: countermeasures prescribed to protect information systems and to meet a set of defined security requirements

security impact analysis: conducted to determine the extent to which change will affect the security state

security plan: document that provides an overview of the security requirements for an information system and which describes the desired security controls

security requirements: criteria an information system must meet in order to be trusted

tailoring: process by which security control baselines are implemented or modified

tailoring assessment procedures: process by which assessment procedures defined in SP 800-53A are adjusted to a given environment

threat assessment: process of formally evaluating the degree of threat

vulnerability assessment: examination of an information system to determine the adequacy of security and privacy measures

References

CCA. (1996). The Information Technology Management Reform Act of 1996 (Clinger-Cohen), 40 U.S.C. 1401 et seq.

DoD Directive 8500.01. (2002). Information Assurance.

DoD Instruction 8500.2. (2010). Information Assurance Implementation.

The E-Government Act. Pub.L. 107–347, 116 Stat. 2899, 2002.

The Federal Information Security Management Act, 44 U.S.C. § 3541, et seq, 2002.

FIPS PUB 199. (2004). *Standards for Security Categorization of Federal Information and Information Systems.* Gaithersburg, MD: Computer Security Division Information Technology Laboratory, National Institute of Standards and Technology.

FIPS PUB 200. (2006). *Minimum Security Requirements for Federal Information and Information Systems.* Gaithersburg, MD: Computer Security Division Information Technology Laboratory, National Institute of Standards and Technology.

NIST. (2006). SP 800-18 Revision 1, *Guide for Developing Security Plans for Federal Information Systems.* Gaithersburg, MD: Computer Security Division Information Technology Laboratory, National Institute of Standards and Technology.

NIST. (2013). SP 800-53 Revision 4, *Security and Privacy Controls for Federal Information Systems and Organizations.* Gaithersburg, MD: Computer Security Division Information Technology Laboratory, National Institute of Standards and Technology.

NIST. (2014). SP 800-53A Revision 4, *Assessing Security and Privacy Controls in Federal Information Systems and Organizations: Building Effective Assessment Plans.* Gaithersburg, MD: Computer Security Division Information Technology Laboratory, National Institute of Standards and Technology.

NIST RMF. (2014). *Risk Management Framework (RMF)*. Gaithersburg, MD: Computer Security Division Information Technology Laboratory, National Institute of Standards and Technology.

OMB. (2000). Office of Management and Budget, CIRCULAR NO. A-130 Revised, Transmittal Memorandum No. 4.

PRA. (1995). Paperwork Reduction Act of 1995. Report on the Committee of Governmental Affairs United States Senate. Available at: https://www.congress.gov/104/crpt/srpt8/CRPT-104srpt8.pdf.

Saltzer, J.H. and Schroeder, M.D. (1974). The protection of information in computer systems, *Communications of the ACM* 17(7), 388–402.

Appendix

(ISC)² Certified Authorization Professional (CAP) Certification

Anyone who has worked within the information and communication technology (ICT) industry for a period is aware of the importance of the vast assortment of certifications that can be earned in order to be competitive in achieving each successive level as they move up in their career. The discipline of cybersecurity is probably the one area of ICT providing the greatest number of certifications. Organizations such as the International Council of Electronic Commerce Consultants (EC-Council), Global Information Assurance Certification (GIAC—formerly SANS Institute), CompTia, and CISCO have provided for many years security specializations in areas such as A+, network security, ethical hacking, forensics, audit, and secure software development. For 25 years, the International Information System Security Certification Consortium, more widely known as (ISC)², has produced thousands of certified security professionals.

(ISC)² was established in 1989 and has become the largest nonprofit membership organization recognizing certified information and software security professionals in the world. Internationally, membership has grown to over 100,000 members across 160 countries. The organization is known across the world as "The Gold Standard," issuing the Certified Information Systems Security Professional (CISSP) credential and other ICT-related credentials including Certified Secure Software Lifecycle Professional (CSSLP), Certified Cyber Forensics Professional (CCFP^{SM}),

Certified Authorization Professional (CAP), HealthCare Information Security and Privacy Practitioner (HCISPP), and Systems Security Certified Practitioner (SSCP) to qualifying candidates. To its credit, (ISC)²'s certifications were among the first ICT-recognized credentials to conform to the requirements of ISO/IEC Standard 17024. In addition to certifications, (ISC)² provides other services to their members, such as education programs and services based on its Common Body of Knowledge (CBK) that encompasses a comprehensive selection of ICT and software security topics. Their CAP certification has a direct relationship to the National Institute of Standards and Technology's Risk Management Framework (NIST RMF). As such, we feel it is important to introduce the certification as part of this book.

A.1 CAP History

In December 2002, the Congress passed the *E-Government Act of 2002* and with it enhanced privacy management and created new mandates for information security management through a title frequently known as the *Federal Information Security Management Act* (FISMA). FISMA was created to address a number of inefficiencies. However, to provide a partial summarization, in 2003, if you gave three separate teams within the same organization the identical system, the system would have likely been configured and secured in three completely different ways. The problem was that there was no common and repeatable standard. Additionally, there was no requirement for organizations to invest in the security of federal systems. As a result, prior to FISMA, organizations would submit their investments and requirements to the Office of Management and Budget (the OMB assists the President in overseeing the preparation of the Federal budget and in supervising its administration in Federal agencies.), and there was no clear representation as to whether security investments would or would not be made.

Throughout this book, you have learned that security is actually an enabler that protects the ICT system, the ICT process, and the overall mission of the organization. After all, we do not have ICT within the federal government just for the sake of having an ICT system. Rather, the investment in ICT systems is made to enable, optimize, and support the mission and business processes. Likewise, when a security objective (confidentiality, availability, or integrity) is disrupted, there is a significant impact. The objectives and strategies of each business function are adversely impacted, and that is a fundamental goal of risk management, and in some cases compliance management.

Considering the state of ICT systems, the Government Accountability Office (GAO) made a series of observations and recommendations to Congress. As might be expected, since the GAO reports to Congress, all of these observations and recommendations were integrated into FISMA. Shortly after FISMA was enacted, (ISC)² analyzed the complexities of the act, and recognized the need for a credential. The credential became what is known as the CAP.

The (ISC)² put together a CAP training course that initially lasted 1 day. Then, as NIST published more standards and guidelines to comply with the FISMA, the course evolved to 2-day course. Eventually that 2-day course began to be offered as a 3-day course to help students absorb the large range of materials. In 2010, the CAP training course was revised to accommodate even more NIST publications forcing it to become a 4-day course. As we write this book, the training has evolved to 5 days. Since the 2010 revisions, NIST has increased the number of related guidance materials substantially (more than 600 pages of documentation). When you factor in the 600 pages of relevant NIST materials that existed prior to 2010, 1200 pages of NIST materials must be understood in order to achieve the CAP credential.

The road to successfully implementing standardized risk management within ICT systems has not been completed. As Congress continues to update and revise legislation that will impact FISMA, the industry has begun to label those changes currently happening and those in the future as FISMA 2.0. The ICT industry can expect a migration from compliance-based security management to a performance model where security is measured on the construct of NIST SP 800-55, *Performance Measurement Guide for Information Security*, which deals with performance management with a focus on measures of efficiency, measures of effectiveness, and impact measures. In short, it neither matters what the system looked like in the past, nor the extent to which documentation supported the system. What will matter are the results and reality. The main question that will be addressed is: Does the system have the capability to ensue real-time risk management? Based on the answer to this question, a follow-up question will be asked. Does the system, on a day-to-day basis, continue to be authorized to operate? Organizations are going to be forced to ask those questions, not on a periodic review schedule, but rather on a day-to-day basis.

A.2 CAP Coverage of the NIST RMF

Recall from our discussion in Chapter 2 that the NIST RMF goes beyond the implementation of tasks corresponding to categorize the select, implement, assess, authorize, and monitor steps. In order to complete those tasks effectively, considerable consideration must be given to the formal architecture of the ICT system. The CAP credential takes the importance of including architecture implications into account, and therefore this must be at the forefront of the knowledge base necessary for the certification.

When most are asked where the NIST RMF starts they respond by saying "Step 1 – The Select step" which is actually incorrect. One of the key points that the CAP credential requires is understanding that you cannot start categorizing the system if you are unaware of the roles, the environment, and the external influences that impact and go as far as to dictate the ICT system. Before even starting into Step 1 of the NIST RMF, the government, for instance, must determine if an information type meets the required criterion for national security systems. This happens at the starting point for organizational inputs. After accounting for the starting point, the NIST RMF has a prescribed model made up of six individualized steps that include two or more tasks that must be completed. Knowledge of all six categories and an understanding of the starting points are required for successful certification. While this book was not written with the intention to be a study guide for the certification, each chapter provides an in-depth discussion of the criteria tested for achievement of the certification, and can be an excellent supplement to the *Official (ISC)² Guide to the CAP CBK*, also published by Taylor & Francis, which serves as a main resource for studying for the exam [(ISC)², 2016].

A.3 CAP Domains

The CAP exam outline [available from the (ISC)² website] identifies coverage of seven distinct domains, each of which are described in Table A.1. Having read through the body of this book, you now know that the RMF is made up of six steps. Yet, the CAP credential requires knowledge of seven domains. The first of those domains is a general overview of the RMF and its impact on the greater scope of cybersecurity. Here is an important tip. At no time will the CAP exam ask what is in domain 1, domain 2, and so on. This credential focuses on the RMF. And the RMF has steps, not domains. Many people studying for the exam completely remove the term domain out of their mind and focus on their understanding based on steps, in order to reduce confusion.

The exam outline focuses on integrating all six RFM steps, not to forget the RMF starting points of architectural description and organizational inputs, and provides an in-depth representation of those activities that make up the RMF. Further, the exam outline provides specific information about the examination itself, which is delivered in a computer-based format.

A.4 Gaining Organizational Value through the CAP Credential

Cybersecurity is inescapable with new demands and new challenges that must be overcome almost on a daily basis. Such circumstances, often out of an organization's control, stem from the growing number of security-based regulations, changes in technology and the implementation of the technology within the organization, and the security implications that exist as professionals evolve in the way they perform each business function. The only way that an organization can address these demands and challenges is through the proper integration of people, processes, technology,

Table A.1   Certified Authorized Professional Domains

CAP Domain and Description
1. Risk Management Framework (RMF)
Security authorization includes a tiered risk management approach to evaluate both strategic and tactical risk across the enterprise. The authorization process incorporates the application of an RMF, a review of the organizational structure, and the business process/mission as the foundation for the implementation and assessment of specified security controls. This authorization management process identifies vulnerabilities and security controls and determines residual risks. The residual risks are evaluated and deemed either acceptable or unacceptable. More controls must be implemented to reduce unacceptable risk. The system may be deployed only when the residual risks are acceptable to the enterprise and a satisfactory security plan is complete.
2. Categorization of Information Systems (ISs)
Categorization of the IS is based on an impact analysis. It is performed to determine the types of information included within the security authorization boundary, the security requirements for the information types, and the potential impact on the organization resulting from a security compromise. The result of the categorization is used as the basis for developing the security plan, selecting security controls, and determining the risk inherent in operating the system.
3. Selection of Security Controls
The security control baseline is established by determining specific controls required to protect the system based on the security categorization of the system. The baseline is tailored and supplemented in accordance with an organizational assessment of risk and local parameters. The security control baseline, as well as the plan for monitoring it, is documented in the security plan.
4. Security Control Implementation
The security controls specified in the security plan are implemented by taking into account the minimum organizational assurance requirements. The security plan describes how the controls are employed within the IS and its operational environment. The security assessment plan documents the methods for testing these controls and the expected results throughout the system's life cycle.
5. Security Control Assessment
The security control assessment follows the approved plan, including defined procedures, to determine the effectiveness of the controls in meeting the security requirements of the IS. The results are documented in the security assessment report.

(Continued)

Table A.1 (*Continued*)   Certified Authorized Professional Domains

CAP Domain and Description
6. IS Authorization
The residual risks identified during the security control assessment are evaluated and the decision is made to authorize the system to operate, deny its operation, or remediate the deficiencies. Associated documentation is prepared and/or updated depending on the authorization decision.
7. Monitoring of Security Controls
After an authorization to operate (ATO) is granted, ongoing continuous monitoring is performed on all identified security controls as well as the political, legal, and physical environment in which the system operates. Changes to the system or its operational environment are documented and analyzed. The security state of the system is reported to designated responsible officials. Significant changes will cause the system to reenter the security authorization process. Otherwise, the system will continue to be monitored on an ongoing basis in accordance with the organization's monitoring strategy.

Source: (ICS)², *CAP SBK Domains*, https://www.isc2.org/cap-domains/default.aspx.

and the 19 security control families we discussed in this book, which make up management, technical, and operational controls. To provide the capability of this integration, organizations require the expertise of properly trained professionals such as those that have earned the CAP credential.

One of the strategies for coping with the substantially large increase in cybersecurity threats and attacks on federal, state, local, and private ICT systems is to have a framework that can put organizational strategy into action; the NIST RMF provides this. However, properly qualified professionals working within an organization's security function are also required, who must demonstrate that they can make competent decisions based on the NIST RMF. Moreover, if they lack the ability to even understand the RMF, the question becomes, how likely is it that the organization's security program is truly optimized? Thus, in considering the increasing number of threats and attacks, mandates and regulations, and changes in technology, it is easy to conclude that cybersecurity (done right) requires a number of properly trained and qualified professionals to manage the issues. The CAP is one of the few credentials focused on addressing the realities of the NIST RMF and all of the NIST references that must be understood to be successful.

The CAP credential is designed to meet the specific needs of civil defense, although it is gradually moving into the awareness of state and local government, in addition to the private sector. It should be noted that since the CAP focuses on NIST publications, it is not surprising that the DoD and the intelligence community were involved in the development of key NIST publications and are therefore able to transition to NIST publication compliance with minor difficulty.

In Section A.5 of this appendix, we will elaborate on the August 14, 2004, DoD issuance of directive 8570.01 entitled *Information Assurance Training Certification and Workforce Management*. This move by the DoD was a direct attempt to steer the workforce toward a competency model. Since its inception, this directive serves as a basis to rely on for security professionals because this is the specific knowledge necessary for success in any area of information assurance. Without this basis to rely on, the DoD realizes that the mission and associated funding could be compromised. So the DoD developed and defined a qualification table and has identified two levels of Information Assurance Managers (IAMs) (Level I and Level II). While the civilian and intelligence sectors do not have a mandate such as DoD 8570, there continues an obvious trend toward recognition of the CAP credential. Moreover, state and local governments are also changing their cybersecurity risk management practices to have a greater alignment with the NIST RMF, as have industries such as health care and power. It is no exaggeration that almost all managers in organizations have gained awareness that their ability to move that organization forward in achieving its mission and objectives requires the use of individuals with the CAP credential across the workforce. Likewise, those individuals with the credential have begun to realize that they are much more competitive and, in some instances, ask for a higher salary.

A.5 Understanding the CAP Relationship to DoD 8570

Since as early as 1992, with the development of the Defense Information Technology Security Certification and Accreditation Process (DITSCAP), certification of compliance to IT security requirements has been at the forefront of priorities set forth by the DoD. In November 2007, directive DoDI 8501.01, *DoD Information Assurance Certification and Accreditation Process* (DIACAP) was published which eventually replaced DITSCAP. The purpose of DIACAP was to establish a process by which ISs are certified for compliance with DoD security requirements and accredited for operation by a designated official. DIACAP provided visibility and control for the secure operation of DoD ISs. In doing so, DIACAP considered the following:

- Mission or business need
- Protection of personally identifiable information
- Protection of the information being processed
- Protection of the system's information environment

In March 2014, directive DoD 8510.01 presented another shift in the DoD compliance standards by providing instructions committing the DoD to move from DIACAP to the NIST RMF. It is important to note that, because the RMF is so significantly different from the DIACAP practices, many CAP candidates struggle with gaining the certification due to an innate tendency to reconcile those differences.

The 2004 issuance of DoD 8570, which serves as a basis for a common security competency model not only just within the DoD but also the entire workforce, provides a substantial degree of reliance for security professionals based on a predetermined knowledge base required for success in information assurance. CompTia, CISCO, Carnegie Mellon University, GIAC, and (ISC)² have worked progressively with the DoD so that the certification credentials offered by these organizations can meet the intent of DoD 8570.

In the case of the CAP credential, you will note that the IAM Level I and II requirements can be satisfied. Understand that the DoD does not expect all of the certifications within a given category be met. Rather, the DoD has determined that once individuals are listed with credentials of certification, they meet the requirements of that category.

Specifically, IAM Level I stipulates ". . . personnel are responsible for the implementation and operation of a DoD IS or system DoD Component within their computing environment (CE). Incumbents ensure that IA related IS are functional and secure within the CE" (Department of Defense, 2005).

Table A.2 provides a brief description of the functions performed by the management at IAM Level I. The individuals performing these functions can include but are not limited to: Information Systems Security Officer (ISSO), Information Assurance Officer (IAO), or Information System Security Manager (ISSM). DoD 8570 stipulates that individuals at this level must comply with all of the requirements in the table.

Likewise, IAM Level II stipulates ". . . personnel are responsible for the IA program of an IS within the Network Environment (NE). Incumbents in these positions perform a variety of security related tasks, including the development and implementation of system information security standards and procedures. They ensure that IS are functional and secure within the NE" (Department of Defense, 2005).

Table A.3 provides a brief description of the functions performed by the management at IAM Level II. DoD 8570 defines individuals performing these functions as the same as those identified in IAM Level II. While it is certainly advantageous, a manager with credentials at one of the two levels does not necessarily have to possess the credentials of the other. Nevertheless, DoD 8570 stipulates that individuals at this level must comply with all of the requirements in the table.

Table A.2   Information Assurance Manager (IAM) Level I

Function
M-I.1. Use federal- and organization-specific published documents to manage operations of their computing environment (CE) system(s)
M-I.2. Provide system-related input on information assurance (IA) security requirements to be included in statements of work and other appropriate procurement documents
M-I.3. Support and administer data retention and recovery within the CE
M-I.4. Participate in the development or modification of the computer environment IA security program plans and requirements.
M-I.5. Validate users' designation for IT Level I or II sensitive positions, as per reference
M-I.6. Develop procedures to ensure system users are aware of their IA responsibilities before granting access to DoD ISs
M-I.7. Recognize a possible security violation and take appropriate action to report the incident, as required
M-I.8. Supervise or manage protective or corrective measures when an IA incident or vulnerability is discovered
M-I.9. Ensure that system security configuration guidelines are followed
M-I.10. Ensure that IA requirements are integrated into the Continuity of Operations (COOP) Plan for that system or DoD component
M-I.11. Ensure that IA security requirements are appropriately identified in computer environment operation procedures
M-I.12. Monitor system performance and review for compliance with IA security and privacy requirements within the computer environment
M-I.13. Ensure that IA inspections, tests, and reviews are coordinated for the CE
M-I.14. Participate in an IS risk assessment during the certification and accreditation process
M-I.15. Collect and maintain data needed to meet system IA reporting requirements
M-I.16. Obtain and maintain IA baseline certification appropriate to position

Source: Department of Defense, *DoD 8570.01-M: Information Assurance Workforce Improvement Program,* Department of Defense, Washington DC, 2005.

Table A.3   IAM Level II

Function
M-II.1. Develop, implement, and enforce policies and procedures reflecting the legislative intent of applicable laws and regulations for the network environment (NE)
M-II.2. Prepare, distribute, and maintain plans, instructions, guidance, and standard operating procedures concerning the security of network system(s) operations
M-II.3. Develop NE security requirements specific to an IT acquisition for inclusion in procurement documents
M-II.4. Recommend resource allocations required to securely operate and maintain an organization's NE IA requirements
M-II.5. Participate in an IS risk assessment during the certification and authorization process
M-II.6. Develop security requirements for hardware, software, and service acquisitions specific to NE IA security programs
M-II.7. Ensure that IA and IA enabled software, hardware, and firmware comply with appropriate NE security configuration guidelines, policies, and procedures
M-II.8. Assist in the gathering and preservation of evidence used in the prosecution of computer crimes
M-II.9. Ensure that the NE IS recovery processes are monitored and that IA features and procedures are properly restored
M-II.10. Review IA security plans for the NE
M-II.11. Ensure that all IAM review items are tracked and reported
M-II.12. Identify alternative functional IA security strategies to address organizational NE security concerns
M-II.13. Ensure that IA inspections, tests, and reviews are coordinated for the NE
M-II.14. Review the selected security safeguards to determine that security concerns identified in the approved plan have been fully addressed
M-II.15. Evaluate the presence and adequacy of security measures proposed or provided in response to requirements contained in acquisition documents
M-II.16. Monitor contract performance and periodically review deliverables for conformance with contract requirements related to NE IA, security, and privacy

(Continued)

Table A.3 (*Continued*) IAM Level II

Function
M-II.17. Provide leadership and direction to NE personnel by ensuring that IA security awareness, basics, literacy, and training are provided to operations personnel commensurate with their responsibilities
M-II.18. Develop and implement programs to ensure that systems, network, and data users are aware of, understand, and follow NE and IA policies and procedures
M-II.19. Advise the designated accrediting authority of any changes affecting the NE IA posture
M-II.20. Conduct an NE physical security assessment and correct physical security weaknesses
M-II.21. Help prepare IA certification and accreditation documentation
M-II.22. Ensure that compliance monitoring occurs, and review results of such monitoring across the NE
M-II.23. Obtain and maintain IA baseline certification appropriate to position

Source: Department of Defense, *DoD 8570.01-M: Information Assurance Workforce Improvement Program,* Department of Defense, Washington DC, 2005.

References

Department of Defense. (2005). *DoD 8570.01-M: Information Assurance Workforce Improvement Program.* Washington, DC: Department of Defense.

(ISC)². (2016). *CAP CBK Domains.* Accessed May 22, 2016. Available at: https://www.isc2 .org/cap-domains/default.aspx.

Index

309